Land Rent, Capital, Rate of Profit

Studies in Critical Social Sciences

Series Editor
David Fasenfest
(*York University, Canada*)

VOLUME 365

New Scholarship in Political Economy

Series Editors
David Fasenfest
(*York University, Canada*)
Alfredo Saad-Filho
(*Queen's University Belfast*)

VOLUME 38

The titles published in this series are listed at *brill.com/nspe*

Land Rent, Capital, Rate of Profit

A Critique of David Harvey's Theory of Urban Land Rent

By

Ilia Farahani

BRILL

This work was supported by Jan Wallanders and Tom Hedelius Foundation (grant number: W22-0017).

The research presented in this work was conducted at Lund University.

ISSN 2666-2205
ISBN 978-90-04-76320-3
ISBN 978-90-04-76321-0 (PDF)
DOI https://doi.org/10.1163/9789004763210

Library of Congress Control Number: 2026936729

Brill and Koninklijke Brill BV are part of De Gruyter Brill.
www.degruyterbrill.com

Questions about General Product Safety Regulation: productsafety@degruyterbrill.com

Cover illustration: Bust of Karl Marx, 1939, by S.D. Merkurov, at the Fallen Monument Park (Muzeon Park of Arts) in Moscow, Russia. Photo courtesy of Alfredo Saad-Filho.

Contents

Acknowledgments

This work would not have been possible without the support of many people and the debts owed to them. At the top of my list is T.S. Faran, from whom I learned so much about many aspects of Marxist theory and practice that it is simply impossible to measure. I thank Eric Clark for introducing me to land rent theory and guiding my academic journey over the past fifteen years. I am deeply indebted to E. Ahmet Tonak, not only for his intellectual feedback during my PhD but also for his continued generous support since then. Without his support, no doubt, this work would not have been possible. The same goes for Jamie Gough, for his always thought-provoking and camaraderie feedback; Raju J Das, for encouraging me to turn my PhD monograph into a book; and David Fasenfest, for helping make that happen. I cannot thank my comrades David O'Byrne, Johan Pries, Liam Campling, Mads Barbesgaard, Stefano Longo, and Peter Rosendal Dau Jensen enough for their constant, invigorating discussions and for reading Marx, Lenin, and Gramsci together. I am especially indebted to David, Mads, and Peter for their generous feedback and comments on later drafts of the book. Thank you to my colleagues at the Department of Human Geography. I feel particularly obliged to express my gratitude to Henrik Gutzon Larsen, Karl-Johan Lundquist, and Tomas Germundsson for their ongoing feedback and invaluable intellectual and pedagogical exchange. I am also grateful to my fellow members of the Social Theory Circle: Alva Zalar, Anna Örman, Daisy Charlesworth, Ingrid Altamirano, Johan Pries, Kristoffer Ekberg, Lorena Melgaço, Mads Barbesgaard, and Peter Rosendal Dau Jensen. Thank you, too, to my Marx reading group friends in Lund and beyond: Helena Pérez Niño, Jostein Jakobsen, Liam Campling, Mads Barbesgaard, Peter Rosendal Dau Jensen, and Trum Daniel Rødvik. Finally, I acknowledge funding and support from the Jan Wallander and Tom Hedelius Foundation (grant number W22-0017) and the Department of Human Geography at Lund University, above all, the head of the department, Ola Hall, for hosting and supporting my postdoctoral research to write this book.

I dedicate this book to my wife, co-author, and go-to alpha reader, Shadi Yousefi, as well as to our little daughter, Nina, who patiently endured my venting, excitement, and frustrations while I worked on it. Their unconditional love and support truly mean everything to me.

Lund, December 2025

Figures

Introduction

Near the bittersweet end of the devastating COVID-19 pandemic, optimism was growing rapidly among industry experts in the southern Swedish city of Malmö about a strong construction industry bounce-back. The reality check, however, came when, by the end of 2021, developers and investors collectively refused to proceed with construction projects, despite land allocated by the municipality, coinciding with a sudden spike in inflation that caught local politicians off guard. What caused these investors to pull back? Why did their reluctance to invest persist even after inflation improved? How common was this trend? And what effects did it have on housing costs and prices for low-income populations? Interestingly, and in stark contrast, 4,755 kilometers to the southeast, in Tehran, the capital of Iran, despite persistently high inflation and the pandemic-induced recession, investing in construction remained not only a safe bet but a more lucrative one than most alternatives.

On the surface, the two cities could not be more different: one is the third-largest city in a wealthy, former social democratic country, while the other is the capital of a semi-isolated, developing nation under mullahs' authoritarian rule. Not to mention their significant differences in population and size. But notwithstanding their different historical, geographical, and political contexts, are there deeper structural economic forces driving these contrasting, seemingly irreconcilable outcomes—sector-wide disinvestment in one case and sector-wide investment in the other? Furthermore, what lessons can be drawn from their stories for other cities? After all, the social consequences of shifting investments in housing and construction, to name but one, are hardly unique to Malmö or Tehran; in fact, over recent decades, they have become everyday concerns in megacities and large metropolitan areas around the world. From New York City and São Paulo to Tokyo and Istanbul, modern cities are increasingly unaffordable for residents with low- to middle-incomes. Housing rents and prices have risen to the point where many working families can no longer afford them. Homeownership, once seen as a realistic goal, now often feels out of reach. For the small number of first-time working-class homeowners who do succeed, holding on to their homes has become a lifelong challenge due to steadily rising housing costs. True, capitalist economies in the Global North and South differ in many ways. Nevertheless, the systemic economic forces that drive fluctuations in investment (in construction or otherwise) remain similar across both.

So, if there is a general "economic basis" underlying these "endless variations and gradations in appearance" (Marx 1991 [1894], 927), how are housing problems theorized? As with other problems in the social sciences involving clashing social interests, debates over housing in contemporary capitalist cities also feature multiple competing explanations that coexist in parallel. These explanations identify different social actors as their primary audiences (e.g., public sector, housing movements, private actors) and interpret the core problem and its key determinants differently. Consequently, the strategies and policy outcomes they suggest also vary. In capitalist economies, investors invest only when they see profit potential. Given that housing is tied to land, overall profitability in the housing sector also includes land rent (i.e., the relative price of land). These parallel explanations then clash over two questions: how is this land rent generated, and how important is it in determining the intensity and direction of future investments in the sector? I argue that answering these questions is crucial to understanding why investments occur in the housing sector and, more importantly, why we experience temporal and sector-wide disinvestments.

Let me discuss some of the most prominent approaches in urban economic geography, starting with the mainstream ones, particularly the neoclassical approach. It boils down to explaining housing prices in relation to supply and demand. Inner-city dwellings are more expensive because demand is high. To balance this out, we need strategies to boost housing supply. Although they acknowledge that increasing supply will not immediately resolve inequality, they argue that sustained growth over time has the most decisive impact. However, some areas may still remain more costly due to higher land rents. But affordability depends on income levels, which are driven by market forces of supply and demand and by efficient resource allocation within labor markets. A rational allocation of resources across these markets and a potential equilibrium between supply and demand will boost economic growth, which, at the societal level, will eventually lead to increased national wealth and benefits for all members of society. Neoclassical explanations are so prevalent that they are often seen as natural. However, as heterodox economists have repeatedly pointed out, these explanations depend on the assumption that all their rather idealistic presuppositions are true, which is unrealistic. While neoclassical theories acknowledge this mismatch with the realities of capitalist markets, they respond by arguing that policy should aim to facilitate the free market, because any extra-economic manipulation of market forces is believed to worsen outcomes.

Heterodox approaches usually start where the neoclassical approach ends—that is, at the limits set by the realities of the capitalist market on its core logic. In this view, housing problems are seen as issues caused by increasing social and spatial inequalities, including reduced effective demand, institutional barriers to free-floating investment in housing, the dominance of short-term financial interests in housing policies and investments, and landlords' monopolistic power to manipulate supply and engage in price-gouging and rent capture. Heterodoxy here is an umbrella term that encompasses many economic theories, including Keynesian, post-Keynesian, institutionalist, and Marxian. What unites them is their opposition to the orthodoxy of neoclassical approaches. They all, in one way or another, emphasize how structural the noted anomalies to the mainstream explanation are to the inner workings of the capitalism system. However, their explanations conflict because their conceptualizations of the structural forces behind housing inequality differ, and their proposed strategies to address them differ accordingly.

One of the most advanced and systematic heterodox analyses of how economic urbanization processes affect housing prices and disparities is presented by David Harvey. Harvey draws on the Marxist political economy tradition and some of Marx's core concepts in Capital to explain how investments in urban space—including housing—are crucial to maintaining capital accumulation. Specifically, he links economic urbanization processes to uneven patterns of capitalist development, recurring economic crises caused by overaccumulation, and capital's need to create spaces of accumulation to absorb surplus capital that created the crises in the first place. This analysis allows him to present a big-picture view of economic urbanization processes under capitalism, with implications for urban land policies and strategies aimed at addressing urban inequalities and supporting the urban poor. He also presents crucial empirical evidence, particularly regarding the implications of neoliberal urbanization and speculative investments in the existing building stock in many advanced capitalist economies.

All the discussed approaches to urban economic geography, in one way or another, address the problem of land rent: that landlords charge rent for urban land investments, and the level of that rent affects the outcome of those investments. The differences between the theories revolve around whether the source and level of rent are determined a) naturally, meaning based on expected variations in the characteristics of the plots, so that their negative impacts can be alleviated by deepening and widening the market; or b) systemically, meaning based on internal needs for further accumulation, expressed through social conflict among different types of capitalists and landowners. Harvey clearly belongs to the latter category of theorists. The puzzle is that, although Harvey begins with Marx's categories of land rent—differential rent I, differential rent II, and absolute rent—he ultimately replaces Marx's most systemic category, absolute rent, with a new concept: class-monopoly rent. Later, Harvey (2010) explicitly states that the category of absolute rent is irrelevant to urban research. Interestingly, although he offered little empirical support for this claim, its conclusion—that the concept of absolute rent is irrelevant—remains popular among many Marxist geographers. But is this popularity due to an unquestioning acceptance of Harvey's assumption, or is the concept truly irrelevant?

In this book, I explore Harvey's reasoning behind this conceptual shift and examine its implications for addressing empirical questions, such as those I introduced at the beginning of this chapter. Using empirical studies, I aim to assess whether his claim that the concept is irrelevant is valid and, if not, whether replacing it would address empirical and theoretical gaps and tensions in his explanation. I also seek to understand how it affects the internal consistency of his argument and the potential for a structural explanation of urban processes under capitalism. To do so, I introduce an alternative approach to the urban land rent question rooted in Marxist political economy, specifically in Anwar Shaikh's theory of real competition. I start with Harvey's own assumption and argue that the leading players in housing production—landlords, builders, developers, and financiers—compete economically over their sources of profit. This raises an important question about how their returns are generated and how these returns relate to the broader economy. Investments follow profits: capitalists invest when and where they expect relatively high potential returns. This means, a) expecting more investment in the housing sector—such as increasing supply and boosting sectoral economic growth—when expected profits in that sector are higher than in other ventures; and b) to explain these dynamics, we need a clear understanding of how this shift in investment occurs. The concept of absolute rent is key to this structural analysis, affecting strategic investment choices in land and changes in land regimes, which are vital for both urban policymakers and social movements.

The timing of this evaluation is not arbitrary, either. Harvey's explanation has been applauded for its compelling account of neoliberal urbanization, its roots in the exigencies of capital accumulation, and its socio-spatial ramifications. Today, neoliberalism worldwide may not yet be entirely in the past, but its dominance is definitely under intense scrutiny. A decade into the phenomenon called deglobalization (or slowbalization) has significantly impacted regional and national economies. The fall of the unipolar world order and the rise of a tri-polar world economy, marked by economic protectionism, techno-industrial policies, calls for energy sovereignty, and various tariff wars, have only accelerated that process. In this context, a Marxist analysis of urban economic processes that goes beyond the peculiarities of neoliberal capitalism is more important than ever.

Structural Analysis

Much of the discussion here concerns structural analysis, so a brief clarification of 'structural analysis' may be in order. A consistent structural analysis, as I try to adhere to throughout what follows, is sometimes viewed as ignoring the active role of conscious agents and is often criticized as deterministic and functionalist—with Harvey's work being on the receiving end of many such criticisms (Barnes 1994; Castree 1995; Anderson 2014; King 1989a). While the term may have been used deterministically in some Marxist writings, a) that is not my approach to consistent structural analysis, and b) such anti-structural views often overlook the importance of structural analysis for the success of agents. Contrary to those claims, in other words, the main point of focusing solely on the internal ('endogenous') dynamics of structures is to offer the knowledge that is indispensable to the actions of the social agents if, in the face of durable social structures, they are going to be successful in bringing about their desired change. That is, I believe, how several great thinkers of social theory, from Marx and Durkheim to Bourdieu, have regarded the role of structural analysis, and it is what I seek to emulate throughout this book. With significant simplification, in the interest of further clarification, one could say that mainstream economic analysis of urbanization processes and Harvey's contribution provide two very different accounts of the structural constraints that social agents face. Whether these social agents are policymakers or social movements, they must seriously consider a coherent structural analysis to devise effective practices for realizing their desired change.

Returning to Harvey, he began developing a Marxist approach to economic geography in the early 1970s by explicitly engaging with structural analysis. He drew on the core principles of Marxist political economy and stated, "[a]ny attempt to create an interdisciplinary theory with respect to a phenomenon such as urbanism has perforce to resort to the operational structuralist method which Marx practices" (Harvey 2009 [1973], 302). A decade later, Harvey reaffirmed this conviction and identified his two main contributions: one to Marxism and the other to the discipline of geography. Concerning Marxism, he saw his contribution in adding the 'spatial dimension' to Marxism (Harvey, 1985, 163; 164). Regarding the discipline of geography—specifically urban economic geography—he believed his role was to challenge "the critics and defectors from the Marxist tradition of urban analysis [who] deny that urban community and its distinctive politics are produced under capitalist relations of production and consumption as these operate in and on geographical space" (ibid. 163). In essence, his main contribution to the discipline has been to introduce the structural dynamics of capital accumulation into an otherwise structure-less geography with its consequential localism and exceptionalism (Harvey 1993; 1995).

Over time, Harvey seems to have moved away from explicitly using the term 'structural analysis' in his later works. This may partly be a reaction to the term becoming more associated with Louis Althusser in academic circles. Additionally, it could be argued that this change in terminology reflects a shift in his empirical interest as he began to align his work more specifically with critiques of place-specific speculative practices under neoliberal regimes in advanced capitalist economies of the Global North over the following decades. I will revisit this point later in the book. Despite the change in terminology, however, he has remained dedicated to the core principles of structural analysis, and his approach continues to influence geographers to "move from a deadening exceptionalism toward generalization, systematicity, and universal explanation" (Barnes and Sheppard 2019, 187). As Kevin Cox pointed out, the operationalization of Marxian political economy into geographic research, culminating in his Limits to Capital (2006 [1982]), highlights Harvey's significant contribution with what Cox describes as a "structured coherence" and a "realist notion of a structure of relations" (Cox 2016, 11; 20; 2013). However, there are two levels of structured coherence in Harvey's explanation that Cox refers to: conceptual and empirical. As Gregory has stated, "[the potency of geographical knowledge] resides, rather, in the use of ideas—if you prefer (and Harvey does prefer), concepts and theories—that produce a systematic and ordered representation of the world that is sufficiently powerful to persuade others of its objectivity, accuracy, and truth" (Gregory 2006, 1, my emphasis). My proposed alternative below begins with this very principle, aiming to offer greater empirical content and thus a more persuasive case than Harvey's explanation for the 'objectivity, accuracy, and truth' of such a structural account in explaining urban land rent through movements of capital, using Shaikh's theory of real competition and the concept of absolute rent.

Critiquing Harvey from a Marxist Perspective

Forty years ago, Harvey outlined his intellectual project as mapping "the rich complexity of a mode of production with greater accuracy" (Harvey 1985, xiii). To achieve this, he aimed to combine two perspectives on capitalism: one "from the perspective of production" in Capital volume one, and the other "from the viewpoint of circulation in volume two" (ibid.). He further submitted that the outcome "should give us a fuller picture of the structure of a mode of production and inner contradictions" (ibid.). However, his engagement with Marx's third viewpoint—which includes competition, relative prices, profit cycles, the movement of capital, land rent, based on his breakdown of surplus value into three forms of profit, rent, and wage (Marx 1991 [1894], 975)—remains much less systematic. More importantly, Harvey's support for this choice remains highly textual. He described Marx's "troubles" with rent theory and stated that "his writings on the subject, all of which were published posthumously, are for the most part tentative thoughts set down in the process of discovery" (Harvey 2006 [1982], 330). Marked by apparent contradictions, Harvey submitted that upon close reading, Marx's work on land rent in Capital Volume Three "is dogged by certain difficulties which do not yield easily to the usual magic of his touch. The result is a good deal of confusion and an immense and continuing controversy among those few hardy souls who have tried to pick their way through the minefield of his writings on the subject" (ibid.). Specifically for absolute rent, he posited that, given Marx spent "hundreds of pages" on differential rents but only a few on absolute rent (ibid. 349), his writings on absolute land rent are of less theoretical significance. In response, and to complement Marx's work toward "a coherent theory of ground rent" sensitive to its contemporary historical and geographical contexts (namely, neoliberal capitalism), Harvey proposed "co-ordinating functions" of "rental appropriation ... in relation to accumulation" that resemble interest-bearing capital, as its role is "bought at the cost of permitting insane forms of land speculation" (Harvey 2006 [1982], 331). He contended that "such an argument is barely discernable within Marx's texts, and he appears extraordinarily reluctant to admit of any positive role for the landlord under capitalism" (ibid.).

This overall textual approach, however, requires careful evaluation. True, proponents of both prominent interpretations of Marx's economic theory discussed here—namely, the Sweezyan monopoly capitalism and the law of the tendency of the rate of profit to fall (LTRPF)—frequently rely on their respective readings and interpretations in debates.[1] But popularity does not necessarily equate to validity. After all, elements of nearly all interpretations can be found in Marx's texts, especially (and naturally) in his various notebooks and unpublished materials, which makes textual analysis less scientifically significant. I would argue, in contrast, that a strong (materialist) critique should demonstrate and challenge the empirical and operational strengths of

1 Examples of the first category include Harvey's (2016; 2021) critique of the LTRPF and Ackerman's 2023 article, in which after outlining the chronological order of appearance of various interpretations of Marx's economic and crisis theory since the 1880s, Ackerman dismisses the LTRPF interpretation because it appeared much later, in the 1930s, through Henryk Grossman, and was not widely adopted by Marxists of the Second International.

its rivals, rather than merely judging how accurate or inaccurate their reading is. This principle also applies to Harvey's own work: it would be a grave mistake to dismiss the empirical and operational merits of his work solely because we may disagree with his interpretation of Marx's writings. Moreover, ever since the publication of his first major book, 'Explanation in Geography' (1969), Harvey's work has addressed numerous topics and debates that remain highly germane and significant to Marxist thought, a notable example being his intellectual struggles with mainstream and later postmodernist geographers. Dismissing all of this because he interprets Marx's economic theory differently would be unscientific. At the same time, recognizing Harvey's interpretation as plausible and scientifically valid on its own does not dismiss the importance of other, equally plausible interpretations of Marx's argument in Capital, as many Marxist economists have demonstrated repeatedly since the previous century (Kliman, 2007, 2012; Moseley, 2016; Roberts, 2009; Shaikh, 2016). In that sense, what this book is definitely not about is claiming to offer a comprehensive critique of Harvey's entire body of work, nor is it claiming to offer a textual critique of his writings. My critique is concerned not with the 'letter' of Harvey (or Marx, for that matter), but rather with the explanatory power of his political-economic framework and the tensions within it for explaining economic urbanization processes through urban land rent theory. This critique, which is decidedly limited in scope to land rent in urban contexts, therefore, is primarily empirical. It seeks to deepen understanding of capitalist urbanization processes beyond the confines of neoliberal capitalism.

All this suggests that, despite its perceived nerdiness, the original puzzle in this book—the omission of the concept of absolute rent in Harvey's explanation of capitalist urbanization—has direct implications for understanding stories like the one I began this chapter with. This hazard of nerdiness, however, must be addressed. After all, Harvey is by far the most influential Marxist geographer and one of the most influential (critical) social scientists of the last fifty years. He is also a popular interpreter of Marx's Capital, whose in-class and broadcast lectures on Capital have inspired thousands of young scholars, intellectuals, and activists over the past five decades. Therefore, it is no surprise that any critique of his work—especially if it comes from other Marxists—is often seen as nerdy, sectarian, or even heretical.[2] In response to such defensive reactions, I advocate for scientific pluralism and note that having many competing (parallel) interpretations of theories—and explanations of real-world problems—in the social sciences greatly contributes to the development and

2 As an (extreme) example, one reviewer once labeled Marxist critics of Harvey as "Harvey's enemies".

growth of science. These competing interpretations coexist because each reflects the social, economic, and political interests of particular social classes or strata—interests that are inherently conflictual. The competitive environment allows these interpretations to modify, expand, and refine their conceptualizations in response to silences, gaps, and tensions identified by their rivals; without this back-and-forth exchange, they risk degenerating into mere reproduction of the same empirical content time and again.

Nevertheless, I write this book not only in the interest of scientific pluralism but also because the times have changed (Farahani 2024; Farahani et al. 2026). Harvey's work on the question of land rent in particular, and his analysis of economic urbanization processes in general, was somewhat deliberately focused on explaining these processes through the dynamics of neoliberal capitalism, with its assumed dominance of speculative activities, amid the de-industrialization of cities in the Global North and the offshoring of manufacturing investments and jobs to the Global South. As Ted Rutland (2010) also noted, Harvey's remarkably lucid insights in the early 1980s into the emerging regime of accumulation—later known as neoliberal urbanization—must be acknowledged here. At the same time, this suggests that his interpretation now needs to be reconsidered and reevaluated, as the neoliberal regime of accumulation is no longer dominant. Even if one agrees with his explanation of capitalist urbanization processes driven by neoliberal strategies and ideologies, it is hardly possible to extrapolate them directly to future regimes of capitalist accumulation or even the current trial-and-error phase with its extreme economic, political, and geopolitical uncertainties. Capitalism existed before neoliberalism emerged and will likely continue after it ceases to exist. A comprehensive theory of land rent in capitalist urbanization must be broad enough to explain the problem regardless of the specific mode of accumulation, while still being concrete enough to incorporate its time- and place-specific forms, including the impact of speculative activities.

Revisiting Harvey's two introductions to the two editions of the Limits, I cannot help but think he wrote the first when the left (in a broader sense) had just passed its peak in many advanced capitalist economies, yet it was still predominantly present in political and intellectual circles, thanks to the "remarkable resurgence" of the "Marxist intellectual tradition" in the 1970s (Harvey 2006 [1982], xxxiii). His second edition was published just before the most significant crisis of the neoliberal era, when all its assumptions still seemed ubiquitous. The political and intellectual context for this book, however, is entirely different. Neoliberal globalization and most of its key regulatory regimes are under constant attack by the rapidly rising alt-right and far-right forces across the advanced capitalist world, and the anti-capitalist left is in one of its weakest positions and deepest existential crises in decades, both politically and intellectually. So why write a book criticizing a fellow Marxist at such a time? For anyone who adheres to Marxism as a theory of scientific socialism, the evolution of Marxist thought is also viewed as a cumulative process. Therefore, all critical engagements with other Marxists, at least in principle, should be seen as positive contributions that add to the overall evolution of Marxist thought and represent a progressive development of the research program in a Lakatosian sense. The intellectual implications of such critical engagements extend beyond narrow academic and disciplinary debates. In this regard, this work should be seen as a continuation of the intellectual project Harvey himself helped initiate in the early 1970s to advance an interdisciplinary Marxist research program in geography. More importantly, looking back over the past four decades, it would be an understatement to say that the practical outcomes of strategies inspired by anti-neoliberal Marxism have been largely limited. At least in part, neoliberal capitalism has remained dominant all these years because the anti-capitalist left (even those few who managed to stay clear of purely academic debates) largely remained in disarray and failed to provide an impactful and effective political challenge to neoliberalism. Now that the decline of the old order coincides with a tumultuous, uncertain trial-and-error phase, it is precisely the time for the anti-capitalist left to reevaluate the legacies (both positive and negative) of anti-neoliberal Marxism and its practical implications.

Over the years, since I embarked on this intellectual project, I have encountered many Harveyan geographers who dismiss criticisms of any aspect of Harvey's work by other Marxists, claiming that they supposedly do not understand Harvey's Ollman-inspired dialectical approach. These Harveyan geographers vigorously defend the core assumptions of Harvey's work against criticism from other Marxists by pointing out his influence from Ollman's interpretation of Marx's dialectics. Ollman (2003, 4) noted that "[the] apparent meanings [of Marx's concepts] varied with context," giving Marx's meaning an "elastic quality" that can be mistaken for inconsistency. Even if we accept that this is true for both Marx and Harvey equally across all their work (which, of course, is a deeply problematic assumption[3]), it still does not mean that either of their works is immune to criticism. Interestingly, such *ad hoc* conceptual protective belts (in a Lakatosian (1978) sense) ultimately fail to preserve

3 Harvey (2006 [1982], 334) himself criticized Marx's lexicon and his conceptualizations of land rent for being "not always consistent," effectively ignoring what Ollman calls the "elastic quality" of Marx's approach to his (dialectical) method of presentation as he outlined in his introductions to both Capital, Volume One (Marx 1976 [1867]) and Grundrisse (Marx 1973).

the hard core of the Harveyan research program, as they dismiss the critique entirely rather than actively engaging with it to expand the program's empirical content. Another claim by the Harveyan geographers is that the alternative interpretation of Marx's economic theory, as opposed to Harvey's, which adheres to the LTRPF, cannot be applied to empirical studies; it is too general, too macro, or even outright irrelevant for geographic research. The problem with such arguments is that they will make no meaningful contribution to the debate unless they demonstrate this alleged irrelevance through empirical evidence. Using Lakatosian terminology, this reaction is also an example of negative heuristics in a degenerating research program, in which the critical expansion of the program's empirical content is sacrificed in favor of the defensive *ad hoc* creation of hypotheses whose only purpose is to temporarily deflect criticism, without any real effort to develop theory innovatively. In contrast, and to expand the empirical scope of the alternative interpretation (LTRPF), some of my colleagues and I have been working on empirical analyses of urban and housing research, as well as global value chains, mining, and agroindustry using a Shaikh-inspired interpretation of Marx's work on competition in Capital Volume Three (Farahani et al. 2026; also, Campling 2025). This book aims to contribute to this overall project.

On the other side of this debate are the Marxist critics of Harvey. Over the last fifty years, well-known Marxist economists from different tendencies have often challenged Harvey's specific interpretation of Marx's economic theory. These criticisms cover a range from his equilibrium model of spatial fix (Lebowitz 1986) to his theory of economic crises (Mattick Jr. 2008; Kliman 2015; Roberts 2014; 2016b), and more recently, to his critique of Marx's labor theory of value (Roberts 2020a). The thrust of many such critiques has been to problematize Harvey's particular *interpretation* of Marx's economic theory (relying principally on Paul Sweezy's well-established reading) and to question how it is used to understand the geographies of capitalist development. This book, however, has a different point of departure. Instead of starting from Marx's theory of rent and pitting it against Harvey's, it begins by examining Harvey's theory of urban land rent on its own terms, with the most significant being its structural treatment of land rent. Harvey's economist critics, who do not limit their critiques to textual interpretation and accuracy, are essential to advancing the debate. However, they still primarily approach it from the perspective of the discipline of economics. This creates a notable research gap that can be filled by expanding the critique to include geographical questions and debates. The critiques offered by Marxists such as Kliman (2015) and Roberts (2014, 2016b, 2020a), while highly detailed in their exposition of Marx's writings, a) remain to some extent at the level of the text itself by aiming to identify issues in Harvey's interpretation of Marx, and b) remain within the disciplinary boundaries of economics, discussing the implications of Harvey's reading for economic research.

I believe the critique of Harvey presented here is not only more relevant scientifically but also more commonsensical. The simple truth is that if several prominent Marxist economists have felt the need to question Harvey's interpretation of Marx's economic theory, it is because he is one of the most influential geographers of our time. Otherwise, they would ignore his allegedly 'inaccurate' interpretation, just as they overlook similar views from many other Marxists. Their high sensitivity to Harvey's interpretation of Marx comes from Harvey's high standing in the discipline of geography (Das 2017a; 2017b; 2023). Harvey is deservedly celebrated as "arguably the greatest living Marxist geographer" and one of the most influential geographers of the 20th century (Castree and Gregory 2006, 97). A systematic critique of Harvey should come from within geography itself, not just because it is "his home discipline" (ibid.) but because Harvey's importance lies in his scientific contributions to geography. As an insightful observer has said, "Harvey's work can be read in many ways, but whatever else it may be, it is surely both an affirmation and a critique of the power of geographical knowledges" (Gregory 2006, 1). His explanation stands or falls with this contribution to geography.

•••

In this book, I aim to challenge Harvey's assertion that the concept of absolute rent is irrelevant to urban research, from both theoretical and empirical perspectives. To do this, I plan to analyze the internal consistency of two Marxist approaches to urban land rent: one, inspired by Harvey, omits the concept of absolute rent; the other includes it. An empirical judgment between them follows this. I investigate the following question: How consistently structural are these two opposing approaches in their explanations of rent creation and appropriation in terms of the macro-dynamics of capital accumulation? Three sub-questions follow: How do they explain the relationship between rent-bearing sectors and the rest of the economy at both macro and micro levels? What analytical tools do they provide? Finally, how do their respective operationalizations of rent theory correspond to their underlying economic theories?

The book is divided into three parts: beginning with an abstract Part 1, followed by a concrete Part 2, and concluding with another abstract discussion in Part 3. Part 1 (chapters 1–3) of the book comprises a brief introduction to the question of land rent, the competing theories of urban land rent around which the book is framed, Harvey's position in the broader intellectual debates on land rent, and finally, a review of post-Harveyan rent debates and urban applications since the 1980s. The primary aim is to identify gaps, tensions, and silences in Harvey's explanation of land rent. It ends by introducing two competing models—Harvey's Spatial Monopoly Model of Land Rent (SMLR) and the Turbulent Inter-Sectoral Model of Land Rent (TILR)—and my criteria for judging between them. Part 2 (chapters 4–9) begins with a critical engagement with Harvey's own empirical evidence and counterposes it with the proposed alternative. It then discusses the empirical gaps and tensions in the SMLR and the relevance of the TILR, using a series of case studies in Sweden and Iran. These studies are organized at both the national and city levels for each of the two countries. Part 2 concludes by revisiting the Lakatosian dilemma that practitioners of research programs often face; they remain tenacious in the face of empirical counterevidence, necessitating further theoretical reasoning to substantiate the comparison between the two models. Finally, Part 3 (chapters 10 and 11) returns to the theoretical discussions, elaborating on the two models' theoretical foundations, their relationship to Marx's economic theory, the connection between the two concepts of land rent, and a detailed presentation of the TILR.

Chapter 1 aims to lay out Harvey's fairly sophisticated line of argument. It introduces central questions in urban research regarding land rent, as initially outlined by Harvey, and their relationship to urban strategies (both short- and long-term). The chapter then situates Harvey in the field. It outlines how his analysis fares with the mainstream neoclassical approaches to urban land rent. Then, it presents the three pillars of his approach to urban analysis in which land rent plays a pivotal role, i.e., his interpretation of uneven geographical development, his dual theses of capital switching and spatial fix, and his conceptualization of land rent categories (differential rent I and II, class-monopoly rent, absolute rent). These will be followed by an exposition of relevant critiques of Harvey's conceptualizations by other Marxist scholars since the 1970s and a discussion on the gaps and tensions within his explanation.

Chapter 2 begins by periodizing the debate over Marxian rent theory in urban economic geography. This will situate the debate between Harvey-inspired geographers and some influential institutionalist urban researchers (such as Michael Ball) from the late 1970s to the late 1990s. The chapter discusses central controversies regarding the categories of land rent (specifically, absolute rent), as well as the empirical corroboration of Harvey's theory by Harveyan geographers, which led to conceptualizations such as the rent gap hypothesis.

The chapter concludes by articulating why the debate has remained unresolved and the project unfinished, setting the stage for the next part to further engage with the debate empirically.

Chapter 3 presents the two competing theories of urban land rent: a) Harvey's theory (reconstructed as the spatial-monopoly model of land rent or SMLR), and b) my alternative, conceptualized as the turbulent inter-sectoral model of land rent or TILR. The chapter ends with outlining my methodological strategy for a critical appraisal and comparison of the two models using immanent critique (to evaluate Harvey's theory on its own terms and identify its internal gaps and tensions) and Lakatosian methodology for the second (to establish that competing interpretations are inevitable, but judging between them is an empirical matter). This brief presentation of the methodological strategy is necessary, as it dictates the dramatic structure of the argument that follows in the subsequent chapters.

Part 2 begins with Chapter 4. The basis of the chapter is revisiting Harvey's original empirical evidence for discarding the concept of absolute rent and replacing it with that of class-monopoly rent. His evidence is then juxtaposed with additional empirical evidence that supports the TILR. Thus, the time frame of this additional empirical evidence is limited to the period covered by Harvey's studies on Baltimore housing markets in the early 1970s. The aim is to identify empirical gaps and tensions in Harvey's evidence for his suggested conceptual change.

Chapter 5 aims to address a gap in Harvey's SMLR, specifically the difficulty of empirically demonstrating capital switching and land rent (resulting from the discontinuation of Swedish municipal site leasehold in the mid-to-late 1980s). It further aims to demonstrate that a modified interpretation of the capital switching thesis can be relevant to the historical analysis of the structural forces driving changes in land policy. The chapter proposes an alternative interpretation of Harvey's capital switching thesis, using the TILR to analyze the discontinuation of the Swedish municipal site leasehold in the mid-to-late 1980s. The three central claims are: a) the cause of capital switching should be extended to other forms of crisis (profitability and productivity), b) inter-sectoral competition over higher expected profit rates determines switching, and c) capital switching is mediated by aggregate land rent rates (as excess profit rates in the land sector), and the fluctuations of land rent rates determine the historical contingency of capital switching, i.e., in this case, lower aggregate land rent rates and higher relative profit rates in the financial sector implied switching to the financial sector, instead of the built environment, and that had implications in terms of disinvestment by private actors (developers and constructors) and intensifying institutional tension between them and municipalities over leasehold costs and land ownership.

Chapter 6 presents an operationalization of the TILR and Shaikh's theory of real competition to analyze, more broadly, the political-economic determinants and structural economic forces contributing to the affordable-housing shortage in Sweden's third-largest city, Malmö. I argue that existing municipal policy recommendations are informed by microeconomic price theory, focusing solely on supply and demand dynamics. I contend that much of the literature criticizing such policies fundamentally shares core assumptions of microeconomic perspectives, treating the shortage as a distributional issue. In contrast, I argue that the problem lies in the inflows and outflows of housing investment. Drawing on Shaikh, I differentiate among various investment types and their associated profit formations, which determine the final price of housing as a commodity. These investment types connect macro-level land and construction dynamics to micro-level housing consumption and inequalities. Finally, I present empirical observations and discuss the strategic implications of Shaikh's theory for understanding the housing shortage in Malmö.

Chapters 7 and 8 extend the discussion to the Global South. Chapter 7 discusses how land relations are rooted in the peculiarities of Iranian capitalism, in which multi-scalar geopolitical conflicts explicitly interfere with both labor relations and investment choices. The analysis incorporates the concept of absolute rent as a structural mechanism governing capital flow into urban land investments, using an inter-sectoral and multi-scalar framework anticipated in the TILR to analyze the country's first state-led public housing initiative. Such a relational analysis is necessary to challenge conventional approaches that assume a clear distinction between macro-level (global) similarities and micro-level (local) differences. The case of Iran is significant, as it adds complexity to the spatiotemporal analysis of aggregate and inter-sectoral rates of return, which are central to measuring the extent and patterns of land rent creation and appropriation in the TILR. Existing studies tend to explain the case of Iran through exogenous mechanisms, such as the backwardness of political and governmental systems, the underdevelopment of capitalist political and economic relations, a lack of expertise, and the restricted influence of technocrats due to the political interference of undemocratic and religious forces. In that sense, the chapter proposes a (structural) alternative approach by drawing attention to the ramifications of the actually existing Iranian capitalism and its economic and geopolitical constraints. Chapter 8 extends this analysis to the urban scale and operationalizes the TILR to analyze gentrification and spatial inequality in Tehran.

Chapter 9 is brief, arguing that Harveyan geographers are unlikely to engage with the concept of absolute rent, despite empirical evidence supporting it. This argument will set the stage for the next part of the book, which will discuss the underlying theoretical assumptions for the SMLR, making the concept of absolute rent internally inconsistent.

Chapter 10 revisits the controversy surrounding the concept of absolute rent, aiming to situate it within competing interpretations of Marx's economic theory and their underlying competition theories. It argues that the concept of absolute rent is internally inconsistent with the interpretation Harvey developed in his project for Marxist geography. In other words, it is not a matter of which interpretation is more *accurate* vis-à-vis Marx's text, but to argue that Harvey's choice of interpretation came with consequences (that rendered absolute rent inconsistent with core assumptions of that interpretation and created the gaps and tensions presented in the previous part). A critical response to Harvey's argument as to why absolute rent is "irrelevant" is also presented here.

Finally, Chapter 11 outlines the TILR, its theoretical presumptions, and its potential implications. The concluding chapter then returns to the book's original puzzle (i.e., the alleged irrelevance of the concept of absolute rent for urban research according to Harvey's theory of urbanization), reviews the argument and its contributions, and discusses some areas for further empirical engagement with the debate.

PART 1

Capitalist Urbanization and the Centrality of Land Rent

CHAPTER 1

Harvey and the Structural Analysis of Capitalist Urbanization

The economic crisis of 2007–08, known as the Great Recession, was sparked by the collapse of the US mortgage markets and viewed by millions of dispossessed citizens primarily as an urban crisis, especially in housing. The devastating impact of the crisis on the lives of the underprivileged is evident. From massive household debt to widespread homelessness worldwide, the person on the street saw the Great Recession not just as a capitalist or financial crisis, but mainly as an urban crisis. One immediate intellectual response to the Great Recession has been a growing interest in rethinking—and in some cases, creating—concepts in urban geography. Since 2008, many papers have been published on different forms of urban struggle and theorizing 'new' kinds of urban uprisings and urban anger (Dikeç 2016; Dikeç and Swyngedouw 2017; Sutterlüty 2014). More relevant to this book's theme, there has also been increasing focus on theories of economic crises and rethinking urbanization processes and their economic drivers, such as land rent (Christophers 2016; Clark 2014; 2018; Haila 2015; Manning 2020; 2023; Park 2014; Slater 2017; Ward and Aalbers 2016). This collective scholarly attention to rent theory and the problem of urban land rent underscores the urgent need to understand and address the urban crisis, which has worsened since the Great Recession as the recovery has become increasingly sluggish and daunting.[1] Historically, interest in modern land rent theory emerged during similar turbulent periods, such as debates over the Corn Laws in England (1815–1846), and again after the 1973 Oil Crisis. Particularly in the case of the latter, the crisis coincided with a revival of the classical political economy approach in economics and later its extension to urban economic geography, which gained popularity during the "remarkable resurgence" of Marxist and heterodox economic thought since the early 1970s (Harvey 2006 [1982], xxxiii). This approach, which centers its analysis on economic crises and land rent issues, is responsible for many detailed analyses of "economic urbanization processes" (Friedmann 2002, 4) and is predominantly shaped by the work of David Harvey.

1 As the crisis has come to seem "less and less like a 'normal crisis,'" some researchers suggest that neoliberal capitalism "may indeed have entered its zombie phase" (Peck 2010, 109).

Harvey's explanation is noteworthy for providing a systemic view of capitalist urbanization, which relates economic urbanization processes under capitalism to the macro-dynamics of capital accumulation. He developed a theory of spatiotemporal fix (reconstructed in Section 1.3 below) "to the crisis-prone inner contradictions of capital accumulation" in response to "a chronic tendency within capitalism … to produce crises of overaccumulation" (Harvey 2003, 87–88). The problem of surplus capital is structural in that "since it is the lack of profitable opportunities that lies at the heart of the difficulty, the key economic (as opposed to social and political) problem lies with capital" (ibid. 88). And he names "geographical expansion and spatial reorganization" as lucrative strategies to absorb surplus capital (ibid.). To put it differently, "since geographical expansion often entails investment in long-lived physical and social infrastructures (in transport and communications networks and education and research, for example), the production and reconfiguration of space relations provides one potent way to stave off, if not resolve, the tendency towards crisis formation under capitalism" (ibid.). Land rent (and rent theory) holds a decisive position in Harvey's analysis. The reason is somewhat straightforward: investments in land require a lease or acquisition, and rent determines the final price of land, thereby restricting the free flow of (the mass of) investments to built environments. This systemic (or structural) analysis of capitalist urbanization, however, was not developed in a vacuum. Harvey explicitly advanced it as a rival to mainstream neoclassical explanations of urbanization processes that relate them to market forces (i.e., the interplay of supply and demand). Let me explain how.

1.1 Pre-Harveyan Urban Analysis and Harvey's Critique

The pre-Harveyan urban economic geography was heavily influenced by neoclassical economics and its principal marginal utility model. Under the assumption of perfect competition (with perfect entry and exit for capital and labor, perfect knowledge, and given price levels), equilibrium is a state in which a perfect market and efficient allocation of resources is possible. The state of equilibrium makes utility maximization rational, given that the marginal utility-price ratio would be the same for all goods. This allows individuals (with their, by definition, limited budgets) to spend according to their subjective (yet rational) evaluation of the value of commodities and helps "link prices to quantities demanded and supplied" (Nicholas 2012, 459). In the urban context, this microeconomic model has been particularly prevalent in New Urban Economics literature (McMaster and Watkins 2006, 904; Richardson 1976, 137).

The neoclassical approach examines the market structures that influence investment choices in urban land markets, where the primary indicator is the cost of land. Furthermore, in the case of residential location, "the general hypothesis is that household trade-off travel costs (which increase away from the city centre), against housing costs (which are shown to decrease from the city centre) in an attempt to maximize utility subject to an overall budget constraint" (Bassett and Short 1980, 27; McDonald 2007, 67). In this trade-off model, budget and time constraints are independent, and travel and housing costs are dependent variables (Bassett and Short 1980, 27–28). Housing production is structured by the household's demand (preference) and the producer's behavior (Muth 1969; 1971). In other words, the elasticity of supply depends on the elasticity of housing demand (Muth 1971, 244). Land rent, in this model, is "a rational allocative device which allocates land to the highest bidder" (Bassett and Short 1980, 28). Like von Thünen, William Alonso builds his monocentric land rent model on a reinterpretation of David Ricardo's differential rent for the urban context (Alonso 1964; McDonald 2007, 68). Land rent in this interpretation is "a function of accessibility" (Bassett and Short 1980, 29). It is explained in terms of differential locational accessibility, which shapes an individual household's willingness to pay away from a commercial city center, such as the central business district, or toward employment centers in other sub-markets, as measured by property and land market prices.

Harvey begins with an immanent critique of such neoclassical models that dominated the field throughout the 1960s, starting with their central assumptions (such as uneven development and monocentric models of urban sub-markets), followed by identifying their gaps and tensions, particularly, their failure to relate "urban development to macroeconomic disruptions" (Harvey 2012, 35). He then counterposes his explanation against this neoclassical research program in his first book of his Marxist period, namely, Social Justice and the City (2009 [1973]). There, he drew upon Marx's "operational structuralist method" and his systemic understanding of the capitalist economy, which Harvey found integral to developing "an interdisciplinary theory with respect to a phenomenon such as urbanism" (Harvey 2009 [1973], 302). This understanding enabled Harvey to go beyond neoclassical analyses of economic urbanization processes by drawing attention to the processes and structures that shape and maintain residential development patterns, which neoclassical models meticulously simulate and describe, but fail to relate to the long-term and systemic movements of capital and tendencies toward crisis formation and socio-spatial conflicts. In response, he developed a rival structural explanation that transcends market structures and connects economic urbanization processes to the macro-dynamics of capital accumulation, thereby providing greater explanatory power. He views neoclassical models as "special cases, which describe conditions when absolute and monopoly rents are insignificant, when absolute and relational concepts of time and space are irrelevant, and when the institution of private property is notably quiescent in the land and property markets" (Harvey 2009 [1973], 188). Land rent, as explained by Harvey, is more than just an allocation device. It is generally levied due to (class) monopoly relations that control land markets and, all other things being equal, act as a barrier to the free flow of capital onto land. The free movement of capital onto land and the built environment plays a vital role in creating spaces of accumulation to offset the systemic and recurring crises of overaccumulation—the inevitable outcome of uneven geographies of capitalist development.

Historically speaking, the appeal of Marx and his economic theory to Harvey and other political-economic geographers in the 1970s comes from the need to a) legitimately establish geography as a scientific discipline; b) move beyond empiricist explanations and incorporate the (economic, historical, and sociological) structures; c) provide a better and more rigorous understanding of the drivers of spatial change; and d) develop a dialectical understanding of the relation between micro-level and local spatial processes and aggregate economic and institutional patterns and forces (Castree et al. 2013, 409; Gregory et al. 2009, 619; Massey 1985; Olsson 1974; Smith 1971, 153–154; Swyngedouw 2000, 42). This last point is crucial, as geographers aimed to find "a way of preserving the truth of premises derived from large-scale data in conclusions about small-scale behavior", most commonly found in neoclassical (microeconomic) explanations (Olsson 1974, 52). The departure from the concept of location and the arrival at the concept of space then seem inevitable, as location is fixed—a specific spot on the map. Inserting space into geographic analysis enabled heterodox urban economic geographers to incorporate social relations and political-economic structures, thereby understanding the structural drivers of geographical differentiation and moving beyond the empiricist descriptions common in urban microeconomic models (Harvey 2006; also see Bandyopadhyay 1982a, 170). Moreover, the resulting spatiotemporal framework was operationalized to delineate the (historical and geographical) dimensions of capitalist urbanization processes. Harvey's contribution culminated in the publication of the Limits to Capital in 1982, whose impact was such that Cox said, "only with the appearance of Harvey's Limits to Capital did things become clearer" (Cox 2016, 13).

Harvey's influence on the establishment of heterodox political-economic geography in the 1970s and 1980s was formative. His immense theoretical and analytical contributions demonstrated the relevance of structural (political-economic) analysis of capitalist urbanization and highlighted the significance of focusing on material conflicts in urbanization processes. Advancing models for spatialities of capital accumulation, he pushed radical geography beyond a framework simply with 'radical values'. He helped establish it as a scientific tradition in urban economic geography capable of (at least to some extent) rivaling non-structural, neoclassical, and institutionalist approaches. He points to the political-economic forces behind both spatial change and urban land strategies. He highlights the role of material struggle in the appropriation of urban resources within a framework specifically designed to address urban inequalities and advocate for the urban poor. None of his contemporary heterodox urban geographers and economists came close to developing a systematic and consistent theory for geographic research and urban political economy that rivals neoclassical explanations by relating spatial differentiation and uneven geographies to capital accumulation processes. Most critiques remain at the theoretical and conceptual levels, highlighting the theoretical differences between political economy and neoclassical urban analyses (Bruegel 1975; Clarke and Ginsburg 1975; Edel 1976; 1977; 1992; Ive 1974; Massey and Catalano 1978; Walker 1974; 1975).[2] His framework, therefore, has proven necessary for urban economic geographers following Harvey to (empirically) operationalize it for urban research.

1.2 Urbanization as Capitalist Accumulation

Harvey is one of the first (and arguably the most significant) urban economic geographers to have successfully advanced a consistent scientific explanation of urbanization processes and spatial change using Marxist political economy. Inspired by Marx's structural explanation of accumulation and circulation in the capitalist economy (as the main viewpoints in Capital, Volumes One and Two, respectively) (Harvey 1985, xiii), Harvey develops a generally consistent explanation of the various ways in which economic urbanization processes relate to the structural forces of capitalist accumulation and development. He

2 "Geography is an eclectic and fashion-prone discipline", Swyngedouw (2000, 41) observed, with a "short-lived" attention span for "major theoretical and methodological perspectives". Radical geography has complied with this rule throughout its history. And even though Marxian political economy functioned as a prominent approach in the early stages of the establishment of radical geography as a coherent intellectual tradition in geography (thanks to Harvey's efforts), it soon lost the ground to first post-structuralist (in social analyses) and then institutionalist and post-Keynesian (in economic analyses) perspectives since the mid-1980s (Cox 2016; see also, Farahani et al. 2026).

relates spatial differentiation patterns to general patterns of capitalist development (best analyzed in *The Limits to Capital* (2006 [1982])). He contends that spatial differentiations are outcomes of inherently uneven geographies of capitalist development. This Marxist interpretation of the (somewhat mainstream) theory of uneven geographical development plays a significant role in his operationalization of Marxian economics into geographic research.

In stark contrast to neoclassical economic theories that assume development on "a flat plain surface endowed with ubiquitous raw materials and homogenous labour supply with equal transport facility in all directions" (Harvey 2006 [1982], 415), Harvey submits that capitalism develops geographically through the movement of capital across space (and regions), producing more spaces for accumulation along the way. That means "actively produced … territorial and regional coherence … arises out of the conversion of temporal into spatial restraints to accumulation" (ibid. 416). A region-specific explanation of capitalist development entails that "surplus value has to be produced and realized within a 'closed' region, then the technology of production, structures of distribution, modes and forms of consumption, the value, quantities and qualities of labour power, as well as all necessary physical and social infrastructure must all be consistent with each other within that region" (ibid. 416–417). It follows that, in such a model, each region would function according to its specific law of value, "associated with particular material living standards, forms of the labour process, institutional and infrastructural structures" (ibid.). However, these spatiotemporal constraints, Harvey maintains, appear as contradictory to capital accumulation, given that "regional economies are never closed" and both capital and labor tend to move to regions with higher relative profits or higher relative living standards, in the forms of capital structure or labor arbitrage (ibid.). That is because capital tends to accumulate in a contradictory and overall uneven fashion as "an opposition between countervailing forces, making for geographical concentration or dispersal in the circulation of capital" (ibid. 417). The spatial limits to circulation are imposed by "immobile physical and social infrastructures" localized to "support certain kinds of production, certain kinds of labour processes, distributional arrangements, consumption patterns, and so on" (ibid. 428).

Harvey draws on Marx to explain the tendency to agglomerate (or concentrate) "productive forces in urban centres [as well as] correlated changes in social relations of production and living … [and] how the forces making for agglomeration can build cumulatively upon each other, drawing new transport investments and consumer goods industries to already established locations" (ibid.). The tendency to concentrate is primarily due to the need to reduce space-related costs, as concentration decreases communication time, transportation costs, and transaction costs (Harvey 2006, 96). At the same time, "the spatial range," between residential and employment centers, "depends upon transportation capacities and the means, cost, and time taken" (ibid.). Harvey criticizes the neoclassical model alluded to above for presuming "an equilibrium arising out of rational trade-offs between rising transport costs over distance and corresponding diminution of demand" (ibid.). Distance, itself, is a function of "time and cost of movement", which puts "intense pressure to reduce frictions of distance by innovations in transportation and communications" (ibid. 100). All this complicates the tendency to reduce circulation time "because the drive to accelerate turnover time through improvements in transport and communication alters relative spaces and so transforms superior into inferior locations and vice versa" (Harvey 2006 [1982], 426).

As the region develops, local costs, such as land values and potential political tensions, increase (ibid.). That is, in part, because concentration increases workers' organizational opportunities (ibid.). Harvey also names "congestion costs, increasing rigidity in the use of physical infrastructures, rising rents and sheer lack of space" (Harvey 2006 [1982], 418). These costs put pressure on agglomeration economies and, as capital begins to move to previously underdeveloped areas, spatial dispersal becomes increasingly inevitable. Harvey's explanation of the geographical mobility of capital is based on his geographical reinterpretation (or more accurately, extension) of Marx's explanation of the movement of capital between spheres or branches of production in Capital, Volume Three, to equalize the rate of profit. He posits that the entire process is (externally) limited by the temporality of the development of communication technologies and transportation (Harvey 2006, 100). Above and beyond the spatial, infrastructural, and technological barriers to the dispersal process, Harvey adds drivers for the inertia of capital to stay put, given that "the large quantities of capital embedded in the land itself, the social infrastructures … restrictions on the mobility of capital tied down in concrete labour processes" (Harvey 2006 [1982], 418). The process becomes even more complicated as "physical and social infrastructures" depend on economies of scale central to the concentration process, making "a stable equilibrium between them" ever more unattainable (ibid.). All this leads capital "towards successive phases of deepening and widening in the spatial configurations of productive forces and social relations" (ibid. 419). Location plays a crucial role in this process as "capitalists occupying superior locations … gain excess profits," as a locational arbitrage (Harvey 2006, 97). These excess profits could prove problematic given that "if the excess profits turn out to be relatively permanent, then they may be 'taxed away' by high land rents/prices: the excess profits will be siphoned off by a landlord class" (ibid.). The existence of excess profits in superior locations rivals other sources of excess profits for capitalists due to technological or organizational advantages (ibid.). Therefore, "trade-offs exist between these two ways of gaining competitive advantage" as capitals with a higher technological advantage might opt to remain in inferior locations (ibid.). This adds complexity to Alonso's explanation of rent and enhances it by linking differential rent levels across urban sub-markets to systemic constraints on capital circulation and reduced turnover time.

Furthermore, the tendency to undermine demand (particularly social demand), combined with systemic barriers to circulation, amplifies the risk of periodic crises of overaccumulation at the aggregate level and shrinks investment opportunities for individual capitals (Harvey 2006 [1982], 424). The tendency to overaccumulation leads to "the devaluation of individual capitals and labour power through crises" (ibid.). Uneven geographical development provides a crucial bedrock for place-specific devaluation of capital, given that it is "produced by differential mobilities of various kinds of capital and labour power, all linked together within temporal constraints imposed by the circulation process of capital itself" (ibid.). Harvey calls this a third-cut theory of economic crisis, which incorporates "the material qualities of social space as defined under capitalist relations of production and exchange" to primarily explain the processes of crisis formation (ibid. 425). In contrast, he refers to Marx's law of the tendency of the rate of profit to fall (LTRPF) as the first-cut theory, and the overaccumulation theory of crisis as the second-cut crisis theory. The latter, he submits, "strives to integrate an understanding of the problems of disequilibrium in production" (ibid. 284). With this, Harvey aims to conceptualize "the manner in which the credit system brings capital together as the common capital of the class, with the potentiality to counteract those errant behaviours of individual capitalists that are a primary source of disequilibrium in production" (ibid. 325) and facilitate a more efficient allocation of resources to correct the temporal disequilibrium. In other words, "the inner contradictions within production are manifest in exchange as an opposition between money and commodity forms of value which then becomes, via the agency of the credit system, an outright antagonism between the financial system and its monetary base" (ibid. 326). The third-cut theory of crisis is "to integrate the geography of uneven development into" the second-cut theory (ibid. 425). The theory explains the trade-off between locational and technological advantage and the subsequent impact on the "place-specific devaluation" of individual capitals on the one hand and a fall in effective demand, on the other (ibid. 425–426). And "since capitalists will be capitalists", they will ignore the social impact of devaluation and continue to accumulate (ibid. 426). The civil society, therefore, in his view, is "destined to experience the social distress, disruption and unrest that accompany the forcible restoration of conditions favourable to accumulation" (ibid. 427).

1.3 The Dual Theses: Capital Switching and Spatial Fix

The theory of uneven geographical development portrays a capitalist landscape, in which "some regions boom while others decline" (Harvey 2006 [182], 428). This unevenness at the aggregate level tends to heighten the risk of overaccumulation, which in turn necessitates geographical restructuring as "temporary resolutions to problems of overaccumulation" (ibid.). Geographical expansion and restructuring, therefore, reduce capitalist crises to "minor switching crises as flows and capital and labour switch from one region to another, or even reverse themselves, and spark regional devaluations (which can sometimes be intense) as well as major adjustments in the spatial structures (such as the transport system) designed to facilitate spatial flows" (ibid. 428). Harvey adds that a general devaluation of capital is "avoided by successive and ever grander 'outer transformations,'" and through the production of new spaces of accumulation (ibid. 427). This process is conceptualized in the spatial fix thesis. The thesis implies "dispersing or exporting capital and labor surpluses into new and more profitable spaces" (Harvey 2006, 96). The process of 'fixing' capitalist crisis, therefore, depends on capital's spatial mobility, i.e., the ability of capital to switch between spaces of investment, which, itself, requires the production of new spaces for investment with longer turnover time, such as built environments (spaces of essential urban services and social reproduction, most notably, housing, as well as office and commercial spaces and infrastructure) to absorb surplus capital slowly (Harvey 2006, 101–102). This gives urbanization a special role in capitalism, making it "a key means for the absorption of capital and labor surpluses ... through speculative activity" (Harvey 2012, 42; 45).

The capital switching thesis explains the flow of capital (as a mass of new investments) from investments in production to investments in built environments to compensate for crises of overaccumulation (as shrinking investment opportunities) by slowly absorbing surplus capital and contributing to fixing the crisis spatially (spatial fix) (Harvey 2006 [1982]). Both spatial fix and capital switching theses are rooted in Harvey's three-fold conceptualization of circuits of capital (primary, secondary, tertiary) (Harvey 1978; 2006 [1982]; 2017). He named Lefebvre's thesis (primacy of investments in urban spaces over productive investments in post-war capitalism) as his main inspiration. One could plausibly argue that Harvey operationalized Marx's notion of the movement of capital to equalize profit rates to provide an economic basis for Lefebvre's thesis. He also supported his capital switching thesis with empirical evidence (specifically, time series for building activities) (Harvey 1978; 1985; 2012). In an interview in 2009, he (2009; also Christophers 2011, 1350) provided context for his thesis and claimed that "particularly since the 1970s," capital surplus has been going "more and more into speculation on asset values" rather than "real production," which in turn has made "every city ... a huge building site for capitalist surplus absorption" (ibid. quoted in Christophers 2011, 1350). His conceptualization of the three circuits was first published in his 1978 article and then expanded and fine-tuned in 2006 [1982], 1985, and 2012 books. Nevertheless, its core assumptions remained the same (also see Christophers 2011). Therefore, it makes sense to use the 1978 piece as a starting point for an exposition of the chain of causality in his conceptualization of the dual theses.

According to Harvey, the primary circuit of capital involves investments in the productive sectors (e.g., manufacturing). In it, "the capitalist captures relative surplus value from the organization of cooperation and division of labour within the work process or by the application of fixed capital (machinery)" (Harvey 1978, 104). This conceptualization centers the primary circuit of capital in "the structure of relations" for the circulation of capital concerning the production *and* consumption of commodities (ibid. 106). He elaborates that within the primary circuit, systematic internal contradictions negatively affect a sustained and "positive rate of accumulation" (ibid. 104). These contradictions "arise out of the tendency for individual capitalists to act in a way which, when aggregated, runs counter to their own class interest" (ibid.). In other words, these internal contradictions warrant the tendency to produce "too much capital ... in aggregate relative to the opportunities to employ that capital" or the tendency to overaccumulate (ibid. 105).

The secondary circuit of capital involves investment in the built environment and finance. That is the circulation of capital (or capital flows) into the "formation of fixed capital and the consumption fund" (ibid.). Certain aspects of the built environment are crucial for "both production and consumption" (ibid.). Harvey stresses that, as fixed capital (i.e., in its productive function), the built environment entails long turnover times that allow slow absorption of surplus capital (a result of the tendency to recurrent overaccumulation). In its unproductive function (e.g., in the case of the existing building stock), it "is immobile in space in the sense that the value incorporated in it cannot be moved without being destroyed" (ibid.). This, in turn, implies that "a whole physical landscape for purposes of production, circulation, exchange, and consumption" must be created for investments in the built environment to be materialized (ibid.). Crucially, a developed credit system is needed to make this immobile (unproductive) capital mobile (i.e., tradable as a financial asset) (Harvey 2006 [1982]). This latter point justifies including finance in the secondary circuit next to the built environment. Finance's role is to coordinate investment flows into the built environment for speculative trading, thereby facilitating the tendency to spatially fix overaccumulation crises by switching capital (as a mass of investments) from the primary to the secondary circuits (ibid. 396).

The third dimension of his conceptualization primarily refers to regulatory and mediating institutional relations. It is referred to as the tertiary circuit of capital, which encompasses the flow of capital into public services, education, research, and development, among other areas (Harvey 1978, 106). Harvey explains, "Individual capitalists, when left to their own devices, tend to under-invest in the built environment relative to their own individual and collective needs at the same time as they tend to overaccumulate" (ibid. 116). The role of state and financial institutions is such that they can siphon off overaccumulation by "the creation of fictional capital within the credit system and put [it] to work to make up the slack in investment in the built environment" (ibid.). And he clarifies that capital switching can be "accomplished relatively smoothly depending upon the efficiency of the mediating institutions" (ibid.).

After this long detour, let me return to his spatial fix thesis (and its associated notion of geographical restructuring). Harvey starts his exposition of spatial fix with a deliberately simplified presumption: that "all production and realization of interdependent capitals occurs within a closed region" (Harvey 2006 [1982], 426). Then, he goes on to explain the process and mechanism of the fix through regional competition as capital tends to explore external spatial investment opportunities "until all external possibilities are exhausted or because other regions resist being treated as mere convenient appendages" (ibid. 427). The regional competition to absorb surplus capital is not straightforward as a) the competition is geographically uneven given that "when a particular civil society creates fresh productive powers elsewhere to absorb its overaccumulated capital, it thereby establishes a rival center of accumulation which, at some point in the future, must also look to its own spatial fix to resolve its problems" (Harvey 1981, 8). Furthermore, b) 'the other' regions can strike back, meaning, "the competitive position of the region as a whole can be eroded because other regions have gone through the discomfort and tragedy of internal restructuring of their productive apparatus, social relations, distributive arrangements, and so on" (ibid.). The external regional competition could potentially force the regions "into even more savage devaluation through outside pressure" (ibid.).

At the economic-geographic level, "interregional competition" is the driving force behind the spatial fix. On the political level, territorial alliance plays a crucial role in regulating the process. Therefore, economic and political forces and reorganization over space/region function as regulatory mechanisms for 'fixing' overaccumulation crises: "the degree to which overaccumulation problems arising in one place can be relieved by further development or devaluation in another place depends upon the intersection of all manner of diverse and conflicting forces" (ibid.). In that sense, spatial fix (and switching crises), and the subsequent spatial reorganization, are mechanisms "to restore the disturbed equilibrium" (ibid. 429). And in the end, the persistent regional "geographical inertia" leaves capital with no other options than moving toward "the total restructuring of the space economy of capitalism on a global scale" (ibid.). Therefore, according to Harvey, geographical restructuring and the production of space are macro-level economic-geographical strategies aimed at resolving capitalist overaccumulation crises. Capitalist crises are rooted in a dual, contradictory strategy of capital accumulation across space (that is, processes of concentration and dispersal). Economic urbanization processes are the outcomes of the production of space and the space economy of capitalism. Unlike what neoclassical models suggest, urbanization processes are not simply the outcome of a trade-off between investors' and consumers' marginal utilities at the micro level. They are deeply rooted in structural patterns and (contradictory) tendencies of capitalist development across space.

Space, therefore, plays a central role in both production and distribution, as they both require "(1) an elaborate social structure (encompassing the division of labour, the provision of socially necessary services, and so on), (2) a structure of social institutions through which individual and group activities can be coordinated, and (3) a certain minimum of physical infrastructure (communication links, utilities and the like)" (Harvey 1974a, 239–240). Thus, Harvey calls for "the integration of the production of space and spatial configurations as an active element within the core of Marxian theorizing" (Harvey 1985, xi). That is an intellectual mission that at the same time seeks to reverse "the predisposition to give time and history priority over space and geography" common in "Marx, Weber, Durkheim, and Marshal", symptomized by a lack of "the conceptual apparatus" required to insert "space and space relations" into social inquiry (ibid.). And especially with Marx, "historical materialism appeared to license the study of historical transformation while ignoring how capitalism produces its own geography" (ibid. xii). "Historical materialism", he goes on, "has to be upgraded … to historical-geographical materialism. The historical geography of capitalism has to be the object of our theorizing" (ibid.). As noted above, he argues (ibid. xiii), "capitalism, as viewed from the standpoint of production in the first volume of Marx's Capital, looks very different from capitalism studied from the viewpoint of circulation in volume two". This observation forms the starting point of his reinterpretation of Marx's theory to accommodate the above-mentioned anomaly, i.e., a lack of a conceptual apparatus to integrate space in the framework. Harvey proposes a synthesis the two viewpoints, in Volume One and Two, as "an understanding of those contradictions and reach out to grasp successive resolutions and internalizations of those tensions within the realms of finance capital, the state apparatus, and the geography of uneven development" (ibid. xiii–xiv). The contradictory process of "creating landscapes" by capitalism is then explained through "studies of the circulation of capital in general" that can be "broadened and disaggregated to encompass problems of fixed capital formation and circulation and the interventions of finance capitals and appropriators of rent" (ibid. xv–xvi).

1.4 Land Rent as a Linchpin in the Analysis of Urbanization

1.4.1 A Brief Introduction to Land Rent Theory

Setting Harvey's review of land rent theories as my point of departure, and at the risk of simplification, let me briefly introduce rent theory and its core concepts and discuss how Ricardian and Marxian rent theories relate rent creation and appropriation to economic structures and policies.[3] Harvey's exploration of land rent theory has evolved since 1973, but he consistently begins with the two most influential modern theorists of land rent: David Ricardo and Karl Marx. Both Ricardo and Marx start with the labor theory of value[4] and treat land as a unique commodity that is not produced by labor, yet it still commands a price. Consequently, the return on any investment in land—whether rural or urban—is partially reflected in land rent. Rent is defined as "that portion of the produce of the earth that is paid to the landlord for the use of the original and indestructible powers of the soil" (Ricardo, 2004 [1911], 33). It can also be understood as "a portion of the surplus value that capital produces [that] falls to the share of the landowner" (Marx, 1991 [1894], 751). Additionally, Marx explicitly refers to rent as "the economic realization of landed property, of the legal fiction 'by grace of which certain individuals have an exclusive right to certain parts of our planet'" (Marx, 1991 [1894], 619, in Murray 1977, 113).

3 For an overview of rent categories in Ricardo, Marx, and Harvey, see Appendix 1.
4 As opposed to the (subjective) price theory of value in mainstream economics.

"The rise of capitalism", Harvey (2006 [1982], 343) writes, "entailed the 'dissolution of the old economic relations of landed property' and their conversion to a form compatible with sustained accumulation". Modern landed property, therefore, differs from feudalist landed property in that in capitalism, "a) property rights could be bought and sold; b) the landlord was transformed from an active agent in production to an unproductive one in distribution; c) the landlord's payment in rent was no longer directly appropriated from agricultural labour, but received as a residual payment in cash from a capitalist farmer; d) landholding was stripped of its former political and social power derived from its direct role in production" (Murray 1977, 113, also, Marx 1991 [1894], 755). Landed property in capitalism, in other words, is repurposed for "a production system which achieves the real subjection of labour to capital (rather than to the landlord) and which liberates the land from the barriers that inhibit the development of the productive forces" (Harvey 2006 [1982], 345). This transition from pre-modern to modern landed property requires "the complete removal of the landowner from any direct power over the use of the land, over the labour power employed thereon, and over the capital advanced, in return for a money payment" (ibid.).

Land ownership is a prerequisite in that the landed proprietor can demand rent for the capitalist's investment in land. That is to say, "the appropriation of rent is the economic form in which landed property is realized and that ground-rent, in turn, presupposes landed property" (Marx 1991 [1894], 772 in Harvey 2006 [1982], 343). At the plot level, rent levels are relative, meaning they are determined by the relative locational advantages between plots, driven by external variables such as soil fertility, mineral deposits, and the like. Ricardo argues that relative rent exists when "two equal quantities of capital and labour" are employed in two plots with different yields, conceptualized as differential rent (Ricardo 2004 [1817], 36). He assumes that the worst (or the least fertile) plot is generally available to all capitalists, which indicates survival conditions of production at the sectoral level. These survival conditions of production in the worst plot regulate production prices, representing the case in which rent is zero, and whose yield is adequate to satisfy demand before the expansion of supply. He further assumes, thus, that a) the worst land yields no rent, while all other (better) plots yield some rent, thereby having higher prices, and b) the expansion of supply requires investments in the better plots. He measures rent, at the aggregate level, as the difference between the production costs of the best land in use and the regulating sectoral price, which itself is determined by the price of the produce on the worst plot (ibid.). For each specific plot, rent is the difference between the costs of production on the worst land and the cost of production on the specific plot of better land (ibid.). Ricardo contends, "because land is not unlimited in quantity and uniform in quality, and because, in the progress of population, land of an inferior quality, or less advantageously situated, is called into cultivation, that rent is ever paid for the use of it" (ibid. 35). In this case, rent levels "depend on the difference in the quality of [best and worst] portions of land" (ibid.). Ricardo concludes that "with every step in the progress of population, which shall oblige a country to have recourse to land of a worse quality, to enable it to raise its supply of food, rent, on all the more fertile land, will rise" (ibid.).

Unlike machinery, which can be reproduced by capital, land is durable and finite, hence monopolizable. This monopolizability justifies the payment of rent. Conditions of production in the land sector are determined by external environmental factors, and location and quality are relative to the context. In the land sector, competition is determined by the generally best available conditions of production, with one caveat: it involves the best generally available method of production and the best generally available land. The level of rent is determined by differential quality (in agriculture, soil fertility), meaning the most fertile plot gains an excess profit that represents the rent. In contrast, the least fertile plot receives no rent. Furthermore, the aggregate price is regulated by the survival conditions (i.e., the minimum acceptable rate of return for a capital of this kind) in the marginal plot that requires the highest labor inputs. In this context, survival conditions of production are regulated by the plot that is the best generally available land (or the marginal land in use), and that determines the expansion of supply (as it represents the minimum production required to satisfy demand), and because it is the condition that gets normal profit, all others get higher profits thanks to rent. For Ricardo, differential natural conditions of production lead to high land rents in the best plots. As the economy grows, more plots will come under cultivation. This, in turn, leads to higher produce prices (due to increased labor inputs), which can lower demand among workers and prompt higher wage demands, ultimately resulting in lower profits for capitalist farmers and an economic crisis.

Both Ricardo and Marx analyze land rent structurally. That is, they aim to relate rent creation and appropriation to the inner workings of the economic system. However, for Ricardo, rent creation depends on a non-economic, natural phenomenon, and its appropriation leads to a fall in aggregate profit and an economic downturn. Hence, in the final analysis, for Ricardo, it is market structures and external factors, such as fertility, that shape rent relations. Nevertheless, Ricardo provides ample material for both neoclassical and Marxian inferences. Marx treats rent at two levels of analysis. At the micro-level (i.e., land ownership), rent creation depends on technological and economic development. It depends on the historical development of agricultural technologies, such as fertilizers and combine harvesters, as well as on the region's level of economic development. At the macro level (i.e., the whole economy), rent is non-relative and applies to all plots within the sector. Here, Marx aims to directly connect the creation and appropriation of land rent with the generation of total surplus value. He splits the total surplus into the producers' profit, the financiers' interest, and the landowners' rent. The level of rent that accrues to all landlords in the economy depends on the movement of capital between branches to equalize the rate of profit (Marx 1991 [1894], 892). This general type of rent, therefore, is independent of the immediate physical characteristics of the land or how intensively it is used (ibid. 894). Its formation relies on competition among capitals seeking higher profit rates and on the flow of capital within and across branches. Rent rates could reach as high as the difference between rates of return in the manufacturing and agriculture (and other rent-bearing) sectors. When that difference widens, all plots, even the marginal ones, yield rents; and when it narrows, for instance, during a manufacturing boom, the excess sectoral profit that constitutes rent disappears. Therefore, at both levels, Marx argues that rent creation and appropriation depend on the health of the overall economy: whether through competitive relationships between sectors or through the development of sectoral conditions of production.

1.4.2 Land Rent in Harvey's Explanation

Land rent plays a decisive role in Harvey's explanation of capitalist urbanization processes, primarily as a barrier to the free movement of capital into land (capital switching), which, in turn, drives social conflicts over landed property. Harvey is distinguished as the first economic geographer to bring land rent to the center stage of urban and spatial analysis. His 1973 classic book (followed by two seminal articles in 1974) includes an entire section on rent and various ways in which Marxian (and Ricardian) conceptualizations of land rent help explain political-economic determinants and mechanisms of investments in urban land. It also appears as the first systematic attempt to update Marx's and Ricardo's rent categories for urban contexts (reviewed in Appendix 1). Some forty years later, Harvey (2010, 183) still insists,

> Rent has to be brought forward into the forefront of analysis, rather than being treated as a derivative category of distribution as happens in Marxist as well as conventional economic theory. Only in this way can we bring together an understanding of the ongoing production of space and geography and the circulation

> and accumulation of capital and put them in relation to processes of crisis formation where they so clearly belong.

To explain how land rent mediates (and limits) switching crises and spatial fix, Harvey turns to Lefebvre. Drawing on Marx's notion of the movement of capital between branches in Capital, Volume Three, he advanced a conceptual apparatus to explain the economic and socio-spatial implications of Lefebvre's thesis that, in late capitalism, productive investments tend to be superseded by investment in the urban. As noted above, this conceptual apparatus sets the basis of his capital switching thesis that implies "'the secondary circuit of capital' is supplanting 'the primary circuit of capital in production'" in modern urban capitalism (Harvey 1974a, 239). Capital switching, Harvey argues, is made possible, primarily given "'the proportion of global surplus value formed and realized in industry declines' while the proportion realized 'in speculation, construction and real estate development grows'" (ibid.). However, this switching could be interrupted by landlords demanding land rent for investments in land ventures, given that land rent is created by the exogenous barriers to entry in the circulation process, i.e., monopoly relations over land ownership. Therefore, Harvey complements Lefebvre's thesis by incorporating an economic explanation for capital switching in terms of rates of return using his spatial interpretation of Marx's notion of inter-sectoral movement of capital. Higher rates of return in "the real estate and property market" will help a mass of investments "shift from the primary productive circuit of capital" to the speculative secondary one (ibid. 241). To illustrate this, he (1978, 106–111) provides a series of historical examples from the 19th and 20th centuries, using a range of variables, including time series on investment in construction (total and percentage of GDP and GNP), building activity, sale prices, and other related metrics. Since the rate of return on investments in space includes land rents, rent must be central to the analysis of urbanization processes.

He (1974a, 240) criticizes the neoclassical solution to the rent question in which "rent is a kind of rationing device through which a scarce factor of production—land and its associated resources—is rationally and efficiently allocated to meet the productive needs of society". He stresses that the neoclassical model fails to treat rent payments as payments to people rather than to land, thereby reifying rent extraction processes (ibid.). It similarly fails to understand that rent is a payment for an exclusively owned 'scarce' resource, resulting from "monopoly power over land" institutionally established as landed property (ibid.). In that sense, he also explains scarcity in terms of monopolistic social relations, a concept absent in the neoclassical framework, as it is presumed 'natural'. Therefore, land rent represents a factor in the realization of surplus value as a transfer payment for land as a scarce and "fixed and immobile capital asset" (ibid.). The two characteristics of land are related "because these relatively permanent fixed capital assets are highly localized in their distribution, the urbanization process has created scarcity where there was none before" (ibid. 240). Land rent represents the price of land and is realized as "a transfer payment to a scarce factor of production" (ibid.). In this context, economic urbanization processes have "multiplied the opportunity for realizing rent" (ibid.). Harvey (2006 [1982], 330) stresses, "rent, in the final analysis, is simply a payment made to landlords for the right to use land and its appurtenances (the resources embedded within it, the buildings placed upon it and so on)". And rent more specifically refers to "the pure payment to raw land, independent of the improvements thereon" (ibid. 331).

Following both Ricardo and Marx, Harvey explains and measures land rent as excess profit, albeit with a modified understanding of the source of profit. He posits that manufacturers operating with scarce resources "stand to receive excess profits in perpetuity by virtue of the natural advantages they enjoy … The level of excess profit (and, by implication, the rent) is fixed by the difference between the individual productivity and the average productivity and price of production prevailing within the industry" (ibid. 336). That gives a significant and unique position to landed property in capitalism: "the ownership of private property in land confers exclusive power on private persons over certain portions of the globe" (ibid. 338). Echoing Marx, he maintains that private landed property "clearly establishes the portion of the earth's surface over which private individuals have exclusive monopoly powers" (ibid.). But he adds a spatial dimension by arguing that an absolute conception of space implied in capitalist land relations entails "a principle of individuation established through exclusivity of occupation of a certain portion of space—no two people can occupy exactly the same location in this space and be considered two separate people" (ibid. 339). This "exclusivity of control over absolute space," according to Harvey, includes both private individuals, but also "states, administrative divisions and any other kind of juridical individual" (ibid.).

Harvey reformulates Ricardo's theory of rent, which explains rent in terms of soil fertility in agriculture, for urban contexts. He emphasizes that in modern capitalist cities, excess profit—land rent—is generated by relative locational advantage, i.e., by producing in more favored locations. Starting from assumptions of Alonso's model, he stresses that "'more favoured' in this case is measured in terms of lower transport costs," but extends that model by interpreting the impact of rent as excess profit for producers in such locations with implications for class conflicts (ibid.). Such excess profit exists, given that for such producers, "production and accessibility costs are lower and their yield higher than on the most marginal field" (Harvey 2010, 81). These excess profits or superprofits, he concludes, "like differences in natural fertility, are to be regarded in the first instance as permanently fixed as compared with the usual transitory form of relative surplus value associated with ephemeral technological advantage" (Harvey 2006 [1982], 338–339).

He extends Marx's theory first, by contrasting the 19th and 20th-century contexts, and maintaining that in Marx's time, landed property was "a residual from feudalism" and that the class power of landlords stemmed from pre-capitalist institutional arrangements. Under urban capitalism, and particularly with the expansion of financial activity and interest in the built environment, "the distinction between capitalist and landlord has blurred concomitantly with the blurring of the distinctions between land and capital and rent and profit," indicating the emergence of a rentier class (Harvey 1974a, 241). Therefore, Marx's theory of rent needed to be reevaluated and updated to analyze modern urbanization processes, incorporating new trajectories that predominantly include financial activities in the housing sector and particularly impact low-income tenants (Harvey 1976, 268). Land rent is appropriated in land markets via monopoly and financial relations that govern them. "What is bought and sold is not the land, but title to the ground-rent yielded by it" (Harvey 2006 [1982], 367). Harvey argues that investments in land are a type of "interest-bearing investment," given that what is to be purchased is "a claim upon anticipated future revenues, a claim upon the future fruits of labour" (ibid.). "Title to the land", therefore, is "a form of fictitious capital" that expands through speculative activity (ibid.). Harvey names two regulatory forces on land prices: interest rates and "future rental revenues" (ibid.). Interest rate (as the price of money) is a crucial variable given that "movements in the interest rate impose strong temporal rhythms and bring land price movements within an overall framework defined by the relation between the accumulation of capital and the supply and demand for money capital" (ibid.).

Landed property assumes "an active role in creating conditions that permit future rents to be appropriated" (ibid. 368). This active role allows landowners to "force production on the land into new configurations and even push surplus value production on a scale and with an intensity that might not otherwise occur" (ibid.). Furthermore, it gives the landowners "co-ordinating functions and thereby legitimates and justifies the appropriation of rent within the overall logic of the capitalist mode of production" (ibid.). Land markets regulate "the allocation of capital to land and thereby [shape] the geographical structure of production, exchange and consumption, the technical division of labour in space, the socioeconomic spaces of reproduction, and so forth" (ibid. 369). Land markets also facilitate the circulation of interest-bearing capital, enabling the coordination of land use for the production of surplus value in general (ibid. 368). The circulation of interest-bearing capital to land markets is crucial given that, as noted above, without it, land rent would appear as a barrier to investments in land, thereby the tendency to spatial fix. With interest-bearing capital circulation in land markets, activities on land will be promoted that "conform to highest and best uses, not simply in the present, but also in anticipation of future surplus value production" (ibid.). That is made possible by treating land "as a pure financial asset" (ibid.). This way landowners "coerce … or co-operate with capital to ensure the creation of enhanced ground rents" (ibid.). Land rent, therefore, appears to be a linchpin of Harvey's analysis of capitalist urbanization processes, via which he aims to structurally relate rent creation and appropriation to exigencies of capital accumulation.

To illustrate this, let me review the central mechanisms of his argument. As noted above, his starting point is that recurrent crises of overaccumulation—i.e., shrinking profitable investment opportunities (particularly at the regional level)—pressure capital to switch to investing in built environments as an alternative investment strategy to absorb surplus capital. That is, due to their peculiar characteristics (as durable types of fixed capital (i.e., physical assets) that require recurrent rounds of reinvestment (e.g., renovations and maintenance) over a long time), built environments help capital find a way out of the overaccumulation crisis to retain equilibrium (Harvey 1978). He refers to this process as a 'spatial fix' (Harvey 2006 [1982], 390). There is a problem, however. Harvey argues that, in reality, the existence of monopoly ownership of land means that rent payment, as an extra expenditure, depending on its level, can appear as a barrier to spatial fix (Harvey 1974a). That is, by and large, because rent has to be paid out of the total expected return on capital. The question is: when and how can this barrier be overcome? Harvey argues that the circulation of interest-bearing capital into land and property markets makes land not only monopolizable but also a fictitious form of fixed capital. A combination of these two characteristics makes excess profit on land (rent) "relatively permanent" (Harvey 2006, 97), enabling landowners to extract relatively high levels of rent on a perpetual basis. This perpetuity of (speculative) rent extraction, in turn, enables rent to facilitate the spatial fix process. This analysis presents a stark contrast to neoclassical models (e.g., Alonso's), as it explains the level and fluctuations of land rent through the forces of finance capital (that the fluctuations of finance determine the fluctuations of land rent, and the price of finance determines the level of rent), rather than consumers' preferences and supply and demand.

Harvey argues that although land rent may appear as a barrier to the spatial fix process since it is "the basis of land price," it can also operate "to allocate capital and labour to land, guides the location of future production, exchange and consumption, fashions the geographical division of labour and the spatial organization of social reproduction" (Harvey 2006 [1982], 396). In other words, land rent can both hinder and facilitate investment flows into land markets. For rent to assume its alternative (positive) role, money capital needs to circulate through built environments to make land (an immobile asset with a long turnover time) mobile and to ensure that property titles can be "freely traded as purely financial assets" (ibid.). That is because capitals with long turnover time "could not be either produced or used without resort to the credit system" as it may take decades "to get that money back through production" (ibid. 225). The penetration of finance into built environments, in turn, renders property markets fictitious capital and "inherently speculative" (ibid. 397). And land rent becomes "a form of interest identified specifically with locational attributes" (ibid. 396). In this process, "landowners must necessarily take an active role in the pursuit of enhanced rents ... The freer interest-bearing capital is to roam the land looking for titles to future ground-rents to appropriate, the better it can fulfil its co-ordinating role" (ibid. 369). Land prices are the key indicator to measure investors' attraction to land and land markets are the "powerful force making for the rationalization of geographical structures in relation to competition" (ibid.). As an example, Harvey maintains, "the stimulus to revolutionize [transport relations] arises out of the need to diminish the circulation time of commodities, to extend markets geographically and so simultaneously to build the possibility for cheapening raw material inputs, expanding the basis for realization while accelerating the turnover time of capital" (ibid.). In this context, "improved transportation" transforms relative locational advantage that determine land rent and further investment in transport will "enhance land values in areas proximate to it" (ibid.). This conditions the gains of the landowners to "the where and when" of investments in transport allowing them to particularly compete in co-ordinating "the patterns of development" (ibid. 370). These dynamics beg the question, "How much appropriation [of rent] is appropriate? To this [however,] there is no clear answer and even if there were there is no guarantee that the forces at work under capitalism could ever achieve it" (ibid. 397–398). That is because, despite potential "factional struggles over distributive share" (ibid. 397) among these agents, they maintain a converging interest to forge "a local alliance to protect and promote local interests and to ward off the threat of localized, place-specific devaluation" (ibid. 420).

In the structural approach to land rent, to which Harvey also adheres, rent generally arises as an excess return on land ownership, itself due to monopoly control over the, by nature, finite land stock for capitalist activities on land. However, the issue of land rent raises empirical questions at both the micro and macro levels. At the micro-level—i.e., the level of individual investors on single plots—an immediate empirical question is: why do some plots have higher rents and others lower? Most urban rent models (neoclassical, Harveyan, etc.) conceptually begin with the Ricardian concept of differential (or relative) rent to answer this question. The concept, as we have seen, refers to the physical characteristics of a plot of land that directly contribute to higher yield, which, in turn, allows the landowner to demand a higher payment than the average in the business (i.e., rent) for investments in such plots. Urban rent theorists maintain that differences in rent levels across plots are explained by locational differences, based on relative locational advantage or proximity to, for example, central business districts, which create better-off and worse-off locations.[5] The concept of differential rent explains the variation in the physical characteristics of land plots. However, it does not provide any clues to deeper (macro-level) analytical questions, such as why rent arises in land rather than in other sectors. This question is crucial, as most rent theorists, since Marx, have documented that all plots within the land sector tend to generate some rent, regardless of their physical characteristics. The question also begs two further questions: what determines the level and fluctuations of land rent? And how do the level and fluctuations of land rent relate to the overall economy? These questions require us to relate land rent to the macro-dynamics of capital accumulation. That seems to be the ambition of Harvey's explanation, too.

Harvey explicitly discusses the relevance of four categories of rent for urban analysis in his 1973 [2009] and 1982 [2006] books. These categories are differential rent I and II, monopoly rent, absolute rent, and class-monopoly rent (see Appendix 1). He explains both differential rent I and differential rent II in terms of relative locational advantage, which is realized through an interplay between extensive and intensive capital flows (Harvey 2006 [1982], 354–355). He aims to bring into the analysis what he contends Marx has left out, namely, "speculation, as well as location, and competition of different uses" (ibid. 354). In defense of location, he posits that differential rent I would disappear "if land is of equal fertility everywhere" (ibid. 355). Besides, "the 'permanence' of locational advantage is perpetually in the course of alteration through investment in transportation and the shifting geographical distribution of economic activity and population" (ibid. 354). To explain the interplay between the two

5 In agriculture for which Ricardo's and Marx's rent theory were originally developed, locational differences have direct implications for productivity. In the urban contexts, this is not as straightforward as location involves a subjective evaluation on the investor or consumer's part. More importantly, attributes to location are subject to continuous transformation in response to intensity and patterns of urbanization.

categories, he also builds on Marx's note in Capital Volume Three that "while the first [differential rent] is the basis of the second, at the same time place limits on one another, leading sometimes to successive investments of capital on the same stretch of land and sometimes to adjacent investments of capital on new additional land" (Marx 1991 [1894], 871).[6] Marx argues that differential rent I arises from variations in fertility, whereas differential rent II arises from successive investments on the same land. The maximum rent created under differential rent II, he elaborates, is limited by the baseline fertility (or differential rent I), and if additional investment leads to diminishing returns, the excess profit from differential rent II declines, reinforcing the original natural (or locational) advantage that created differential rent I (ibid. 871–880).

In his interpretation, Harvey argues that the flow of capital into ventures on land is dependent not only on sectoral concentration of capital, as Marx had envisioned, but is also "highly sensitive to the existence of a credit system," particularly when "landlords are also the financiers" (Harvey 2006 [1982], 355). If differential rent II is determined by successive investments above normal capital, and the normal in this case is defined as "the unequal application of capital to soils of unequal fertility", which means differential rent I is the basis of differential rent II. The nature of differential rent II, a result of "shifting flows of capital onto the land," renders the effects of this rent "transient" (ibid. 356). An active "intervention of landed property and the appropriation of rent" is therefore needed to "prevent the flow of capital down channels that would otherwise be unproductive of surplus value (though not of profit)" (ibid. 357). This is particularly true in modern circumstances where it "becomes impossible for either landowner or capitalist to separate the two forms of rent ... But exactly how the landowner appropriates it does indeed have implications for market prices and the accumulation of capital" (ibid.).

Harvey finds monopoly rent, i.e., "the opportunity of charge a monopoly price" (Harvey 2009 [1973], 179), relevant in two cases. The first case examines a scenario in which "prestige and status locations" create the opportunity for monopoly pricing (Harvey 2006 [1982], 350). And the second case is when "landowners may refuse to release the unused land under their control unless paid such a high rent that the market prices of commodities produced on that land are forced above value" (ibid.). In both cases, "the scarcity of land" and "the collective class power and position of the landed interest" are prerequisites of landed property's direct interference with "surplus value production" and charging monopoly prices (ibid. 350; 353).

6 In contrast, Shaikh interprets Marx's note as the two differential rents function as two investment strategies driven by costs of operation and average expected profit rate.

In his review of the concept of absolute rent, Harvey (2009 [1973], 181) writes, "excess profits can therefore 'fleetingly' emerge in all areas of production ... [but] in agriculture excess profits are institutionalized into absolute rent through the monopoly power of private property" given that absolute rent is responsible for the conditions that "give rise to monopoly price" (ibid.). But Harvey is skeptical of Marx's analysis of sectoral rates of return with his labor theory of value. He writes, "the profitability of housing construction is heavily dependent on speculative movements in housing prices and rent extractions (both land and interest) via the credit system" (Harvey 2016, 48). Absolute rent, according to Harvey, is conditioned through spatiotemporal barriers to "the overall equalization in the rate of profit among the different spheres of production" (Harvey 2009 [1973], 181). Harvey applied an interpretation of the concept of absolute rent in terms of rents in absolute space, synthesizing the concepts of monopoly and absolute rent (Harvey and Chatterjee 1974). In a related article (1974a, 241), Harvey also treats absolute rent and monopoly rent very closely to one another. Elsewhere (Harvey 2009 [1973], 181), he writes, "the distinction between monopoly and absolute rent can perhaps be rescued by regarding the former as operating at the individual level (a particular owner has something which someone particularly wants or needs) and the latter as something which arises out of the general conditions of production in some sector (it is a class monopoly phenomenon which affects the condition of all agricultural landowners, all owners of low-income housing, etc.)". Later Harvey conceptualizes this type of rent distinctively as class-monopoly rent (Harvey 1974a; 2006 [1982]) and calls the concept of absolute rent (in its original conceptualization) "irrelevant" and "meaningless" (Harvey 2013 interview in Barnes and Sheppard 2019, 207); he does "not think it works" (Harvey 2010, 81).

Given this conclusion, Harvey decided as early as 1974 to replace absolute rent with a new macro-level concept of rent: class-monopoly rent (Harvey 1974a; Swyngedouw and Ward 2022). As noted by Barnes and Sheppard, Harvey "quickly realized, though, that absolute rent was *inappropriate*, substituting the term 'class monopoly rent'" (Barnes and Sheppard 2019, 207). Class-monopoly rent is inferred to explain broader, structural power relations that shape and limit rents derived from the monopolistic ownership of land. Such structural relations are, therefore, articulated in class terms. Following Ricardo and Marx, he argues that rent at the macro level arises from landlords' general monopoly over the entire land stock. Harvey explains that the level of class-monopoly rent depends on the power of the landlord class to impose monopoly prices on the land stock (Harvey 1974a; Harvey and Chatterjee 1974, 32). However, there are objective constraints. Thus, he argues, the landlords tend to collaborate as a class to coordinate investments over urban land and ensure that monopoly pricing of land, while remaining feasible, as noted below, is maintained at the desirably high level by, for instance, creating artificial scarcity, i.e., keeping dwellings vacant (Harvey 1974a; Bradley 2023). According to Harvey (1974a, 243), class-monopoly rent is appropriated by a class of "speculator-developers", and it is formulated to explain a socio-spatial conflict between them and a class of consumers of land use. He writes, "the level of class-monopoly rent realized by speculator-developers depends upon the outcome of the conflict of interest between them and the various consumer groups who confront them in the market" (ibid.). The speculator-developer class requires specific institutional and regulatory arrangements to secure their interests, including physical planning measures such as zoning and redlining, as well as systematic taxation that primarily benefits the wealthy (ibid.). He articulates the socio-spatial conflict that regulates the rent with two different scenarios. He (ibid.) argues,

> If the speculator-developer can persuade upper-income groups of the virtues of a certain kind of housing in a particular neighbourhood, gain complete control over the political process, and so on, then the advantage lies with the speculator-developer. If consumers are unimpressed by the blandishments of the speculator-developers and have firm control over the political mechanisms for land-use regulation and the provision of infrastructure, then the class-monopoly power of the speculator-developers will be contained. But if certain minimum rates of return are not realized, the speculator-developer will pull out of the business until rates of return rise.

At the abstract level, all this is required because "with the exception of builders," none of the active agents in land markets "organize the real production of surplus value" (Harvey 2006 [1982], 397). Their revenues (including rent) are to be generated out of the circulation of surplus value produced elsewhere (ibid.). At the concrete level, this process means that the capital required for investments in land is borrowed from financial institutions, with the interest rate serving as the price of money. Investing in land will be feasible when the rate of return on the investment, after paying rent, exceeds the prevailing interest rate. In other words, the level of rent is determined by the price of money, and land rent (as an excess profit on land) fluctuates with the fluctuations of financial profits. This condition also decides the timing of capital switching. But how does it happen in reality? He (2006 [1982], 395) argues that in land markets, the division of labor is such that,

> landowners receive rent, developers receive increments in rent on the basis of improvements, builders earn profit of enterprise, financers provide money

> capital in return for interest at the same time as they can capitalize any form of revenue accruing from use of the built environment into a fictitious capital (property price), and the state can use taxes (present or anticipated) as backing for investments which capital cannot or will not undertake but which nevertheless expand the basis for local circulation of capital.

From the financing process for commercial operations on urban land, it is clear that the landlord's monopoly pricing cannot be set arbitrarily (i.e., not entirely driven by power relations). Therefore, Harvey introduces the coordinating role of financial institutions in maintaining and conditioning the landlords' (and, by extension, speculator-developers') monopoly ownership of the land stock. In that sense, the rent level is a function of the cost of finance (i.e., interest). The deviations of the rent in different plots of land from this general level of rent are, of course, determined by the "relative locational advantage," e.g., in "the 'right' neighborhoods" (Harvey 2006 [1982], 389; 1974a, 242). However, landlords' investment choices depend on the availability and level of coveted interest rates, due to factors such as zoning practices and existing land-use regulations (Harvey and Chatterjee 1974; Harvey 1974a). And the higher the interest rates, the higher the costs for landlords, and thereby the higher rents for tenants. For this reason, mortgage prices become politically significant because they affect housing affordability (Harvey and Chatterjee 1974).

To summarize, Harvey maintains that in modern urban settings, with adequately developed financial systems, "the distinction between capitalist and landlord has blurred," which practically unifies the two classes as "speculator-developers" (Harvey 1974a, 241). Speculator-developers "treat the land as a pure financial asset" for primarily speculative investment with the hope of future higher returns (Harvey 2006 [1982], 368).[7] Harvey later elaborated on this category as "an activist alliance between landowner and capitalist" in an actively speculative land ownership venture in modern urban land markets (ibid. 368). Such landowners perpetually strive to "put land to its 'highest and best use,'" thereby coordinating the circulation of interest-bearing capital in land markets (ibid. 368). The "temporal rhythms" of land prices, he maintains, are imposed by "movements in the interest rate" (ibid. 367). However, the finite nature of urban land, the monopolistic ownership of land stock, and the inherently speculative nature of investments in built environments mean that the

7 The introduction of the new category of speculator-developer seems to be a generalization based on Harvey's noted fieldwork in Baltimore with Chatterjee. I am not aware of any further empirical corroboration of this category by them. Yet, the category and the corollary concept of land as a pure financial asset have been frequently used by some influential urban geographers (e.g., Haila 1990; Park 2014; Purcell et al., 2020; Ward and Aalbers 2016).

trend of land rent is never downward. This feature is necessary for land rent to facilitate the spatial fix process.

1.5 Gaps and Tensions in Harvey's Theory

Ever since his famous and well-documented Marxist turn in the early 1970s (Harvey 2000), Harvey has faced challenges from other Marxists, many of whom, as noted in the introduction to this book, have been inspired by interpretations of Marx's economic theory other than his own. Interestingly, except for a handful of instances, these Marxist critics have seldom advanced a coherent and exhaustive alternative explanation to rival Harvey's analysis for 'another' Marxist geography. Instead, the focus has primarily been on pinpointing the difference between Harvey's interpretation of Marx and the others. The most influential critiques of Harvey can be usefully categorized into two fronts at different levels of abstraction: on the level of economic theory, stand critics of Harvey's competition theory and his theory of economic crisis. More elaborate critiques by 'Marxist' economists challenge Harvey's rejection of the law of the tendency of the profit rate to fall and his proposed (equilibrium) spatial fix (Kliman 2015; Lebowitz 1986; Mattick Jr. 2008; Roberts 2014; 2016b; 2020a). On the level of geographic theory, stand the far fewer critics of his theory of capitalist development (i.e., theory of uneven geographical development) and accumulation by dispossession (Das 2017a; 2017b). I could add a third front to this list, characterized by attempts to operationalize economic theory in geographic research, specifically in urban economic geography. That is the realm of rent theory, where fluctuations in other aspects of the economy (e.g., sectoral differential profitability) drive (dis)investment in land at the macro level and govern investments at the micro level. This front requires elaboration, as although Harvey's rent theory has been subject to criticism by various Marxist economists since the late 1970s, a coherent alternative for geographic research has yet to be presented. Before discussing this third front in detail in the next section (Section 1.5), let me discuss some gaps, tensions, and silences of Harvey's theory of uneven geographical developments, his conceptualization of the three circuits of capital, and his dual theses of capital switching and spatial fix.

1.5.1 Capitalist Development and Unevenness

Only recently have Marxist geographers begun to critically engage with Harvey's interpretation and development of uneven geographical development. This section is dedicated to one of the most systematic and unequivocally Marxist critical re-examinations of Harvey's theory of uneven geographical development set forth by a geographer (Das 2017b). Raju J Das (2017b, 517; also, 2023, 1081) counterposes Harvey's theory with Trotsky's theory of uneven and combined development and posits that Harvey "conflates capitalism-in-general with capitalism at a specific stage of development (advanced capitalism)" (Das 2017b, 518). Das writes, Harvey "generally equates capitalism to the capitalism where productive forces are advanced and technological change is constantly happening" (ibid.). While interesting, this comparison with Trotsky risks overlooking the intellectual origins of Harvey's uneven geographical development (i.e., his rivalry with the mainstream approach to uneven development in the field of geography). Notwithstanding, Das questions Harvey's epistemological choice, which takes an ideal (i.e., the most perfect) case of capitalist development, in which investment in fixed capital is evenly distributed across space and economic and technological developments are also at a high level. For Harvey, Das argues, unevenness is an outcome of the absence of such an ideal case. Das (ibid.) questions "this implied underlying linearity and the associated tendency to generalize on the basis of the experience of a few capitalist countries which currently have an advanced level of productive forces, rather than thinking about capitalism-in-general and thinking about capitalism internationally". "What is uneven", Das (ibid. 519) continues, "is not just the development of the physical properties of capital (e.g., built environments, etc.) but also the non-linear transition from one stage to another".

Das draws on Marx's mechanisms of exploitation in terms of formal subsumption of labor (i.e., extracting absolute surplus-value through prolonging the working day) and real subsumption of labor (i.e., extracting relative surplus value through intensifying the working day by incorporating labor-efficient technologies). He contends that the shift from formal to real subsumption of labor (as capitalist productive forces develop) "varies in space, producing spatial unevenness in whether and how the transition to real subsumption of labour associated with a developed capitalism based on systematic technological change happens" (ibid. 519). In other words, uneven geographical development "cannot be seen merely in terms of *where* capital investment is/occurs/moves to. What capital accumulation/investment *does* to labour must be taken into account in a much more rigorous way than Harvey's approach allows" (ibid. emphasis in original). Therefore, Harvey's theory is deemed inadequate because: a) the role of technological development and real subsumption processes in capital accumulation, which historically varies over space, is not central to it. Harvey discusses some technological relations. But he (2006 [1982], 134–135) finds Marx's explanation of the organic composition of capital, which indicates overall productivity and where production-related technological development is central, "mathematical" and therefore inadequate, because he believes "the necessary limits here are social", meaning "the need to maintain the consuming power of the workers as a necessary source of effective demand for the realization of capital through exchange." Harvey also questions the lack of substantial argument in Marx's works "about technologies of realization and circulation" (Harvey 2017, 107). And b) Harvey's theory does not adequately distinguish formal and real subsumption processes. Das (2017b, 523) maintains that Harvey's "distinction between areas where there is an overaccumulation of capital and areas which receive overaccumulated capital, and between capital that is fixed/immobile and capital that is not" is necessary but inadequate. So, he complements Harvey by suggesting "to think about geographical areas in terms of the organic composition of capital: areas where there is a higher-than-average ratio of organic composition of capital (c/v) and areas where the ratio is lower" (ibid.). That is, areas in which sectors with a higher or lower organic composition of capital are dominant.

Das says, "for Harvey, [uneven geographical development] is about cutting costs (including especially costs of geographical movement), which is associated with an increase in the ratio of immobile to mobile capital" (ibid.). Das criticizes Harvey for explaining "contradictions of capitalism using an approach that applies to *all* class societies rather than deploying a broader, a more totalizing, approach which combines mechanisms that apply to all class societies with those that are associated with capitalism as such, and with advanced capitalism" (ibid. 520, emphasis in original). He also criticizes Harvey for identifying "competitive relations in an anarchic market", and not class relations, as the most significant set of relations shaping and forming capitalist development and crises (ibid. 519). Das goes on, "the disequilibrium happens unevenly; the overaccumulation crisis is localized. That is in part because of the geography of fixed capital. If for neo-classicals, market is the solution to ills, for Harvey market causes problems" (ibid. 521).[8] Das (ibid. 523) provides a counterexample to Harvey's explanation of cost-cutting processes, which Harvey noted occurred in cases where cutting wages led many capitals to stay put (most typically in the Third World and other underdeveloped regions within global capitalism). Das (ibid.) posits,

8 Elsewhere, Edel (1992, 6) is similarly cautious about the risks of reformism in Harvey and notes, "Harvey's notion of analyzing disequilibrium to devise policies for equilibrium also failed to distinguish between unresolvable conflict and conflict leading to reform solutions within capitalism".

> Capital's more general tendencies/mechanisms operating at the level of capitalism-in-general and at the level of capitalism at a higher stage of development—these include competition, including in geographical space, exploitation of labour, tendency towards crisis via technological changes, imperialism, etc. which are, more or less, independent of time and place within the history of capitalism—interact with the time-and-place-specific features of capitalism.

Uneven geographical development is a consequence of the interaction between the general and the specific. By summoning the central themes of Trotsky's theory of uneven and combined development, Das proposes an alternative approach that incorporates "uneven transition to the real subsumption of labour in production at multiple scales" and examines "the dialectics of urbanization of capital and ruralization of capital" (Das 2023, 1081).

1.5.2 Conflating Circuits

Harvey's conceptualization of the three circuits of capital aims to explain how masses of investment circulate throughout the entire economy to realize the total value created. This much is agreed upon in most interpretations of Marx's theory and is evident in his notion of the movement of capital to equalize the profit rate, as presented in Capital, Volume Three. Harvey's contribution is in demonstrating the spatial manifestation of this movement. In doing so, he emphasizes that elements of both production and consumption are to be included in all three circuits. The benefit of this inclusion for his explanation is straightforward: it enables him to incorporate the tendency to overaccumulation (and shrinking investment opportunities) into his concept of the primary circuit of capital, which involves implications of both supply and demand, and to argue that the fall in demand drives the formation of surplus capital. One conceptual problem with Harvey's interpretation is that he collapses circuits of capital, household revenue, commerce, exchange, and so on into a single category of primary or secondary circuit of capital. This approach creates tensions not because it seems counterintuitive in comparison to, for instance, classical political economy, in which these circuits are not regularly collapsed into fewer categories, but because the noted concepts of circuits in economic theory are specifically distinguished to explain various types of investments in production and consumption of commodities, including the built environment, their underlying drivers, corresponding types of return, and pricing mechanisms (for more discussion, see Chapter 6). Conflating these circuits may have been necessary for his conceptualization of the capital switching thesis and, more importantly, the spatial fix. Nevertheless, it has ramifications for empirical analysis (see Chapter 5).

In Shaikh's interpretation of Marx's analysis in Capital, Volume Two, the general circulation of commodities is presumed before the three central circuits are conceptualized: 1) circuit of productive capital, 2) circuit of money capital, and 3) circuit of commodity capital. The aim is to distinguish three social classes and, consistent with the labor theory of value, to single out the significant role of exploitation and unpaid labor in the production of commodities and the formation of profit (Shaikh 2016, 206; Marx 1992 [1978], 181). In the circuit of productive capital (M-C-M'), which can be more accurately demonstrated as M-C ... P ... C-M', money (M) is invested in labor, raw material, overhead, and machinery (as commodities) to produce (P) more commodities (C) with the purpose of exchange for more money (M') (Marx 1973; 1992 [1978]). In the circuit of commodity capital (C-M-C), labor enters the process to sell labor power as a commodity in exchange for money (wages), "then uses this money to buy consumption goods and financial assets" (Shaikh 2016, 206). This difference between the two conceptualizations of the circuits implies two parallel understandings of what drives investments. One starts with the labor theory of value, highlighting unpaid labor as the primary source of profit to explain the underlying mechanisms of class conflict between labor and capital. In contrast, the other approach begins with speculative activity—specifically, unproductive speculative investments in the built environment—to explain the class conflict between developers, financiers, and the property-less (more on this below). The point is that the latter approach must be corroborated by empirical evidence that this is universally the case in contemporary capitalism (that the labor theory of value is no longer relevant) to prove the former approach wrong. Otherwise, the former approach can be equally detailed in its explanation of the concrete.

As an example, in their interpretation, Shaikh and Tonak further concretize Marx's circuits to clarify that "[t]he goods of a household, both durable and nondurable, are part of the consumption [or revenue] circuit, those of the government are part of social administration [while] business R&D and exploration costs" are a part of the circuit of capital (Shaikh and Tonak 1994, 14). This conceptual clarification is crucial to highlight "the differences between capitalist enterprise, personal consumption, and social administration" and stress that only the first one is a profit-generating category (ibid.). This first category also encompasses the productive component of investments in the built environment. An interesting empirical implication of this conceptualization, as Shaikh (2016, 207) argues, concerns savings. He says, "[i]n the circuit of revenue, which applies to household expenditure, savings is a means to expand reserves of financial assets ... But in the circuit of capital, which applies to business operations, savings is a means of expanding capital", which appears as a form of future investment and is determined by the profitability of the production process in earlier steps or the expectation of profit rates in future steps (Shaikh 2016, 207; also Marx 1973, 467). In other words, the increase in productivity and subsequently in the creation of surplus value means that in a growing economy, investments in Department I (means of production) have to grow faster than in Department II (means of subsistence) (Marx 1992 [1978], 597). That creates an inherent "imbalance," leading to inharmonious and turbulent growth in capitalist economic reproduction (Das 2017a; 2023; Kliman 2011; 2015; Roberts 2021c; Shaikh 2016).[9] On the other hand, Harvey appears to assume equilibrium to be the 'normal' case,[10] the center of gravity, thereby assuming disequilibrium or an imbalance within the circuits created by accelerating accumulation as a cause for capital mobility.

To explain the difference between the operational logic of the two circuits, Shaikh provides some examples, starting with the notion of transfers between circuits of capital and revenue. He argues that a stolen commodity from a household would increase the aggregate profit as a "vibration between the circuit of revenue and the circuit of capital" without altering the general stock, provided that the burglar sells the item to a seller (Shaikh 2016, 209–210). Marx refers to this as "profit on alienation," as opposed to "profit on the production of surplus value," which itself encompasses land rent and interest (ibid.; also Duman and Tonak 2024). If the burglar keeps the item for personal consumption (as an internal transfer within the household sector) or, in an alternative scenario, the item is stolen from one business by another, the aggregate profit will not change (Shaikh 2016, 209–210). The second example is for "transfers within the circuit of capital" (ibid.). The production profit "will go down," if the production sector pays a portion of "its operating surplus to banks as interest," while the total bank revenue (a sum of banking profit and costs) will go up (ibid.). That means the magnitude of profit is distributed between the two entities while its total level remains the same. The same logic applies to profit and land rent (as "costs and profits of land or building rental firms") or taxes and transfers (ibid.). Transfers within the circuit of capital can "increase or decrease aggregate profit insofar as the transactions cross the boundary between current and capital cost accounts" (ibid.). All this is to say that the

9 Lenin draws a similar conclusion: that in capitalist economies "the increase in means of production outstrips the increase in articles of consumption" (Lenin 2004 [1899], 54).

10 A similar observation led Das to characterize Harvey's theory as "a complex version of what is effectively under-consumptionism" (Das 2023, 1082).

revenue generated in the second entity is, in effect, "the recirculation of revenues without any change in surplus" (ibid.).

This transfer between circuits of capital and revenue, which, in Shaikh's interpretation, generates profit on vibration, is similar to Harvey's conceptualization of the switching from primary to the secondary circuits (the latter being unproductive, therefore, within the realm of revenue), with one caveat: as Marx pointed out in Capital, Volume Two, transfers are not the source of industrial profit; they are generated out of the redistribution of the surplus created during the production process (Marx 1992 [1978], 32). And even if the aggregate profit is increased (in the case of transfers between circuits of revenue and capital), "no new value is created or destroyed"; it is only transferred (Shaikh 2016, 224). This reading aligns with Harvey's decision to disregard the law of value in his explanation of economic urbanization processes and examination of investment flows into the built environment, focusing on prices driven by speculative activity. At the same time, it means that a transferred value to, for instance, the built environment can only partially and temporally contribute to the aggregate rate of return and cannot function as a general 'fix' to capitalist crises.

1.5.3 Capital Switching and Overaccumulation

Harvey's concept of capital switching explains the movement of capital (defined as a mass of new investments) from the primary circuit (productive investments) to the secondary circuit (investments in built environments). Since the 1980s, Harvey's capital switching thesis has attracted more interest among Harvey-inspired geographers than it did among Marxist scholars. Many of these sympathetic critics pointed out difficulties in ascertaining whether and, if so, which capital switched to investments in the built environment (Beauregard 1994; Christophers 2011; King 1989a; 1989b; 1989c). And Harvey's limited indicator to demonstrate capital switching (the periodic rise of building activity) certainly did not help. The two contributions by Ross King (1989a) and Robert Beauregard (1994) are noteworthy. Both criticized Harvey for failing to provide sufficient empirical support for capital switching and overaccumulation crises that caused it. But as noted in the most comprehensive critical engagement with the thesis to date, i.e., Brett Christophers (2011), their attempt to provide additional evidence was not compelling, either. In response, Christophers casts doubt on the idea of having "a comprehensive and watertight empirical substantiation of switching" (Christophers 2011, 1351). Instead, he aims for "a clear indication" of the switching using a "proxy measure" that combines "investment in labor and investment in noninfrastructural fixed assets" to be later compared with "the temporal trends" in the two investment types Harvey envisioned in his primary and secondary circuits of capital, and specifically the speculative activities of "fund managers" (Christophers 2011, 1351–1352). Nevertheless, two crucial gaps remain. In a reversal of the chain of causality in Harvey's original formulation, Christophers (like Rutland (2010, 1171) before him) seeks to indicate a capital switching that occurs before the crisis (Christophers 2011, 1352). Therefore, he, too, fails to demonstrate the type of crisis that led to switching empirically. More germane to our current discussion, Christophers omits the mediation of land rent that Harvey carefully included in his original conceptualization of the capital switching thesis.

For Harvey, the underlying assumption is that recurrent crises of overaccumulation in the primary circuit force capital to flow to the built environment (as fixed assets with long turnover times) to absorb the surplus capital created in the primary circuit slowly, provided the built environment is financialized, and the investments in it are speculative. However, this presumption also implies that investments in built environments are categorically unproductive and, hence, excluded from the primary circuit of capital. Harvey explicitly argues that of all (five) economic actors in built environments (landlords, developers, financiers, builders, and state), only builders "organize the real production of surplus value" (Harvey 2006 [1982], 397). However, even if one accepts his categorization, at least investments in construction (of residential and commercial built environments as well as physical infrastructure) should have been included in the concept of the primary circuit of capital. Construction is a significant contributor to overall sectoral investments and rates of returns, as evidenced by the current wave of dual recessions in construction and real estate across many advanced capitalist economies (see Chapter 6). More importantly, construction involves an intricate chain of intermediate inputs and their associated productive, value-creating processes, each determined by its internal competitive dynamics at every moment. The overall process (and its associated relative price and rate of return), therefore, is determined as "the vertically integrated unit labor cost associated with the production" of buildings as commodities (Shaikh 2016, 69). It is measured as "the sum of the unit labor costs of the industry producing the commodity in question, plus the unit labor costs of the set of industries producing the inputs (raw materials, etc.) of this particular industry, plus the unit labor costs of the industries producing the inputs for the industries producing the inputs, and so on" (ibid.). That is because the general concepts of this process in its totality "only show themselves when it appears as real, as many capitals" (Marx 1973, 520). A crucial tension in Harvey's conceptualization is that excluding construction from the primary circuit makes it internally inconsistent. However, if one factors in investments in the built environment (or at least a significant portion of it, such as construction) in the primary circuit, there would be no (general) spatial fix to the (general) overaccumulation crisis.

The second problem concerns the source of returns in Harvey's secondary circuit of capital. Does capital flow to the secondary circuit in search of higher (sectoral) profit rates due to the productive (value-creating) aspects of investments in built environments? Furthermore, if the presumption is that the productive part of the sectoral investment is only a small portion (a one-fifth), then is the high return generated in the secondary circuit a result of the transfer of revenues, i.e., similar to Shaikh's explanation of a "vibration between the circuit of revenue and the circuit of capital" that increased the aggregate profit, thereby compensating for the overaccumulation crisis elsewhere? If that is true, then does it mean that it is not, in fact, a capital flow between circuits but a transfer of revenues? Harvey does not begin with Marx's value theory (as he elaborated recently (Harvey 2018)), which is scientifically legitimate, nor did Sweezy (1970 [1942]). Nevertheless, he needs to have addressed these empirical problems or at least anticipated them in his conceptual apparatus. Harvey does mention investments in physical infrastructure and specifically names "transcontinental railroads, and highways, dams, and the like" as areas of investment in the secondary circuit of capital (Harvey 2012, 42). But the specific type of investment he attributes to the secondary circuit is "speculative" (ibid. 45). In that sense, it can be argued that his explanation overlooks the significant contribution of construction profits (as a productive, value-creating process) to aggregate profit rates, as well as intra-sectoral competition among constructors and inter-sectoral competition between constructors and other productive capitalists.

Rutland observed this tension and writes, "[t]he primary circuit, for Harvey, pertains strictly to the capital, labor-power, and means of production involved in a single production-to-consumption cycle (even plant and equipment, as fixed assets, are excluded from this category)." In contrast, the secondary circuit includes, "the built environment, along with a diverse range of 'aids' to production and consumption" (Rutland 2010, 1171). However, he did not explore this further. Belina (2025) also notes this tension and attempts to address it in his recent reinterpretation of Harvey's conceptualization. However, his solution—integrating construction into the secondary circuit of capital, not the primary—completely diverges from Harvey's original formulation, save for the terminology. It suggests that the primary circuit only differs from the secondary by containing commodities with a "longer-term temporality," rather than representing specific types of activities (productive, non-productive, etc.), as Harvey assumed (Belina 2025, 149). This suggests that Harvey's secondary circuit is now directly tied to a specific branch (i.e., the built environment), rendering the original categories (primary, secondary, etc.) redundant, given that it excludes other commodities with "longer-term temporality" as well as finance in general.

There are two noteworthy implications of this conceptual tension in Harvey's explanation. First, the failure to relate capital switching to intersectoral profit rate cycles and the general rate of profit, as noted by Das (2017a; 2023), led Harvey to overemphasize the roles of spatial and financial forces (also see Duman and Tonak, 2024). Second, it renders the terminology (primary, secondary, tertiary) somewhat arbitrary, as it implies a spatial and temporal hierarchy among various spaces of economic activity. The fact of the matter is that the types of investment (productive and non-productive) flowing into the three levels Harvey describes stem from different social relations and are driven by their expected rates of return (profit, interest, rent). Each of these return types is determined and partially realized within its respective circuit. They all contribute to the overall sectoral activity, with none being inherently superior, and their contributions are also influenced by intermediate inputs generated in other circuits. Harvey's conflation of these investment types and the implied hierarchy, as discussed earlier, muddies this important analytical distinction.

Harvey (2023, 39) attempts to concretize his notion of capital switching in his brief analysis of the Chinese economy after the 2008 crisis, drawing on Marx's (1973, 90) concepts of final consumption and productive consumption in Grundrisse. He surmises that in response to the falling magnitudes of Chinese exports to the US (in part due to the falling purchasing power of the lower-income population in the latter), indicated as a general overproduction problem for the economy, the Chinese state attempted to shift to investments in infrastructure (as a form of productive consumption) to compensate for the fall in final consumptions (Harvey 2023, 39). Even if we leave aside the accuracy of this analysis of the Chinese case, there are two empirical problems with this explanation for the present discussion. Firstly, as Harvey noted (ibid. 34), Marx's productive consumption refers to reinvestments as such and not merely in the built environment. In other words, it includes all types of reinvestments (including the production of intermediate inputs) as a constant constituent of the circulation of capital, and its potential periodic rise is not attributable merely to compensating for a potential fall in final consumption. Secondly, in Harvey's explanation, general overproduction is presumed to be a precondition for the rise of productive consumption (in this case, infrastructure). However, this formulation is not adequately explanatory, as it does not explain the more frequent (short- and mid-term) investments in urban built environments (i.e., Harvey's thesis's principal empirical objective) that follow much faster and briefer cycles than the longer-term cycles of general overproduction. Instead, it tends to limit investment flows into the built environment to long cycles of general overproduction.

An alternative approach to capital switching is plausible to avoid the noted tension, using Shaikh's notion of incremental profit rates (gross profit divided by lagged gross investment), which indicates the year-end sectoral shift of investments in response to higher profit expectations in different branches as "profit rate equalization in its true form" (Shaikh 2016, 68). Here, the shift in investment is explained at the sectoral level (i.e., disaggregated but not at the firm level) and analyzed in terms of profit rate expectations. The underlying presumption that this is still a macro-level indicator is crucial. It allows for anticipating investment fluctuations at the level of individual capitalists, recognizing that not all individual investors behave the same way. The aggregate explains the overall behavior and its causes. So if we agree with Shaikh's interpretation that aggregate profit only changes if the transfer occurs between circuits of capital and revenue, then Harvey's notion of capital switching and its positive impact on rates of return means that for Harvey, the built environment (secondary circuit) is in fact treated as external as a revenue circuit which makes sense only if we treat the entire sectoral investments in built environments as non-value creating. That does not exhaust the evidence, as detailed in Chapter 5 below.

A note on the overaccumulation crisis (i.e., Harvey's assumed precondition of the movement of capital between circuits) is due here. While Harvey allocates a few passages to explaining different types of overaccumulation crises (partial, sectoral, geographical, and global) (1978; 2006 [1982]), he does not engage with other potential types of economic crisis in the primary circuit beyond overaccumulation itself. Nor does he provide any empirical evidence for overaccumulation and the subsequent movement of capital to the secondary circuit (a point also raised by Beauregard (1994) and Christophers (2011)). Nevertheless, his exposition strongly implies that the tendency towards overaccumulation in the primary circuit is the primary type of economic crisis we need to factor in to explain the flow of capital into urban space, as overaccumulation is reinforced by a supply shock (of sorts) of available spaces for further investments. In other words, in Harvey's conceptualization, capital switching is restricted to overaccumulation crises, monopolistic competition, and a neoliberal (and financialized) regulatory context. This restricted formulation, I argue, has led many scholars to characterize it as borderline functionalistic (Barnes 1994; Castree 1995; Anderson 2014; King 1989a).

There are three problematic implications for this: a) it implies a rather monocausal (to use Harvey's own words (Harvey 2016)) explanation of capitalist economic crisis (to treat overaccumulation as the only relevant type of crisis to analyze capitalist urbanization). To put it differently, Harvey, on the one hand, declares that there is no leading cause of capitalist crises (Harvey 2014; 2016; Tapia 2023), which implies the futility of developing a crisis theory (Roberts 2016b). On the other hand, when it comes to explaining concrete processes of capitalist urbanization, he limits the analysis to discussing the implications of overaccumulation, prioritizing it over all other forms of crisis. Furthermore, b) it implies that there would be no capital switching if overaccumulation does not happen in the primary circuit. However, as presented in Chapter 5, empirical evidence indicates that capital switching may occur under certain economic and historical conditions. This capital switching (as indicated by Shaikh's incremental rate of profit) does not depend on overaccumulation of capital, but rather on profitability cycles and inter-sectoral competition over future (expected) profit rates (Farahani 2025). It is also not limited to investment flows to built environments (Watterton 2023). Finally, c) as noted by Lebowitz (1986, 388), Harvey proposes that "the fundamental contradiction in capitalism is the contradiction between the interests of capital in general and the interests of individual capitalists," and the actions of individual capitalists may "destabilize capitalism" (Harvey 2006 [1982], 188, quoted in Lebowitz 1986, 388). This proposition implies "a perfectly planned capitalism (on a world scale)" would help the system "to return to its equilibrium path and spatial configuration," despite crises being "inherent in the system," making his argument "overdetermined" (ibid. 388–389).

1.5.4 Value, Profit, and Class Conflict

It is generally accepted that the processes of circulation of capital in Marx's work are explained at the aggregate, i.e., a whole-economy level, which is the level at which the law of value applies. He noted in Volume Three of Capital that the analyses presented in the first two volumes of the book were at the level of "values of commodities" (Marx 1991 [1894], 263). Marx insists that this whole-economy (or capital-as-such) analysis needs to be disaggregated in competition and argues that "capital exists and can only exist as many capitals" (Marx 1973, 414). By the level of value, Marx means "the normal, average situation for capital invested in this branch of production" and/or "the average of total capital" in the whole economy (Marx 1991 [1894], 243). By market price, he means "the individual value of particular commodities produced by the different producers," which could stand below or above values depending on individual conditions of production (ibid. 279). To put it differently, "value is the centre of gravity around which price turns and at which its constant rise and fall is balanced out" (ibid. 279). And to analyze its impact and to "capture the total industrial" average (Shaikh 2016, 69), Marx suggests starting with "*one* branch of production, as a *single* commodity, and add together the sum of the prices of many identical commodities to arrive at *one* price" (Marx 1991 [1894], 283, original emphasis).

This indicates that, in addition to considering value and price as separate levels of abstraction, it is also worth explaining how they influence the economy at various scales. Inspired by Marx's analysis of competition in Capital, Volume Three, Shaikh expands on this interpretation. Engaging with long-term sectoral dynamics (between and within "each particular sphere of production" (ibid. 257)), he argues that the aggregate reflects expectations and overall tendencies (Shaikh 2016, 76). That is to say, at the whole-economy level and in the long term, in which "actual conditions … express their own general type" (Marx 1991 [1894], 242), these "structural factors predominate" (Shaikh 2016, 730). However, individual capitalists' behaviors, performance, or "desired outcomes" may or may not carry such aggregate tendencies (ibid. 31). In each moment in the competition, thus, only a few will gain while others will lose. However, individual capitalists continuously adjust (or else move) in response to aggregate expectations (e.g., fluctuating aggregate profit rates) (ibid.). The aggregate, in other words, is determined by "the relative weight which these different rates of profit assume in the formation" of the average (Marx 1991 [1894], 262).

There are practical implications, too. As we have seen, to conceptualize capital switching, Harvey draws on Marx's notion of "uninterrupted emigration and immigration of capitals that takes place between various spheres of production produces rising and falling movements in the profit rate which more or less balance one another out" (ibid. 310). The rate of profit is central to this movement as "capital withdraws from a sphere with a low rate of profit and wends its way to others that yield higher profit" (ibid. 297). The problem for Harvey, however, is that without the concept of the competitive (intra-sectoral and inter-sectoral) profit rate, his interpretation fails to explain the upper limit of aggregate (speculative) expectations. The profit rate dynamics and their associated "competition of capitals in different spheres" (ibid. 281) are central to what Harvey once called "the operational structuralist method" of Marx, which Harvey argued is crucial for analyzing phenomena such as urbanization (Harvey 2009 [1973], 302). The notion of competitive profit rates, which explains how fluctuations of intra-sectoral and inter-sectoral profit rates relate to aggregate (value-level) forces, for Marx is aimed at demonstrating that "each individual capitalist, just like the totality of all capitalists in each particular sphere of production, participates in the exploitation of the entire working class by capital as a whole, and in the level of this exploitation; not just in terms of general class sympathy, but in a direct economic sense, since, taking all other circumstances as given, including the value of the total constant capital advanced, the average rate of profit depends on the level of exploitation of labour as a whole by capital as a whole" (Marx 1991 [1894], 298–299).

1.5.5 Urban Land Rent

That final point is further explored in Marxist political economy through the theory of land rent. In the sphere of economic production and reproduction, the theory seeks to explain how the land rent component of the overall profit rate is generated—outlining the conditions under which this occurs—and how the interconnected fluctuations of these profit rate components are tied to the creation of surplus value by workers in the productive sectors. In social reproduction, the focus is on how workers' everyday struggles to secure food, shelter, and other essential services in their living spaces are also linked to their struggles in the workplace. The central question, therefore, is how the profits capitalists make in residential areas relate to the general rate of profit and to profits from manufacturing, and how these profits are affected by crisis cycles. Irene Bruegel highlighted the importance of the labor theory of value in addressing such questions, notably in one of the earliest critical analyses of Harvey's land rent theory from a Marxist urban political economy perspective.

Bruegel (1975, 36) began her critique of Harvey by disputing his interpretation of the labor theory of value and exploring various ways it could be operationalized to explain urban processes and development under capitalism. Harvey had criticized neoclassical urban rent models (e.g., Alonso 1964) for their failure to explain urban structures in terms of use value. According to Bruegel, Harvey's application of value is limited; as "by exchange value, Harvey means market prices, [and] by use value he means the individual's subjective valuation" (Bruegel 1975, 36). The difference between the two (as Anne Haila (1990) also points out) creates "consumer's surplus", which Harvey defines as "the difference between what an individual actually pays for a good and what he or she would be willing to pay rather than go without it" (Harvey 1973, 169). The concept explains how lower-income groups in the city systematically tend to lose favorable locations (including better housing conditions) to the urban rich. Bruegel says, "labour power is paid for at its value, i.e., the costs of reproducing it and *not* at the value of the commodities it produces" (Bruegel 1975, 36 emphasis in original). Harvey's treatment of exchange value in terms of the market price of commodities (here housing and property values), according to Bruegel (ibid.), implies that for him, the social tension over urban resources is explained at price levels (income gaps) and the tension between landlords and tenants is equivalent to the social tension between the wage laborer and the capitalist. This analysis is also shared by Matthew Edel (1976; 1992). However, Bruegel continues, one need not equate tenant-landlord conflict to worker-capitalist conflict to develop a Marxian urban theory. She maintains, "the tenant may be 'cheated' under capitalism, but this is not fundamental to the system: the exploitation of the worker is" (Bruegel 1975, 37). More importantly, as Bruegel (ibid. 38) points out, if Harvey explains urban socio-spatial tension based on income levels, his critique of neoclassical models (Alonso and Muth) loses its strength because their models do not 'ignore' income stratifications; in fact, the phenomenon of increasing housing expenditure due to rising rents can also be derived from neoclassical models of urban land rent. The question they fail to address is why they find "no reason to ask why there are huge disparities of income under capitalism" rather than whether income disparities exist (ibid.). It should be noted here that Harvey dealt with this anomaly in his later works since the late 1970s (especially in the *Limits*) by explaining the urban process in terms of expansion into the secondary circuit of capital (the capital switching thesis) and the tendency to treat land as a financial asset, thereby relating it to broader processes of capital accumulation.

Bruegel (ibid. 39) stresses that for Marx, rent is construed at the macro-level as an outcome of productive relations over land. "Unlike Harvey, [Marx] keeps quite separate the question of the rents paid for by workers for their housing and does not appear to have considered rent for unproductive [speculative] activities explicitly" (ibid. 39–40). Therefore, she also refutes Harvey's attempt to analyze high housing rents in the inner-city as differential rent. Harvey, according to Buegel, argues that the concentration of unproductive (and speculative) activities in central urban areas with "highest rental values" implies "rent determining use," similar to absolute rent, rather than "use determining rent," as is the case with differential rent. Bruegel asserts that such an argument implies "capitalists are acting irrationally in locating offices in city centres" (ibid.). She, however, maintains that differential rent remains pertinent as land users compete for more productive uses. But that does not mean that differential rent has a direct impact on housing prices. On the contrary, it means that differential rent is "probably the main influence which the factor of location has on [housing costs]" (ibid.). Bruegel (ibid. 41) finds the concept of monopoly rent "to be something of an aberration" with "limited importance" for Marx. The reason is that it indicates monopoly pricing, unlike the concepts of differential rent I and II and absolute rent, which are explained structurally in terms of the dynamics of productive capital. She further argues that the existence of monopoly power (central to most land and resource relations) cannot be easily translated into monopoly prices and, therefore, monopoly rent. She (ibid.) contends,

> It is not clear that revenue varies with location independently of the variation of productivity with location for activities other than shops and consumer services, so while there may well be instances where the monopoly profits of such enterprises are transformed into monopoly rent, there seems to be no basis for asserting that this is a generalised phenomenon.

She (ibid. 41) identifies a few gaps in Harvey's treatment of the concept of absolute rent. First, the precondition for absolute rent is competition driven by differences in the organic composition of capital between branches (also see Fine 2019), which creates excess profits. The second point concerns historically specific conditions that allow absolute rent to arise; that is, if the excess profit disappears, so does absolute rent. The third point is that, unlike differential rent, absolute rent affects the prices of commodities produced on the land with implications for class conflict: "[t]his excess price then cuts into the surplus value of the capitalist class as a whole by raising the costs of producing the labour force, i.e., costs of subsistence" (Bruegel 1975, 43). In other words, absolute rent is directly involved in the distribution of surplus value between sectors. Besides, for Marx, Bruegel submits, absolute rent "is not just any form of excess rent payment, i.e., it is a long run rather than a short run phenomenon" (ibid. 43). Similarly, Graham Ive contends, the difference between differential rents and absolute rent is that in differential rents, the landowner intercepts excess profits "that could otherwise go into 'the private capitalist (farmer's) pocket'" (Ive 1974, 26). In the case of absolute rent, such excess profits intercepted by landowners "would otherwise go into the general capitalist fund to raise the general rate of profit but reduce the rate of profit in that branch to the general rate" (ibid.).

Bruegel further criticizes Harvey for introducing an overly generalized category of class-monopoly rent, "which, as defined, could include all rent" (Bruegel 1975, 43; also Edel 1976). She stresses, "Marx's distinctions or categories are important if one is to understand whether any particular rent payment is a temporary, chance phenomenon or whether it is a long-term, structural feature of the system. The argument is not for orthodoxy as such—that Harvey is wrong *because* he departs from Marx's analysis of any particular phenomenon—but rather that Harvey's account is incoherent" (Bruegel 1975, 43, emphasis in original). According to her, with class-monopoly rent, Harvey "is trying to show that finance capital acts to create distinctive submarkets in housing, which themselves increase frictions of distance and so the possibility of extracting absolute rent, or a form of it, class-monopoly rent" (ibid. 44). Instead, she (ibid. 43–44) calls for further empirical engagements on, for instance, planning practices as preconditions of rents' existence. For example, she suggests the construction sector "with its traditional low organic composition of capital, may well be a source for such surplus profits, and planning controls of the British type—development control, green belts and industry and office development permits—could well act as a barrier to capital investment and hence promote absolute rent" (ibid.). According to Bruegel (ibid. 46), three presumptions are behind Harvey's reasons to replace the concept of absolute rent with class-monopoly rent: a) his focus on income rather than value to explain socio-spatial conflicts; b) his understanding of class as a group with common interests; and c) his emphasis on space rather than sector and scale in creation and appropriation of rents.

The main problem with Bruegel's account is that, in the end, she fails to propose a heuristic or analytical framework to rival Harvey's for operationalizing rent theory in urban research. Instead, she exemplifies potential scenarios regarding barriers to the equalization process while also providing a remarkable elucidation of Marx's formulation of rent and the development of rent theory in class and inter-sectoral economic relations. However, she does not take it further and remains at the conceptual level in her critique. Ideally, her propositions should have been explored by other Marxist urban scholars, but they were not.

Murray (1977; 1978) similarly emphasizes the centrality of the labor theory of value in his seminal, exhaustive two-part review of Marx's land rent theory. Geography and the urban, so central to Harvey, Bruegel, or Edel, are only briefly discussed in Murray. Nevertheless, the central debate in Marxist economics over the primacy of production versus distribution, and their relation to value theory, seems to be a primary critical concern for Murray (1977). He writes, "it is only through starting from value, and never losing its thread, that we can adequately understand the determination of distribution by production, and the contradictory development of their forms" (ibid. 119). He diagnoses that starting from production prices and not values is central to all rent theorists "who adopt monopoly rent in preference to absolute rent" (ibid.). Discussing urban applications of rent theory, he (ibid.) writes, "in urban theory, for instance, the dominant approach is barely distinguishable, save in terminology, from traditional monopolistic competition and bilateral monopoly theory". He particularly criticizes Harvey (2009 [1973]) for analyzing capitalist cities "as aggregations of sub-markets strategically separated by landed proprietors" like "man-made islands" and then calling "the rent earned from them absolute rent". Murray (1977, 119) says, Harvey "is in no way seeking to connect rent to value, or to see how labour in these sub-sectors is commensurated with the rest of social labour. The barriers to the free flow of capital to which he refers are similar to the traditional 'barriers to entry' that can apply to any temporary monopoly. The resulting rent is merely a version of monopoly rent" (ibid.). Furthermore, Murray argues such an interpretation lacks a "theoretical basis" to adequately "engage with bourgeois theory on the major issues of rent theory" (ibid. 120). Murray (ibid. 122) identifies this issue in the work of other urban political economists, including Clarke and Ginsburg (1975), Byrne and Beirne (1975), Walker (1974), and Edel (1976). According to Murray (1977, 120), such an interpretation tends to generalize rent "to all sectors[11] with diminishing returns". It fails to relate it to long-term contradictions of the capitalist economy, including inter-sectoral competition and crisis.

It is also interesting to note that Harvey shifts his focus from concepts of monopoly, class monopoly, and absolute rent in his early 1970s writings to differential rent I and II, particularly in The *Limits*. I suspect this could partly be a response to the criticism set forth by Bruegel, Edel, and Murray. Though this suspicion cannot be verified from the book itself, given that Bruegel and Murray are not even mentioned in the book, and Edel is only mentioned once (Harvey 2006 [1982], 330) in an acknowledgement of his extensive survey on the urban applications of Marx's rent theory. Harvey insisted that Marx struggled in both Capital, Volume Three, and Theories of Surplus Value with "a good deal of confusion" (Harvey 2006 [1982], 330). Particularly, in the case of absolute rent, this textual interpretation serves as the basis for his conclusion that Marx began to assign greater significance to monopoly rent. However, it is equally clear that Marx dedicates as many passages (if not more) making a case for absolute rent and brushing off monopoly rent as "a mere monopoly price" (Marx 1991 [1894], 902) driven by "the demand of the purchasers and their ability to pay," investigation of which belongs to the realm of the market price (ibid. 898). Thus an entirely different reading is also possible, and that is: typical in his explanatory approach in sections on land rent (and value as noted by Ollman (2003) this style is central to Marx's dialectical thinking), Marx aims to address all possibilities, including monopoly rent, which he decidedly leaves out of his three main categories (differential rent I, differential rent II, and absolute rent). He aims to refute all such possibilities in favor of the cases consistent with the rest of his theory, and specifically the labor theory of value. This gives more significance to absolute rent. A textual investigation, however,

11 Manning (2020) makes a similar argument (see Chapter 2 below).

is insufficient. What is to be advanced is an empirical evaluation of such readings, not their textual accuracy.

Harvey's theory of land rent promised to relate rent to the overarching capitalist structure, i.e., Marx's law of capital accumulation. One significant tension is that, according to his theory, the fact that investors (in response to shrinking investment opportunities) move to urban land indicates that he presumes urban land was outside the process of capital accumulation at the whole-economy level. In other words, he first excludes construction from his concept of the primary circuit of capital, then he regards the overaccumulation crises of capital as occurring in industrial, service, or other non-land branches, and only then does capital overspill into the urban land sector. In this conceptual exposition, the urban land sector is exempted from shrinking opportunities and the general rate of profit. The urban land sector (and the built environment, for that matter), thus, is given a unique position in Harvey's somewhat linear process of spatially fixing overaccumulation crises. In other words, the logic of his argument, in effect, depicts the routine movements of capital in search of higher rates of return, and overaccumulation does not seem to be the necessary condition for this process. As noted by Lebowitz (1986, 389), this makes his argument for spatial shifts similar to technical shifts (to increase productivity or cut wages), which implies, again, no necessarily unique role for either land or the built environment. If this reading of his argument is valid, then it makes sense, as Callinicos (2009) argues, to draw the analogy between his explanation and Rosa Luxemburg's theory of capital accumulation (1951), which argues that "the capitalist process of accumulation is inherently dependent on dominating a non-capitalist 'other'" (Callinicos 2009, 36).[12] The crucial difference is that for Luxemburg, the 'others,' to which the international capital moved to absorb its surplus, were pre-capitalist societies that remained outside of the global capitalist market in the early 20th century. Harvey, however, treats a sector within the capitalist economy as an 'other' external to it.

Conceptually, as noted above, Harvey's theory aspires to structural analysis as an alternative to the neoclassical explanation of the level and fluctuations of land rent. Consistent with the structural analysis, he incorporates

---

12 Of course, Luxemburg's underconsumptionist theory of crisis is not the same as Harvey's theory of overaccumulation. However, as Callinicos (2009) argues, their similarities in the causes of the crisis remain strong. For example, in their respective interpretations of Marx's reproduction schemes, both Luxemburg and Harvey presuppose an equilibrium between the two departments and attribute eventual disequilibrium to crises. However, while one (Luxemburg) blames the crisis on demand and underconsumption, the other (Harvey) attributes it to supply, arguing that the imbalance caused by accelerating accumulation pushes capital to move elsewhere seeking new investment opportunities.

financing practices into the analysis, thereby rejecting an arbitrary rent level driven solely by monopolistic power relations and collusion. Instead, as we saw, he explains the rise of rent through financial practices over land and the mediation of speculator-developers who treat land as a pure financial asset (Harvey 2006 [1982]). This auxiliary mediation, however, would not have been necessary had he not excluded land from the general rate of profit. Even then, the argument remains anomalous, as it overlooks the crucial productive component of the venture on land and the built environment—namely, construction, as noted by Bruegel, and specifically new construction—as a source of the sectoral rate of return and land rent. His explanation of the rise, level, and fluctuations of rent in relation to the macro-dynamics of capital accumulation, therefore, is not consistently structural. True to the model reconstructed below (Chapter 3), his only extensive empirical study of urban land rent (the Baltimore study) suggests that he relates it not to the accumulation of capital per se but to the dynamics of finance capital. Harvey does not explicitly put it this way. However, a more sympathetic reading is possible, assuming his initial premise is that shrinking investment opportunities are due to a falling rate of profit in the productive sector, that the spatial fix is due to the dynamics of the financial sector in particular, and that financial profits determine rent levels.[13] It remains unclear, however, what determines financial profits. That is to say, are the interest rates (thereby financial profits) determined internally in the economy (i.e., in response to fluctuations of the rates of return in other sectors) or independently (i.e., in response to exogenous interventions such as changes in monetary and fiscal policies)?

As Harvey's empirical studies of Baltimore testify (see Chapter 4), his answer leans toward the exogeneity of financial profits as "the ability to obtain a mortgage under suitable terms is also a function of the policies of financial and governmental institutions," whose interaction "filters" and "transmits" national housing and monetary policies to the local level (Harvey and Chatterjee 1974, 23–24). The valuation of interest rates, according to Harvey and Chatterjee, depends on a preexisting "geographical structure" that determines each area's land values, and this geographical structure forms a "decision environment" for price setting (ibid. 25). At the same time, the noted geographical structure itself is created and maintained by the interaction of "governmental and financial institutions" (Harvey 1974a, 245). Elsewhere, he outlines the state's practices regarding finance capital. He (2006 [1982], 321) writes,

13 Neil Smith (1996b) attempted a similar reconstruction of Harvey's model in his analysis of the gentrification process, as he tries to relate it to the general rate of profit (even though Harvey is not explicit on this point).

> It fixes the legal and institutional framework and often designs the highly differentiated channels through which interest-bearing capital circulates into the different activities such as consumer debt, housing finance, industrial development and the like. It often regulates flows down the different channels by fixing interest-rate differentials or direct allocations of credit. The degree of centralization or decentralization of money wealth and control is likewise highly sensitive to state fiscal and redistributive taxation policies as well as to monetary strategies that affect inflation.

This is hardly the consistently structural explanation that he had initially promised: his model assumes that returns on financial activities (i.e., interests) mediate the relationship between land and the overall economy, and the price of land (i.e., rent) and the rate of interest are not directly related to the dynamics of productive investment. Instead, land and money prices are determined at the micro level through the interaction between landlords who take loans from financiers and changes in monetary policy. At the level of individual landlords and investors, this might indeed be the case. Individual investors' and landlords' investment choices might be influenced by their access to favorable financing terms. But "micro features do not necessarily carry to the macro level and any given macro pattern may be consistent with many different (even contradictory) micro foundations" (Shaikh 2016, 31). The model should, instead, have explicated the structural determinants of land prices and financial activities at the aggregate level. Another crucial empirical challenge is that rent levels fluctuate over time. For Harvey, rent levels are determined (and, by extension, investment choices are coordinated) by the power of landlords as a class to maintain monopoly pricing on the land stock, itself determined (and coordinated) by the availability and the price of secured loans (such as mortgages) offered by the financial institutions (Harvey and Chatterjee 1974). Therefore, in the final analysis, fluctuations in rent levels are determined by changes in financial profits. And, for him, as we have seen, the level of interest rate and financial profits are determined by changes in policy (e.g., zoning practices and "neighborhood biases," deregulations, financialization, and the like) (ibid. 24). Undoubtedly, policy matters. Nevertheless, a consistently structural model of land rent needs to explain (at the macro level) the structural determinants of the noted fluctuations and corresponding policy changes.

1.6 Summary

Harvey provides a systematic and structural analysis of capitalist urbanization processes in which rent creation and appropriation are central. His theory extends significantly beyond neoclassical models by relating investment choices and rent relations to broader structural and contradictory processes of capital accumulation, rather than focusing on the behaviors and preferences of individual investors and households. His analysis, however, is not consistently structural, as it ultimately relies on exogenous monopoly power relations and explains rent levels in terms of the landlords' class power. More importantly, the historical contingency of rent creation and appropriation is absent from Harvey's model. He conceptualizes the capital switching thesis to explain capital flows into land as a sectoral shift in investment. But beyond the monopoly pricing mechanism and indicators like construction activity, he does not provide adequate analytical tools for empirical analyses of rent rates, ceilings, magnitudes, and capital switching. His analysis also lacks a conceptualization of macro-level dynamics governing micro-level investment decisions. The alternative model I propose here (Chapter 3), therefore, aims to improve on Harvey's explanation by offering a consistently endogenous structural analysis of rent relations.

The concept of class-monopoly rent is pivotal in Harvey's theory of urban land rent, as it relates land rent to spatial fix and financial practices (Park 2014; Purcell et al. 2020; Swyngedouw and Ward 2022). I argue that the gaps and tensions within his theory necessitated the introduction of this concept and the other noted mechanisms into his model (and led to the subsequent conflation of macro and micro dynamics). Nevertheless, these auxiliary concepts and mechanisms (e.g., financial practices and favorable regulatory frameworks) still fail to relate rent structurally to the macro-dynamics of capital accumulation. These gaps and tensions would be resolved and his theory improved by incorporating the concept of absolute rent, a concept Harvey repeatedly rejects as irrelevant (Harvey 2013, interview in Barnes and Sheppard 2019, 207; Harvey 2010, 81; Ward and Aalbers 2016). The point is not that rejecting the concept of absolute rent is problematic because it makes Harvey's theory less true to Marx's original text, but that this rejection has implications for his proposed structural explanation of the level and fluctuations of land rent. Absolute rent is a conceptual tool to keep urban land within the economy (as a multi-sectoral whole), and I argue that incorporating it renders Harvey's auxiliary concepts and mechanisms for consistently (and structurally) relating the rise of land rent to macro-dynamics of capital accumulation redundant.

The difference between the two concepts lies in the fact that the level and rate of absolute rent are determined by competition between sectors over higher expected (productive) profit rates and the potential excess profits in the entire land sector (in urban contexts, primarily as a sectoral average across all constructions). In other words, the level and rate of absolute rent, unlike Harvey's concept of class-monopoly rent, consistently fluctuate and are determined comparatively in relation to inter-sectoral dynamics at the whole-economy level (Fine 2019; Murray 1977; 1978). Empirically, this argument suggests that financial speculation and monopolistic land ownership can sustain high investment in the urban sector only when overall sectoral profit rates (and, consequently, absolute rent rates) are high. It also implies that, particularly in low-income neighborhoods where most plots struggle with minimal differential rents, the cyclical patterns of investment flows are determined by fluctuations in the absolute rent rate. In other words, low rates of absolute rent (i.e., the rent for the entire sector) mean higher rates of disinvestment in marginal plots in low-income residential areas, where differential rents are also minimal.

The realization of land rent depends on the level of investment, and rent contributes to the overall rate of return on the investment. The upper limit of absolute rent is determined by the difference between excess profits in construction and those in other sectors, such as manufacturing. That means that the level and rate of rent could be minimized or maximized in response to such macro-dynamics of (productive) capital. In this competitive context, investments constantly shift between sectors in search of higher profits, and the urban land sector is just one of many destinations for this movement. Therefore, explaining the rent's share/contribution to the total rate of return on the investment in the venture on land is particularly crucial, as it determines expectations at both firm and sector levels. As Marx argues, "the profit of capital does not depend on its magnitude, but rather, given an equal magnitude, on the relation between its component parts" (Marx 1973, 761). This contribution of land rent to the sectoral profit rate is absent in Harvey's explanation because he excludes rent creation and appropriation from overall sectoral profitability. That is, he assumes that the source of land rent is unproductive revenues, as landlords and developers respectively receive rent and increments in rent, but "builders earn profit of enterprise" (Harvey 2006 [1982], 395).

CHAPTER 2

The Evolution of Rent Applications by Harveyan Geographers since the 1980s

Harvey provided a single analytical tool (monopoly pricing mechanism) to explain (and determine) the rise of non-relative rents. He advanced an innovative explanatory apparatus, thanks in no small part to the introduction of new concepts, most notably class-monopoly rent, for his structural political-economic analysis of capitalist urbanization processes. Nevertheless, aside from the monopoly pricing mechanism, he did not offer many analytical tools consistent with his structural point of departure for measuring monopolistic rates of return. He regards these rates as the source of rent and capital switching, which explains the sectoral movement of capital. In response, the next generation of urban economic geographers, inspired by his systematic and structural critique of neoclassical models of rent and urbanization, began to focus on problem-solving within the research program. It was up to them to operationalize his theory, modify and apply it to various urban cases, resolve its potential empirical anomalies, explain newly discovered (social, political, economic) aspects of capitalist urbanization processes, demonstrate its methodological superiority against competing explanations advanced by the institutionalists, and potentially take it to new frontiers.

2.1 Periodizing Rent Applications

A survey of 250 scholarly works on land rent by urban economists and geographers between 1970 and 2021 (Figure 1) indicates three main periods (also see Farahani 2021). The first period pertains to the theoretical foundations. It involves initiating the debate and elaborating building blocks by early heterodox urban economic geographers, led prominently by Harvey from 1973 to the early 1980s. The second period (which comprises the second and third periods of Haila's (1990) taxonomic periodization) encompasses the debate over the application of mostly Marxian (but also Ricardian) land rent theory to urban settings. The debate engaged the Harveyans on the one hand and the institutionalists on the other, spanning from the late 1970s to the late 1990s. The first and second periods epitomize a "progressive" phase, in a Lakatosian sense (see Chapter 3 below), expanding the research program's "excess empirical

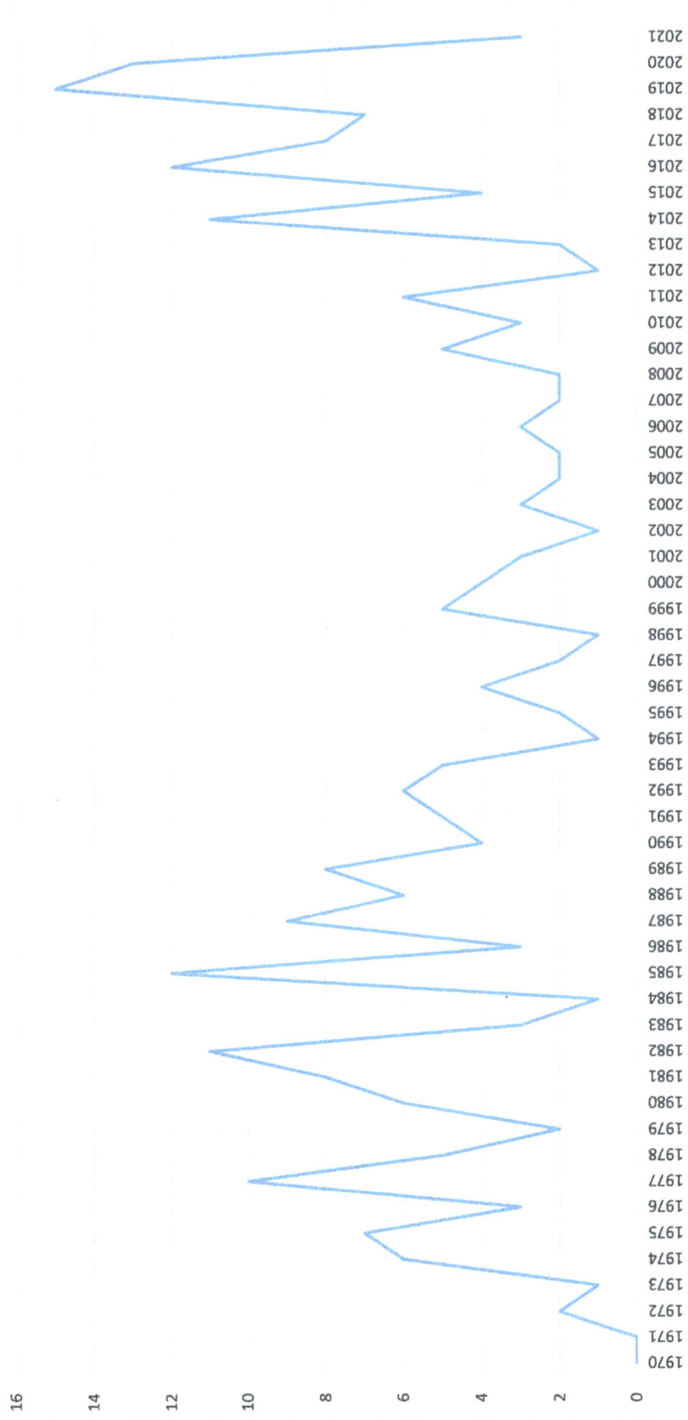

FIGURE 1 Studies on land rent—frequency 1970–2021

content." Finally, in the third period, since the late 1990s, with the institutionalists abandoning rent theory altogether (largely thanks to Michael Ball's (1985) intervention), a mutated version of Harvey's explanation arose, incorporating some central arguments of post-Keynesianism concerning the increasingly prevalent financialization thesis, which promised a post-Keynesian-Harveyan synthesis (see Manning 2020; 2023 for a good survey on this transition). The third phase marks a "degenerating" stage of the research program, involving the development of "protective belts" to address gaps and tensions raised by competing explanations, which indicate a slight shift in the research program's core assumptions toward post-Keynesian hypotheses. After a brief overview of the first period, this chapter provides a more extensive examination of the second and third periods, revisiting some prominent applications of Harvey's theory. It primarily focuses on how Harvey-inspired urban economic geographers addressed the aforementioned anomaly and the analytical tools they developed for the empirical operationalization of his theory.

The first coherent periodization of rent debates[1] in urban geography was developed and presented by Haila (1990). Her taxonomic periodization of three periods—consensus (the 1970s), transition (late 1970s and early 1980s), and rupture (mid-1980s to early 1990s)—aimed to consolidate the strengths of institutionalist interpretations and address the weaknesses of Marxian interpretations for urban applications. Accordingly, while her taxonomy has been highly influential since its publication, it has also been subject to perpetual criticism. Haila, for instance, has been criticized for diverging from rent theory and adopting an empiricist stance against general theories (Kerr 1996, 294; Ward and Aalbers 2016, 1772). Moreover, although she borrows her main explanation for rent realization from Harvey, i.e., landowners treating land as a financial asset, she "departs from him in arguing that it cannot be theoretically deduced from posited tendencies internal to the logic of capital but instead must be empirically investigated with an account of landlords' behaviour" (Ward and Aalbers 2016, 1772). Haila was also criticized for treating rent as both a consequence of the dynamism of real estate markets and a coordinator of such markets (Kerr 1996, 82). Three influential contributions from the mid-1990s stand out for their critical engagement with Haila's scholarly project. The central element common in these works (Kerr 1996; Park 2014; Ward and Aalbers 2016) is to evaluate 'the explanatory power' (á la Lakatos) of dominant approaches during each period for geographic research. Therefore, their studies serve as a

1 Another interesting periodization presented by F.T.C. Manning characterizes contributions of the 1970s and 1980s as "the Golden age of ground rent theory" (Manning 2023, 357).

starting point for my critical examination of Harveyan geographers' innovative methodological strategies for operationalizing Harvey's theory.

In his extensive survey of the historical development of rent theory within geography and urban research, Joon Park (2014, 93) echoes Haila (1990) and identifies three stages of consensus, transition, and rupture in the debate. The first stage marks the beginning of debates within geographical thought on the economic mechanisms of land investment, primarily influenced by discussions among Ricardian, Marxian, and neoclassical theories in the 1960s and 1970s. The second stage represents the divergence between contending theories and the rising popularity of the notion of "social relation around land" (Park 2014, 99) that led to a "premature stagnation" since the 1980s. The academic scene during the 1990s was dominated by neoclassical interpretations of rent theory, followed by a hiatus in the 21st century until the Great Recession. Park's diagnosis of the etiology of stagnation is similar to mine. That "a few fundamental problems in the theory were revealed during the period of heated [abstract] debates and the lack of empirical analysis also contributed to the decline" (ibid. 106). Therefore, he proposes establishing "a consistent theory of the mechanism of land rent" informed by "a detailed analytical approach to the categories of land rents", i.e., operationalization of the theory, reexamining "the debates about the condition of absolute rent and the relationship between it and monopoly rent" lest remaining within "abstract discussion[s]" (ibid. 106). In his evaluation of the debate in the 1970s over absolute rent and monopoly rent, Park (ibid.) declares the debate "technical" and, to a certain degree, unnecessary. The main problem is, Park (ibid. 100) points out, "the deficiency in the analytical approaches to the mechanism of land rent impeded further development of the theories and turned them in the direction of abstract discussion, without concrete empirical research".

Derek Kerr contextualizes the rent debate of the 1970s in "the rapid increase in land and housing prices coupled with a boom and subsequent bust in the commercial and industrial landed property" (Kerr 1996, 59). He reviews the debate over land rent in urban contexts, involving key figures such as Harvey, Ball, and Haila. What inspires him to develop this taxonomy is Haila's (1990) taxonomical periodization that identifies three potential tendencies at a crossroads: a) "dogmatic" attempts to develop a general theory of rent, b) empirical attempts to measure urban rent and its social impacts, and c) an "unbiased" attempt as an alternative to the other two tendencies. Kerr agrees with Haila that "[t]he 'crossroads' exist, but, contrary to Haila, this emerged in the early 1970s, not in the 1980s" (Kerr 1996, 63). Instead, he suggests "the way forward is to 'return' to one particular classical authority, Marx, as the point of departure and not to attempt to develop, as does Haila, the dominant tendency within the contemporary debate" (ibid.). Haila's approach, Kerr clarifies, "leads from the crossroads to the magic roundabout" (ibid.) as it "starts and ends with the activities of landowners, rather than with capital accumulation and the capitalist users' of landed property" (ibid. 80). Contra Haila, Kerr (ibid. 79, emphasis in original) argues that debates over rent theory and its relation to classical political economy categories should instead point to the "possibility that: (a) previous attempts to develop a theory of rent in terms of the categories of *Capital* have *misapplied* Marx's method; (b) capital, value and profit are *not* categories belonging to 'several other theories' but dialectically related categories internal to the 'theory' of capitalism; and (c) the development of categories such as rent may presuppose others in order to render the nature of rent in capitalist society intelligible". As Kerr points out, Haila's 'unbiasedness'[2] has much more in common with empiricism and represents a shift to neoclassical economics.

Kerr's critique of both Ball and Harvey is methodological—though he is, in principle, more sympathetic toward Harvey. His main critique of Ball targets Ball's failure to appreciate Marx's theory of rent and its categories in terms of different levels of abstractions (ibid. 64). He (ibid. 67), for example, writes, "contrary to Ball, Marx's categories of rent were not categories of market structure but of how landed property mediates the production and circulation of surplus value". Marx conceptualized them "at a higher level of abstraction than the contingencies of the market" (ibid.). And Kerr establishes his argument by saying that Ball's call for deserting rent theory, instead of refuting Marx, refutes Ball's model, as it fails to provide any explanatory tool for the existence of any rent.[3] Kerr's critique of Harvey follows a similar methodological approach. Harvey is criticized for identifying "dualisms" instead of dialectically engaging with them (ibid. 70). And in the case of rent, such a dualistic approach tends to neglect the dialectical relationship between production and circulation as well as landowners' role in class relations over land, based on which Harvey (2006 [1982], 331–332) criticizes Marx. According to Kerr, Harvey shares a problematic understanding with Ball and Haila that to explain the presence of rent in capitalist cities today, one needs to depart from Marx's understanding of

2 Haila's critique against the limited applicability of Marxist urban rent literature, however, is crucial. She says, "if one cannot apply the theory of rent in explaining land prices of the 1980s without first solving the transformation controversy and the like, the relevance of the theory of rent is understandably at stake" (Haila 1990, 280).

3 Ball (1985, 504) argues that instead of rent, social relations of building provision are to bridge the theoretical gap "between ultimate land use and initial land ownership", while "the competition between potential users of land" determines its price (ibid. 503).

landed property as a parasitic class force and understand its "active and coordinating role within capitalism" (Kerr 1996, 71; also, Harvey 2006 [1982], 361). Kerr maintains, "this leads Harvey to state that 'it is plainly in the interest of capital in general to keep absolute and monopoly rents strictly within bounds, to ensure that they remain small (as Marx insisted, they must be) and of sporadic occurrence'" (Harvey 2006 [1982], 361 in Kerr 1996, 72). However, according to Kerr, "Marx did not 'insist' that those forms of rent must be kept within bounds but rather pointed to their tendential limits and subordination to the competitive movement of capital" (ibid. 72). Kerr (ibid. 73) criticizes Harvey for interpreting modern landed property as "a superlative set of arrangements totally adapted to capital's requirements" (Harvey 2006 [1982], 361 in Kerr 1996, 73). Kerr also questions the causal relations implied in Harvey's interpretation and his explanation of how such arrangements give rise to absolute or monopoly rents, and therefore Kerr finds Harvey's treatment of them anomalous. He further clarifies, "this interpretation appears to miss the point that the forms of landed property in other epochs were suitable for, and constituted in terms of, these epochs, as is the case in capitalism" (ibid.).

In their evaluation of the 'rupture' period of the 1980s, Calum Ward and Manuel Aalbers (2016) agree with Kerr's assessment that institutionalist interpretations dominated the debate at that time. Three interpretations, according to them, stood out: capital switching (Bryson 1997; Scott 1982; Smet 2016), institutionalist (Ball 1998; Guy and Henneberry 2000; Healey and Barrett 1990; Needham et al. 2011), and rent gap (Bourassa 1993; Clark 1995b; Hammel 1999; Smith 1979), all aiming to extend the empirical applications of urban rent theory inspired by Harevy and to a lesser extent, Ball. Ward and Aalbers criticize institutionalist interpretations for conflating land and capital, thereby obscuring their distinct sources of return—rent and profit—and their distinct origins and characteristics (Ward and Aalbers 2016, 1773). This conflation, they argue, "in actual practice is a fundamental contradiction of capitalism exactly for this reason and ends in disastrous rounds of market 'rationalisation' being applied to socio-spatial configurations" (ibid.). And to avoid such conflations, contra Ball (1985), one needs a proper theory of rent that explains patterns and logic behind empirically corroborated mechanisms. Ward and Aalbers (2016, 1761) submit that the ongoing marginalization of rent theory (with all its variations) in urban political economy is due to the failure of its main contributors since the 1970s to unearth "the explanatory power [of rent theory] in understanding the geographies of capitalism". They (ibid.), in response, distinguish between land rent as the total rent paid by the capitalist tenant to the landowner for the right to use land and improvements built on it and "ground rent … paid for the use of the land, minus that paid for the fixed capital on the land (buildings and other appurtenances)" (ibid.).[4] Ward and Aalbers acknowledge that such a distinction might not be crucial. Nevertheless, it constitutes what has been at stake in the entire rent debate during the first and second periods, which both methodologically and theoretically focused on ground rent. Whereas, for them, land rent represents "a straightforward return on capital invested"—making ground rent "the major determinant of both the contracted rent paid by tenants and the land's purchase price" (ibid.). Moreover, that, in effect, has shaped the central question of rent theory around justifying or questioning its existence: "why does land command large values, the largest portion of which cannot be attributed to labour or interest on capital investment but seemingly appears for nothing" (ibid.)?

2.2 Theoretical Challenges and Controversies over Rent Categories in Urban Contexts

2.2.1 Absolute Rent

The concept of absolute rent, if not entirely ignored (e.g., in Huber 2022), has been reinterpreted by geographers many times over the past five decades. These reinterpretations (many of which inspired by post-Keynesian theories) are not immune to confusion. Stripped from its origins in Marx's theory of value (which incidentally was Harvey's main point of criticism), the concept has been reintroduced to the literature to explain monopolistic relations in land and property markets, driven by various forms of financialization and assetization, and creating artificial scarcity (Bradley 2023). In one of the more consistent expositions of this trend, Ward and Aalbers contend that absolute rent "has been rejected in the literature but should be the basis of a critical theory of monopolies" (Ward and Aalbers 2016, 1762). They maintain that absolute rent, "as the form of rent that arises only through the violence of asserting property rights or class position," should be "rehabilitated" and extended "beyond land to an increasingly extractive financialised capitalism rife with distributional

4 I have reservations about their distinction between land and ground rent. I do not define land rent here as a price paid for 'the right to use land and improvements built on it'. For me, land rent refers to the relative price of land as such. And I consider the conceptual distinction between ground and land rent perhaps even superfluous. That is why classical political economists did not make that distinction. Nevertheless, Ward and Aalbers's analysis of the analytical implications of shifting the focus away from "the explanatory power" of rent theory in understanding capitalist urbanization processes is crucial.

conflicts" (ibid.). Therefore, they propose a consistent incorporation of "a theory of monopoly pricing" into rent theory. This proposed synthesis, they argue, seeks to explain in tandem a) "the existence of 'natural' monopolies … where the unavoidable scarcity of something means that its price is limited only by effective demand" and b) "the existence of 'absolute rent', where the barriers imposed by the existence of a rentier class in itself is the source of rent" (ibid.). The synthesized view thus views rent as a general form of extraction encompassing financial and non-financial, as well as land and non-land gains, where monopoly rent is the general type and absolute monopoly rent is the specific type. Monopoly rent, so the argument goes, depends on "the impairment of competition," in general, and its fluctuation "affects the price of the commodity produced" given that it "enter[s] into the costs of production" (ibid.). In the specific form, absolute monopoly rent, "the impairment is attributed to the existence of the class of rentiers themselves" (ibid. 1763–1764). They draw on Harvey's conceptualization and write, "Harvey's work on the notion of class-monopoly in the 1970s showed this to be possible in a modern urban context" (ibid. 1771). The challenge is, according to them, that before Harvey's "rediscovery" of absolute rent as class-monopoly rent, such a general analysis of monopolies was "for a long time ignored" and "not integrated into wider rent theories nor acknowledged to be a form of absolute rent" (ibid. 1771). Therefore, they maintain, notwithstanding Harvey's attempt to reintroduce the concept of absolute rent in his notion of class-monopoly rent, "a Marxist theory of monopolies" has been omitted from the debate, whereas "it should have been highly applicable to a contemporary economy rife with rentiers of immaterial goods in a financialised 'knowledge' economy" (ibid.).

Ward and Aalbers's alternative (viewing absolute and monopoly rents as a single category) echoes Ramirez (2009). He (ibid. 89) states that absolute rent will not "disappear altogether" even if the organic composition of capital in agriculture (its "social productivity") reaches manufacturing levels: "as long as land is privately owned, landowners will continue to receive a rental payment for the use of the indestructible powers of the soil." Absolute rent, in such a scenario, "becomes a form of monopoly rent (surplus profit)" (ibid.). The source of such rents "is found outside of agriculture and is redistributed to landowners via the price mechanism from more competitive sectors (including wage-goods industries)" (ibid.). Similarly, Purcell et al. (2020) analyze categories of absolute rent and monopoly rent as a single category of monopoly rent, which they find helpful for explaining the patterns and drivers of the financialization of land.

Such interpretations are received more critically in recent interventions. Manning (2020, 35), for instance, diagnoses a crucial (empirical) tension in such interpretations, as they tend to conflate rent and interest, a conflation she traces back to Harvey and to his conceptualization of the "rentier class." "This conflation", clarifies Manning, "obliterates all that is specific about the form of ground rent—especially the finitude of land (key to its monopolizability)" (ibid.). In a similarly critical intervention, Park (2014, 92) calls for returning to the theoretical origins of the concept in classical political economy to explain the impact of rent and measure its magnitudes. For absolute rent, he writes, "the amount of absolute rent is explained as the difference in value over the price of production of the product in a sector", where "value is the sum of constant capital, variable capital, and surplus value" and "price of production is the sum of cost of production [C + V] and average profit". He defines value as "the average value of a product in a sector", and absolute rent is defined as the difference between excess surplus value and average profit. However, Park (2011) abandons those theoretical underpinnings in his empirical study and, like Harvey and Chatterjee (1974), divides the city into housing submarkets organized around employment and residential centers. Absolute rent, it is argued, arises due to scarcity in stock and "favorable economic condition[s]" in certain groups of houses (ibid. 84). The most vigorous defense of the concept of absolute rent, however, appeared much earlier by Kerr, who (1996, 81, emphasis in original) argued, "*absolute rent* is not some aberration, but a *necessary* barrier posited by capital". Absolute rent is "a *necessary* form through which capital appropriates and commands space while at the same time enforcing labour's exclusion from that space, thereby reproducing the commodity status of labour power" (ibid. emphasis in original). The relationship between differential rent and absolute rent is such that "differential rent subsists within the frame of absolute rent and yet it also tends to limit the magnitude of absolute rent as capital continually transmutes its geographic mode of existence through crises of overaccumulation" (ibid.). His intervention, however, did not include concrete suggestions for operationalization and stayed at a conceptual level.

2.2.2 Class-Monopoly Rent

The concept of class-monopoly rent is, in principle, advanced as an alternative to absolute rent to explain rent on the marginal plot (a non-relative category). This rent is accrued to the landlords due to "the monopoly control that landlords as a class have over land, a necessary input of production" (Sheppard and Barnes 1986, 504). The level of class-monopoly rent depends on the landlord class's power to impose monopoly prices (ibid.). Wyly et al. argue that the realization of class-monopoly rents depends on "risk-based pricing" as "credit flows etch out intricate urban and regional geographies of class-monopoly rent that are rooted in generations of racialized inequalities" (Wyly et al. 2009, 334). Land rent is extracted from "unimproved land" because although "the cost 'production' for the landowner is zero, … the owner receives a price for its use; the class of landowners, by definition, enjoys a monopoly that commands rent" (ibid. 335). They elaborate on the two components of the concept, class and monopoly. Class is the general social form. It "matters because, in all capitalist societies, the rights and privileges of ownership are central to power relations, political conflict and social inequality" (ibid. 336). And monopoly is the general legal form. It "matters not primarily because, as Marx suggests, the supply of land is limited, nor because landowners can become price-makers, but rather because of the inherent monopoly associated with the legal status of ownership" (ibid. 336). Class-monopoly rent for Wyly et al. (ibid. 336–337) is understood in local terms in that "the use of highly mortgaged 'homeownership' [connects] national and transnational capital markets to the lucrative profit margins of local class-monopoly rents". That differs from Harvey's notion of class-monopoly rent, in which the rent performs a regulating, macro-scale role. They argue that subprime lending itself stems from an extensive, deregulatory shift in policy in the United States since the 1980s, which favored "predatory" and reckless lending on the one hand and increasingly limited "publicly subsidized affordable lending" on the other (ibid. 337). The result is "an unprecedented wave of capital investment targeted mostly but not exclusively to low-income people and places, racially and ethnically marginalized borrowers and communities, and other 'new markets'" (ibid.). Wyly et al. treat class-monopoly rent as, in effect, a localized monopoly pricing.

Despite the empirical significance of Wyly et al.'s (2009) study in mapping the spatiality of racial inequality, it fails to connect the creation and appropriation of class-monopoly rents to broader accumulation tendencies in contemporary capitalist cities. This connection, as we have seen, plays a crucial role in Harvey's formulation. This task is taken up by Anderson (2014). Anderson (ibid. 14) argues, "the conditions through which class monopoly rents are realized have changed since first discussed by Harvey". Anderson elaborates that "the ascendency of neoliberalism represents a return to market-oriented practices mobilized by the very neoclassical economic principles sharply critiqued by Harvey", which renders class-monopoly rent "acutely relevant to the critical project of fracturing the resilience of neoliberal hegemony" (ibid.). Class-monopoly rent illuminates "the complex relationships between landowners, producers, and consumers within such processes of change", and neoliberalism functions as a context to highlight "the historical trajectories of political-economic transformation over the past four decades" (ibid. 14).

Anderson (ibid. 15) begins his operationalization of the concept of class-monopoly rent with Harvey's framing in which urban land and housing markets are collectively and individually controlled by a class of "actors", which Anderson elaborates as "developers, landlords, homeowners, and financial institutions". This class of actors produces an "'artificial scarcity' within urban housing markets" through "active manipulation of supply/demand conditions by landowners … who legally possess the *monopoly* power to collectively (but competitively) exert their 'class interest' over the use of their property" (ibid. emphasis in original). Harvey's example of this process is in "removing rental units from circulation to maintain acceptable rates of return" (ibid.). This class-monopoly power is rewarded through class-monopoly rent payments, whose creation and appropriation have implications for the socio-spatial differentiation of "residential landscapes" (ibid. 16). This process could, at the same time, "harm the collective" as due to its dependence on financial institutions, it can "lead to speculative bubbles, oversupply of units and lowered rents, and invariably crisis, the effective regulator of the market absent active or conscious coordination" (ibid. 15). Anderson (ibid. 18–19) exemplifies policies "such as public housing demolition, historical preservation and tax-increment financing" that in Chicago "have unequivocally unfolded in the service of clearing disinvested structures (and their low-income inhabitants) and stimulating private market investment and rising land values in spaces targeted for gentrification". This process culminates through disinvestment in demolished building areas, ensued from "stockpiling of vacant land", reduction in "the supply of high demand affordable housing" and public housing production in general, and finally, increasing property values (ibid.). The local state and developers, therefore, constitute "the class of actors" Harvey anticipated in his formulation of class-monopoly rent, and land rent itself is analyzed in terms of "revenue streams" due to "supply-reducing strategies and the value-enhancing 'uses'" (ibid. 19).[5]

2.3 Urban Applications of Rent Theory

In addition to debating the theoretical and empirical power of rent theory for urban research (as discussed in the somewhat tacit debate with institutionalists in the second period above), heterodox urban economic geographers since the late 1970s have begun to extensively operationalize Harvey's theory for a

5 Anderson also uses these variables and indicators in his study of Portland (2019).

variety of contemporary urban issues. They collectively helped to relate urban economic geography to urban social geography. However, I contend that they cannot by any means be considered successful in their debate with the institutionalists. Harveyan geographers' theoretical (and analytical) dominance in the field since the late 1990s is primarily due to institutionalists forsaking rent altogether, moving instead toward microeconomic analyses of urban land markets, rather than to an ostensible methodological superiority of Harvey's explanation.

Connections to urban social geography were consolidated by developing a series of mid-range theories in most cases and incorporating already existing ones in others. To name a few, most urban problems discussed and analyzed by urban geographers deal with various forms of socio-spatial inequality, unevenness, suppression, and marginalization. In other words, the focus of inquiry in this period is on the ramifications of capitalist urbanization processes. The aim is to relate these ramifications to broader processes of capital accumulation, primarily using Harvey-inspired conceptual apparatus, such as uneven geographical development, the production of space, and accumulation by dispossession. In most, if not all, cases, inspired by Harvey and other Marxist urban theorists such as Lefebvre, various forms of oppression—such as racial, ethnic, and gender—are understood and analyzed through the lens of economic inequality, which itself originates from the imperatives of capital accumulation and the social and ideological structures that shape it. The context of the inquiry is primarily, if not exclusively, residential areas (housing and public spaces surrounding them), and it spans from gentrification, filtering, segregation, differentiation, displacement, and homelessness, to migration, marginalization, and even the prison system (Beitel 2016; Gilmore 2007; Harris and Lewis 2001; Hedin et al. 2012; Mitchell 1997; Smet 2016; Smith 1996b; Wyly et al. 2009). The aim of the next generation, therefore, was to extend Harvey's theory to analyze concrete urban processes and associated spatial transformations driven and shaped by general processes of capital accumulation and its need for the continual production of space, as "Harvey provided limited empirical evidence, mostly at the aggregate national level" (Wyly et al. 2004, 630). Alternative urban strategies implied in their analyses include the right to the city, reclaiming public space, squatting and occupying space, community development, as well as urban riots (e.g., Cox 1982; Cox and Mair 1991; Cox and Wood 1997; Dikeç 2016; Dikeç and Swyngedouw 2017; Harvey 2008; Lauria 1984; Mitchell 2003; Smith 1996b).

The interest in the financialization thesis for urban geographic research escalated since the Great Recession and exposed, among other things, the bubble-prone nature of the financialization of built environments and its quintessential examples in the subprime mortgage crisis, various mortgage securitization processes, and extensive household debt (Aalbers 2008; 2009a; 2009b; 2012; Aalbers and Christophers 2014; Charnock et al. 2014; Christophers 2010; 2014; 2016; 2019; 2020; Gotham 2006; 2009; Purcell et al. 2020; Tapp 2020; Teresa 2016; Weber 2002; 2010; Wyly et al. 2009; Wyly 2002; 2015). Harvey (2012, xv) argued that this process results from "overinvestment and speculative activity" by financiers. He viewed the problem as a prime example supporting his theory of capitalist urbanization. He stated, following the Great Recession, "fiscal difficulties of the states (and proposed austerities) were derived from a global crisis of capitalism that arose out of the near collapse of a financial system that was caught in a tangled web of property market speculation that reflected malfunctioning processes of urbanization driven by the need to find outlets for overaccumulating capital" (ibid.). Such processes of financialization of land and built environments, so the argument goes, are governed by the creation and appropriation of class-monopoly rents (Anderson 2014; 2019; Charnock et al. 2014; Smet 2016; Wyly and Hammel 1999; Wyly et al. 2009; Wyly et al. 2012). In both capital switching and rent gap models discussed below, monopoly rents play a decisive role. Smet (2016), for example, contends that uneven price development results from a shift in the dominant (spatial) accumulation strategy in late capitalism, driven by the dialectics of differential and monopoly rents and their financial basis. In another example, Charnock et al. (2014, 199) discuss "how attempts to manage the vicissitudes of capital accumulation through a variety of regulatory and institutional means—geared, for instance, to facilitating the increased liquidity of real estate in many parts of the world in the years preceding the current crisis—serve to fuel the process of crisis formation, and expose the contradictions of national and local state strategies" a process that is "driven by the rentier compulsions of state agencies, financiers and developers—all in the pursuit of profit-maximizing opportunities through the mobilization of land and property as a financial asset". All of this materialized through the rentier and speculative behavior of financiers and developers, who set monopoly prices and extract monopoly rents, thereby overinflating property prices (e.g., ibid. 201; 204).

Methodologically, two analytical contributions (as two 'auxiliary hypotheses') stand out for their innovative approaches to concretize the processes Harvey explained at the conceptual level. First, the capital switching thesis aims to explain the long-term tendency for capital to shift from the primary to the secondary circuits. Second is the rent gap theory, which provides a method to measure rent creation and appropriation underpinning urbanization processes.

2.3.1 The Capital Switching Thesis

Harvey (1978; 2006 [1982]; 1989) had conceptualized capital switching from the primary (productive) circuit to the secondary (built environments) circuit of capital in response to the overaccumulation of capital in the primary circuit, through which rent appropriation—as a barrier to the free movement of capital—was related to long-term structural tendencies of capital accumulation. His explanation, however, remained primarily at the conceptual level. Although he provides a series of historical examples (from the 19th and 20th centuries) to support his thesis (Harvey 1989), he does not offer analytical tools beyond time series of investment in the built environment or sale prices for measuring or historicizing it. None of the indicators Harvey (1978, 106–111) suggested, including time series for investments in built environments and building activity, directly point to inter-sectoral switching. Furthermore, the indicators discussed are not compared with the primary circuit patterns and investments therein.

The first critical examination of Harvey's capital switching thesis was presented by King (1989a; 1989b; 1989c). King (1989a) finds Harvey's formulation inadequate for operationalizing his empirical study of Melbourne since the early 1970s. He argues Harvey's argument is "very generalised" given that "the timing of the processes of investment and disinvestment …, their spatial scales, the interrelationships between them, or the social conditions that will accompany them" are not concretely presented (ibid. 451). King complements Harvey's framework with a socio-cultural explanation, borrowed from Bourdieu and Habermas, for the rising rents and the resulting capital switching. He suggests that Harvey's framework be taken as a context and then disentangled for analyzing housing sub-markets (ibid. 456). However, the crucial indicator of rising rents, he (1989c, 879) says, is "attitudes and expectations" of both housing suppliers and consumers. A few years later, Beauregard (1994, 718) criticizes Harvey for not documenting overaccumulation and not providing "direct evidence attesting to the switch of capital from the primary to the secondary circuit, …, [but only offering] indirect evidence on the countercyclical relation of production activity and construction investment that would indicate, or at least be consistent with, switching" (ibid. 719). As a concretized improvement to Harvey's framework and to analyze capital switching in the 1980s US construction boom, Beauregard then suggests comparing "temporal patterns of private construction investment with various measures of nonconstruction investment activity" for built environments, machinery and equipment, and structures (ibid. 724). He concludes that the primary circuit of capital grew less rapidly than the secondary during that period, to no small extent due to the mediation of finance capital, pointing cautiously to a capital switching similar to what Harvey had conceptualized (ibid. 729; also Beauregard 1991).

More recent studies have elaborated on these two conceptual and empirical approaches. The most comprehensive study, presented by Christophers (2011), agrees with King (1989a) and Beauregard (1994) that there is an empirical gap in Harvey's original formulation of the thesis, specifically, Harvey's failure to provide empirical evidence that the switching occurs. However, Christophers contends, "a comprehensive and watertight empirical substantiation of switching" may not be "attainable," though "a clear indication" could be feasible without "bulletproof [quantitative] verification" (Christophers 2011, 1351). Therefore, he proposes a "proxy measure" as a calculation method, that is, "the combination of investment in labor and investment in noninfrastructural fixed assets," and a comparison of "the temporal trends" for both productive investments (Harvey's primary circuit) and investments in built environments (Harvey's secondary). He also suggests supporting the results with an analysis of the activities of "fund managers" (ibid. 1351–1352). Nevertheless, as I noted elsewhere, "his evidence as to whether the switching originated from an economic crisis (overaccumulation or otherwise) remains inconclusive" (Farahani 2025, 4; also, see Christophers 2011, 1360). Christophers also leaves out both the intermediary role of land rent and an "evaluation of causality" (ibid. 1353). More important, he reverses the chain of causality Harvey used in his formulation and argues that capital switching needs to be traced "before" the crisis, as "economic crisis is frequently preceded by a switching" (ibid. 1352). He also omits the implications of competition between productive and non-productive activities within the built environment, specifically between construction and real estate (Farahani 2025, 4). Nevertheless, his empirical strategy inspired others, such as Kutz (2016), who extended it to explain contemporary activities in private rental markets and the various ways they relate to regulatory structures and geographical variations. Similarly, Yrigoy (2023) extends Christophers' input by incorporating the dynamics of new construction. The latter is also interesting, given that it is the only other contribution (the first being Beauregard's (1994)) to engage with the dynamics of the construction sector in capital switching.

Karl Beitel (2016) connects capital switching to rent relations and extends this concept by assessing multiple circuits of capital in housing markets. He (2016, 31) defines ground rent as "the portion of the total rent payment on existing buildings that represents a payment for the right to occupy a given site or plot of land". He argues that urban land rent is derived from "the site's location" (ibid.). Rent is different from land price, which is "the price paid to acquire rights to use and build upon, or modify existing structures on, a given site" (ibid.). Land price is a component of the building's production costs and is paid at the time of acquisition (ibid.). Rent, however, is "an income flow derived from ownership of a rent-bearing property over a longer time horizon" (ibid.). Beitel maintains that rent cannot be "directly measured" as rent is "a theoretical category that captures the processes that determine the modulation of the ground rent surface and formation of surplus profits within a segmented system of residential housing" (ibid. 35). However, rent is reflected in "some mixture of increased land prices and developer's surplus profit realized over and above the profit that would accrue to a capital of equivalent magnitude invested at the average rate of profit" (ibid.). The property circuit responds to the fluctuations of total housing prices as a sum of "developer's surplus profit and rising land price, and the locational component of ground rent" (ibid. 39). Therefore, high rents and surplus profits play a key role in urban development. Their presence renders "the advanced metropoles ... magnets that function to attract massive sums of investment-seeking surpluses circulating through the global banking and financial circuits, a significant share of which is absorbed by property investments" (ibid. 41).

Smet (2016, 497–498) understands rent as "a monetary transfer" between investors and owners. This monetary definition implies that, by paying rent, the investor also acquires the right to "future revenues" from land use, which constitutes "the financial basis of rent" (ibid. 498). Since rent is a component of housing prices, these prices should be analyzed in terms of the interaction between the circulation of capital and the circulation of revenues (ibid.). In other words, housing construction is to be analyzed as an interaction between productive capital accumulation and fictitious capital accumulation (ibid. 499). "The restructuring of city economies" since the 1973 crisis is analyzed in terms of "declining profitability and increasing international competition" that translates into a shift in employment from the manufacturing to the service sector (ibid. 503–505). This structural shift was assisted by "the liberalization of financial markets" and "the emergence of secondary capital markets" (ibid. 504). The shift means the rise of bubble-prone speculative investments in housing markets is rooted in rent appropriation processes that "became detached from the surplus-value created in these cities and could tap into the money flows of places of consumption and services, which were embedded in global capital and revenue circulations" (ibid.). Inspirations from the post-Keynesian literature, evident in recent decades, are also apparent in this case. As Ted Rutland (2010) noted, several aspects of this interpretation already existed in Harvey's early works on the thesis, as he "anticipate[d] accounts of financialization—decades later" (Rutland 2010, 1171). The aim here is to incorporate financial profits into capital switching by adding, for instance, a "quaternary circuit of capital" mediated by credit (Ward 2021, 249). This reinterpretation aims to explain "the possibility that financial institutions might simply channel capital into its most profitable, short-term venue," which, in a similar conclusion to Christophers (2011), implies that capital switching may "cause rather than help to avert crises" (Rutland, 2010: 1171).

2.3.2 Rent Gap Theory

The rent gap hypothesis was first introduced by Neil Smith (1979) as an economic mechanism underlying gentrification. The idea was to provide an objective explanation for the pressing question of why and when gentrification happens, while also analyzing its impacts as social, economic, and physical changes (Smith 1987, 463). He also aimed to explain the relationship between land and property values (Smith 1979, 542). The hypothesis entails that in "a well-developed capitalist economy", financial institutions providing the outlay are necessary for the commodification of land and improvements built on it (ibid. 541). The value of the built environment "influences" the land rent, and "since land and buildings on it are inseparable", the building sale prices reflect the level of land rent (ibid.). Unlike the land, the built environment is subject to physical deterioration and, "patterns of capital depreciation will be an important variable in determining whether and to what extent a building's sale price reflects the ground rent level" (ibid.). Gentrification theory, therefore, should "explain the detailed historical mechanisms of capital depreciation in the inner city and the precise way in which this depreciation produces the possibility of profitable reinvestment" (ibid. 542). "In a capitalist economy," Smith contends, "profit is the gauge of success, and competition is the mechanism by which success or failure is translated into growth or collapse ... This search for increased profits translates, at the scale of the whole economy, into the long-run economic growth" (ibid. 541). Capital tends to flow onto built environments in search of higher returns "when economic growth is hindered elsewhere in the industrial sector ... as is particularly apparent with this century's suburbanization experience" (ibid. 541). This "spatial expansion", i.e., capital switching, secures "the continual need for capital accumulation" (ibid.). This is a double-sided process as the investment in built environments is at the same time "a vehicle for capital accumulation" and "a barrier to further accumulation" (ibid.). The reason is that investment in built environments is characterized by "near-monopoly control of space, the fixity of investments, the long turnover period" (ibid.). Smith (ibid.) elaborates,

> Near-monopoly control of space by landowners may prevent the sale of land for development; the fixity of investments forces new development to take place at other, often less advantageous, locations, and prevents redevelopment from occurring until invested capital has lived out its economic life; the long turnover period of capital invested in the built environment can discourage investment as long as other sectors of the economy with shorter turnover periods remain profitable.

Smith disentangles two categories of property and land value and reclassifies them into four categories: "house value, sale price, capitalized ground rent, potential ground rent" (ibid. 542). He elaborates that "capitalized ground rent is the actual quantity of ground rent that is appropriated by the landowner, given the present land use," whereas "potential ground rent is the amount that could be capitalized under the land's 'highest and best use'" (ibid. 542). He (ibid. 545) defines the rent gap as "the disparity between the potential ground rent level and the actual ground rent capitalized under the present land use" mainly in response to the depreciation of building value over time in (market) price terms. The gentrification process (which includes investment in the physical environment), therefore, is assumed to *potentially* kick off "once the rent gap is wide enough" (ibid.). Prior to that point, the opposite process of disinvestment and abandonment of the physical environment occurs. This way, Smith a) articulates an economic mechanism missing in demand-side explanations of urbanization that turned their focus to cultural and individual consumer preferences (e.g., Ley 1987), and b) operationalizes Harvey's model of uneven geographical development for concrete housing research. And in a crucial reference to Harvey's capital switching thesis, as Clark noted elsewhere, "fundamental to the rent gap is the condition that investments in the built environment involve a spatial 'fix'" (Clark 2004, 152).[6]

This hypothesis sparked a debate regarding the relevance of rent gap theory to gentrification theory and, more broadly, capitalist urbanization processes (Bourassa 1993; Clark 1995b; Hammel 1998; Ley 1987; Smith 1987, 1996a). The debate helped consolidate the rent gap as a mechanism underlying urbanization processes, thereby also being conducive to empirical analyses of housing markets. Rent gap theory, therefore, inspired many urban geographers to relate urbanization processes to the political economy of space and, by extension, to general processes of capital accumulation, all inspired by Harvey

6 Interestingly, Clark and Pissin (2020) also find Harvey's concepts of the rentier class and landed developer interests particularly crucial for analyzing potential rents.

(Clark 1988; 1992; 1995a; 1995b; Clark and Gullberg 1991; Diappi and Bolchi 2008; Hammel 1999; Hedin et al. 2012; Porter 2010; Slater 2017; Wachsmuth and Weisler 2018; Yrigoy 2019). Rent gap theory complements Harvey's explanation by providing an analytical mechanism for measuring rent creation and appropriation. However, it deviates from some of Harvey's structural hypotheses regarding land rent in its method of operationalization, regardless of the type (absolute, differential, or class-monopoly): it depends on (market) sale prices, adjusted by the taxed land and building values, to measure the level of rent. (Clark 1987; Clark and Gullberg 1997).

Further elaborations using the financialization thesis and the category of class-monopoly rent contribute to the analysis. Highlighting the processes of the financialization of land, Wyly and Hammel operationalized rent gap theory to explain the "rapid acceleration of reinvestment in fringe areas" (Wyly and Hammel 1999, 738). In inner cities, they argue, "capital began to fill the vacuum left behind by a wave of disinvestment that rippled outward from the urban core as metropolitan expansion boosted potential land rents far above the levels capitalized through prevailing local land uses" (ibid.). Wyly and Hammel draw attention to the historical role of "the spatial allocation of mortgage credit" in creating rent gaps, and argue "biased lending practices, often explicitly rooted in ecological theories of neighborhood change, as well as blatant racial and ethnic discrimination, were instrumental in prompting disinvestment and selective outmigration from older residential districts near the urban core" (ibid.). However, there is a temporal discrepancy in the timing of the impact of different financial instruments on creating rent gaps. Wyly and Hammel (ibid. 755–756) further clarify, "while mortgage capital flows may have been responsible for disinvestment and the creation of rent gaps in an earlier generation (and may still be doing so in other inner-city neighborhoods), in the boom of the late 1990s, lending now appears to be leading the reinvestment process in the established outposts of gentrification". Wyly and Hammel further complement rent gap theory with the concept of class-monopoly rent to explain the relationship between rents and the rest of the urban economy (ibid.).

One crucial anomaly that was put forth against Smith's formulation of rent gap challenged the theory's identified preconditions of rent gaps, as developed capitalist urban land relations and a developed finance capital active in land markets (Darling 2005). The focus of inquiry has recently begun to shift from advanced capitalist cities to global capitalist cities, where finance capital may not be highly developed, or urban land relations may not be advanced (Slater 2017). Nevertheless, it is argued that rent gaps exist and that their presence could trigger gentrification. In this latter literature, the rent gap is described as an economic mechanism for investing in land, with its social ramifications including displacement and dispossession. A substantial body of empirical evidence from around the world supports the existence of rent gaps. Studies from India (Maringanti and Jonnalagadda 2015; Whitehead and More 2007), to South America (Borsdorf and Hidalgo 2013; López-Morales 2010; 2011; 2013; 2016a; 2016b; López-Morales et al. 2019), to the Middle East (Balta and Eke 2011; Krijnen 2018a; 2018b) have been presented to this aim.

Moreover, Smith had theorized that the magnitudes of rent (whose character he did not specify) increase over time and that this potential attracts investment to land. In the early 1990s, Bourassa (1993) criticized Smith's articulation of capitalized ground rent as a price component of rent. Bourassa (ibid. 1731) problematized the concepts of actual (or capitalized) and potential land rents, arguing that Smith allegedly conflated land rent and land value (ibid. 1733). Bourassa (ibid.) distinguishes an accounting sense of rent (immediate rent payments) from an economic sense of rent (land rent). He argues, "the concept of rent that is relevant to changes in land use is land rent as an opportunity cost, which is a function of the potential use of a site rather than its actual or current use" (ibid. 1732). Then, he contends that Smith's theory could benefit from incorporating an analysis of differential rent. Clark (1995b) responded to Bourassa's critique and argued for the relevance of rent gap theory as an economic and not an accounting theory. He (ibid.) contends that Bourassa's microeconomic model "is based on an empiricist fallacy of equating an abstract concept with a naïvely observable event", disabling it from acknowledging the importance of the gap for the time before redevelopment (ibid. 1490). Furthermore, concerned with patterns of capital flows onto land, Clark complements rent gap theory with Harvey's interpretation of the (spatial) interplay between differential rent I and II in an empirical study in Malmö, Sweden (Clark 2004, 150). The interplay between two types of differential rent hinges on "the distinction between 'normal' capital investment in 'equal' sites and above-normal investment of capital" (ibid. 155). Rent gap theory, on the other hand, is based on "the distinction between capital investment appropriate for a site's 'highest and best use' and historically dated investment which has become below-normal investment for 'equal' sites" (ibid.). Rent gap theory helps explain economic mechanisms of spatial change at the micro-level, which, as Clark's studies show, could be complemented by introducing the interplay between differential rent I and II. Nevertheless, the empirical similarities with the concept of appraised value in real estate accounting raise concerns for a theory that aims to rival the mainstream, neoclassical understanding of land and property relations. It also needs to explain the structural preconditions of the rent level (at $t = 0$ and at different points in time).

2.4 An Unresolved Debate and an Incomplete Project

Urban geographers, inspired by Harvey's theory, have developed innovative methodological strategies (as 'problem-solving within the research program') to study rent and its relation to urbanization processes. Two of these strategies stand out. First, the capital switching thesis explains the long-term tendency for capital to flow into land. Furthermore, the second is the rent gap theory, which provides methods for measuring rent creation and appropriation. As crucial as they are to the evolution of Harvey's explanation as a systematic approach to analyzing rent relations in capitalist urbanization, these attempts remain inadequate because they fail to complement his explanation by structurally addressing rent relations with the inner workings of the capitalist economy. Their problem-solving strategies, except for a few cases, are generally limited to creating protective belts such as innovative conceptualizations to explain social consequences of urbanization processes, further elaborations of the role of finance capital in built environments, empirical operationalizations of Harvey's theory for more cases across the globe and particularly in the global South, and elaborations of monopolistic land relations shaping the geographies of rent creation and appropriation in specific studies. These studies complement Harvey's explanation by relating rent to other social and political structures of capital accumulation. However, these applications have not resolved the anomalies discussed earlier, i.e., 1) a lack of analytical tools to measure and explain rent rates, ceilings, and magnitudes, 2) a lack of a dialectical analysis of macro and micro dynamics of rent creation and appropriation, 3) a lack of a historically contingent analysis of the movement of capital across sectors, and 4) a lack of a consistently structural explanation of economic urbanization processes. Their inadequate response to the anomalies is indicated by a) the shift to microeconomic measurements (using market prices of plots and buildings to determine the level of rent) and exogenous monopolistic power relations (referring to the power of landlord class to determine the level of rent), in the case of rent gap theory, and b) the shift to the mediation of financial and institutional relations, in the case of the capital switching thesis. More importantly, the inadequate response (limited to theoretical and conceptual clarifications) to the crucial anomaly raised by institutionalists in the 1980s—concerning the empirical impotence of Harvey's model (see Chapter 3) as a political-economic model for explaining economic relations over urban land—leaves the debate unresolved and the project incomplete.

CHAPTER 3

Two Models of Land Rent

The two competing models I reconstruct here are predicated on Marx's economic theory. I will discuss the empirical comparisons of the models in Part 2 and their theoretical foundations in Part 3. The purpose of this reconstruction is to highlight their methodological and conceptual similarities and differences, and to accentuate their respective central mechanisms, drivers, and determinants. It is built on the gaps and tensions of Harvey's theory, identified and presented in the earlier chapters. The common assumptions are: first, both models start with Marx and his structural analysis of the capitalist economy; second, both aim to explain economic urbanization processes structurally and in close connection to processes of capital accumulation; third, both identify land rent as a central mechanism to explain the dynamics of investment in urban space; fourth, both models treat land monopoly ownership as a precondition and a general characteristic of land rent; finally, both aim to explain the structural processes of rent creation and appropriation in terms of the dynamics of capital. Nevertheless, as we will see in Part 2, they relate differently to the empirical evidence.

3.1 Harvey's Spatial Monopoly Model of Land Rent (SMLR)

Building on the merits and tensions of Harvey's theory presented in the first two chapters, I argue that he essentially seeks to explain how long-term trends and processes of capital accumulation create, shape, and transform space and existing spatial configurations. Harvey deliberately avoids formulating his explanation as a model. He refers to it at times as a framework (Harvey 1978). Nevertheless, I argue that reinterpreting and reconstructing his explanation as a model could still be worthwhile without sacrificing its complexity. This approach helps isolate its central mechanisms and conceptualizations, highlighting their drivers, determinants, internal logic, and implications for empirical analysis. All other things being equal, land rent, in his model, acts as a barrier to the free movement of capital into space and is significant at two stages. First, it drives and limits investments in urban development processes, as the spatial expression of capital accumulation in the form of differential rents I and II, and class-monopoly rent (see Appendix 1.1 and 1.4). Second, it drives and limits investments in the production of space as the spatial solution to its impending crisis in the form of class-monopoly rent. Finance capital orchestrates the extraction of class-monopoly rent, which restricts productive activities and promotes speculative activity in land.

According to the Spatial Monopoly Model of Land Rent (SMLR), urban land rent arises in response to a "relative locational advantage" (Harvey 2006 [1982], 389). Therefore, owners of plots in favored locations are entitled to rent. The reason is somewhat intuitive. Units (residential or commercial) in those plots could have high monopoly prices, allowing investors to potentially gain above-normal (monopolistic) rates of return on their investment in the built environment in those areas. Excess returns in land markets are due to two factors. First, land is scarce and monopolizable, a consequence of capitalist social relations over the land (Harvey 1974b, 272). Second, it is spatially fixed with relative permanence. Land rent, thus, appears as "a transfer payment" for the use of a scarce and spatially fixed asset (Harvey 1974a, 240). Land rent is a central component of the analysis. Given that all other factors remain the same, it appears as a barrier to the free movement of capital, i.e., the free flow of investments across branches, which Harvey conceptualized as capital switching. Therefore, the model explains the economic reasoning behind investments in urban land markets characterized by monopolistic excess returns (Harvey 1982). As discussed in Chapter 1, Harvey (1985) built his capital switching thesis on his conceptualization of three circuits of capital (primary, secondary, and tertiary) to explain the tendency to switch from the primary circuit (i.e., productive investments) to the secondary circuit (i.e., speculative investments in real estate and built environments). Harvey (1974a) explicitly names Henri Lefebvre's (2003 [1970]) thesis—the primacy of investments in urban spaces over productive investments in late capitalism—as his main inspiration. It can be plausibly inferred that Harvey reinterprets Lefebvre's thesis using Marx's concept of the movement of capital to equalize profit rates, thus providing an economic basis for it (Harvey, 1978; 1985; 2012). Capital switching is crucial in explaining the economic mechanisms of producing space, particularly through the flow of capital onto land to resolve overaccumulation crises spatially (Harvey 1978; 1985; 1989). He maintains that this tendency arises from excess returns in the secondary circuit. And this excess return constitutes rent. In an interview in 2009, he (2009; also Christophers 2011, 1350) provided historical context for his thesis and argued that "particularly since the 1970s," capital surplus has increasingly gone "more and more into speculation on asset values" rather than "real production," which has turned "every city ... [into] a huge building site for capitalist surplus absorption" (ibid. quoted in Christophers 2011, 1350).

Crucial to the analysis, too, is the role of landed property. Since circulation and distribution hold a "strategic co-ordinating role" in capitalist accumulation and development (Harvey 2006 [1982], 331), the existence of the institution of landed property secures class-monopoly ownership of land at the aggregate level. Monopoly relations, in turn, limit the free movement of capital, which is crucial for shifting to the secondary circuit. Their class monopoly secures the power of the landlord class to interfere with the free movement of capital by imposing monopoly prices and demanding rents. The level of this rent depends on the vigor of the landlord class to ensure the excess profit is maintained, and in that sense, it affects prices (ibid.). In the final analysis, rent is the outcome of a class conflict between a class of housing producers (i.e., speculator-developers) and a class of consumers (i.e., tenants) (Harvey 1974a, 1976). Along with these monopolistic power relations, spatial relations also preexist the processes of rent creation and appropriation. The SMLR analyzes these spatial relations through the concept of relative space to explain how spatial reconfigurations in the surrounding area influence the development of the area under study. These spatial reconfigurations include the development of infrastructure, an abrupt upward change in the type of tenure, intensive investment in luxury commercial or residential development, and so on, which put pressure on and eventually appreciate the land values of the entire region and mount the expected productivity for individual investments (Harvey, 2006 [1982], 336). The aim is to explain the material preconditions of the interplay between differential rents I and II, which Marx introduced[1] in Capital Volume Three, and Harvey extended in the *Limits* for geographical analysis and examining "the contradictory role of landed property and rental appropriation" to have "positive, negative, or neutral effects upon market prices, the accumulation of capital, the degree of dispersal of production, and so on" (Harvey 2006 [1982], 358). The intensity of development in the surrounding area depends on regional economic development and the class-monopoly power relations that govern it. Class-monopoly power relations determine the reach and type of local land regimes, including urban policies and governance, as well as the regulatory mechanisms for investments in land markets.

He argues that in what we today call neoliberal capitalism, governing contemporary "advanced capitalist countries," landed property comprises "motley

1 He wrote of the relationship between differential rent I and differential rent II, "while the first is the basis of the second, at the same time place limits on one another, leading sometimes to successive investments of capital on the same stretch of land and sometimes to adjacent investments of capital on new additional land" (Marx 1991 [1894], 871).

and heterogeneous groups ranging all the way from ancient institutions (the Church, the Crown, large aristocratic estates), through financial institutions (banks, insurance and pension funds) to a wide range of individual and corporate owners (including workers who own their own homes) and government agencies" (ibid. 346–347). In this context, land is transformed into "a form of fictitious capital," freely tradable as "a pure financial asset which is bought and sold according to the rent it yields," and as "a claim upon future revenues" (ibid. 347). Land markets function as "a particular branch ... of the circulation of interest-bearing capital" (ibid.). And rent, as a "stream of revenue," functions as "interest on money laid out," meaning it is "no different from similar investments in government debt, stocks and shares of enterprises, consumer debt, and so on" (ibid.). A monopoly ownership of urban land, therefore, appears as financial land ownership. Financial instruments ensure that land, as a fixed asset, is liquidated. Liquidation is necessary for speculative investments in the built environment and to make land tradable. Financial institutions, for instance, manipulate land markets using various regulatory tools, such as zoning restrictions and redlining. As interest-bearing capital enters land markets, landowners acquire financial tools to perpetually strive for the "highest and best use" of land and capitalize on potential returns, and in "an activist alliance[2] between landowner and capitalist" (ibid. 368). The "temporal rhythms" of land prices, he maintains, are imposed by "movements in the interest rate" (ibid. 367). However, the finite nature of urban land, the monopolistic ownership of land stock, and the inherently speculative character of investments in built environments mean that land rent trends are typically never downward. This characteristic is essential to sustain processes of spatial fix. The SMLR analyzes rent as an offshoot of monopolistic competition between productive and speculator-developer capitals, serving to secure above-normal profits from land use as a long-term response to overaccumulation crises.

The SMLR begins with a structural analysis of rent creation and appropriation, promising to relate these processes to the macro-dynamics of capital accumulation. In a decisive shift, however, the model diverges from its economic structural point of departure, adopts an alternative analytical strategy to explain the source of rent and the movement of capital through exogenous mechanisms of market imperfections created by monopolistic and uneven power relations, and limits rent creation and appropriation to

2 This conceptualization, as noted in Chapter 1, is built on Harvey's earlier analysis that in such a context, and with adequately developed financial systems, "the distinction between capitalist and landlord has blurred," and the two classes are practically unified as "speculator-developers" (Harvey 1974a; 241).

peculiarities of neoliberal capitalism in highly financialized parts of the global North since the late 1970s. The model's proposed analytical tools for empirical (political-economic) analysis of land markets are limited because they explain only the characteristics of rent, not its rates, ceilings, or magnitudes. Beyond innovative conceptualizations, the model's crucial analytical tools include the monopoly pricing mechanism, which explains the rise of rents and the power of the landlord class in determining their level. More importantly, the model's conceptualization of the dynamics between micro-foundations and macroeconomic patterns remains tenuous. It formulates a structural yet somewhat temporally static (King 1989a; Anderson 2014) explanation for capital switching, relating micro-level spatial changes and market imperfections to macro-level movements of capital between branches. The model also lacks a macro-level mechanism required for a consistently endogenous structural analysis of land rents. This mechanism is necessary to explain the historical contingency of rent creation and appropriation, as well as their relation to the dynamics of capital at the whole-economy level.

3.2 The Turbulent Inter-sectoral Model of Land Rent (TILR)

The proposed Turbulent Inter-Sectoral Model of Land Rent (TILR) improves on the SMLR by offering a conceptual apparatus that integrates long-term inter-sectoral and multi-scalar dynamics of capital. Thanks to this sectoral and scalar interpretation of Marx's rent theory, the TILR is designed to avoid the aforementioned theoretical and empirical tensions in the SMLR's explanation of the source of rent and the movement of capital. Incorporating Shaikh's theory of real competition (Chapter 10), this inter-sectoral and multi-scalar framework enables the TILR to articulate an economic structural mechanism that explains rent creation and appropriation endogenously, i.e., in relation to the whole economy, particularly to the dynamics of productive capital. The theory of real competition that underlies the TILR posits that "competitive firms are active price-setters and aggressive cost-cutters," and that creating techniques to lower production costs typically requires greater investment in fixed capital per unit (Shaikh 2016, 327). This distinction is crucial for analyzing "the choice of technique and the time path of the average rate of profit" in a context of turbulent disequilibrium (ibid.). The equalization of prices across sellers and "profit rates on new investments ... over somewhat longer periods ... result in perpetual fluctuations around various centers of gravity" (ibid. 260). Price equalization occurs as "buyers gravitate toward the lowest price," and profit rate equalization happens as "investors flock to higher rates of return" (ibid.

260). One unintended consequence of these dynamics is the acceleration of "supply relative to demand in the favored industries [which] drives down their prices and profits" (ibid.).

In the TILR, rent represents "a deduction of value[3] produced elsewhere" in the economy (Murray 1977, 102). It is "a deduction from total social value and is limited by the total value produced by labour" (ibid. 102). Land ownership allows landlords to "extract surplus profit which in other circumstances would accrue to capital" (ibid. 102). All things being equal, rent arises where there is an above-normal rate of return (e.g., in plots with more fertile soils). That is to say, the excess return for non-reproducible and monopolizable lower-cost conditions of production constitutes rent, particularly for non-regulating capitals operating with a mixture of lower profit rates for their higher-cost conditions of production (e.g., technology and machinery) and higher-profit rates for their lower-cost (non-reproducible) conditions of production. The TILR views land rent as a relative price of land and measures it as the difference between the value and the price. Like other factors of production, the nature and patterns of this price are to be explained theoretically and in relation to the competitive interrelationship between micro-foundations (many capitals, i.e., the local level) and macro patterns (capital-as-such, i.e., the aggregate, whole-economy level). Aggregate rent rates, like interest rates or wage rates, determine the expected (or 'normal') levels for individual enterprises. The nature of rent rates, as well as those for wages and interest, is explained theoretically at both the aggregate and micro levels. Individual land prices are set at the micro level, while macro-level forces govern them. The latter determines the upper and lower bounds of expectations, above or below which the rate is considered abnormal by proprietors. Rent theory explains the nature and patterns of rent creation and appropriation at the micro and macro levels.

To analyze the rate and ceiling of rent, the TILR draws on Marx's critique of Ricardo. Ricardo analyzed agricultural rent in terms of the natural

3 Shaikh defines Marx's notion of value as integrated labor times, that is, "the labor required to produce the given commodity plus that required to produce its inputs and the inputs to its inputs, and so on" (Shaikh 2016, 20). He defines direct prices as "prices proportional to integrated labor times" (ibid. 21); relative price as "the vertically integrated unit labor cost associated with the production" of any two commodities (ibid. 69); production prices as "competitive relative prices generated by three essential outcomes: selling prices equalized across sellers, labor incomes equalized across workers, and profit rate equalized across regulating capitals, all equalizations being turbulent" (ibid. 381); natural prices as classical economists' equivalent for Marx's production prices (ibid. 194); and regulating prices as production prices set by the regulating capital as the frontier capital in each sector around which sectoral market prices gravitate (ibid. 380).

characteristics of the land. That is, rent arises from the differential quality of land plots in terms of soil fertility; the least fertile land sets the regulating condition and the (regulating) price of the product, and the more fertile ones get an excess profit that constitutes rent, which he conceptualized as differential rent. In response, Marx first distinguished between potential scenarios of differential rent and argued that differential fertility could be socially and historically surmounted by extending the land in use or intensifying its investment, for example, through the use of chemical fertilizers (see Appendix 1). Drawing on this, the TILR assumes that Ricardo's analysis of land rent can only provide magnitudes and rates of rent at the micro-level, but not their macro-level rates, magnitudes, and ceilings. Macro-level rent rates, magnitudes, and ceilings can be best analyzed in a long-term, competitive economic context, i.e., inter-sectoral dynamics. Marx conceptualizes this macro-level category, through which he relates rent creation and appropriation to broader economic structures, as absolute rent. Inter-sectoral competition secures excess profits in rent-bearing sectors, which constitute land rents, and drives capital onto the land. Assuming all other factors as equal, not only does land rent function as a barrier to productive activities on land, but it also could stimulate the movement of capital as an excess profit on new constructions (as productive activity) and compensate for a fall in the rate of profit elsewhere in the economy.

The TILR defines rent at two (micro and macro) scales: 1) at the level of land ownership and 2) at the whole-economy level. These micro- and macro-level rents are regulated by the state of competition within and between sectors (Fine 2019). Rent rates tend to gravitate around the regulating prices (Shaikh 2016, 330–337). Regulating prices are determined by the regulating production conditions in the worst (or least fertile) land in use (ibid. 330–337). And the state of competition equalizes rates within and between sectors (ibid. 330–337). In other words, rent is "generated by evening out the price for the resultants of varying production costs" and is determined by inter-sectoral and intra-sectoral competition (Marx and Engels 2010 [1982], 262). This interpretation enables viewing the built environment at the whole-industry level (involving landlords, constructors, developers, financiers, etc.) and analyzing its relational dynamics with the rest of the economy. According to the TILR, land rent, at the macro level, is created and regulated in response to inter-sectoral dynamics of capital. These inter-sectoral dynamics are measured as the differential sectoral profitability. The rate of profit is measured as net operating surplus divided by net capital stock. It, then, is to be calculated for the manufacturing and construction sectors. Their difference (i.e., higher profit rates in the construction sector) represents the macro-level rent rate. Land rent appears as an excess profit rate on newly added value (particularly in new construction) for land-owning investors (e.g., developers). However, it appears as a land cost for non-land-owning capitalists who need to acquire land from a landlord. The ceiling of rent is "the excess above the average profit," governed by equalization of profit rate, i.e., "the distribution of capital among the various spheres" of production (Marx 1991 [1894], 1022–1023).

In the theory of real competition that informs the TILR, "the profit motive plays the central role," and competition is understood as "antagonistic by nature and turbulent in operation" (Shaikh, 2016: 6; 14). The theory assumes "that all social phenomena are constantly subject to [tendential] movement," meaning the movement is regulated by "tendencies and counter-tendencies" (Carchedi 1991, 4). The tendencies "are the state toward which the counter-tendencies gravitate," and the counter-tendencies are "deviations from the tendency" (ibid.). The model returns to Marx's notion of inter-sectoral movement of capital to equalize profit rates, aiming to broaden its scope and avoid being limited to the peculiarities of neoliberal capitalism. In this interpretation, the movement of capital to ventures on urban land (and built environments) depends on aggregate land rent rates, which appear as a sector-wide excess profit rate, relative to expected profit rates in other sectors. Essentially, even if an underlying profitability crisis necessitates an inter-sectoral movement of capital (switching), switching to the built environment may not occur if land rent rates remain lower than the expected profit rates in other sectors. Geography matters as it determines the investor or consumer's choice with the mediation of land rent (or in exceptional cases, geographic arbitrage), "but the initial tendency of capital to move into a specific space depends on whether investing in land at that moment is more profitable than engaging in ventures in other sectors, even in the absence of speculative interests or a full-blown (neoliberal) financialization" (Farahani et al. 2026, 100). This way, the model aims to stay true to Harvey's initial call to "create an interdisciplinary [structural] theory" for urbanism (Harvey 2009 [1973], 302).

A critical analytical point is that "it is the rate of return on new investment, not the average rate of profit on all vintages, which is relevant to the mobility of capital" (Shaikh 2016, 264). New investments will focus on the profit rate of what Shaikh calls "regulating capitals" (ibid. 265). Regulating capitals represent "the best generally reproducible conditions of production in [each] industry," or regulating production conditions that represent "lowest reproducible (quality-adjusted) costs in the industry" (ibid.). A more detailed exposition of different possibilities for these regulating conditions will be discussed in Chapter 10. Here, it is crucial to note the case when "the reproducible conditions of production are the highest cost ones in use" (ibid. 266). This scenario allows for incorporating land as a non-reproducible production condition and land rent as excess profit, "given that competition among producers will enforce a common price, lower cost producers [with better lands] will tend to have higher profit margins and higher profit rates" (ibid.).

The TILR incorporates the viewpoint of competition from Marx's Capital, Volume Three (see Introduction above) into the analysis (also see Farahani et al. 2026). This viewpoint crucially highlights the scenario in which rent can be minimized if the manufacturing (or other competing) sector's profit rates do not fall below those of the construction sector. As Edel (1976, 102) points out, for Marx, rent creation and appropriation are historically contingent. That is, they depend on spatiotemporal contexts. Historical contingency in land rents is most typically captured in the concept of absolute rent. Sandemose (2006, 363, emphasis in original) points out that the existence of absolute rent for Marx is not absolute; "[the] main point is that it is necessary to prove its *possibility*." That possibility depends on long-term inter-sectoral competitive relations at the whole-economy level. Rent rates, at the macro level, fluctuate in tandem with fluctuations in manufacturing profit rates. In other words, rent rates fluctuate with changes in the rates of return in the two sectors. This historical contingency also applies to capital switching. Switching from manufacturing investment to investment in built environments needs to be contextualized. It depends on inter-sectoral competition and fluctuations in sectoral rates of return. However, a retrospective analysis of rates of return alone cannot empirically explain the process. To empirically explain the process, the TILR proposes Shaikh's (2016) notion of incremental rate of return on capital, built on Marx's notion of capital mobility and measured as the change in gross profits (gross operating surplus) divided by lagged nominal gross investments (fixed capital formation), to indicate the most recent sectoral shift in investments. The capital switching thesis conceptually explains shifts in investment and the direction of capital flows. However, it needs to be historicized and concretized, using incremental profit rates, to explain the processes empirically and incorporate new constructions as the sectoral regulating capitals driving intra-sectoral competition.

That said, as Edel (1976, 119) argues, absolute rent is a macro-level concept, and Marx did not design it to explain the micro-level fluctuations in the market prices of land and improvements built on it. The relation between the category of absolute rent and micro-level magnitudes and rates of rent (explained by Marx through differential rent I and II) is similar to the relation between value and prices of production. It explains long-term structural patterns that govern fluctuations of rent rates and magnitudes at the micro-level. Micro-level rates and magnitudes gravitate around these long-term structural patterns. Similar to the scalar dynamics that Harvey envisions for class-monopoly rent on the one hand, and differential rents I and II, on the other, in the TILR, too, absolute rent and differential rents I and II operate on two scales: absolute rent at the macro (whole-economy) and differential rents I and II at the micro (plot) level. When absolute rent arises, plots with higher fertility or relative locational advantage yield absolute rents on top of differential rent I and II (depending on their extensive or intensive investment strategies), and plots with inferior fertility or relative locational advantage also yield rents, even though differential rent I and II could be zero. When absolute rent is minimized, plots with higher fertility or relative locational advantage *could* still yield differential rent I and II. But rents in plots with inferior features will be zero. Generally, differential rents I and II function as investment strategies, meaning whichever appears less costly will be prioritized by the investors. They arise in plots with a higher relative locational advantage, provided both spatial and regional development allow them, and regional intra-sectoral competition determines the extent and intensity of both.

By incorporating the concept of absolute rent into the analysis, the TILR eliminates the need for exogenous monopoly power relations to mediate the link between rent creation and appropriation and the macro-dynamics of capital. It offers economic mechanisms to connect macro- and micro-level tendencies, acknowledging the historical contingency of rent creation and appropriation through a constantly turbulent interaction between sectors at both levels. Fluctuations of land-based investment in the TILR are endogenously related to the dynamics of productive capital. It provides specific (political-economic) methods for measuring and explaining rent rates and ceilings, as well as capital switching. The model, therefore, provides a consistently endogenous structural explanation of rent creation and appropriation, which is missing in the SMLR. That, by no means, implies that the TILR relies on a deterministic structural explanation. On the contrary, the model suggests that agents' knowledge of economic structures informs their actions and policy choices. And as the reader shall see in Part 3, to do so, the TILR needs to incorporate an alternative interpretation of Marx's economic theory.

3.3 Judging between the Two Models

The principal assumption behind the critique of Harvey's theory of land rent I present here, is the Marxian notion of immanent (or internal) critique. It implies demonstrating the limits of a system of thought according to "its own avowed norms," i.e., "norms whose acknowledged validity is part and parcel" of that system of thought (Buchwalter 2012, 42). The process starts with "accepting the premises of a system of thought, then spotting the gaps, silences and contradictions in it, and finally showing the necessity of introducing new concepts in order to resolve such tensions" (Boda and Faran 2018, 10). Theory development is due to overcome the identified anomalies (gaps, tensions, contradictions, and inconsistencies). Immanent critique is a common approach in Marxist scholarship. And, more relevant to the present discussion, Harvey himself incorporated it into his critique of mainstream approaches to urban economic geography in Social Justice and the City (2009 [1973]) and The Limits to Capital (2006 [1982]).

My suggested metric for this critique is Lakatos's methodology of scientific research programs. Lakatos (1978) develops his methodology through an immanent critique of logical positivism and constructivism, resulting in the synthesis of Kuhn's historical development of scientific theories and Popper's development of scientific methods. Lakatos rejects the Kuhnian argument that successful paradigms create a consensus (or monopoly) among scientists, but acknowledges Kuhn's point about the subjective (theoretical) character of research programs, highlighting the tenacity of scientists in protecting their programs. Lakatos also rejects what he calls naïve falsification, which claims that empirical facts can easily falsify and dismiss a paradigm. The choice of research programs, he argued, is not arbitrary. Nor is it a result of some intellectual consensus among scientists. Instead, it is an outcome of competitive interaction between research programs to explain empirical facts, anticipate future counterexamples, and turn them into corroborative reasoning. For Lakatos, science evolves around co-existing, competitive research programs, which comprise "a characteristic hard core [or core assumptions] stubbornly defended" … a "more flexible protective belt" … and an "elaborate problem-solving machinery" or heuristics (Lakatos 1978, 5). Core assumptions must be kept intact. Otherwise, the program begins to degenerate (ibid. 47). Scientists generate auxiliary hypotheses as a "protective belt" and redirect the *modus tollens* to these hypotheses instead of the core assumptions (ibid. 48). This strategy is known as negative heuristics. Alternatively, scientists develop positive heuristics by generating hypotheses to anticipate future anomalies (ibid. 49). He maintains, "[t]he negative heuristic specifies the 'hard core' of the programme which is 'irrefutable' by the methodological decision of its protagonists; the positive heuristic consists of a partially articulated set of suggestions or hints on how to change, develop the 'refutable variants' of the research-programme, how to modify, sophisticate, the 'refutable' protective belt" (ibid. 50). A research program progresses as long as it can anticipate more anomalies, and it degenerates when it fails to do so. The 'hard core' may crush under too many protective belts against coming *modus tollens* instead of progressing toward new assumptions. The theoretical development in a progressive research program "leads to the discovery of hitherto unknown novel facts" (ibid. 5). On the other hand, a research program degenerates if "theories are fabricated only in order to accommodate known facts" using only *ad hoc* explanations (ibid. 5; 39). Lakatos argues that a competing program is successful if it "explained everything" that the other "had successfully explained"; if "it explained also to some extent some known anomalies and, in addition, forbade events … which had been permitted by other well-corroborated scientific theories of the day"; and if it corroborated at least some "unexpected excess content" (ibid. 39). Only then can an alternative research program surpass its rival.

Harvey's analysis of economic urbanization processes, in which land rent is central, highlights the core anomaly of neoclassical approaches: their failure to explain the structural forces (i.e., capital forces) that stimulate or limit urbanization processes. His explanation is methodologically superior to pre-Harveyan, i.e., neoclassical, approaches because it is specifically designed to analyze structural forces in urbanization processes. Harvey's model of urban land rent, the SMLR, however, breaks with its structural aspirations and, in the final analysis, explains structural mechanisms with agential and institutional relations by incorporating monopoly and power relations as the driving force of rent creation and appropriation and explaining the level of rent with the power of the landowner class to impose monopoly prices. This tension was discussed in detail in Chapter 1, followed by a further examination of conceptual inconsistencies in the Harvey-inspired scholarship (Chapter 2). Since the 1980s, subsequent generations of heterodox urban economic geographers have operationalized and expanded Harvey's framework, taking on the task of problem-solving within the research program. The absence of a conceptual framework to explain macro-level rent relations, rates, magnitudes, and ceilings prompted the next generations to develop and innovate alternative conceptualizations, such as the rent gap hypothesis, to complement the SMLR. Nevertheless, the aforementioned anomalies remain unresolved.

Following Lakatos's criteria for comparing (and judging between) research programs, I conducted a series of empirical studies in Part 2. The empirical studies aim to examine the empirical strength of both models in explaining the source of rent (or rent creation) and the movement of capital (or rent appropriation) in a structural and dynamic context, with a focus on the dynamics of productive capital. One crucial question, however, remains. If incorporating the concept of absolute rent could resolve all anomalies identified in the SMLR, why have Harvey and Harvey-inspired geographers remained reluctant to operationalize it for five decades? Answering this question requires a theoretical comparison of the economic theories underlying each model. The aim is to explain why and how the underlying economic theory of the SMLR, rooted in Harvey's interpretation of Marx's economic theory, deems the concept of absolute rent inconsistent and, therefore, "irrelevant" (Harvey 2013 interview in Barnes and Sheppard 2019, 207). Conversely, it aims to explain how the underlying economic theory in the TILR, rooted in another interpretation of Marx's economic theory, enables the model to consistently incorporate the concept of absolute rent and rival the SMLR for a consistently structural and endogenous explanation of economic urbanization processes. This will be the task of Part 3.

PART 2

Empirical Comparisons of the Two Models

CHAPTER 4

Harvey's Empirical Evidence Revisited: Inter-sectoral Profitability and US Cities

This chapter revisits Harvey's two seminal empirical articles (1974 with Chatterjee; 1974a), which form the basis of his urban land rent model (SMLR) and have influenced many of his supporters and critics alike. The same database used in these two key papers in 1974 underpins Harvey's core conceptualization of both absolute rent and class-monopoly rent. Here, I aim to identify empirical gaps and tensions in Harvey's evidence for his proposed conceptual change. These empirical anomalies are built on the conceptual ones identified earlier in the first two chapters and include a) tools for measuring and explaining rent rates, ceilings, magnitudes, and capital switching at the macro level, and b) the historical contingency of rent creation and appropriation. The two models are compared based on their capacity to address these anomalies. For the sake of argument, and following Lakatos, I start with the hypothesis that Harvey's data (1974, with Chatterjee; 1974a) represent land rents, which had been purportedly increasing during the period of his two studies (i.e., the early 1970s). His evidence is then juxtaposed with additional empirical evidence supporting the TILR, using national and inter-sectoral measures of rates of return (as alternative analytical tools to gauge the rate, ceiling, and magnitude of rent), which Harvey's studies overlooked. To maintain consistency, the timeframe for this additional empirical counterevidence is limited to the period covered by Harvey's studies of Baltimore's housing markets in the early 1970s. The supplementary data presented here show the historical and inter-sectoral dynamics that influence and generate land rents, which are then used to place Harvey's treatment of land rents in a historical and economic context.

4.1 Absolute Rent or Class-Monopoly Rent

Let me start with a review of the methodological approach used in the two studies, followed by an examination of Harvey's SMLR's analytical and conceptual tools for assessing the source of rent and capital switching. Harvey and Chatterjee's (1974, 22) solution to a key scalar problem in urban economics—namely, linking aggregate, national patterns to local, micro-level behavior—involves analyzing "the structure of governmental and financial institutions."

They identify three significant challenges for housing research at the national level: the connection between construction and economic growth, the issue of capital switching, and the question of housing provision and welfare. They recognize land rent as the primary driver of all three processes (ibid. 22–23). Expanding on their analysis of this scalar problem, Harvey and Chatterjee state, "[a]t the national level, then, policies are designed to maintain an existing structure of society intact in its basic configurations, while facilitating economic growth and capitalist accumulation, eliminating cyclical influences, and defusing social discontent" (ibid. 23). These policies, then, are "filtered and transmitted" to the local level through the interaction between financial and government institutions (ibid.). This creates a central conflict in controlling funds for homeownership (via loans and mortgages), which in turn is regulated by federal fiscal and monetary policies. Lastly, at the individual level, they maintain, "the ability to obtain credit and a mortgage," especially "under suitable terms," influences housing choices (ibid.). They clarify that this ability "is a function of the policies of financial and governmental institutions," since private financial institutions "prefer to finance the more expensive housing," leaving less expensive (and more costly) dwellings to federal and state financial institutions (ibid. 24). Notably, the latter are also affected by "neighborhood biases," which is standard for private institutions (ibid.).

Harvey and Chatterjee divide Baltimore City's housing market into 13 submarkets. With this, they aim to illustrate the geographical structure underpinning the previously mentioned institutional service preferences (private versus state/community-based) in relation to "housing prices and socioeconomic composition" (ibid. 25). They assert, "[t]his geographical structure forms a 'decision environment' in which individual households make housing choices" (ibid.). The geographical structure itself is linked to inherited patterns of social differentiation based on income and race, while also presumed to create preconditions for the realization of land rent through excess monopoly returns (ibid.). To analyze landowners, Harvey and Chatterjee (ibid. 30) restrict their study to "professional landlords who own and manage about a quarter of Baltimore City's rental inventory." Based on interviews with four landlords, Harvey and Chatterjee (ibid. 31–32) find that landlords make investment decisions rationally, depending on "the availability or non-availability of landlord finance." They calculate the return rate for rental properties based on directly collected annual housing rent (ibid. 32). According to their interviews, they report that "[p]rofessional landlords in Baltimore, in fact, seek a 20 percent return on their capital, regard 15 percent as 'normal,' and remain operative at 11–12 percent (after expenses, including interest payments and an imputed managerial wage for the landlord as manager)" (ibid.). Harvey and Chatterjee do not provide further evidence or explanation as to why these numbers (as monopoly prices) are valid, nor do they clarify how macro-level interest rates could influence these figures. They appear to rely on their interviewees' assessments. Nonetheless, they argue these figures represent the city's regulatory benchmarks. Consequently, especially in areas with cheaper housing, tenants generally pay higher rent relative to the property's market value. The "decision environment" where landlords make housing choices is thus shaped and influenced by the selective and somewhat arbitrary practices of financial institutions (both private and public) that provide mortgages (ibid.).

For Harvey and Chatterjee, absolute rent is understood as a form of class monopoly over housing markets, realized when "absolute limits of some sort operate over different segments of the housing market" (ibid. 33). Geographical and structural patterns of differentiation shape these limits. They start with a hypothetical scenario where "a sub-market is completely isolated from all other sub-markets so that consumers and providers of housing are all locked into a specific situation" (ibid.). They then add two conditions to this scenario: a) the area is "an inner city sub-market where low-income tenants cannot possibly find alternative accommodations and from which landlords cannot possibly extract themselves", and b) "financial institutions and government intervention play no role" (ibid.). They conclude that "in such a sub-market, rent levels will be set by the relative power of the landlord over the tenant" (ibid. my emphasis). By adding complexity, they argue that the power balance between landlord and tenant depends on the extent of intervention by financial institutions. As tenants gain more power, landlords' returns drop (below the somewhat arbitrary 12 percent they asserted in the interviews), since their power is influenced and limited by financial institutions and institutional practices that finance housing markets. This often leads landlords to withdraw from the sub-market, such as through abandonment, particularly if the tenant's increased power is not supported by government regulation, such as "rent control legislation" (ibid.).

In a subsequent article using the same data set, Harvey (1974a) expands on and diverges from some of the main theoretical ideas presented in his earlier article with Chatterjee. In that initial article, Harvey and Chatterjee stated, "[r]ent is not, after all, inherent in production but arises only because the legal institution of private property is a necessary feature in the capitalist mode of production and because it proves difficult or impossible to restrict that legal right to production solely" (Harvey and Chatterjee 1974, 34). In the second article, Harvey maintains all assumptions regarding the nature of rent, its creation, and appropriation, but interprets its character as class-monopoly rent. For Harvey (1974a), rent is represented by transfer payments for the use of built environments. He defines rent as "a transfer payment realized through the monopoly power over land and resources conferred by the institution of private property" (ibid. 240). His goal in the analysis is to explain the "social consequences" of rent as "an actual payment to people" (ibid.). The primary factor for the existence of rent is the "scarcity" of urban land (ibid.): "If rent is a transfer payment to a scarce factor of production, then the urbanization process has also multiplied the opportunities for realizing rent" (ibid.). The next factor in this process is the typically long turnover period of housing as a commodity.

He measures rent based on monopolistic excess rates of return and writes, "[i]f rates of return are high in the real estate and property markets, then investment will shift from the primary productive circuit of capital to this secondary circuit in a manner that would be consistent with Lefebvre's thesis" (ibid. 241). He is, however, quick to add, "[w]hat has to be explained, however, is how returns can be higher on the secondary circuit over any length of time" (ibid.). He does not explain how different rates of return are calculated or what other economic mechanisms are involved in potential capital switching. Furthermore, the preconditions for capital switching are merely presented and analyzed spatially, rather than historically. Key variables in both articles include spatial scarcity and monopolistic power relations. The level of rent depends on the landlord class's ability to impose monopoly prices. In both articles, monopoly relations observed at the local (micro) level are generalized to national (macro) level patterns of capital mobility across the economy. However, macro patterns are separated from fluctuations of rent at the local level. Another issue is that, although rent relations are discussed alongside economic relations in both articles, the analysis is limited to sources of housing financing rather than to housing production.

King (1987; 1989a) criticizes Harvey for the invariant and static causal mechanisms he lists to explain how economic relations at the national level influence spatial and social relations at the local level. However, ultimately, King rejects the influence of macroeconomic forces entirely and describes Harvey's approach as "economically determinist" (King 1989b, 712). This critique (economic determinism and functionalism) has remained influential in the literature (Barnes 1994; Castree 1995; Anderson 2014). Beauregard's (1994) critique of Harvey's capital switching theory is more analytically interesting because he tries to a) analyze production processes in the construction sector, and b) historicize Harvey's analysis. However, as Christophers (2011) pointed out, Beauregard a) fails to explain fluctuations in investment in the construction sector in terms of rates of return and b) limits his analysis to the size of investment.

4.2 Measuring Aggregate and Sectoral Rates of Return

A key difference between SMLR and TILR concerns how they measure the rate of return, which in turn influences land rent levels. As mentioned earlier, according to Harvey and Chatterjee (1974, 30), a self-declared, nominal rate of return is sufficient to demonstrate landlords' ability to set monopoly prices, provided it exceeds the interest rate they pay to lenders. For the TILR, this expectation is gauged (on multiple scales) by average sectoral levels at the national level and in comparison with other sectors. Let me start with a standard mainstream indicator of corporate profits: corporate profit before tax (Figure 2[1]).

Even within its limited scope, the competitive dynamics among the manufacturing, construction, and financial sectors are recognizable. More importantly, as the figure shows, the observed patterns constantly fluctuate. The FIRE (i.e., Finance, Insurance, Real Estate) sector's corporate profits follow the trend of the manufacturing sector, while the construction sector may move in the opposite direction. A closer look reveals that a rise in construction mirrors the L-shaped, prolonged recovery after the 1969 recession in manufacturing. In contrast, the recovery of 1975 is reflected in a decline in construction. The fact that the construction sector's share of total corporate profits remains lower than that of manufacturing highlights the latter's central role in inter-sectoral competition. As Figures 3 and 4 demonstrate, investment patterns in structures for the manufacturing and residential sectors are counter-cyclical. All of this suggests a correlation that the SMLR fails to account for.

Nevertheless, the TILR method for calculating and analyzing rates of return is fundamentally different from these mainstream methods. Here, I compare three leading methods for calculating and analyzing rates of return, as outlined by Andrew Kliman, Michael Roberts, and Anwar Shaikh. This comparison is important because it highlights the complexity of measuring profit rates and shows that they can be concretely demonstrated despite minor methodological differences. However, the main challenge of connecting national (capital-as-such) levels to local levels still remains. I will discuss this further in Section 4.4 below.

Kliman (2015) calculates the US rate of profit as net profits divided by the net stock of fixed assets. He considers what he calls property income to be the most "inclusive" indicator for profits, calculated as "gross value added minus

---

1 I used official data (e.g., BEA) for all figures in this chapter, mainly with my calculations. To avoid repetition, I present the detailed description of the sources (with tables, lines, etc.) in Appendix 3.1.

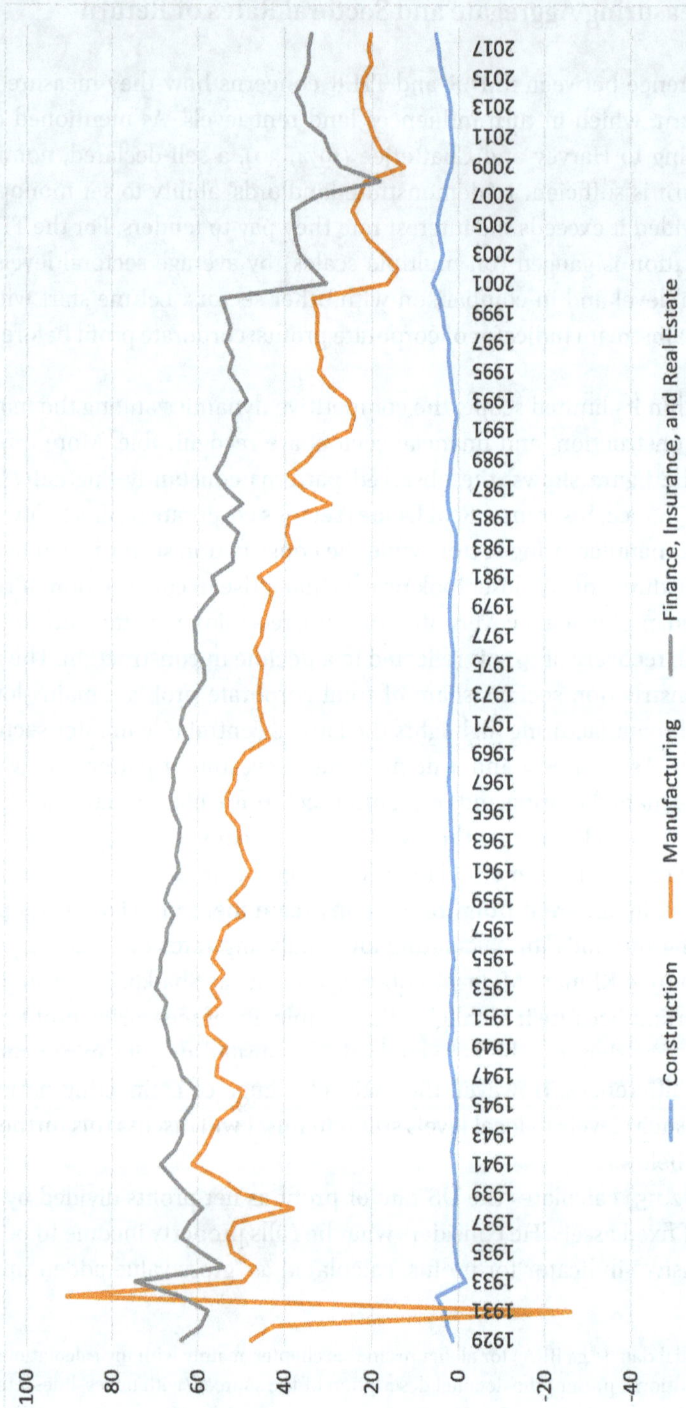

FIGURE 2 US—corporate profits before tax by industry—share % (Source: BEA online database (my calculation))

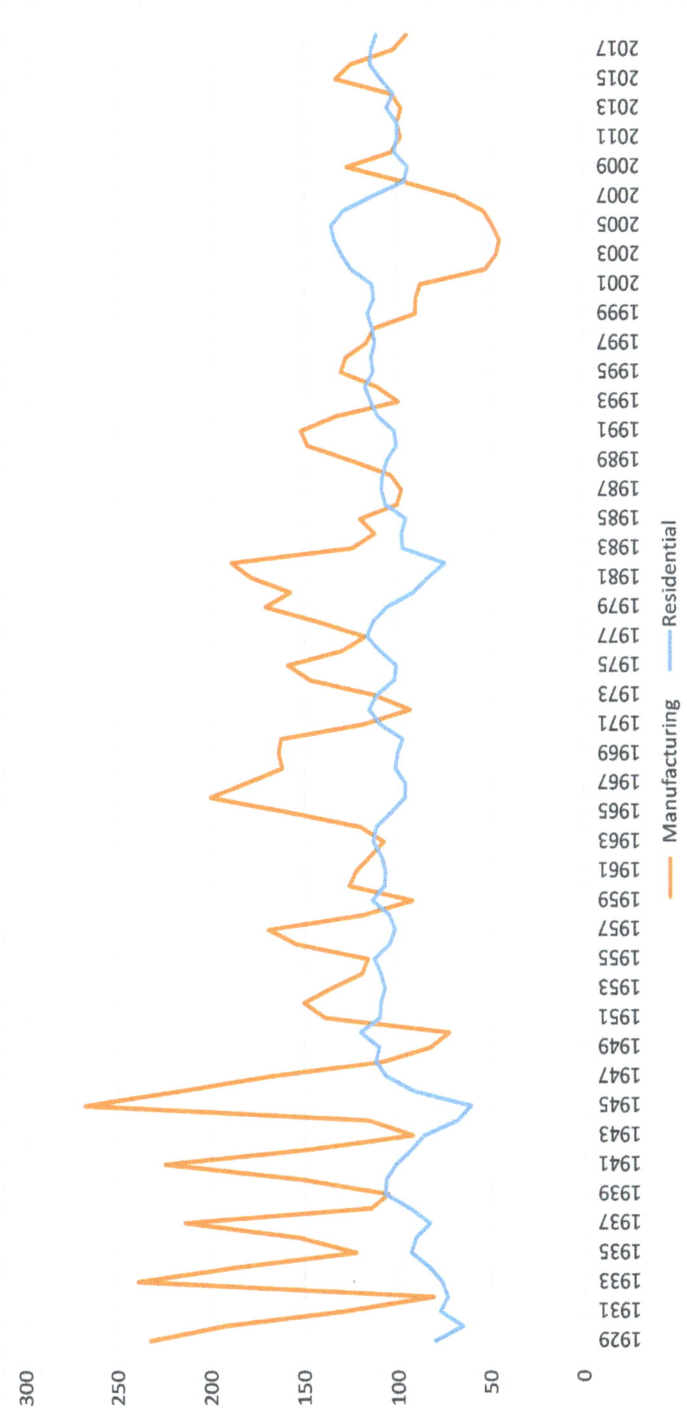

FIGURE 3 US—real private fixed investment in structures by type, quantity indexes—share % (Source: BEA online database (my calculation))

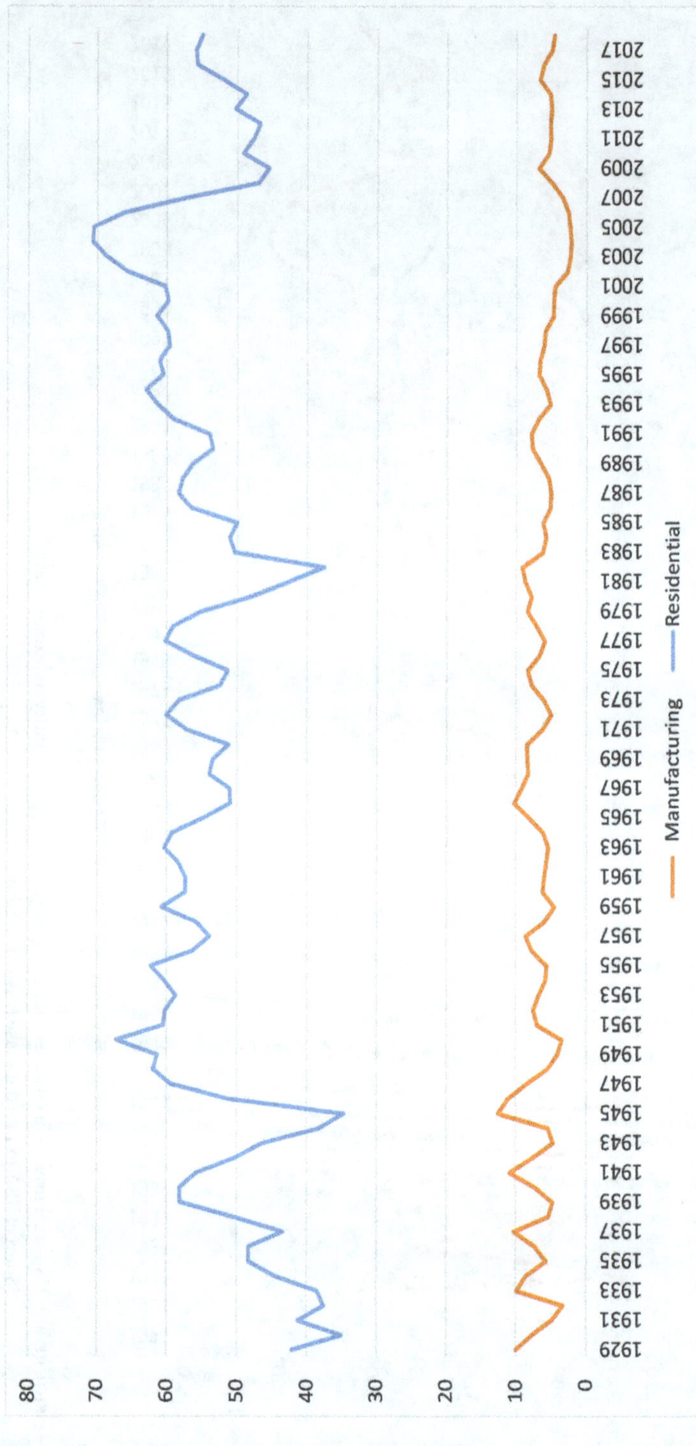

FIGURE 4 US—private fixed investment in structures by type—share % (Source: BEA online database (my calculation))

depreciation and compensation of employees" (ibid. 246; also 2012, 75–76). A less inclusive indicator is net operating surplus, figured as property income minus "net indirect business taxes (sales tax, etc.)" (Kliman 2015, 246). Kliman (ibid.) calculates "corporations' profits as a percentage of their accumulated investment in (or 'net stock of') fixed assets". Thus, the net stock of private fixed assets reflects total constant capital. Both profit and accumulated investment are measured net of depreciation at historical cost (ibid.). I have replicated Kliman's calculations for both property income and net operating surplus for corporate and private-sector profit rates (Figures 5 and 6). The U.S. National Income and Product Accounts (NIPA) define net operating surplus as the sum of proprietors' income, rental income, corporate profits, net interest, and net business current transfer payments, all adjusted for capital consumption. Kliman's property income is defined as net operating surplus plus taxes on production and imports. Therefore, the rate of profit equals profit (property income or net operating surplus) divided by the net stock of private fixed capital, valued at historical cost. The results display similar patterns.

Kliman (ibid. 249–250) criticizes measuring the rate of profit "as a percentage of the replacement cost (or current cost) of fixed assets, the amount of money that would currently be needed to replace them." He elaborates, "[w]hen the rate of inflation rises (falls), the amount of money that would be needed to replace all of the fixed assets in use rises (falls) relative to the amount of money that was actually invested to acquire them in the past, and the replacement-cost rate of profit therefore falls (rises) in relation to the rate of profit based on actual accumulated investment" (ibid.). That leads him to argue, "the acceleration of inflation during the 1970s depressed the replacement-cost rate and the deceleration of inflation during the 1980s boosted it, and this—not the putative economic success of neoliberalism—is the source of the difference in the trajectories of the two rates of profit" (ibid.). In Figure 7, I have updated his equation for sectoral profit rates. As the figure shows, the period during which Harvey made his observations in Baltimore (roughly 1970 to 1974) coincided with a decline in the manufacturing sector's profit rates, while the overall profit rates of the construction sector began to rise. The data, however, does not point to any causation, I should emphasize. Nevertheless, it provides a clear indication of the historical context upon which Harvey's analysis was made.

The difference in profit rates across sectors influences investors' decisions about where to invest. Theoretically, it determines the flow of capital between sectors on a macro, whole-economy level. More complex issues arise at the micro and local levels, as smaller capitalists might not be able to switch to other sectors. More importantly, those with bounded capital, who have already

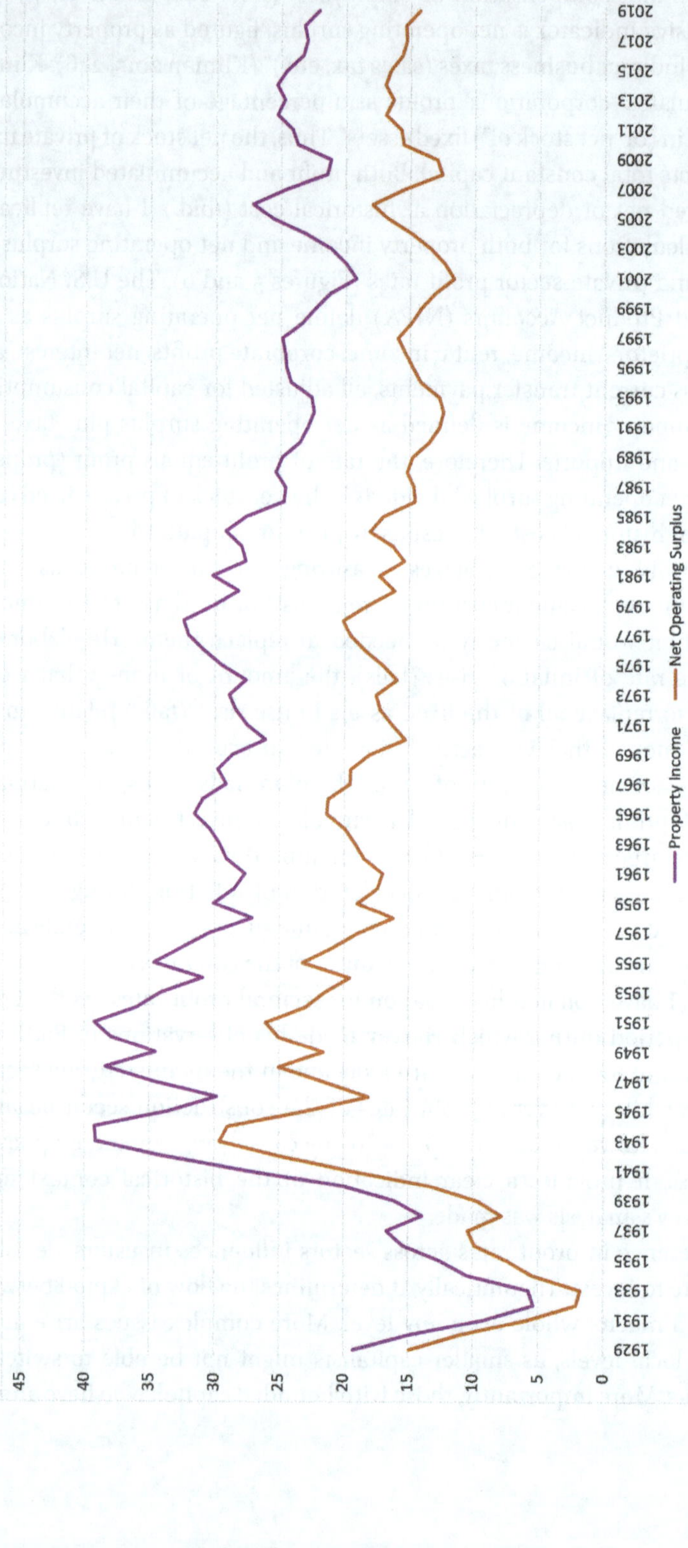

FIGURE 5 US—corporate rate of profit (%) (Kliman-inspired) (Source: BEA online database (my calculation))

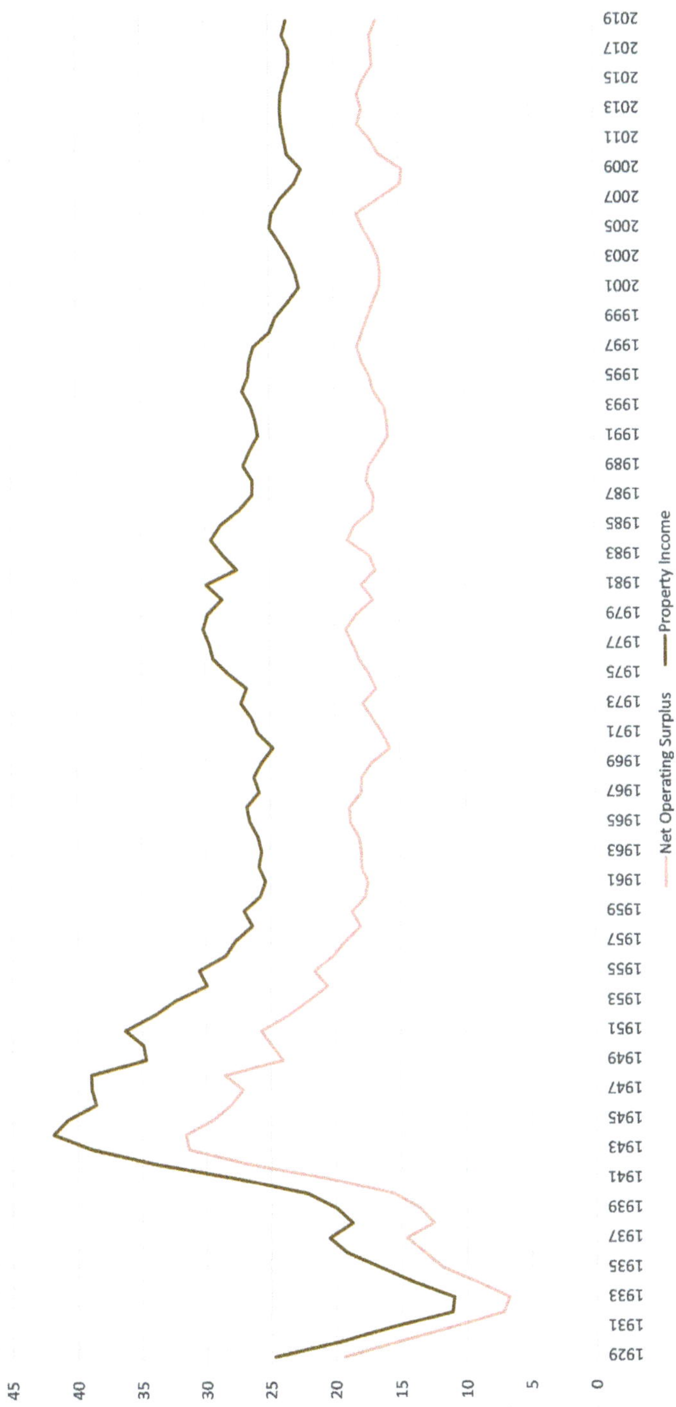

FIGURE 6 US—aggregate rate of profit—private sector (Kliman-inspired) (Source: BEA online database (my calculation))

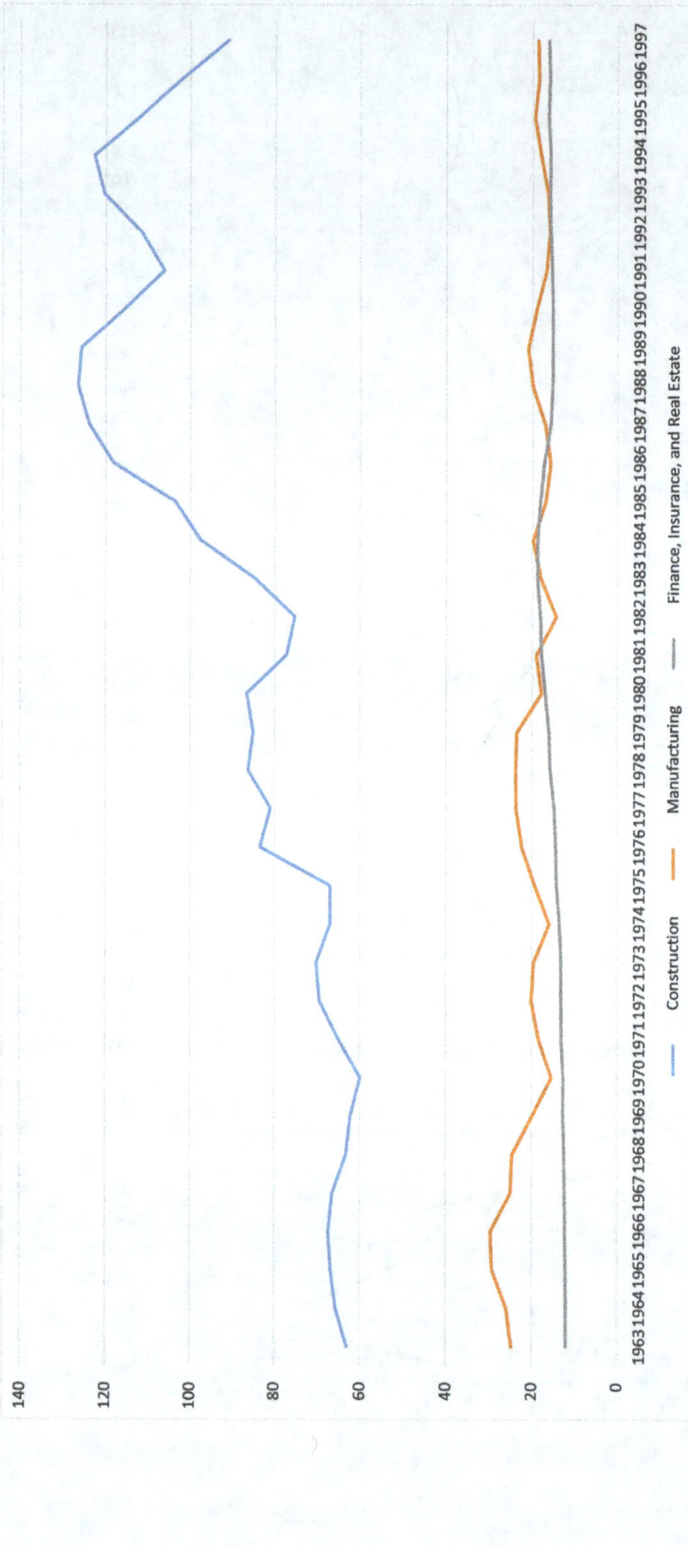

FIGURE 7 US—sectoral profit rates (Kliman-inspired) (Source: BEA online database (my calculation))

heavily invested in constant capital (machinery, equipment, etc.), may also prefer to stay put and hope for the best. The overall difference in sectoral profit rates explains why capital tends to move to more profitable sectors at an aggregate level. Generally, the manufacturing sector's profit rate moves closer to the overall rate. I should note that aggregate rates only reflect historical processes and do not reflect the most recent investments. I will revisit this in Section 4.3.

Roberts (2019) calculates the general rate of profit somewhat differently, "by looking at total surplus value in an economy against total private capital employed in production; to be as close as possible to Marx's original formula of s/c + v." He measures the rate at the whole economy level and calculates it as "total national income (less depreciation) for surplus value [i.e., GNI/GNP with capital consumption adjustment]; net non-residential private fixed assets for constant capital; and adds employee compensation for variable capital" (ibid.).[2] He (ibid.) further explains, "[m]ost Marxist measures exclude any measure of variable capital on the grounds that employee compensation (wages plus benefits) is not a stock of invested capital but a flow of circulating capital." Roberts rejects this view. However, he argues that "the value of constant fixed capital compared to variable capital is five to eight times larger (depending on whether you use a historic or current cost measure); the addition of a variable capital measure to the denominator does not significantly alter the trend or turning points in the rate of profit" (ibid.). Roberts (2016c, 274) clarifies that he follows "a simple formula. S = net national product (that is GDP less depreciation) minus v (employee compensation); c = net fixed assets (either on a historic or current cost basis); and v = employee compensation, that is, wages plus benefits." He calculates this rate for the entire economy, unlike Kliman, who does so for the corporate sector. According to Roberts, Kliman's approach excludes "employee costs or the product appropriated by government from the private sector through taxation" (ibid.). The whole economy approach "also includes the value and profits appropriated by the financial sector, even though it is not productive in the Marxist sense" (ibid.). Roberts further explains that his calculation of "constant capital is for the capitalist sector only and thus excludes household investment in homes and government investment" (ibid.). I again replicate Roberts's method, using national income as GDP minus depreciation (consumption of fixed capital), divided

2 Roberts's method is reminiscent of Brenner's. Brenner calculates the rate of profit as net profits divided by net capital stock. "Net profits = net value added minus the sum of compensation and indirect business taxes, with net value-added equivalent to gross value-added minus depreciation or capital consumption" (Brenner 2006, 345).

by net non-residential fixed private assets in both historical and current costs, plus employee compensation (Figure 8).

The rate is then similarly calculated for post-war sectoral profits (Figure 9). Once again, similar patterns are observed: a decline in aggregate profit rates since 1965, which, when broken down, is reflected by a sharp decrease in manufacturing sector profit rates and a slight rebound in the construction sector during the early 1970s.

Using a slightly different approach, Shaikh (2016, 65) defines the rate of profit "as the aggregate net operating surplus divided by the net capital stock, both in constant dollars" (cf. Kliman's historical cost method). Shaikh (ibid. 65) explains that "the total net stock of fixed capital consists of the surviving vintages of all past investments in plant and equipment." This means that at the time of calculation, "the capital stock encompasses capital ranging from that which was put into place (say) thirty years ago, to that which came online only one year ago" (ibid.). The difference in profitability levels across these periods indicates that "the overall rate of profit represents the average of the rates of profit on the various vintages still in operation" (ibid.). Shaikh (ibid. 66) emphasizes, "[t]he profit rate is central to accumulation because profit is the very purpose of capitalist investment, and the profit rate is the ultimate measure of its success." Furthermore, the essential role of economic growth in capitalist production and reproduction means sectors are continuously influenced by new capital flow: "[t]hus, when sectoral profit rates are unequal, new capital tends to flow more rapidly into sectors where the profit rate is higher than the average, and less rapidly into those where the profit rate is lower" (ibid.). He also notes a tendency toward the equalization of profit rates across branches, stating, "[i]t is not a question of entry and exit, but of acceleration and deceleration" (ibid.). The sectors experiencing rapid growth enjoy a "faster influx of new capital [raising] supply relative to demand, and [driving] down prices and profits" (ibid.). This "search for higher profits tends to diminish high profit rates and raise low ones" and "gives rise to a general tendency for profit rates to be equalized across sectors" (ibid.).

Similar to Kliman and Roberts' methods for calculating profit rates, I have replicated Shaikh's method at the aggregate, corporate, private, and sectoral levels (see Figures 10, 11, 12, and 13). Once again, the results show similar patterns for the early 1970s (Harvey's period of study): a decline in the profits of the aggregate and manufacturing sectors, and an increase (and higher levels) in the profits of the construction sector.

In Figure 13, I calculated profits as gross value added (GVA) minus depreciation and compensation of employees, divided by the current cost of the net stock of private fixed assets. GVA is computed as GDP minus taxes on

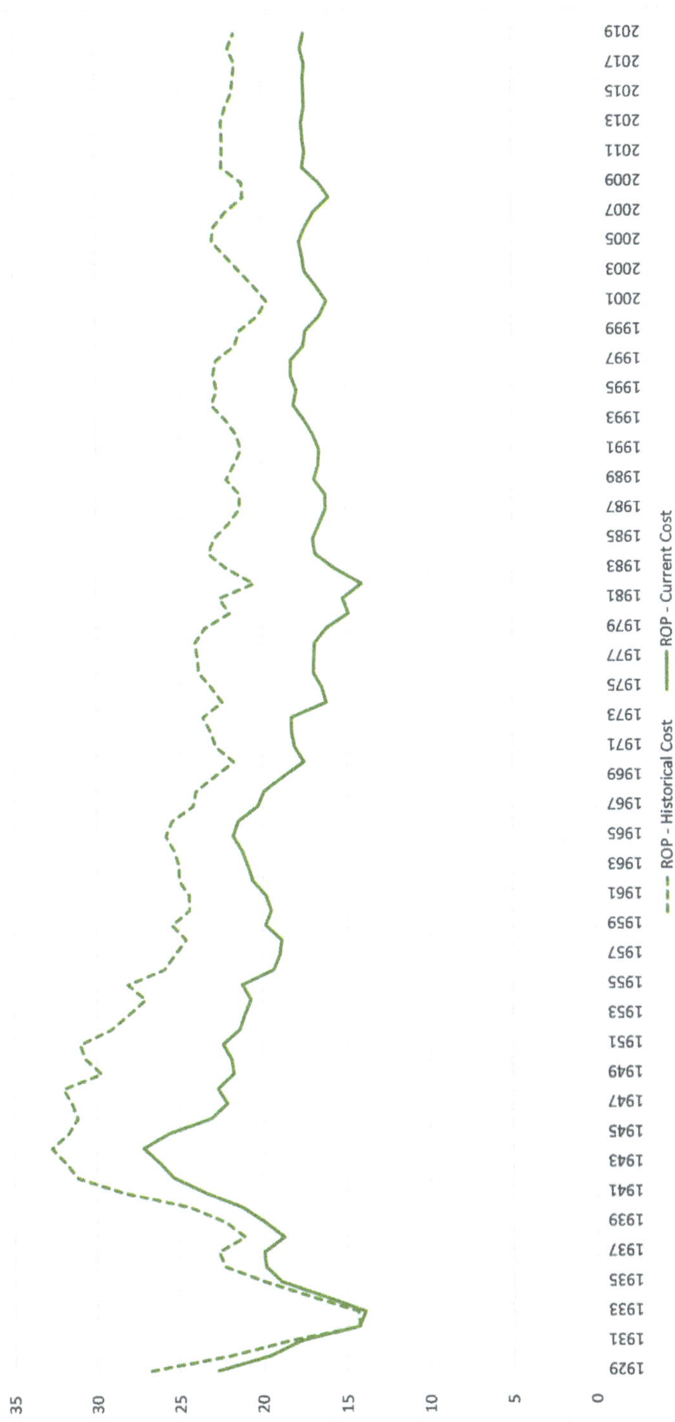

FIGURE 8 US—general rate of profit (%) (Roberts-inspired) (Source: BEA online database (my calculation))

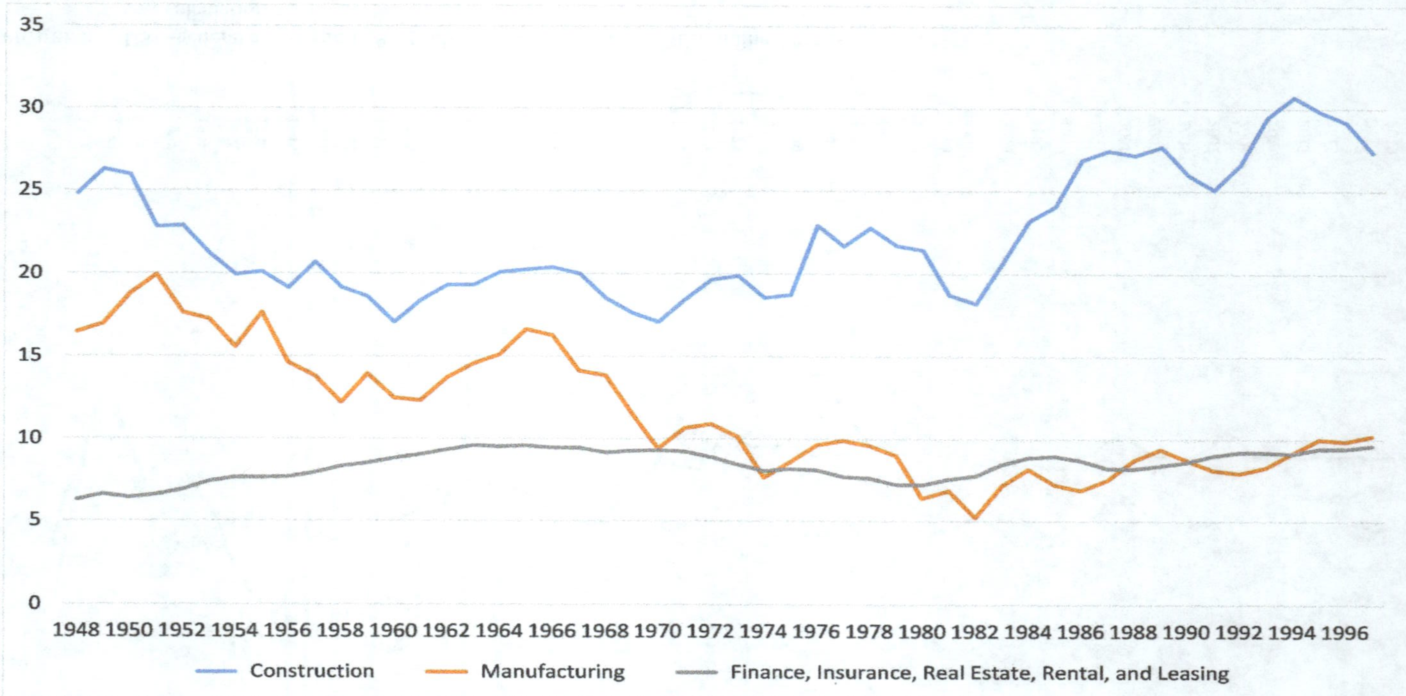

FIGURE 9 US—sectoral rates of profit (Roberts-inspired) (Source: BEA online database (my calculation))

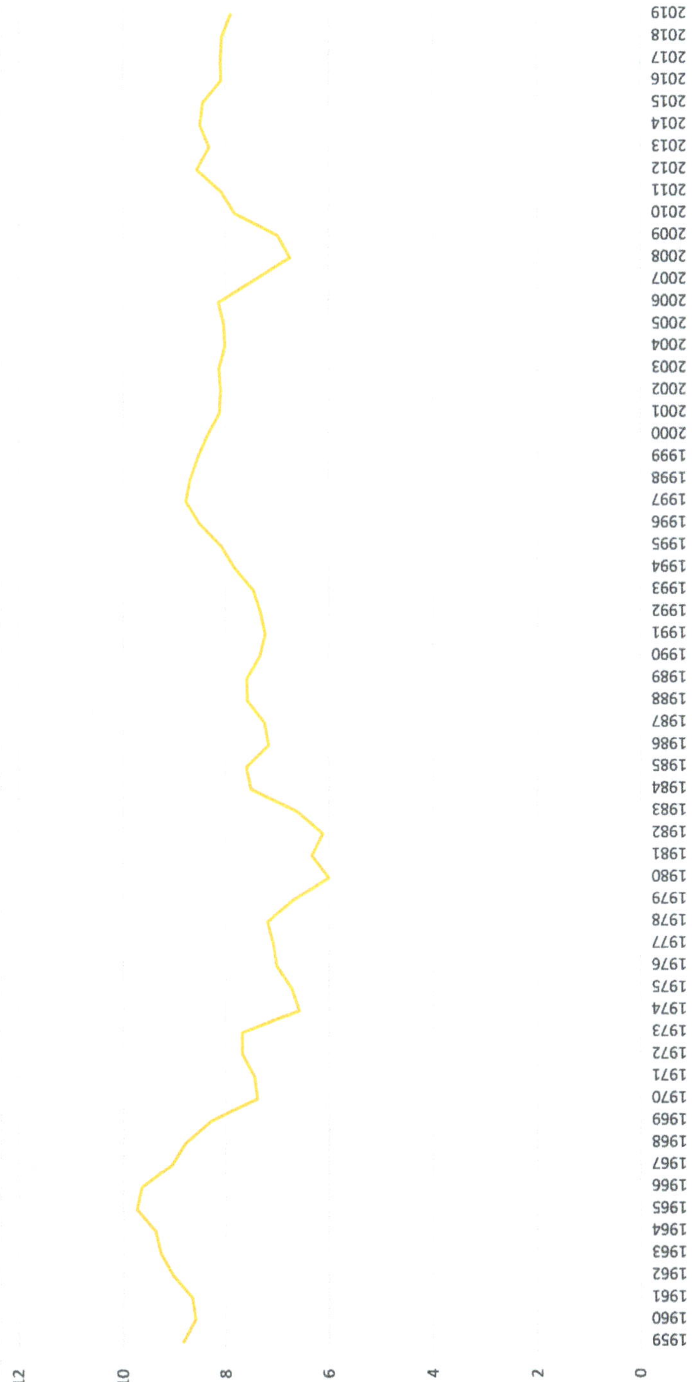

FIGURE 10 US—aggregate rate of profit (Shaikh-inspired) (Source: BEA online database (my calculation))

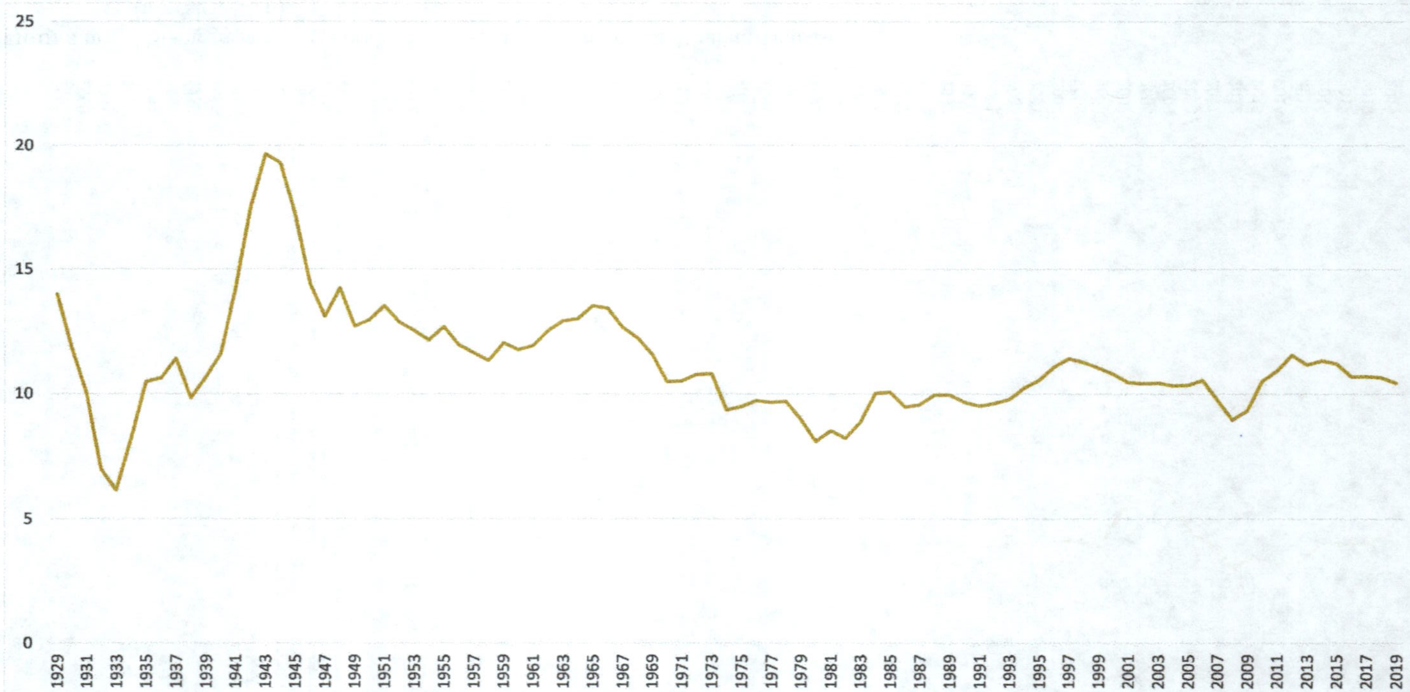

FIGURE 11 US—aggregate rate of profit—private sector (Shaikh-inspired) (Source: BEA online database (my calculation))

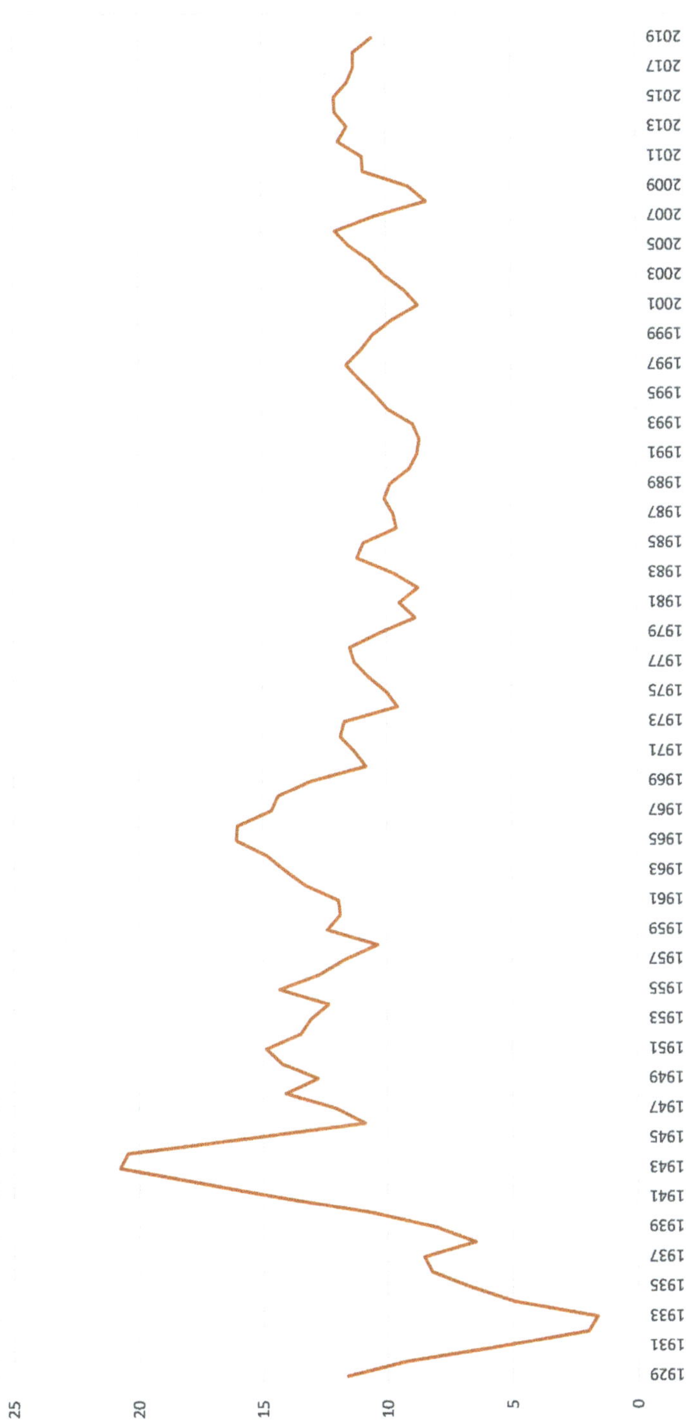

FIGURE 12 US—corporate rate of profit (Shaikh-inspired) (Source: BEA online database (my calculation))

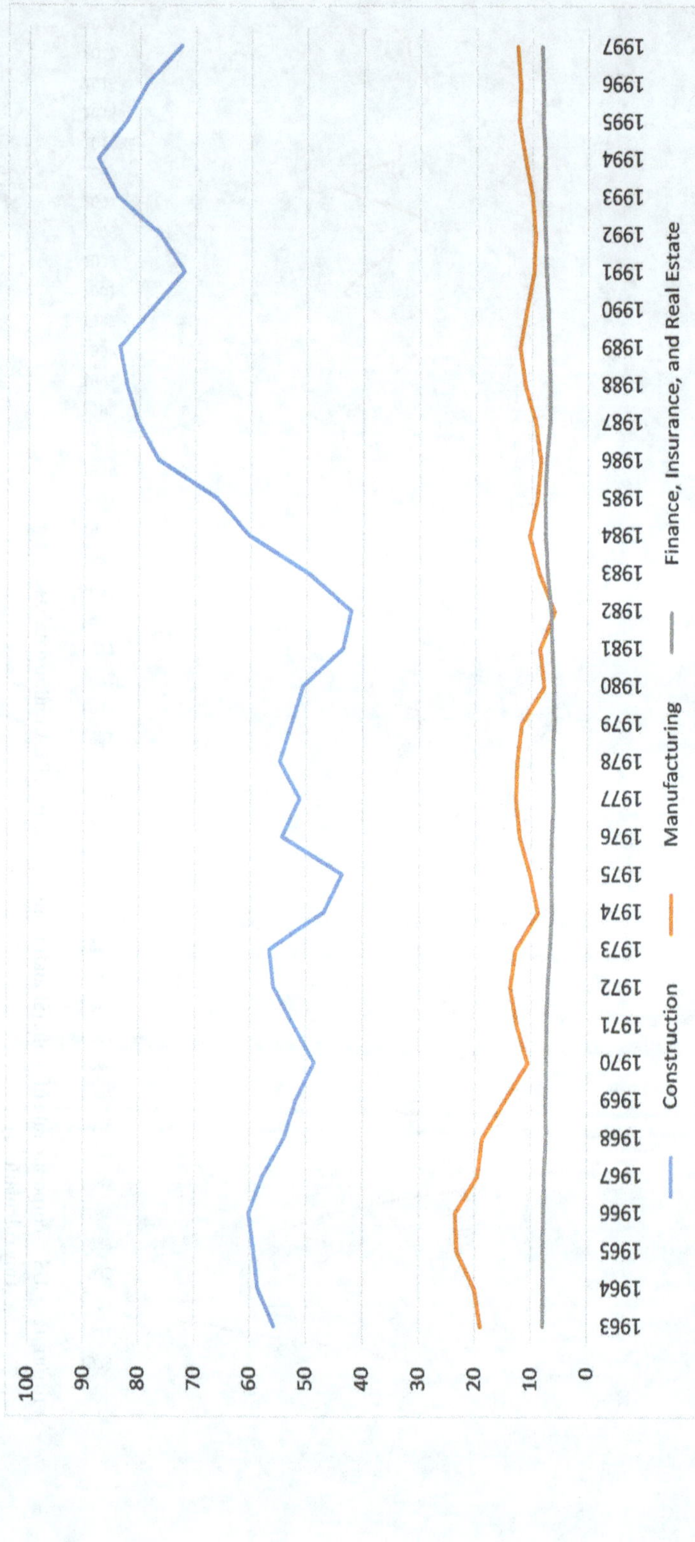

FIGURE 13 US—sectoral rate of profit (%, current costs) (Shaikh-inspired) (Source: BEA online database (my calculation))

production and imports, plus subsidies. Note that, as Shaikh and Tonak (1994) argue, the values of compensation of employees are higher than the values of variable capital (in its traditional Marxian sense). Therefore, the resulting profit rate (calculated with compensation of employees) will be slightly lower than the profit rate calculated with the traditional variable capital; however, the trend remains unchanged.

The calculation method in Figure 13 resembles Kliman's property income indicator. The difference is that Kliman determines his net operating surplus by subtracting taxes on production and imports from this indicator. At the same time, Shaikh considers a similar definition (as Kliman's property income) for net operating surplus. However, there is a discrepancy between the two definitions of NIPA's net operating surplus and Kliman's property income, even though their patterns are similar. Shaikh's preferred measure of profit is operating surplus, which he (2015, 125) states is NIPA's equivalent of classical surplus value in monetary form. Now, suppose we define profit as the net operating surplus (i.e., gross operating surplus minus depreciation of private fixed assets in current costs) and divide it by the current cost of the net stock of private fixed assets. In that case, we get (Figure 14).

The excess profit in the construction sector, as shown in Figure 14, determines the macro-level rate and ceiling of land rents.[3] Harvey does not ignore the difference between sectoral rates of return (or differential inter-sectoral profitability). However, he believes that excess sectoral profits result from monopolistic excess returns. He interprets monopolistic excess returns as the source of land rent, attributes the rent level to the (monopoly) power of the landlord class, and sees this as the driver of the transition to the secondary circuit of capital to address the overaccumulation crisis (via a spatial fix). Shaikh's approach differs from the equilibrium state implied in Harvey's model (conceptualized as the spatial fix thesis). For Shaikh, the inter-sectoral "movement is a never-ending one, with profit rates always overshooting and undershooting their ever-changing centers of gravity" (ibid. 66). It represents "an average balance achieved only through perpetually offsetting errors" (ibid.). Shaikh calls it "turbulent arbitrage, characterized by recurrent fluctuations, [through which

3 Shaikh and Tonak (1994, 269–270) calculate the magnitude of land rent for real estate and rental sector, indirectly, as gross output of "land-rent component of total rents paid" after subtracting "dealers' commissions on real estate activities" and "direct payments of royalties and land rent" using a proxy of the ratio of land costs to "total sale price of new and existing homes". They (ibid. 268) reckon that land rent accounts for 25–30 percent of total real estate revenues. Their method could be of use for calculating the magnitude of absolute rent in the marginal plot, provided other types of rent are zero, and to analyze geographies of absolute rent in the housing sector. However, this is beyond the scope of the present monograph.

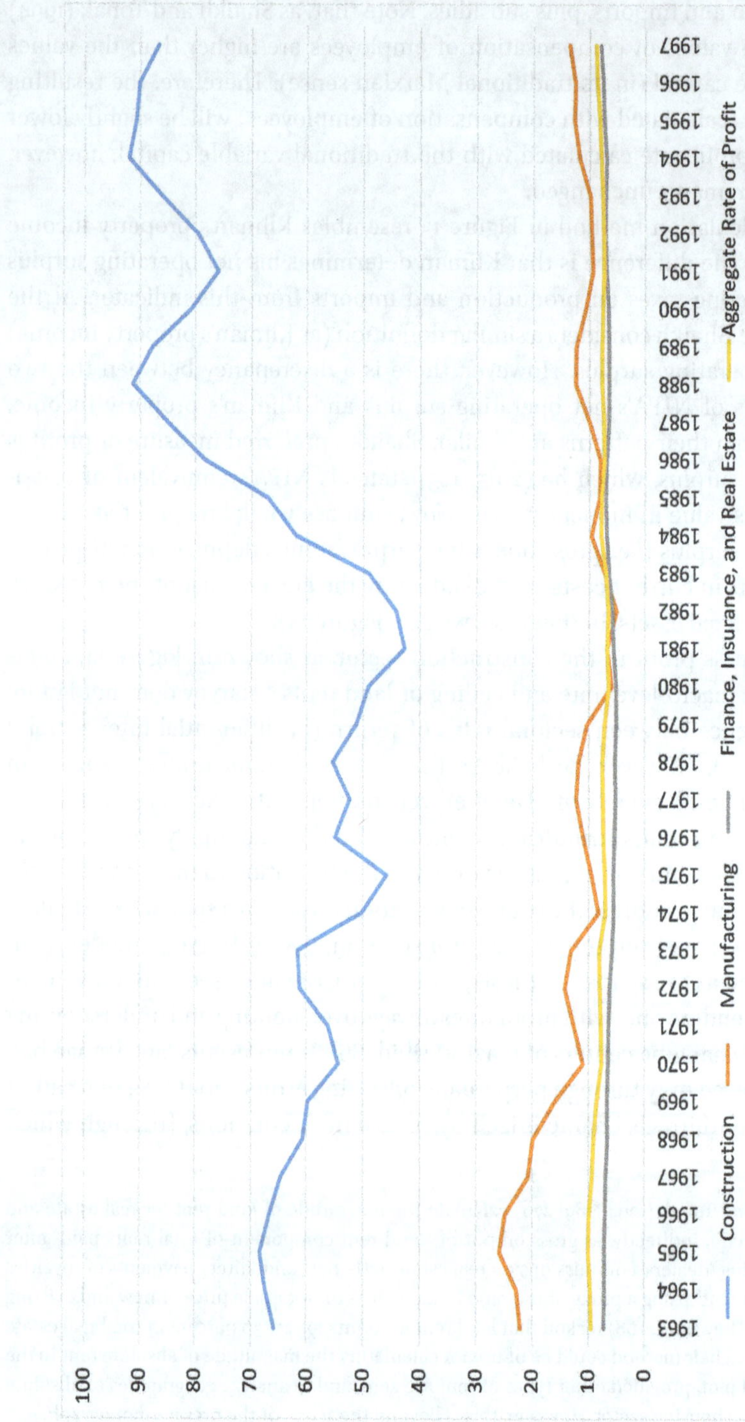

FIGURE 14 US—sectoral rate of profit (Shaikh-inspired) (Source: BEA online database (my calculation))

instead] of a uniform rate of profit, competition actually produces a persistent distribution around the average" (ibid.). More importantly, "because this process is driven by the movement of new capital, the relevant profit rates are those on new investment" (ibid.). Profit rates of new investments are expected to equalize across sectors (ibid.). However, since the capital stock includes capital from various investment periods, "it would not be a useful guide to the future profitability of any investment under current consideration. Current investment (i.e., accumulation) is regulated by the estimated profitability of its future performance" (ibid. 65–66). As we will see in the next section, the profit rates of the most recent investments determine future profit expectations (ibid. 65–66).

4.3 Profit Rates on the Recent Investment and Capital Switching

In such a turbulent competitive environment, according to Shaikh (ibid.), "firms make their decisions about investment in new capacity and new methods of production ... [and] given that profit rates normally fluctuate a great deal from year to year, all new investment must embody a substantial margin of error." His solution is to measure "the incremental rate of return on capital" as gross sectoral profits "divided by gross investment in the previous year" (ibid. 67–68). He (ibid.) emphasizes, "incremental profit rates, unlike average ones, do 'cross over' a great deal, again and again." That could serve as an economic mechanism for Harvey's somewhat abstract and ahistorical case for switching from primary to secondary circuits of capital. Shaikh also argues that incremental profit rates play "a crucial role in explaining the movements of stock and bond prices, and hence in those of interest rates" (ibid. 68). He calculates incremental profit rates as gross profit divided by lagged gross investment (ibid. 857). To determine gross profits for the 1970s, I used NIPA's gross operating surplus, which includes all types of income (including wages) as profit-type income. I limited my calculation to gross operating surplus because the impact of employment types on the overall trend is not significant. Shaikh uses historical cost investment in fixed private assets for gross investment, scaled up with the quantity index. The results for a selection of industries are shown in Figures 15 and 16. As seen, investors tend to switch as expected profit rates fluctuate, including rising incremental profits in the construction sector compared to manufacturing in the 1970s. The figures also reveal that, in retrospect, the construction sector was not the only destination for investment, as other industries also benefited from capital switching. It is also notable that profits

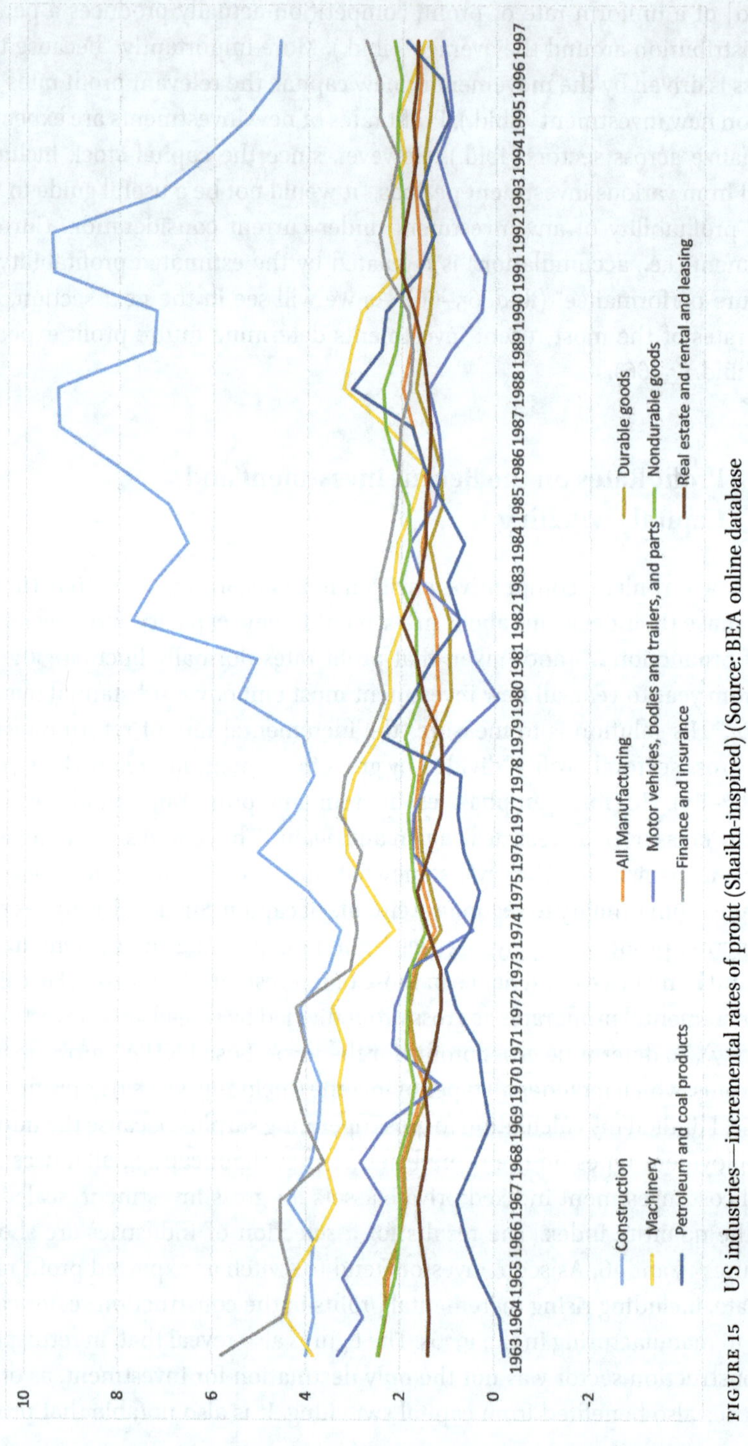

FIGURE 15 US industries—incremental rates of profit (Shaikh-inspired) (Source: BEA online database (my calculation))

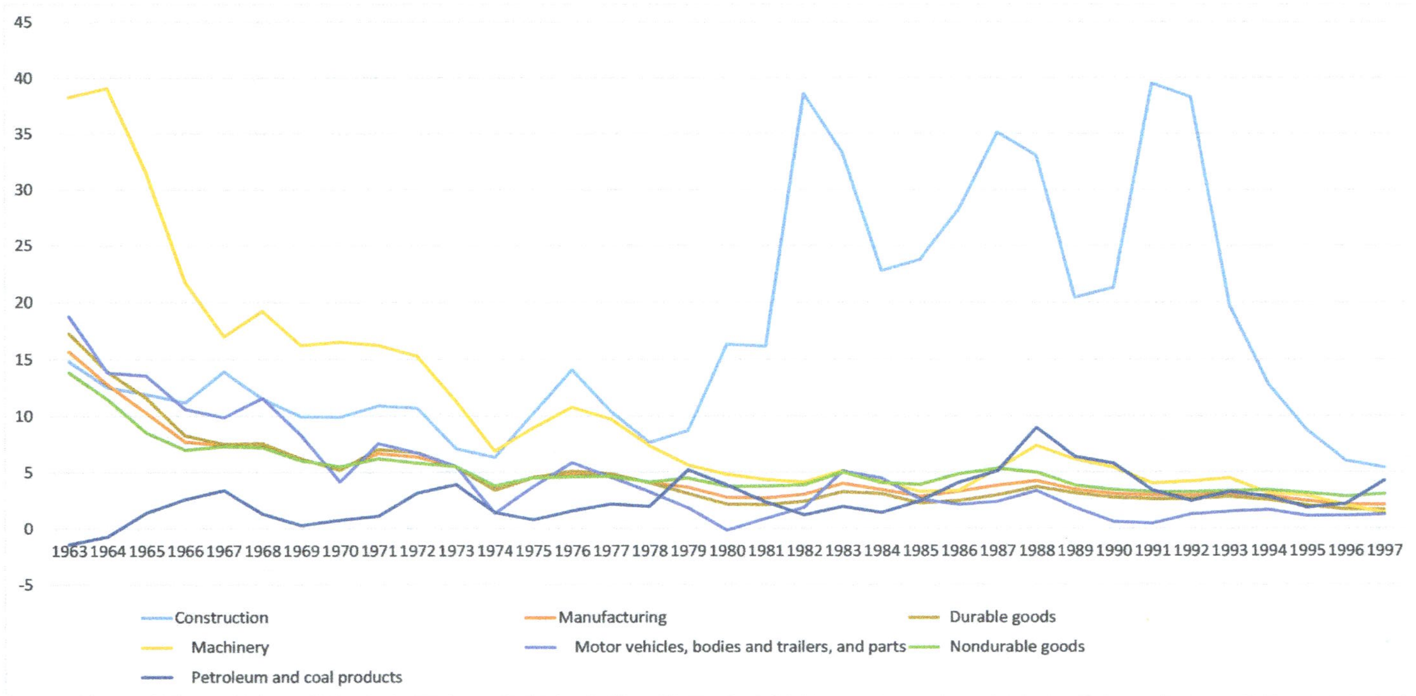

FIGURE 16 US industries—incremental rates of profit (Shaikh-inspired)—simplified (Source: BEA online database (my calculation))

in finance and insurance began to decline below profits in construction in the early 1970s, making Harvey's presumption that the financial sector dominated and shaped investment in fixed space even more historically and geographically contingent.

Now, excluding different branches of the manufacturing sector, we have (Figure 17). It shows that when Harvey conducted his study in the early 1970s, the construction and financial sectors dominated the competition. However, finance soon lagged behind the construction sector.

All three methods and definitions show similar patterns in the historical changes of profit rates (see Figures 5–17). I slightly prefer Shaikh's definition for a few reasons. His main difference from Kliman is that Kliman uses historical costs, while Shaikh uses current costs. Both argue that the net operating surplus is a more comprehensive indicator of corporate profits, although Kliman defines it differently. Kliman does not deny that the NIPA net operating surplus could also apply to more specific profit types. For my purpose, however, the comprehensive nature of property income is advantageous. Shaikh's net operating surplus, calculated as gross value added minus compensation and depreciation, appears similar to Kliman's property income. The key difference is that Shaikh's gross operating surplus (which he interprets as gross surplus value) is computed as gross value added minus compensation. Regarding the use of historical or current costs, I contend that Kliman's definition aligns with my argument about the transformation problem, which I borrowed from Kliman (see Chapter 10). Kliman's and Shaikh's definitions differ from Roberts's because Roberts favors general profit rates; hence, he uses GNI/GNP with a capital consumption adjustment, whereas Kliman and Shaikh prefer specific corporate or private rates. Kliman and Shaikh's approach is closer to my analytical focus here. Additionally, as Roberts notes, including compensations in the denominator would not significantly alter the trend, as its effect is minimal. Shaikh's calculations align with his concept of incremental profit rates—an alternative to Keynes' marginal efficiency of capital—that reveal shifts in investment and recent capital mobility. His analysis of incremental rates also supports his theory of real competition, which underpins the TILR (see Chapter 10). All three approaches show a long-term decline in the overall profit rate and manufacturing sector profitability since the mid-1960s. Kliman's figures indicate a slight recovery in the 1970s; however, this does not alter the overall downward trend.

Harvey's data depends on current cost measures of only one segment of returns, namely transfer payments. As demonstrated by the three methods, transfer payments are an inadequate indicator of rates of return, whether aggregate or sectoral. It might be said that Harvey's use of transfer payments is not

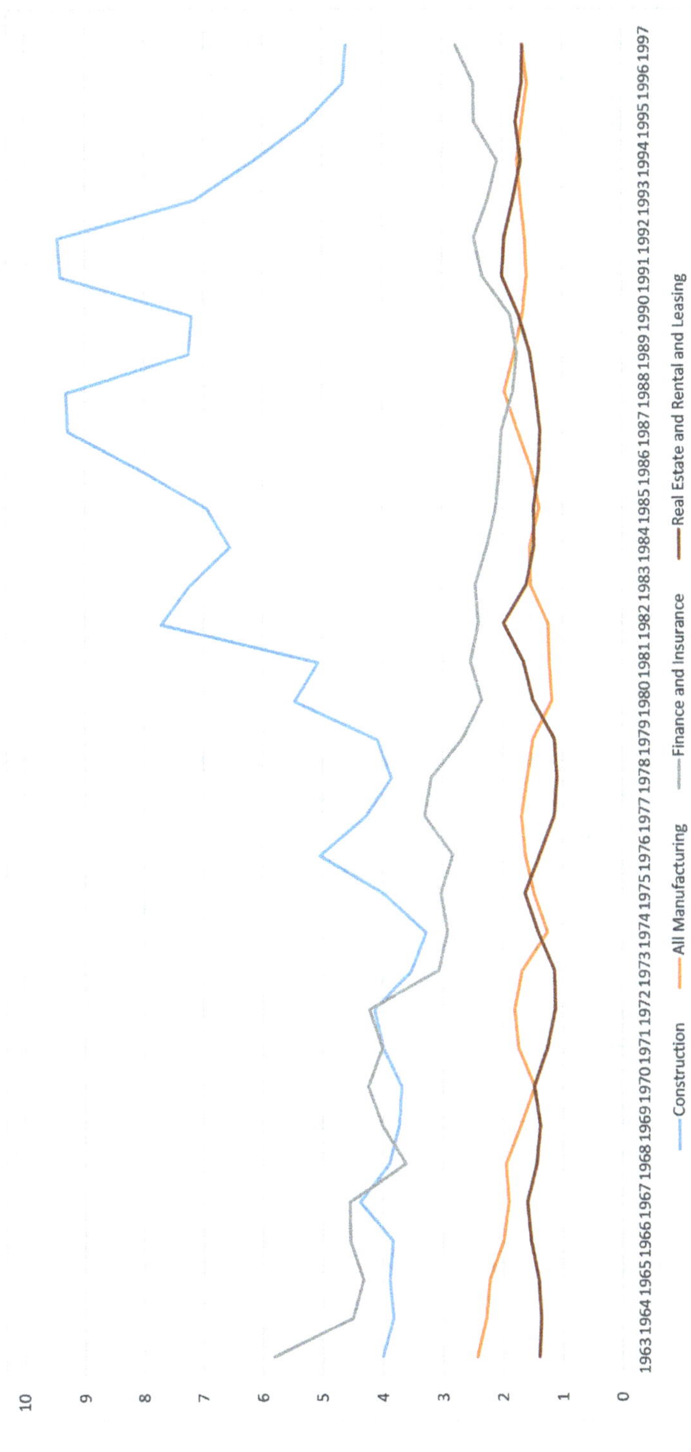

FIGURE 17 US industries—incremental rates of profit (Shaikh-inspired) (Source: BEA online database (my calculation))

meant to be taken literally as an indicator. Nevertheless, a critical question (an empirical anomaly) remains unanswered: how could transfer payments—or any other micro-level, isolated indicator of profit—indicate capital switching, which is central to the SMLR? Furthermore, Harvey does not explain the economic drivers behind higher returns in housing as the cause of rising rents; instead, he attributes rent levels to the power of the landlord class to impose monopoly prices. These measurements are crucial for a consistently endogenous, structurally and historically conscious analysis of rent creation, appropriation, and capital switching. Without these measurements, such processes are seen as exogenous influences stemming from monopoly and power relations within the SMLR. Regardless, it is likely that Harvey observed a steady increase in non-farm proprietors' income relative to a sharp rise in dividends, interest, and rent. He might have interpreted this disproportionate change as an indication of escalating monopolistic price-gouging in Baltimore's property markets (Figure 18). More importantly, the TILR underscores the historical contingency involved in land rent creation. As the study of profit rates reveals, the influence of rent is either minimized or maximized at specific periods, depending on competitive relations with the manufacturing sector and varying inter-sectoral profitability. I will return to this point in Chapters 5 and 7.

One important aspect of Marx's original explanation for the rise of absolute rent is the lower organic composition of capital (the capital-wages ratio indicating sectoral productivity) in rent-bearing sectors. The conceptual importance of this assumption for the urban land sector has often been debated since the 1970s. However, I argue that this is a matter for empirical analysis rather than a purely conceptual debate. The sectoral organic composition of capital (measured as the net stock of private fixed capital divided by the compensation of employees in each sector) shows (Figure 19) that, first, as Marx explained, it is a historical process that depends on the context (such as differential profitability and technological development). Second, as profit rates in the manufacturing sector started to decline, investment in the construction sector's constant capital (the net stock of fixed capital) slowed, as the rent component in the sectoral rate of return became more influential. Moreover, this process should be understood in light of technological advancements (notably information and communication technology) that began in the 1970s. It also reflects the rising costs of constant capital over time, especially in the 1990s, for manufacturing and information, communication technologies (ICTs), which contributed to declining profitability and the onset of the Great Recession (see, e.g., Jones 2021; Kliman 2012; Roberts 2016c; Shaikh 2011; 2016).

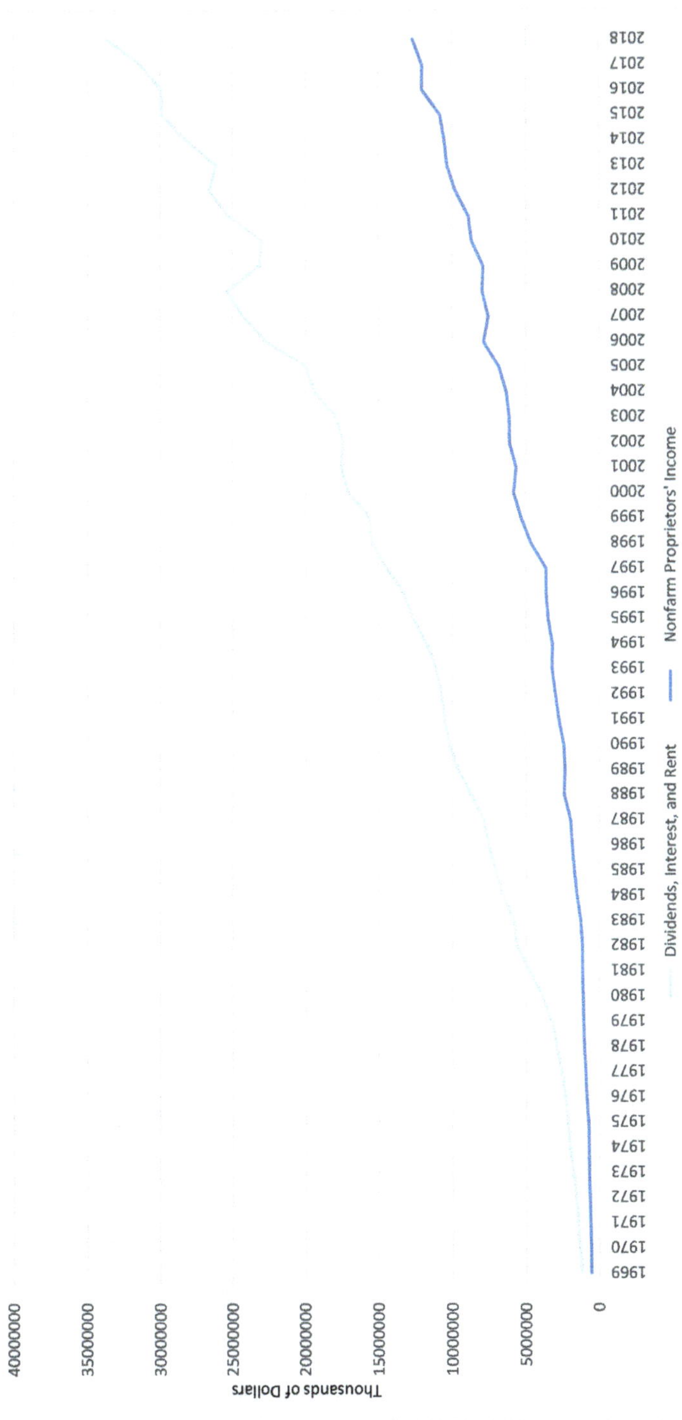

FIGURE 18 Baltimore metropolitan area business income (Source: BEA online database (my calculation))

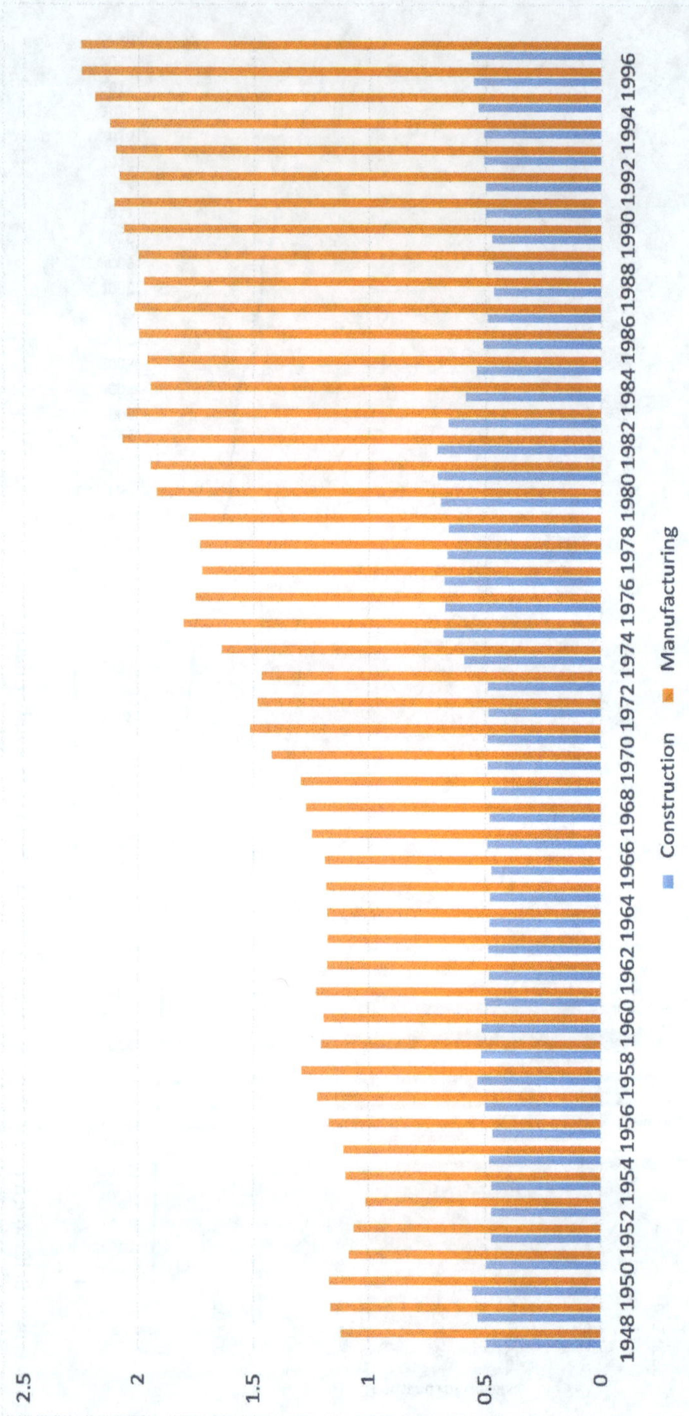

FIGURE 19 US—sectoral organic composition of capital (Source: BEA online database (my calculation))

4.4 From Macro to Micro

The data presented and trends analyzed so far operate at the national level. However, it is still necessary to explain micro- and local-level mechanisms and processes, along with how they are influenced and managed by national-level drivers. Harvey's empirical material provides only limited insights, as his starting points differ. A key empirical difference is that, beyond construction and building activity, Harvey (1974a; 1978; 1989) does not really focus on the construction sector, a point also criticized by Beauregard (1994). According to Beauregard (1994), Harvey does not support his data on construction activity and related phenomena with empirical evidence for overaccumulation. To supplement Harvey, I paid closer attention to construction data for two main reasons. First, from an analytical perspective, construction represents productive activity on land. This explains why the return on investment in construction, especially when the developer also owns the land, could reflect land rent. Second, as shown in Figures 20, 21, 22, and 23, most constructions are private, and a significant portion of the total constructions are dedicated to residential buildings.

The TILR provides alternative analytical tools to measure and explain rent rates, ceilings, magnitudes, and capital switching, not by referencing monopolistic power relations, but through turbulent inter-sectoral competition. The differential inter-sectoral profitability determines the rate and ceiling of land rent at the whole-economy level. The TILR analyzes this process using the concept of absolute rent, which establishes a structural relationship between the dynamics of investment in urban space and those of productive capital. As Shaikh and Tonak (1994) point out, although it is conceptually important to distinguish between royalty payments on land (as land rents) and building rents, it is not easy to do so empirically. The differential inter-sectoral rates of return determine whether land rents can emerge at a given time and place on a macro level (indicating the presence of absolute rent). The existence of absolute rent accelerates investment, especially in new construction. As Figure 21 shows, investment in new housing units (part of overall new construction investments) follows a cyclical pattern. It aligns with rising incremental profit rates in the national construction sector during the 1970s (an increase in the early 1970s, a slight recession in the mid-1970s, then an increase again). However, these macro-level trends alone do not explain the extent of land rent at the micro-level. The micro-level magnitude of land rent should be analyzed in relation to local investment opportunities (see Footnote 3 above). In housing, differential rent I and II account for potential rent levels for each investment in apartment buildings (or single-family homes). Their influence

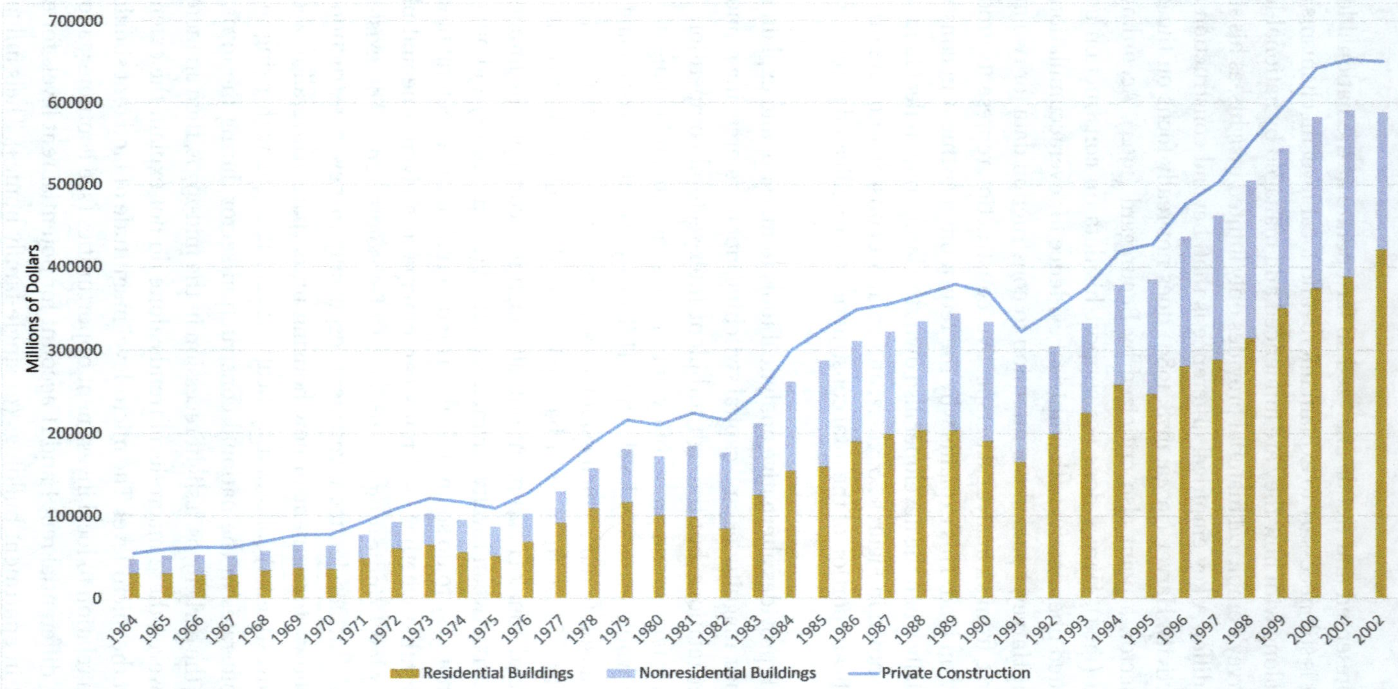

FIGURE 20 US—annual value of construction put in place, current US dollars (Source: Census Bureau (my calculation))

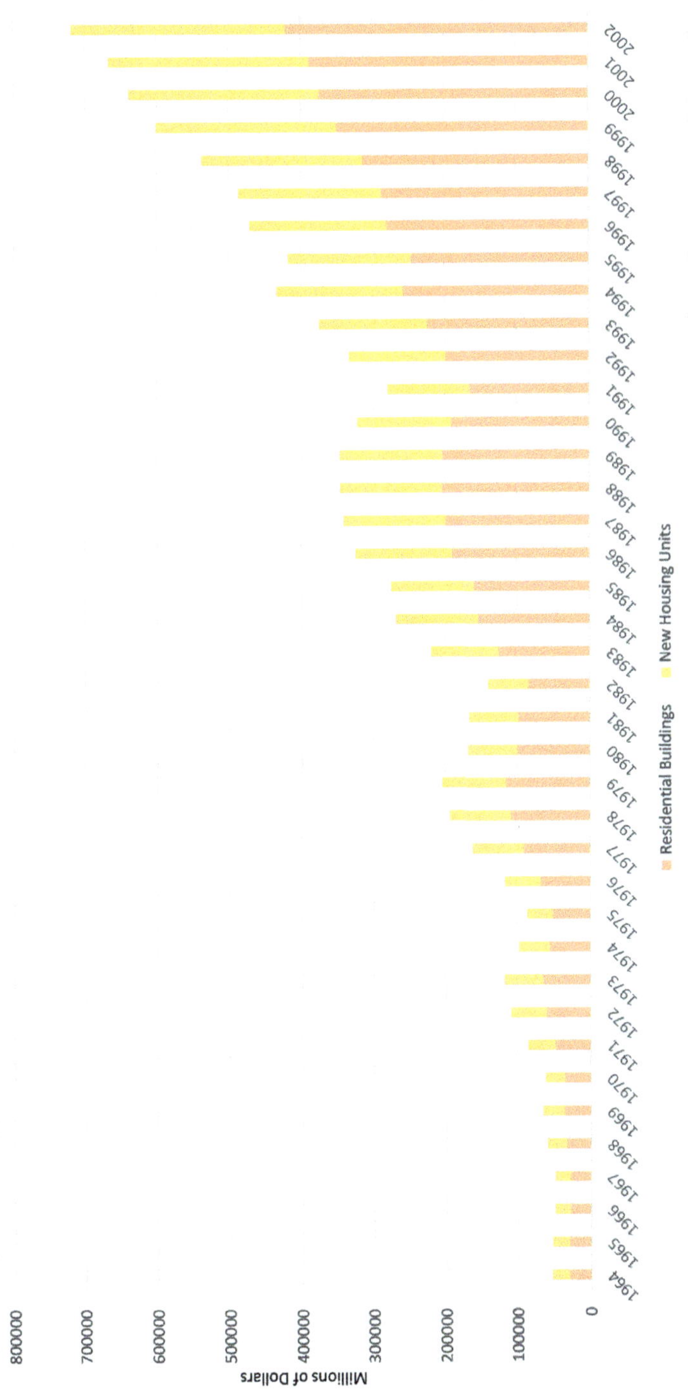

FIGURE 21 US—annual value of construction put in place, current US dollars (Source: Census Bureau (my calculation))

FIGURE 22 US—annual value of construction put in place, current US dollars (Source: Census Bureau (my calculation))

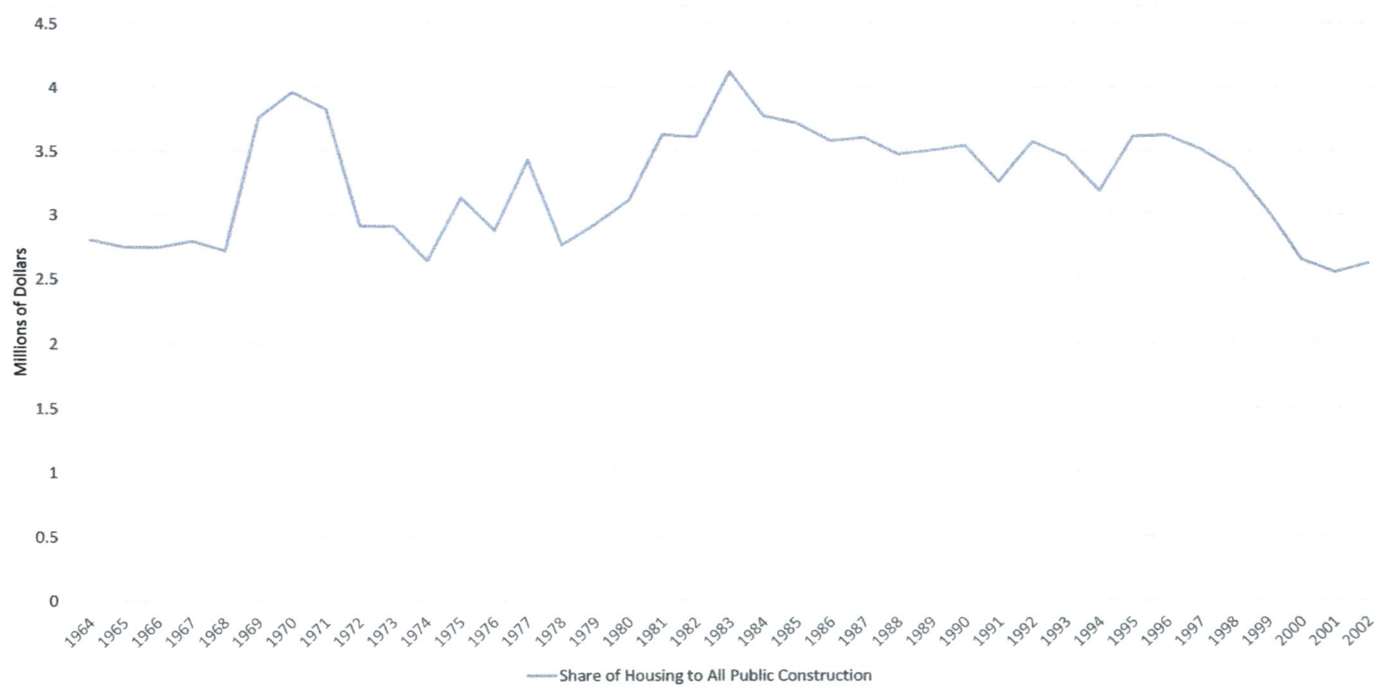

FIGURE 23 US—annual value of construction put in place, current US dollars (Source: Census Bureau (my calculation))

depends on the overall sector-level land rent (which I will revisit in Chapter 6). The value of apartment units is set at the micro level (i.e., price) and partly determined by supply and demand (see Shaikh 2008). This makes them susceptible to financial and speculative practices, especially when mortgage interest rates are low, as in the wake of monetary policies such as quantitative easing implemented by many OECD countries, including the United States and Sweden, after the Great Recession. Harvey's material is insufficient for understanding common investment strategies and practices among local developers regarding differential rents I and II (see also Bruegel 1975; Edel 1992). His case study needs additional data to show whether active individual investors in the market could overcome, for example, racial stigmatizations (which he and Chatterjee (1974, 24) refer to as "neighborhood biases") through more focused investment in the area (potentially leading to gentrification) (via differential rent II) or by acquiring more blocks (via differential rent I). Such an analysis requires field-based qualitative data collection, which should have been done at that time. Therefore, I can only conceptualize these as building blocks for future research. However, if he and Chatterjee had gathered such data, it would have been possible to identify specific practices of Baltimore's local developers in the early 1970s aimed at generating excess profits in the housing market through land rent appropriation, a process enabled nationwide by the declining profitability of the manufacturing sector. In the subsequent four chapters, I will operationalize the TILR at both the national and city levels for cases in the Swedish and Iranian economies.

CHAPTER 5

Swedish Municipal Site Leasehold: Capital Switching and Land Policy

In this chapter, I analyze the historical contingency of capital switching, the mediation of land rent, and their relational dynamics with aggregate and sectoral economic crises, all of which help explain the necessary context upon which the Swedish land policy, more specifically, its central instrument, Municipal Site Leasehold—a lease agreement between municipalities and developers over the right to build on municipal owned land plots—was revised and modified.[1] I have two reasons for choosing Sweden. First, Sweden experienced a rapid transformation from a primarily public land regime to a generally private one since the 1980s. Second, Sweden has historically experienced a relatively successful municipalized land model, which, interestingly, includes many exceptions and agential conflicts. As noted in Chapter 1, Harvey's capital switching thesis continues its powerful influence on social and economic geographers who aim to explain the structural determinants of investment flows on urban land and the built environment (Beauregard 1994; Castree and Christophers 2018; Charney 2001; Ekers and Prudham 2017; Kutz 2016; Webber et al. 2022; Yrigoy 2023). The thesis, in a nutshell, addresses the tendency of capital to switch from productive investments to investments in built environments. This tendency, according to the thesis, is triggered by the overaccumulation crisis but allows for the slow absorption of surplus capital and for potential recovery from it.

One crucial contextual transformation to note, as noted earlier, is the underlying regulatory regime, neoliberalism, which Harvey presumed for the switching of capital and is now under severe scrutiny (Alami 2023; Alami and Dixon 2024). In this chapter, I propose an alternative interpretation of Harvey's thesis, grounded in the TILR's core assumptions, to address the existing gaps and silences in the literature, highlight its continued explanatory value, and liberate it from Harvey's overly specific contextualization. To do so, I revisit the historical case of the discontinuation of Municipal Site Leasehold and explain how inter-sectoral capital switching contributed to the transformation of the policy. Harvey notoriously offered limited empirical support for the thesis

1 The chapter encompasses a summary of my article (Farahani 2025) on the discontinuation of Swedish Municipal Site Leasehold in the mid-to-late 1980s.

and provided only illustrative examples based on long waves of construction activity (Beauregard 1994; Christophers 2011; King 1989a). Interestingly, as noted in Chapter 1, the empirical evidence offered by subsequent scholars persists as unconvincing. Except for King (1989a), these scholars a) leave out the mediation of land rent in the process of capital switching, b) specifically, in the case of Christophers (2011) and Rutland (2010), reversed the chain of causality in the thesis in its original conceptualization (from overaccumulation to the switching), c) "fail to relate capital switching to (productive) profit rate cycles and the general rate of profit" (Farahani 2025, 5). To complement, I aim to address the gaps regarding 1) what causes the switching and 2) how inter-sectoral competition determines the historical contingency of capital switching. Addressing these gaps, in turn, requires modification of Harvey's original conceptualization of the capital switching thesis by "integrating the role of land rent, inter-sectoral competition, and crises of profitability" as outlined in the TILR (ibid. 3).

In addition, Harvey's (2005) view of the Swedish economy as a "circumscribed" neoliberalism faced criticism from scholars who argued that the shift to neoliberalism, which gained momentum in the late 1980s, was partly influenced by the transformation of Swedish land policy and notably in the housing sector, both of which Harvey's assessment overlooked (Clark and Heddin 2009; Lund Hansen et al. 2015). Municipal Site Leasehold was identified as the main policy instrument and driving force behind Swedish land policy in the 1960s and 1970s (Caesar 2016; Clark and Runesson 1996; Duncan 1985; Olsson 2018; Passow 1970; Ratzka 1981). Its beneficial distributional effects on the housing market earned Swedish housing policy during this period the label of a social democratic "success story" (Lundqvist et al. 1990; Pries 2022; Tomasson 1969). Municipal Site Leasehold is not unique to Sweden; similar policies exist in the Netherlands, Australia, and Singapore (Clark and Gullberg 1991; Haila 2015; Neutze 1989; Olsson 2018). However, what makes the Swedish version particularly interesting is the rapid transformation of Municipal Site Leasehold into a market-oriented and neoliberal land regime beginning in the mid-to-late 1980s, a change seen as a key event in the broader neoliberalization of the Swedish economy (Clark and Hedin 2009). Here, I argue that a modified version of Harvey's thesis, using the TILR, could help explain this transition.

Shaikh's theory of real competition,[2] elaborated in Chapter 10 below, and his interpretation of Marx's analyses of relative prices, competition, capital

2 Shaikh's work oddly remains marginal in the field of geography. The rare exceptions are Campling (2025), Berry (2023), and Barbesgaard et al. (2024). Christophers (2024, 136)

mobility, and profit cycles in Capital, Volume Three, informs my analysis and suggestion to modify Harvey's capital switching thesis. As noted in Chapter 1, Harvey builds his thesis on two foundations: a) Lefebvre's (2003 [1970]) thesis (primacy of urbanization in post-war capitalism), and b) his geographical reinterpretation of Marx's notion of the movement of capital to equalize the rate of profit in Capital, Volume Three. His reinterpretation, while innovative, has one crucial drawback: it made the notion of capital switching "too specific (limited to overaccumulation crisis, monopolistic competition, and neoliberal regulatory context)" (Farahani 2025, 4). Harvey was subsequently criticized for his functionalistic approach toward the flow of capital into urban space (Anderson 2014; Barnes 1994; Castree 1995; King 1989a). Such critiques, however, "fail to distinguish between the explanatory merits of the capital switching thesis and Harvey's relatively limited contextualization" (Farahani 2025, 4). Shaikh's theory, and specifically, his notion of incremental rate of profit (introduced in Chapters 1 and 4 above), is crucial in broadening the scope of Harvey's thesis to incorporate other types of economic crisis and "to make it sensitive to the temporal rhythms of switching to the built environment, as well as other sectors" (ibid. 5). The underlying assumption is that capital moves to the built environment only if it is relatively more profitable, and that potential profitability is neither inherent nor guaranteed in this sector. It will be subject to regular inter-sectoral competition.

Similarly, I rely on the structural approach to urban land rent (Bruegel 1975; Edel 1992; Feldman 2017; Flamant 2021; Kerr 1996; Manning 2023; Murray 1977) as outlined in the TILR, which assumes "land rent rates are determined by competitive dynamics within and between sectors that equalize rent rates at the plot and whole-economy levels" (Farahani 2025, 5). Land rent rates contribute to the total sectoral rate of return. These rates matter because they reflect investor expectations. Sectoral rates of return influence sectoral investment rates, which in turn drive sectoral growth rates (Kliman 2012; Roberts 2019; 2021b; Shaikh 1998; 2016; Tapia 2018). Land rent manifests in two ways, depending on the type of land ownership: a) as excess profit for landowning (mostly large) capitalist investors, and b) as land costs for those capitalists who do not

finally recognized the relevance of Shaikh's work in 2024. He writes "the economic key for renewables in winning out against fossil fuels" lies in fossil fuel investments, indicating higher expected profits, as capitalists must "foresee profitability" to invest. However, this recognition was limited to a) the validity of the notion of profit, which should have already been clear, and b) the field of renewable energy transitions, not urban issues—particularly housing—where he still depends on Harvey and post-Keynesian theories.

own the land. In this view, land rent mediates "the macro dynamics of capital accumulation and micro-foundations of housing provision" (ibid. also, Moreno Zacarés 2024, 2). Importantly, as noted in Chapter 2, the macro-level concept of rent in Marx's theory—namely, absolute rent, which signals "above-normal rates of return in rent-bearing sectors" (Farahani 2025, 5)—is overlooked by urban economic geographers following Harvey and his SMLR model (Anderson 2014; 2019; Anderson et al. 2024; Bradley 2023; Charnock et al. 2014; Park 2014; 2023; Swyngedouw and Ward 2022). Harvey's concept of class-monopoly rent replaces it, representing "a microeconomic interpretation of rent as an excess monopoly price" created by market imperfections and landlords artificially keeping dwellings vacant (Farahani 2025, 5).

Land rent is also pivotal for inter-sectoral competition that determines the extent and direction of capital switching. This is because "the return on investment in built environments (from a production perspective) is partially levied by landowners (or landowning capitalists) in the construction sector in the form of land rent" (ibid.). Due to its generally labor-intensive character, the net capital stock and, consequently, the capital cost-labor cost ratio (i.e., organic composition of capital) are generally lower in the construction sector. The sector's "temporal above-normal rates of return in the construction sector … can be attributed to its double feature as a rent-bearing (land rent component of total returns) and (generally) labor-intensive sector (absolute surplus value component of total returns)" (ibid.). Figure 24[3] shows the organic composition of capital for manufacturing and construction in Sweden, from 1993 to 2018. It is calculated as net capital stock divided by compensation of employees. The data are limited to 1993–2018 because Sweden's capital stock data are only available from 1993 (Wolf 1997).

The case of Swedish Municipal Site Leasehold is significant to the overall argument here because: "First, it highlights a major economic crisis (profitability and productivity) peculiar to the Swedish economy, although not necessarily exceptional to the overall tendency. Second, it underscores an inter-sectoral dimension (and associated institutional tensions with implications for capital mobility) that the capital switching thesis did not anticipate (in Harvey's original formulation or later developments). Third, it illustrates that capital flows follow a more turbulent and historically contingent pattern, shaped by inter-sectoral dynamics" (Farahani 2025, 2). In Sweden, in the mid-to-late 1980s, "capital likely flowed from the manufacturing sector to other

3 I used official data (e.g., SCB, OECD, CBT) for all figures in this chapter, mainly with my calculations. To avoid repetition, I present the detailed description of the sources (with tables, lines, etc.) in Appendix 3.2.

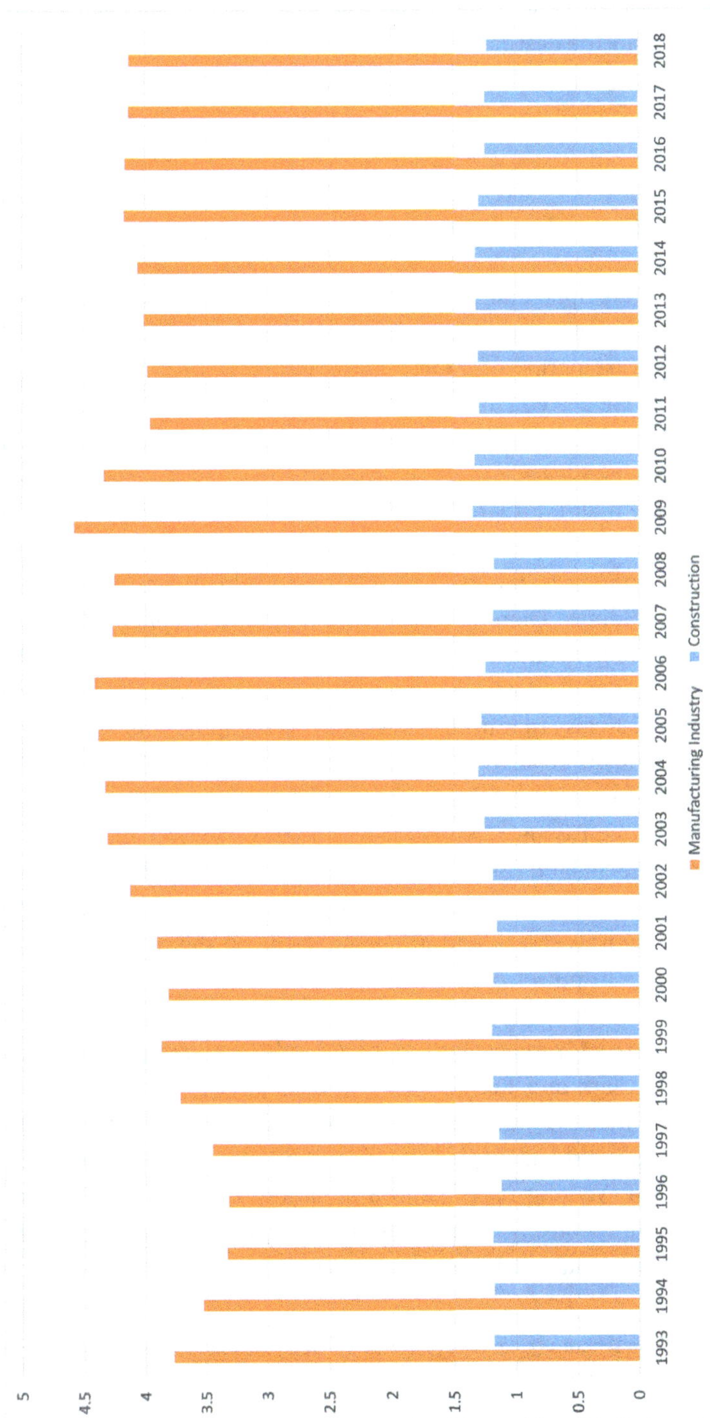

FIGURE 24 Swedish sectoral organic composition of capital 1993–2018 (Source: SCB online database (my calculation))

sectors in pursuit of higher profit rates; however, (a) the built environment was not necessarily the destination, and (b) mobility was not merely limited to absorbing surplus capital" (Farahani 2025, 3).

5.1 Municipal Site Leasehold and Its Macroeconomic and Institutional Tensions[4]

The Swedish Municipal Site Leasehold is a lease agreement between a municipality and a private developer that grants the rights "to use and build on" a site for a lease period of 26 to 100 years in exchange for an annual fee (Boverket 2022). The fee was initially fixed for the entire lease period, but later reforms in 1954 and 1967 established 20-year and then 10-year revision intervals for newly signed lease contracts (Boverket 2007, 68; Runesson 1997, 11). The municipality maintains land ownership rights and claims on increases in land value (partly reflected in leasehold fees and re-evaluated between payments). At the same time, the leaseholder retains rights to land use and ownership of the buildings. Therefore, it is considered a form of municipal land banking (Boverket 2022; Ratzka 1981). The policy instrument and its underlying municipalization strategy were initially introduced in 1907 with backing from the capitalist class to limit the effects of "geographic spillovers" (higher property values due to relative locational advantage) and land rents (as a portion of total returns on capital) to promote perfect competition (Clark and Runesson 1996, 204; Passow 1970; Swenson 2002). This was achieved by redirecting increments in land values to municipalities (Clark and Runesson 1996; Duncan 1986; Olsson 2018). In turn, developers obtained rights to land use and building disposals (Clark and Runesson 1996). In the 1940s, social democrats (who were in power continuously from 1932 to 1976, and again from 1982 to 1991) shifted the policy to systematically use municipal proceeds from land value increases for redistribution, partly aided by the 1947 Building Act (Boverket 2023; Clark and Runesson 1996; Misgeld et al. 1992; Olsson 2018; Ödmann 1973). Since 1967, under pressure from social democrats, a series of policies were proposed and implemented as Land Stipulations (*Markvilkoret*) from 1974 to 1991 (Vedung 1993). Land Stipulation, regarded as essential for the central state's housing loan system (*Markförvärvslånefonden*), urged municipalities to engage actively in urban land markets, obtain urban land

4 The following two sections (5.1 and 5.2) have been largely reproduced from Farahani (2025) with minor modifications.

through the state loan system, and lease it to private developers via Municipal Site Leasehold (Boverket 2007; Vedung 1993). However, because land values remained market-driven, most inner-city land plots were deemed too expensive for municipalities to purchase (Vedung 1993), which contributed to uneven effects of Municipal Site Leasehold on the overall land markets, potentially causing institutional tensions.

Beyond the potential allocation of municipal returns from Municipal Site Leasehold for welfare spending, the policy instrument helped municipalities control "the distribution of development gains and increments in land value" (Clark and Runessson 1997, 204). The policy also allowed municipalities to retain a planning monopoly (*Kommunalt Planmonopol*) (Clark and Gullberg 1991). However, municipalities had limited control over "the distribution of land uses over space, [and] the distribution of building and property rights among presumptive developers and users" (Clark and Runesson 1996, 204). The Municipal Site Leasehold policy also empowered municipalities' productive capacities in housing provision (Olsson 2018), evident during the massive public initiative for social democrats' "state-led housing production" (Olsson 2018, 636), including the Million Program (1965–1974) encompassing low-income, multi-dwelling, rental projects across the country (Blücher, 2006; Duncan 1986; 1989; Hall and Vidén 2005; Hård 2010). Increments in land value were central to municipalities' distributional and productive ambitions during the social democratic period (Duncan 1985; 1989). The municipal share of land rent as a portion of total returns eventually triggered conflict between developers and municipalities over (notably, though not exclusively, administrative) costs, formally resulting in the discontinuation of Municipal Site Leasehold in the mid-1980s, and creating a more market-friendly land policy (Clark and Runesson 1996; Clark and Gullberg 1997).

Two main factors contributed to later institutional tensions around Municipal Site Leasehold. First, implementation was voluntary, and municipalities could choose not to enforce it (Clark and Gullberg, 1991; Clark and Runesson, 1996). Second, municipalities were expected to streamline planning processes, invest in costly regional transportation networks, and periodically offer discounts on leasehold fees to private developers (Clark and Gullberg 1997). These challenges emerged throughout the late 1970s and into the 1980s when social democrats regained power. When expected rates of return on investments in land, whether for specific plots or land in general, were low, developers anticipated significant discounts on leasehold fees. Without these discounts, municipalities faced waves of disinvestment from developers (Clark and Gullberg 1997). This was followed by slow bureaucratic procedures and increasing legal fees for denied construction permits (Ratzka 1980). Rising costs reduced expected profits, making it harder to sustain the policy during the 1980s (Ratzka 1980). These observations are noteworthy, as far as they go, as the rising disinvestments since the late 1970s prompted the liberal Minister of Housing, Birgit Friggebo, to propose a motion (CU 1980/81:40–41, 12) in 1980 to discontinue state loans system for Municipal Site Leasehold lands (*Markförvärvslånefonden*) to "facilitate competition" and "stimulate construction activities" (Swedish Parliament, 1981, my translation). By 1975, 34% of all multi-dwelling buildings in the country were on leasehold land (SCB BO 1995, 61). This share dropped to 22% in 1983 and further down to 8% by 1989 (SCB BO 1995, 61). On average, the proportion of multi-dwelling buildings for the 1975–1979 period was 28.2%, but decreased to only 10.8% in 1985–1989 and 8.8% in 1990–1994 (SCB BO 1995, 61). Slight improvements have been seen since 2000, driven by the outsourcing of responsibilities envisioned in the policy, although its distributional aspect was completely halted (Mattsson 2006; Olsson 2018). Therefore, a significant downside of Swedish Municipal Site Leasehold is that, because its influence is geographically dispersed and implementation is not mandatory, only a portion of total rent revenue is remitted to the state. The diverse landscape of Swedish Municipal Site Leasehold means municipalities are constantly competing with developers over land rent revenues. Even in the 1960s, municipalities had to undertake more expensive activities (such as building transport networks) to attract investment and secure developers' expected profits (Meidner 1993). As a result, maintaining this policy can be challenging amid economic volatility and shifts in capital between sectors.

5.2 Capital Switching, Economic Crisis, and Land Rent

Let me now explain the impact of economic structural forces behind the discontinuation of Municipal Site Leasehold using the TILR. This will be done by specifically examining aggregate crises of profitability and productivity, which drive inter-sectoral competition and fluctuations in aggregate land rent. These factors influence the direction and historical contingency of capital switching. To empirically demonstrate these forces, the following macroeconomic variables and indicators are used: aggregate and sectoral rates of return, productivity, investments, land costs, and incremental rates of return. A key aspect of the capital switching thesis for both Harvey and Christophers is the type and timing of the economic crisis that triggered capital switching. While both characterize the type of the relevant crisis as overaccumulation, the switching happens before the crisis for Christophers. A closer look at Sweden's aggregate and sectoral profit rates in the 1980s shows that a) Swedish capitalism experienced a structural economic crisis of profitability and productivity, especially in the latter half of the 1980s, and b) this crisis preceded an inter-sectoral switching of capital.

5.2.1 The Economic Crisis of the 1980s and Its Sectoral Implications

The analysis of rates of return indicates two notable peaks and troughs in the Swedish economy from 1975 to 2000 (Figures 25 and 26). The first trough happened in 1978, followed by a peak in 1984. The second sharp drop in (aggregate and non-financial) profit rates occurred between 1984 and 1990. Then, there was a visible recovery in 1995, followed by another decline in 2001. Looking back, the overall trend has been downwards since 1995, despite two recoveries in 2006 and 2015. Figure 2 displays only return rates since 1980 because data on capital stock before 1980 are unavailable in Sweden (Wolf 1997). Therefore, I use gross capital formation in place of net capital stock in the denominator of Figure 3 to approximate trends before 1980. The results align with the trend shown in Figure 2. In the latter half of the 1980s, the Swedish economy experienced an evident decline in both aggregate and non-financial profitability.

The lack of sectoral capital stock data in Sweden before 1993 also limited the ability to demonstrate sectoral rates of return in the 1980s accurately. Nevertheless, the overall trends shown in Figures 25 and 26 match the sectoral trends for manufacturing and construction (Figure 27). This similarity suggests an increasing rate of return for the manufacturing sector from 1993 to 1995, while the construction sector's rates of return stayed constant. This allows for cautious generalizations of pre-1993 data trends. The rate of return in the construction sector (as a productive activity on land) includes a significant land-rent component. Essentially, the above-normal rate of return in the construction sector indicates the aggregate rate of land rent (conceptualized as absolute rent). The national-level ceiling (maximum limit) of this macro-level rent is set by the competitive inter-sectoral dynamics shown in Figure 27. The construction sector's rate of return increased around the turn of the century until the Great Recession of 2007–08, then dropped sharply until 2013. The rate stayed relatively stable even as manufacturing profit rates increased during the early 1990s. However, the rise at the start of the 21st century reflected a decrease in manufacturing profit rates.

It is worth noting that between 1985 and 1990, the financial rates of return (Figure 28) showed a trend opposite to that of the aggregate and non-financial

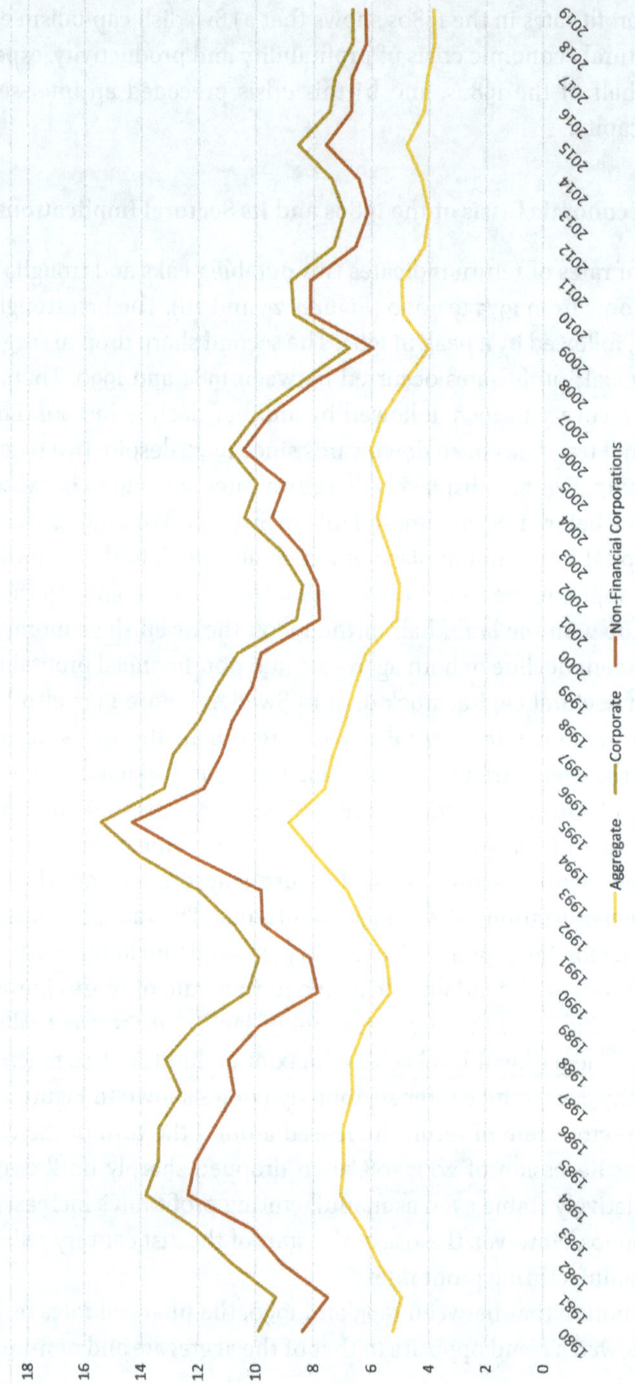

FIGURE 25 Swedish aggregate, corporate, and non-financial rates of return, 1980–2019 (Source: SCB online database (my calculation))

FIGURE 26 Swedish total and non-financial rates of return (alternative calculation), 1950–2019 (Source: SCB online database (my calculation))

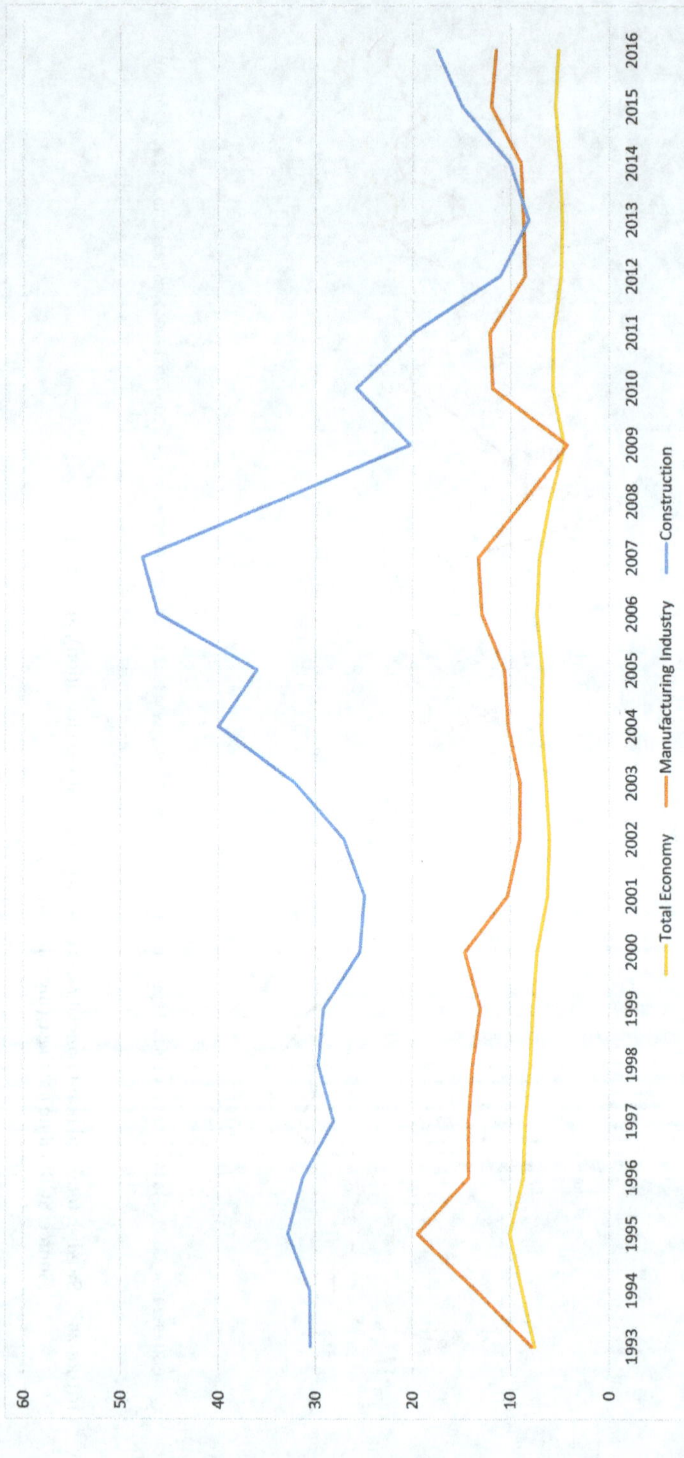

FIGURE 27 Swedish total and sectoral rates of return 1993–2019 (Source: OECD online database (my calculation))

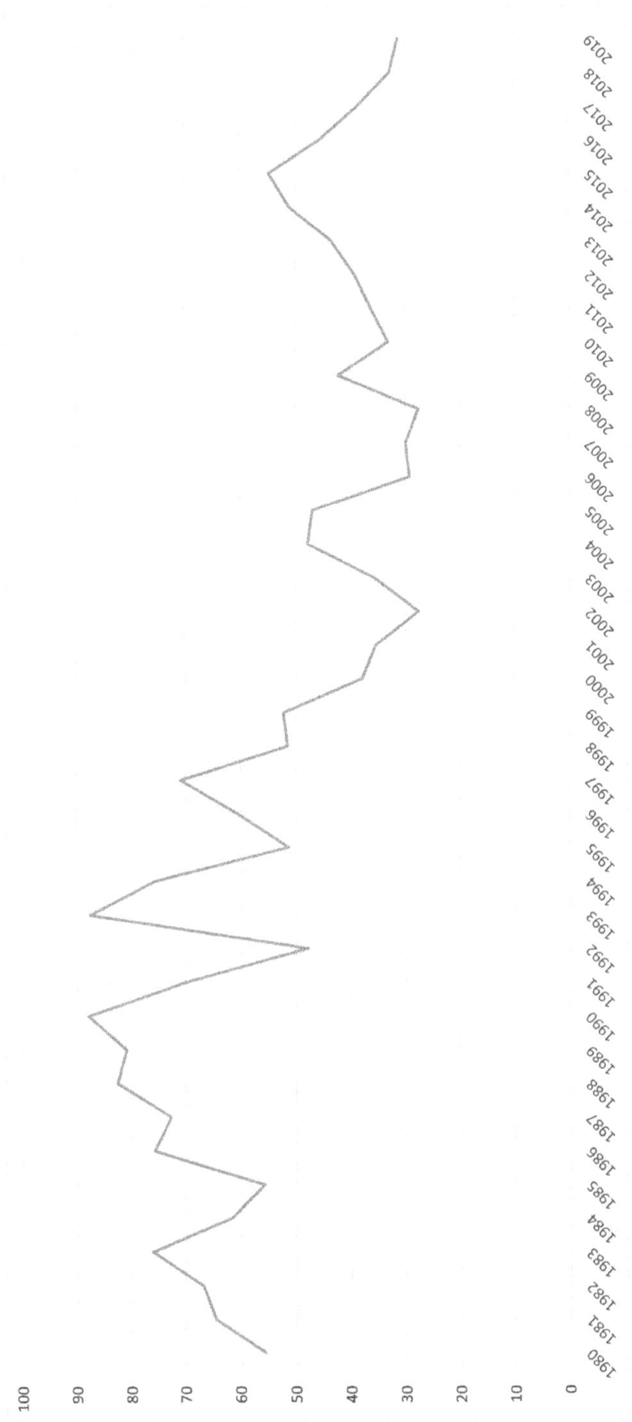

FIGURE 28 Swedish financial rates of return, 1980–2019 (Source: SCB online database (my calculation))

rates. The decline in 1985 was followed by a relatively strong recovery until 1990, largely due to the 1985 deregulation that lifted the ceiling on interest and lending (Englund 2015, 10). Deregulation positively affected private non-financial borrowing, which averaged 16% from 1985 to 1990, compared with 8–13% from 1980 to 1985 (ibid.). Employment in the banking sector increased by 20% (ibid.). Corporate borrowing (in aggregate) also rose by 56% from 1985 to 1988 and by 51% from 1988 to 1990, while household borrowing grew by 65% during 1985–1988, but only 14% during 1988–1990 (ibid. 12–13). This sectoral recovery aligns with the decline in aggregate and non-financial profit rates during the same period, indicating a cautious flow of capital into the financial sector rather than manufacturing or construction. Specifically, the share of investments in the financial sector in the second half of the 1980s responded positively to rising sectoral profit rates. Conversely, profit rates and investments in manufacturing and construction decreased, suggesting capital was switching to the financial sector (Figure 29). Rising profit rates in manufacturing from 1990 to 1995 subsequently led to increased investments in that sector.

The flow of capital to the financial sector in the mid-to-late 1980s negatively affected construction-sector profit rates (and thus sectoral rent rates), leading to increasing tensions and disinvestment between municipalities and developers, as discussed earlier. Stagnant investment rates in construction are also reflected in private investors' share of completed buildings, which dropped from 57% in 1980 to 39% in 1988 (SCB BO 1990, 66). The switching of capital toward finance is implied in Harvey's original concept of the capital switching thesis and a few others (Christophers 2011; Rutland 2010; Ward 2020), with one caveat: for these scholars, finance's role is to mediate switching to the built environment and property markets, whereas, in the Swedish economy of the 1980s, the switching to finance mainly came at the expense of construction and built environments. This finding underscores the importance of capital switching in explaining why tensions between municipalities and developers over the costs of Municipal Site Leasehold (which eventually was discontinued) increased in the mid-to-late 1980s, going beyond existing explanations (micro-level bureaucratic inefficiencies).

The financial sector's recovery in the second half of the 1980s ended with the 1991 financial bubble burst, which triggered the Banking Crisis (Riksbanken n.d.). Bank lending decreased by 6.3% in 1991, down from 15.3% in 1990. "By the end of 1990, the stock price index had fallen by 37 percent from its peak on August 16, 1989" (Englund 2015, 19). Commercial property prices declined by 6% in 1990 and 40% in 1991 (ibid.). Mortgage markets were especially affected as "real interest rate rose from 1–2% in 1991" to about 10% in 1992 (Riksbanken

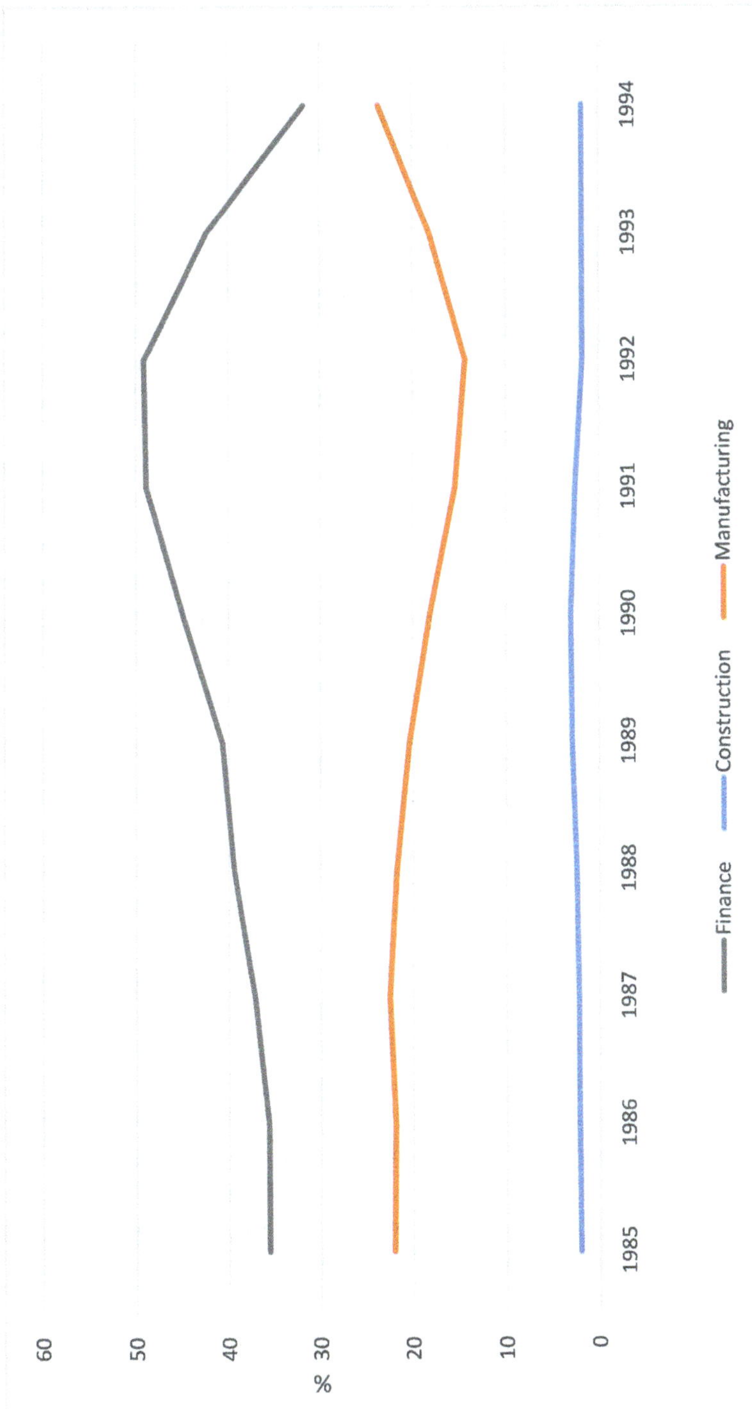

FIGURE 29 Share of construction, manufacturing, and finance in Swedish gross fixed capital formation (Source: SCB Yearbooks 1991, 230, Table 255; 1996: 235, Table 269 (my calculation))

n.d.). As Englund observed, "The timing—with production and investment stagnating in 1990 but loans still increasing—suggests that the real crisis started before the financial crisis" (Englund 2015, 19). It also indicates that "the real crisis" occurred before the inter-sectoral switching of capital.

The "real" crisis of Swedish capitalism in the late 1980s had deeper roots. Shaikh demonstrated that a common factor contributing to declining profitability in many welfare states was the slow growth of productivity compared to real wages. This disparity led to the Great Stagflation, which persisted until "real wages [began] rising more slowly than productivity" (Shaikh 2016, 674). The Swedish economy is no exception. Starting in the mid-1970s, unit labor costs rose sharply, peaking in 1991, and labor costs per hour worked matched the real value-added per hour in 1985 (Figure 30). This suggests that, although profit rates slowed in the 1970s, the combination of this slowdown and the decline in productivity in the late 1980s worsened the crisis, requiring swift and systematic policy changes. However, this does not mean that changes in land policy, financial regulations, and other factors were unavoidable. As Englund (2015) showed, understanding these structural economic forces, including inter-sectoral capital switching, partly influenced policy decisions in the mid-to-late 1980s. This finding is consistent with Roberts' view of the shift to neoliberalism in the US and UK, driven by falling aggregate and sectoral profitability and productivity (Roberts 2021a).

An immediate result of the crisis was the rapid decline in compensation, including pensions, since 1990 (Gustafsson et al., 2009; Zetterlund, 2022: 105). This decline contributed to the recovery of both productivity and profitability in the first half of the 1990s (Figure 31), marking the start of "an era of negative wage-share growth" (Shaikh 2016, 674). This process was linked to capital outflows from both the manufacturing and construction sectors (see below), leading to the discontinuation of Municipal Site Leasehold. After 1990, the net disposable income of households (both nominal and real) decreased rapidly (Figure 32). During the late 1980s, both the household debt (net lending-to-borrowing ratio) and the savings ratio were negative. In contrast, interest payments as a percentage of net disposable income increased (alongside rising financial rates of return) until the 1991 Banking Crisis, when these trends reversed. The decline in compensation and income, which affects consumer demand, is a response to the earlier dual crises in profitability and productivity. This also supports the overall argument about the timing of capital switching and the economic crisis that triggered it.

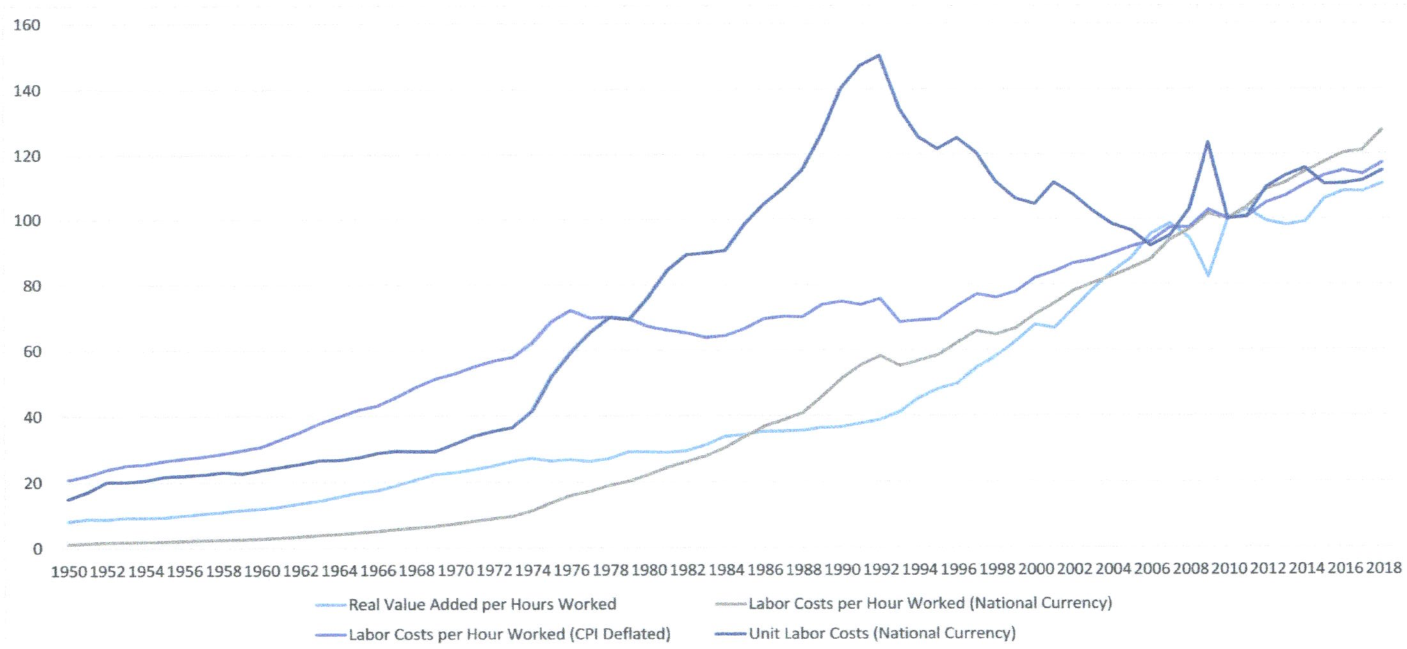

FIGURE 30 Swedish manufacturing sector, output, compensations, unit labor cost, 1950–2018, 2010 = 100 (Source: CBT online database (my calculation))

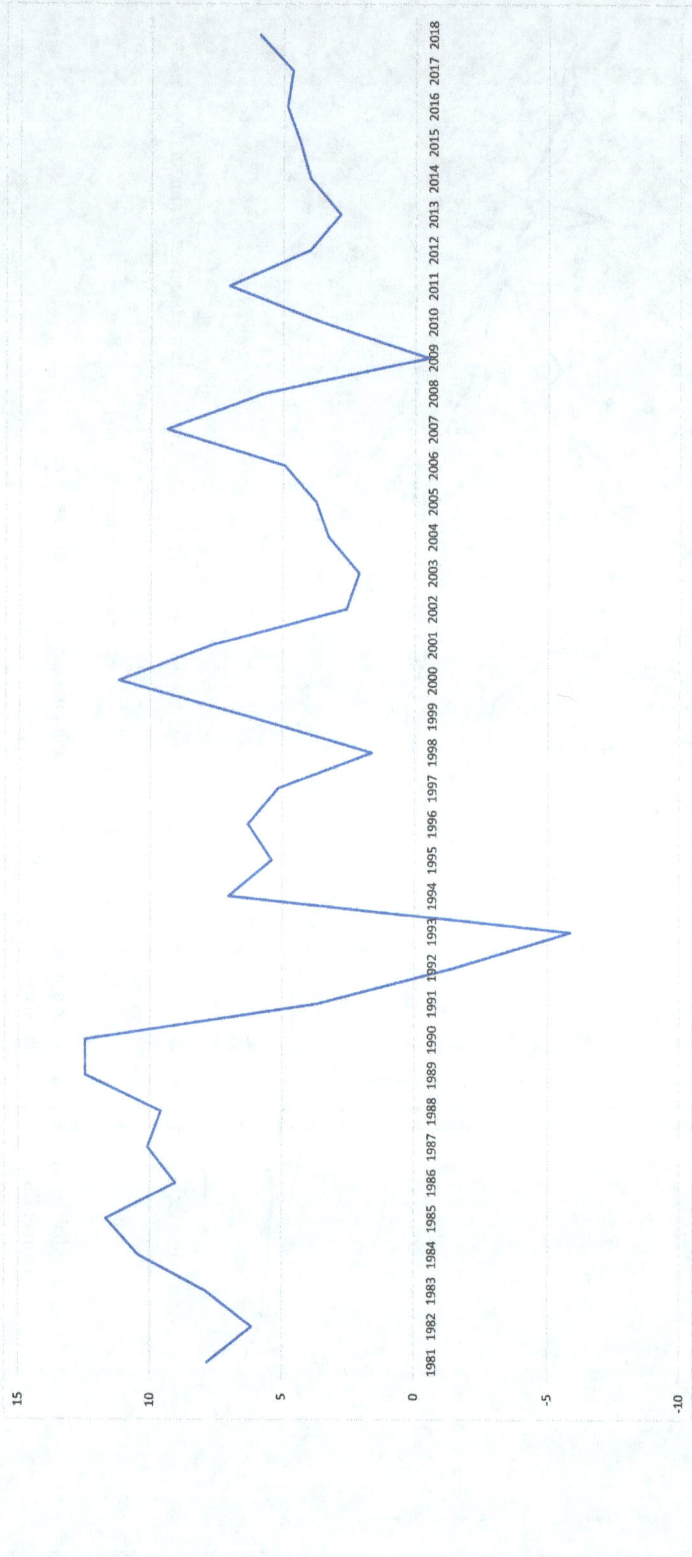

FIGURE 31 Swedish compensation of employees (growth rate) 1981–2018 (Source: SCB online database (my calculation))

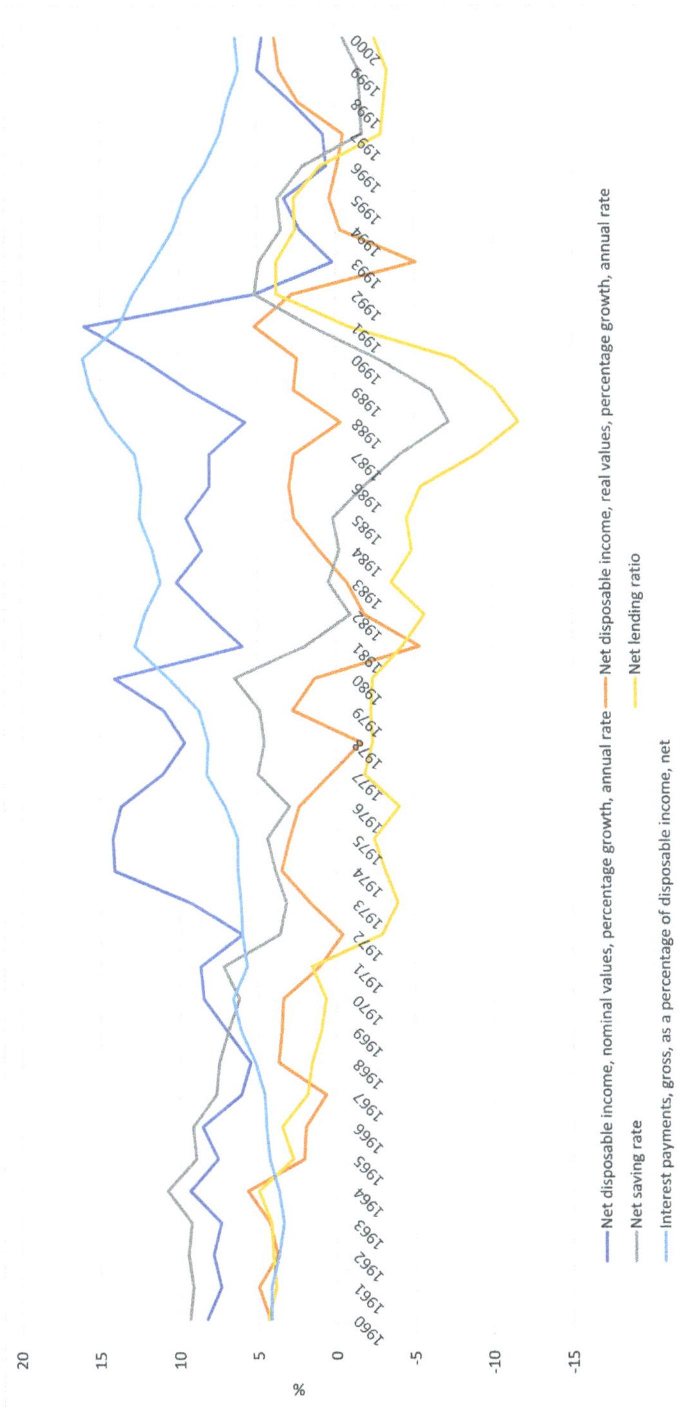

FIGURE 32 Swedish household income growth, savings ratio, debt ratio, interest ratio (Source: SCB online database (my calculation))

5.2.2 Implications of the Crisis for Land, Construction, and Built Environments

Construction activity, indicated by completed dwellings in new construction, also declined in response to capital switching to the financial sector (Figure 33). There was a rapid drop from the mid-1970s to 1987, followed by a relatively slow increase in new construction since 1987, as manufacturing profitability decreased and the process of discontinuing Municipal Site Leases began. Another decline occurred in the first half of the 1990s, despite an increase in manufacturing profitability. However, since the data in Figure 33 aggregates all completed dwellings regardless of lease or title type, it does not display the impact of the Municipal Site Leasehold discontinuation on construction activity.

Conceptually, land rent is essential in Harvey's idea of capital switching in the SMLR. The same applies to King (1989b). This crucial mediating role of land rent has been overlooked in other contributions to Harvey's thesis. Both Harvey and King examined land rent in terms of monopoly pricing. They insisted that it acts as a barrier to the free movement of capital between branches controlled by the landowning class. Specifically, this suggests that the two are inversely related: higher land rent leads to slower switching to the built environment, and vice versa. Using a Shaikh-inspired whole-economy interpretation of rent theory, aggregate land rents are viewed as the excess sectoral profit rate on productive activity on land. This determines the expected return on future ventures and indicates that the relationship between capital switching to the built environment and sectoral land rents is linear. In the case of Municipal Site Leasehold, one consequence of capital flowing into the financial sector (at the expense of construction) was that, in the late 1980s, as municipalities increased leasehold fees, developers began disinvesting from leasehold projects (Clark and Runesson, 1996). This analysis, combined with the data shown in Figure 28 (recovery in financial profit rates), indicates a possible decline in overall land rent rates as capital shifts toward finance and excess profits in the land sector diminish.

According to the TILR, land cost data reflect land rent levels for investors who do not own the land and need to acquire it from a landowner, who could be a large landowning construction firm or a private or public landowner. The Swedish urban land sector is highly concentrated. Since the 1980s, four large construction firms with extensive landholdings in Sweden have dominated the sector: Peab, NCC, JM, and Skanska (Blackwell et al. 2023). The shares of these large (landowning) construction firms in aggregate land rents are shown in the sectoral profit rate data mentioned earlier. Meanwhile, the share of smaller

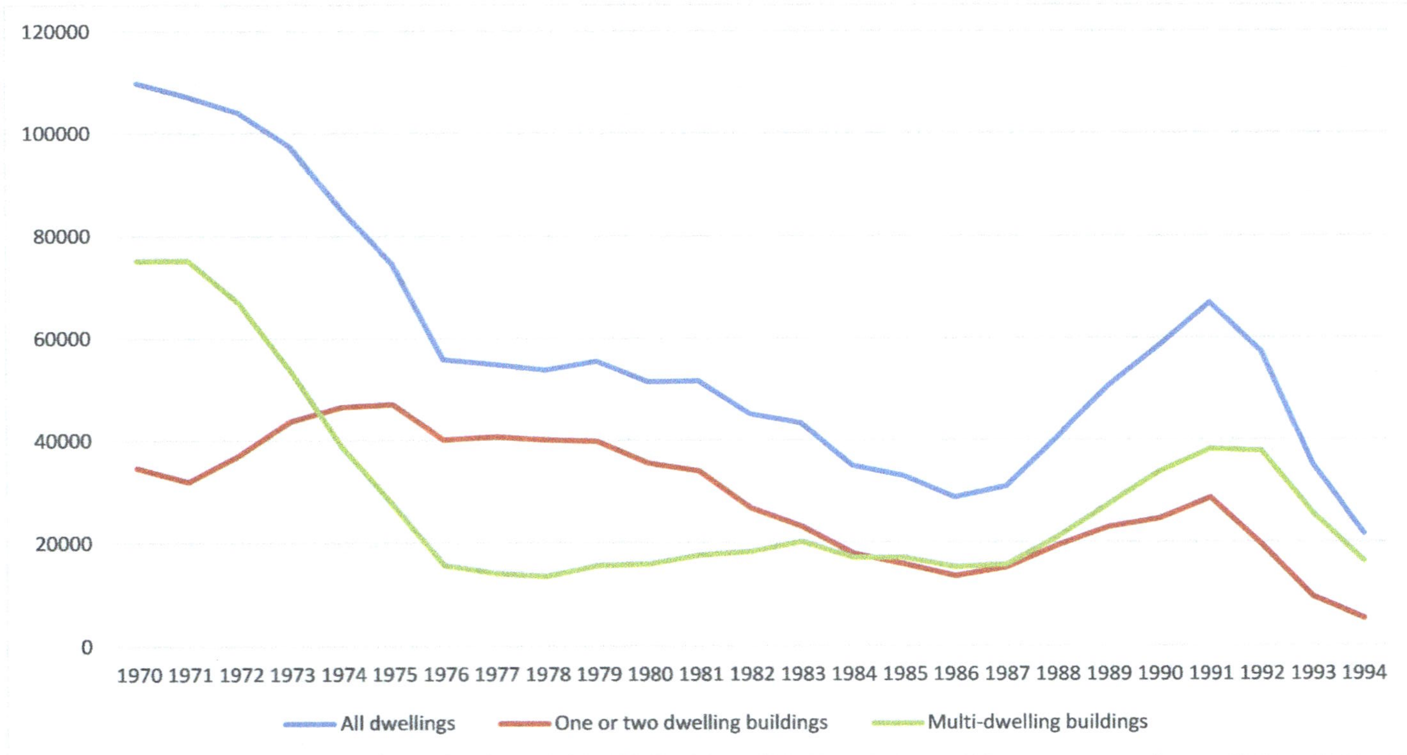

FIGURE 33 Dwellings in completed buildings (number of units) (Source: SCB BO, 1990: 50 and BO, 1995: 42 (my calculation))

(landless) construction firms appears in the land cost data (Figure 34). The stagnant construction profit rates and land costs in the latter half of the 1980s reflect stagnant land rent rates. At the same time, stagnant land costs also suggest lower returns on land assets (i.e., land rent) for larger landowning construction firms (SCB BO 1995, 128; SCB SM 1995, 17). Statistics Sweden (SCB) defines land costs as total production costs minus construction costs (SCB SM, 1995: 8). A similar trend is observable in land costs within reconstruction and development areas (SCB BO 1995, 130; 131). Figure 35 illustrates the substantial share of investors' costs relative to total construction costs—excluding labor and even plant and equipment—that began rising rapidly in 1987, including bureaucratic costs of the construction process. Essentially, throughout the 1980s, revenues from multi-dwelling buildings (both private and public) remained steady (Figure 36). However, these revenues started to increase in 1990 as the process of discontinuing Municipal Site Leasehold began. By the mid-1990s, private companies' revenues even surpassed those of public companies as regulations were further relaxed. In other words, less profitable land investments in the 1980s led to lower municipal returns from Municipal Site Leasehold, which contributed to the growing conflict between municipalities and developers.

Housing rents also surged significantly in the latter half of the 1980s, especially at the start of the 1990s, when the discontinuation of Municipal Site Leases began (Figure 37). It appears that when aggregate sectoral rents were low, maintaining profits required substantial cost cuts—including the bureaucratic costs of Municipal Site Leasehold, as shown earlier in Figure 35—and perhaps an increase in housing prices (Figure 37), which became possible after the discontinuation of Municipal Site Leasehold. Additionally, in the mid-to-late 1980s, the total number of vacant units rapidly decreased (Figure 38), reflecting the expansion of financial markets into the real estate business (Figures 28 and 32), but this also limited overall monopoly pricing. The level of overall monopoly in the land market—indicated by the presence of four large construction firms—may never entirely disappear. However, low investment and profit rates in the latter half of the 1980s suggest low land rent rates, despite partial monopoly ownership in land markets. This challenges the microeconomic view that interprets land rent as an excess monopoly price caused by artificial (intra-sectoral) scarcity created by landlords, framing it as class-monopoly rent (Anderson 2014; Bradley 2023; Harvey 1974).

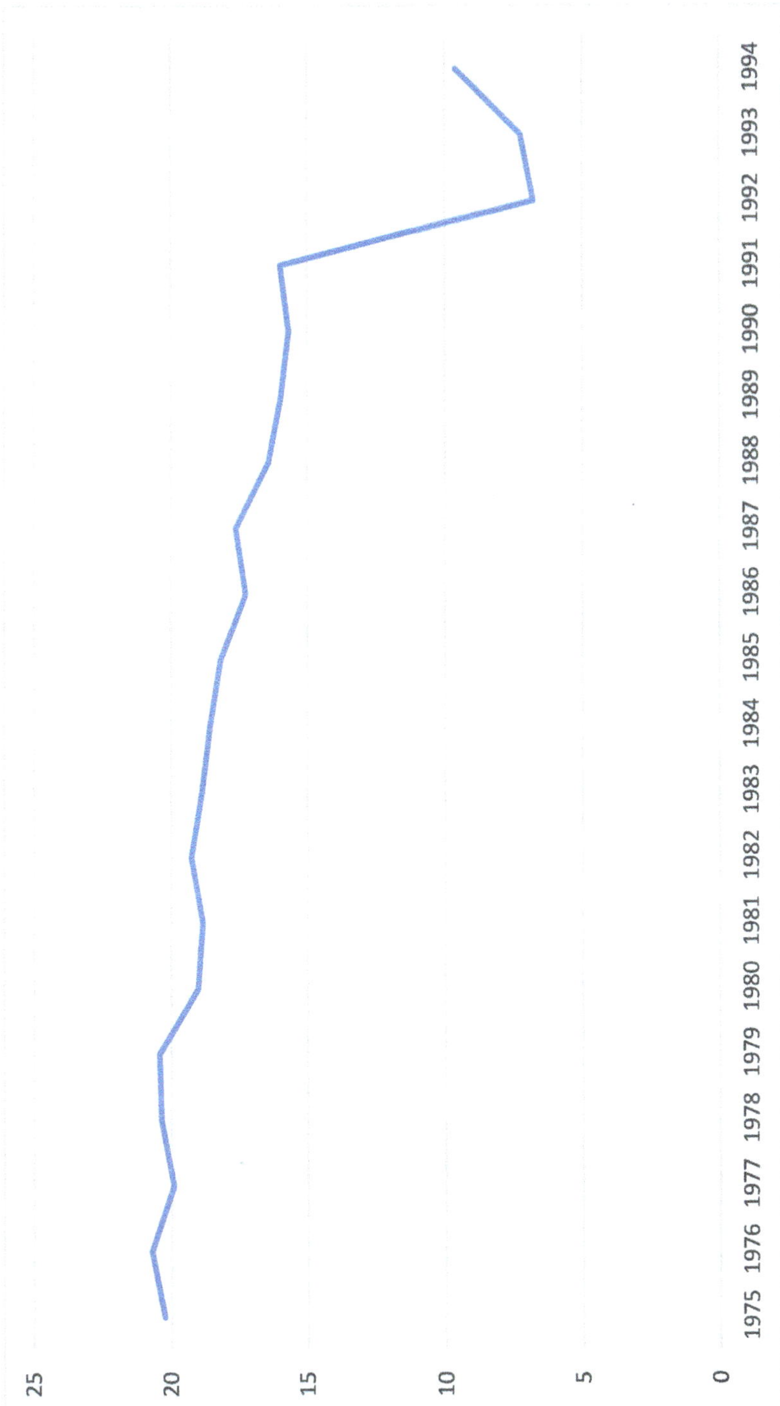

FIGURE 34 Swedish average land costs per square meter for dwellings in multi-dwelling buildings with granted government aid (Source: SCB BO, 1995)

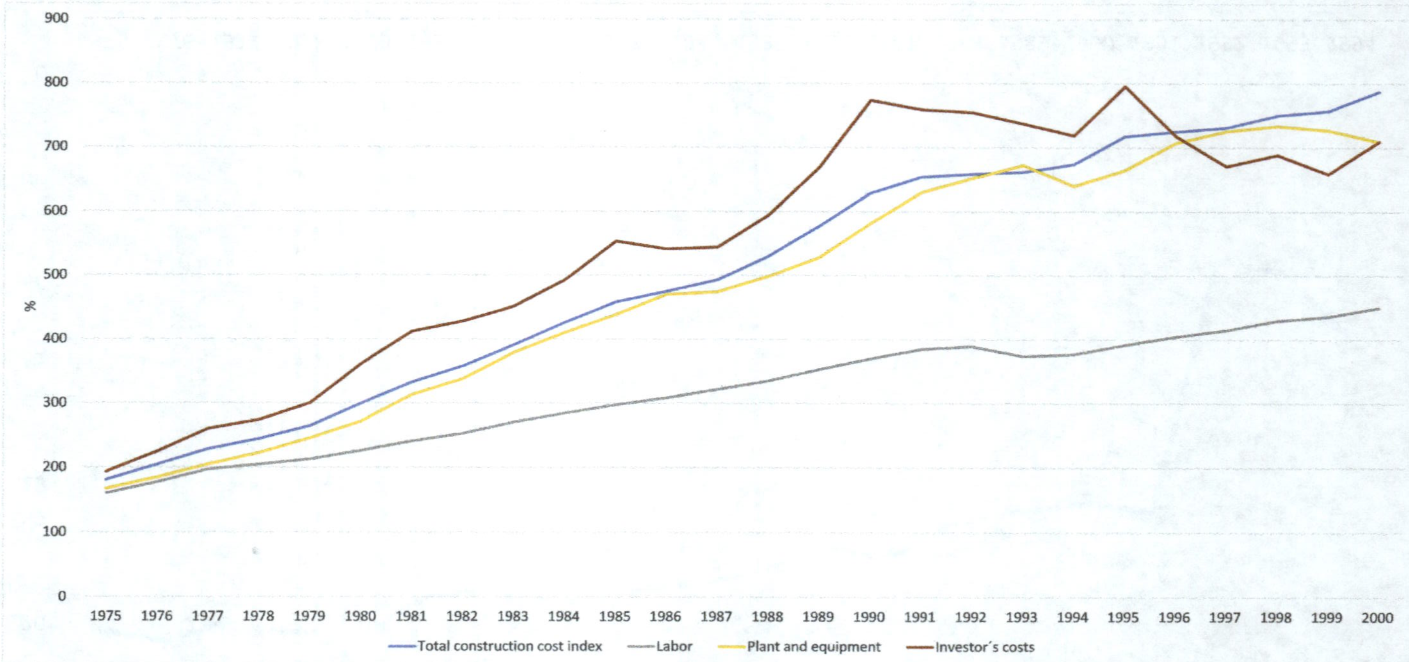

FIGURE 35 Swedish construction cost index (excluding wage drift and VAT) for multi-dwelling buildings (1968 = 100) by type of expenditure (Source: SCB online database (my calculation))

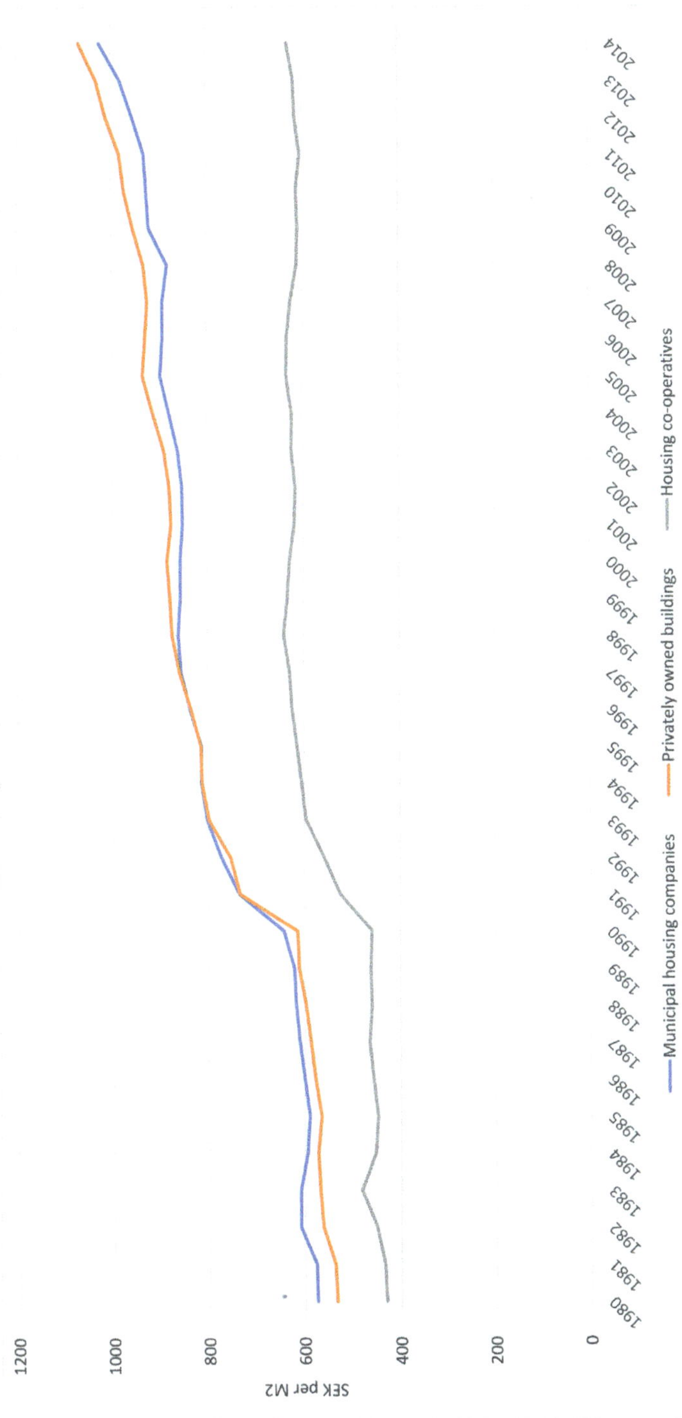

FIGURE 36 Swedish revenues for dwellings 1980–2015, SEK per square meter dwelling space, constant prices (Source: SCB online database (my calculation))

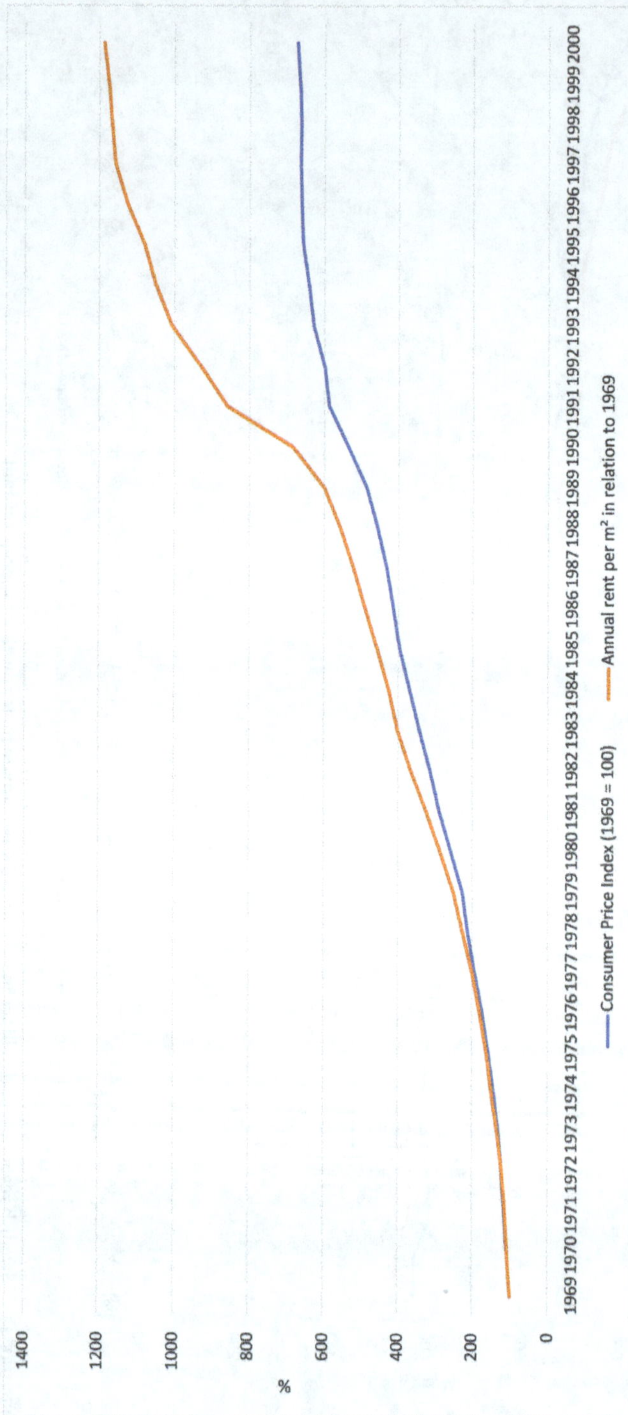

FIGURE 37 Swedish housing rents and general price level 1969–2000 (1969 = 100) (Source: SCB online database (my calculation))

FIGURE 38 Vacant dwellings available to Let, 1 March 1981–2003, 1 September 2004–2009, municipal housing companies and private bodies (Source: SCB online database (my calculation))

5.2.3 Empirical Demonstration of Capital Switching

The empirical data so far show the connection between rates of return and investments, as well as the relationship between the manufacturing and construction sectors. Additionally, the data suggest that investments follow expected profit rates in the sector; in construction, this process is driven by land rent as part of sectoral profits. But does this connection imply a shift in investments toward new construction? Once more, the explanation resides in Harvey's capital switching thesis. Harvey does not identify a specific indicator beyond construction activity for measuring capital switching. However, I propose using Shaikh's notion of incremental rates of return to indicate the most recent (previous year) shift in investments, as investors (at the aggregate level) tend to pursue more profitable ventures by updating their expected rates of return based on actual outcomes, avoiding the issues discussed earlier (Shaikh 1998; 2016).

Figure 39 displays incremental rates of return for Swedish industries from 1993 to 2017 (data on gross profit before 1993 are unavailable). These data complement statistics on sectoral rates of return and show that after sluggish growth in the 1990s, incremental rates of return on construction began to increase noticeably after 2000, peaked during the Great Recession, and stayed relatively constant afterward. However, these data also highlight another important aspect. The incremental rates of return show turbulence, as capital frequently switches between sectors in search of higher returns. This reflects the historical contingency of land rent creation (resulting from excess return on land) and the switch of capital to land. Unlike Harvey's seemingly functionalist interpretation of capital switching, construction is just one of many sectors to which capital moves; in this sense, there is nothing unique about the built environment. For example, the information and communication industry took over construction in 2008. In contrast, during specific periods (such as 2000–2007), the textile industry led a shift in investments, and after the Great Recession, the manufacturing of coke and petroleum products became more prominent. These are aggregate data. Individual capital may or may not move due to individual constraints. Still, the overall trend influences investment decisions.

5.3 Final Remarks

A historical assessment of the Swedish economy using the TILR model shows that Sweden's shift to neoliberalism was not smooth. First, financial

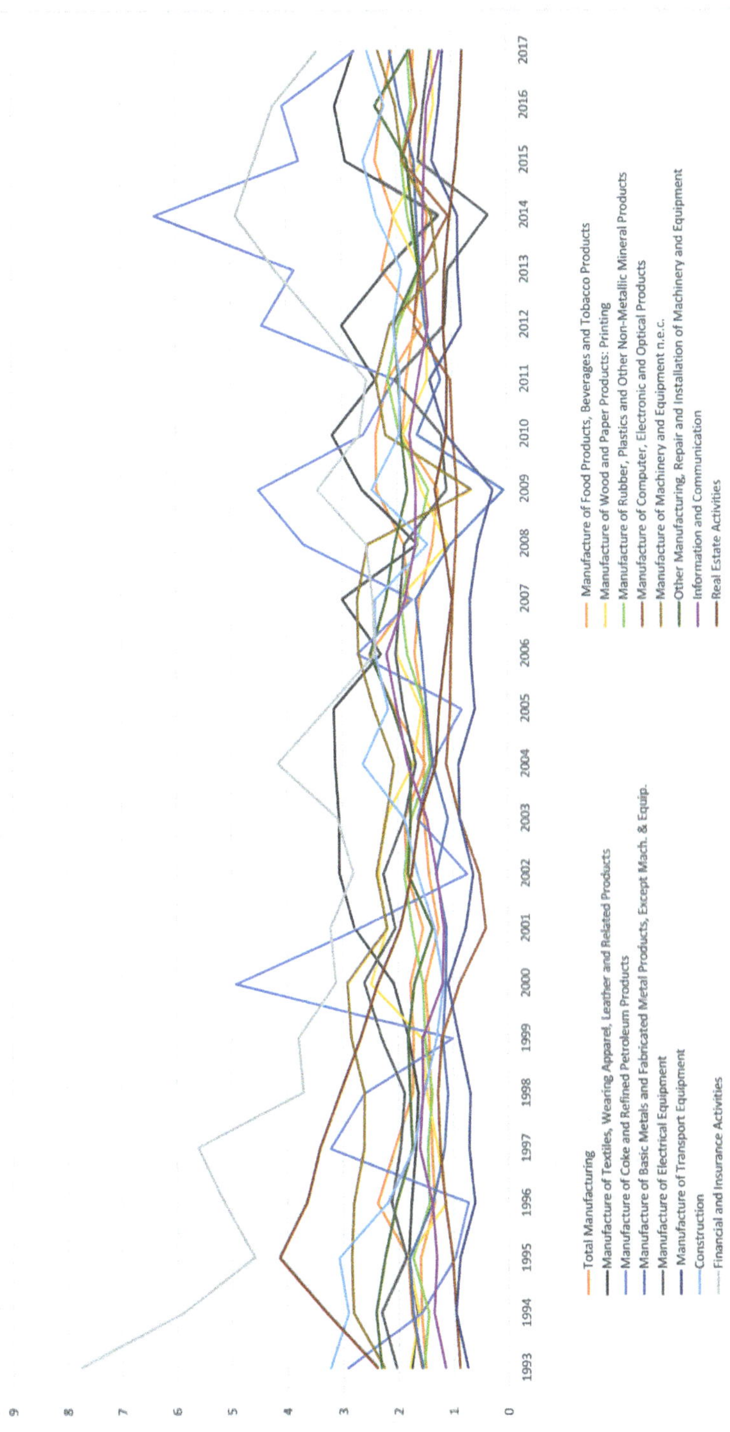

FIGURE 39 Swedish industries' incremental rates of profit 1993–2017 (Source: OECD online database (my calculation))

deregulation, which facilitated capital shifting into finance, caused the 1991 Banking Crisis. Second, regarding manufacturing profits, the recovery from the 1980s crisis—mainly driven by wage cuts to increase productivity rather than investments in labor-efficient technologies—lasted only about five years (1990–1995). This assessment aligns with Roberts' (2021a) view that the rise in neoliberalism was a response to a decline in overall and manufacturing profits, as well as a productivity crisis. Concerning Municipal Site Leasehold, the economic structural forces discussed above provide a material context for local decision-making and explain the macroeconomic barriers strategists face periodically. These macroeconomic forces restrict policy options and influence microeconomic responses. During economic turmoil, Swedish municipalities and private developers competed to control land, viewing it as a key source of economic power in construction. Like in other capitalist economies, Swedish municipalities rely on external support from the central government. Therefore, during the economic crisis, which negatively affected land rent rates, the central government focused on addressing the downturn, leaving municipalities unable to counter private disinvestment in land markets. Looking back, the shift in strategy and the eventual discontinuation of Municipal Site Leasehold may not have been the best choice (and certainly not the only one). Still, assuming it was likely the result of trial and error (which warrants further study), there is enough evidence to suggest it helped reverse key aspects of the severe economic crisis Swedish capitalism was facing. Studies on Sweden's transition to neoliberalism have highlighted the emergence of a neoliberal state characterized by shifting ideological dominance (Baeten 2017, 105), evolving neoliberal subjectivities (ibid. 112), social regulations (Pries 2017, 19), and social technologies of rule (ibid. 219), following political and ideological crises. Others have pointed to changing international trade policies and their effects on "an export-dependent country with a small internal market" (Zetterlund 2022, 105). However, the structural economic forces and their effects on this transition have not been thoroughly analyzed. Therefore, further research is needed: a) to understand how aware key policymakers were of these economic forces (similar to Copley's study of the Thatcher government's policy trial and error to recover manufacturing profits); b) to explore how political and parliamentary debates relate to these economic forces; and c) to see if different Swedish municipalities responded differently to these forces and the discontinuation of Municipal Site Leasehold.

Another implication of this study needs to be discussed. In recent years, urgent needs for public investments have sparked growing interest among urban and economic geographers in examining the legacies and prospects of municipalization (Albalate et al. 2021; Clifton et al. 2021; Gradus and

Budding 2020; McDonald 2024; Voorn et al. 2021; Warner 2023). This relates to decades of privatization and marketization of urban land and housing, which have posed significant challenges for the public sector in working with private developers and landlords on land use policies and affordable housing in many advanced capitalist countries (Mironova and Stein 2018; Summers 2006; Weiler 2008). As seen in the case of Swedish Municipal Site Leasehold, a primary reason for these challenges is quite apparent: it is not cost-effective for the private sector to invest in affordable housing for low-income groups, and the state generally lacks the resources or authority to force the private sector to do so. Policy tools like Swedish Municipal Site Leasehold relied on a strong (and ideally thriving) national and regional economy to provide the public sector with sufficient funds for large-scale intervention in land markets or to ensure low costs and high profits for landowners. This idea aligns with the standard view that welfare economies tend to function best during periods of economic growth (Concidine and Dukelow 2010; Lambertini et al. 2013; Lipsmeyer 2011).

Land ownership has become essential for the public sector to achieve any reliable and sustainable impact on land markets (Bua and Davies 2023; Mironova and Stein 2018; Stein and Mironova 2020). The private sector's growing control over land (as the key resource in the urban economy) significantly limits the influence of the public sector. Moreover, where the public sector still maintains some influence (at least bureaucratic), it often loses it due to market-regulated land prices and repeated waves of disinvestment, which again weaken the public sector's ability to serve low-income populations, regardless of political or ideological goals. Re-municipalization is increasingly being proposed as a way for local governments to address social issues arising from marketization more systematically. However, it is worth noting that remunicipalization strategies should be based on thorough historical and geographical analyses of previous de-municipalization efforts, including how and why they occurred. In other words, we need to understand better the structural economic and geographical conditions that might limit future attempts at municipalization.

Finally, the case of Swedish Municipal Site Leasehold cautiously highlights the advantages of nationalizing land as a key policy for the state to regulate rent relations. In a nationalized land market, all rent revenues go to the state (Hall 1980), reducing conflicts over individual plots or between municipalities. Capitalists face different production conditions. Owning land and collecting land rent means those who benefit from this advantage may invest less in higher-cost (more labor-efficient) technologies and still enjoy excess returns if sectoral land rent rates are high. This creates conflicts over land policy, which explains why developers fought municipalities fiercely over Municipal Site

Leasehold costs (e.g., leasehold fees) in the late 1980s when overall rent rates were not high. This suggests that strategies should be adjusted to consider these challenges and ensure effective policymaking. The empirical evidence here indicates a link between the discontinuation of Municipal Site Leasehold and the dynamics of return and rent rates. If this is correct, depending on whether agents were aware of the macroeconomic context, reversing the trend would require a structural transformation of the economy.

CHAPTER 6

Shortage of Affordable Housing in Malmö

This chapter[1] extends the national-level analysis presented in the previous chapter to the urban level. It outlines my propositions for the affordable housing shortage problem in Sweden's third-largest city, Malmö. I aim to advance a realistic understanding of the problem by using the TILR (and Anwar Shaikh's theory of real competition that underlies it) to examine the flow of investments in and out of the housing sector. To do so, I draw on Shaikh's (2016) theory of relative prices, which he develops as part of his broader theory of real competition. A crucial implication of his theory is its explanation of the relationship between supply and demand in price formation. While Shaikh's real competition theory explains prices in the context of structural (turbulent) disequilibrium, its two main competing theories—neoclassical and heterodox—do so in the context of a presumed state of equilibrium or a (temporary) lack thereof.

The Great Recession of 2007–2009 revealed significant income and wealth disparities, especially in housing (Arundel 2017; Waldron 2023). These gaps widened during the COVID-19 pandemic, with draconian impacts. The pandemic primarily affected densely populated, low-income areas and the increasingly vulnerable homeless population across many OECD countries (OECD 2023), both already limited in their ability to cope due to deep-rooted inequalities. Monetary policies following the Great Recession, such as quantitative easing, aimed to stimulate investment by reducing borrowing costs (Roberts 2017). Particularly in Sweden, these measures, coupled with housing policies favoring homeownership over rentals, contributed, among others, to speculative activity in housing markets (Christophers 2021, 574). Interestingly, the subsequent rapid shift to quantitative tightening—reversing easing policies—mainly to curb post-pandemic inflation—worsened housing inequality, increased insecurity for low- and middle-income homeowners, and sparked concerns about affordable housing shortages.

The case of Malmö is interesting for two reasons: The municipality's main recent policy to address housing shortages is likely based on neoclassical (microeconomic) views of price formation, focusing solely on balancing supply and demand in the housing market (Malmö Municipality 2021). This traditional approach primarily encourages private investment in constructing new high-rise buildings (Borgegård and Kemeny 2004). It aims to increase the

1 This chapter comprises a modified version of a forthcoming article.

current housing stock to meet present needs while also preparing for future population growth. This fits into broader densification efforts in crowded, low-income neighborhoods, many of which feature low-rise structures (Boverket 2017; Malm and Jenning 2019). Second, many critiques point out the unequal distribution of the current housing stock within the city (Listerborn and Baeten 2022; Madureira and Baeten 2016). They argue that the problem is not just how housing is produced but how it is unevenly distributed among residents. Essentially, they see the housing shortage as a distribution problem, caused by demand inequalities, and view it as a temporary disequilibrium. Interestingly, this perspective appears to share core assumptions with the neoclassical view that underpins the policies it seeks to criticize. However, I contend that a more straightforward explanation can be reached by operationalizing the TILR and its underlying theory of real competition and relative prices. The TILR differentiates between various types of investments and their profit sources, which influence the relative price of housing as a commodity in market economies. These investment types link macro forces affecting land markets and construction with micro-level housing inequalities.

6.1 Real Competition and Relative Prices

Shaikh's theory of real competition, detailed in Chapter 10, aims to analyze capitalist relations amid the complex, turbulent intra- and inter-sectoral movement of capital, driven by a continually higher expected profit rate that never reaches a static equilibrium. Price equalization among sellers and the equalization of profit rates over (longer) time cause "perpetual fluctuations around various centers of gravity," resulting in structural (turbulent) disequilibrium and structural inequalities (Shaikh 2016, 260). Shaikh recognizes that supply and demand influence these processes but considers them not decisive, since both can shift in response to profit opportunities (Shaikh 2016, 260). Price equalization occurs as buyers seek the lowest prices, and profit rates equalize as investors pursue higher returns (ibid. 260). One unintended consequence is the accelerated supply in favored industries, which lowers their prices and profits (ibid.). The theory suggests that competitive capitals (as plants and equipment) actively set prices and aggressively cut costs, moving within and across industries to maximize profits, primarily by increasing investment in fixed capital per unit (ibid. 262; 327).

Shaikh highlights the significance of price, considering it the firm's key "weapon" in this competitive, war-like scenario (ibid. 261). He (2016, 69) explains that "the price of any commodity" hinges on two main factors: a) the vertically integrated unit labor cost involved in production, which encompasses the combined labor costs across the entire industry chain—from the primary industry, its input suppliers (raw materials, etc.), to the industries supplying those inputs (ibid.). This metric captures the total industrial labor costs to produce a specific commodity (ibid.). b) the vertically integrated "ratio of profits to wages" within the same industry, which reflects an average weighted profit-wage ratio across the industry producing the commodity and its input industries, including their suppliers (ibid.). Shaikh asserts that the three classical political economists—Smith, Ricardo, and Marx—agree that "market prices tend to gravitate around, but remain different from, natural prices (production prices)" (ibid. 17). This divergence mainly results from competition that tends to equalize wage and profit rates (ibid.). Referencing Marx's analysis of capital mobility, relative prices, and profit cycles in Capital, Volume Three, he notes that the "gravitational fluctuations" of market prices around production prices are inherently "anarchical" (ibid.).

Shaikh's theory of relative prices posits that "temporal changes in relative prices are primarily driven by shifts in relative integrated labor times," aligning with Marx's concept of relative labor values (ibid. 242; Shaikh 1990, 254). He states that production costs "depend on the length and intensity of the working day, wages paid to workers, and the technology in use" (Shaikh 2016, 261). Additionally, he notes that "capitals (plant and equipment) differ in their cost structure," enabling the creation of new capitals "often with new, lower-cost methods of production" (ibid. 262). In intra-sectoral competition, "profit margins and profit rates" tend to become unequal because competition tends to "equalize selling prices" (ibid. 261). This competition "creates an average price and a corresponding dispersion of profit rates across firms and across capitals" (ibid. 264). Conversely, profit rate equalization between sectors occurs "because it promotes entry and exit of capitals in response to profit rate differentials" (ibid. 265). This inter-sectoral "mobility of capital implies that new investment will accelerate relative to demand in industries with higher profit rates and decelerate relative to demand in industries with lower profit rates" (ibid. 264). This process continues until the inflow of investments causes supply to grow faster than demand, leading to a slowdown in relative prices and profits.

As noted in Chapter 3, a crucial point in this discussion is that "it is the rate of return on new investment, not the average profit rate across all vintages, that influences capital mobility" (ibid.). New investments are primarily driven by the profit rate of what Shaikh terms "regulating capitals" (ibid. 265). These are "capitals representing the best generally reproducible production conditions in [each] industry," or those that reflect "lowest reproducible (quality-adjusted) costs in the industry" (ibid.). The concept also considers land as a non-reproducible production factor. Land rent essentially reflects the relative land price, which, for landowners, correlates with an excess profit rate. Consequently, "competition among producers will enforce a common price, causing lower-cost producers (including landowners) to tend to have higher profit margins and profit rates" (ibid.). This mechanism enables land-based ventures, such as residential development, to attract private investors when the land rent component of expected profits is sufficiently high. This results in a higher overall profit rate compared to other industries.

6.1.1 Operationalizing the TILR for Housing Research

The TILR posits that the mobility of new investments into and out of the housing sector, which depends on expected inter-sectoral profit rates, determines the timing and intensity of supply and relative prices of housing. In the housing sector, regulation of investments—following a Shaikhian perspective—can be effectively indicated by investments in new construction. Importantly, the long-term investment patterns in housing are also geographically influenced, as profits include a significant land-rent component because land is a non-reproducible condition of production. Specifically, as noted earlier, larger land-owning construction companies gain land rent as excess profit, especially in relatively low-cost production. Short-term investment flows and their spatial distribution depend on intra-sectoral capital mobility and competition for lower costs and higher profits. These core assumptions of the real competition theory allow the TILR to incorporate macroeconomic relations and forces shaping investments in the housing sector. Additionally, given housing's unique status as a commodity, total profits comprise a sector-wide profit rate plus additional profits from land rents. The profit rate can further be divided into two types: profit on exploitation—gained from surplus value during construction, materials, equipment production, and maintenance—and profit on alienation, derived from property transfers, especially in real estate and finance (Shaikh 2016, 232; Duman and Tonak 2023, 236–237).

The TILR framework categorizes housing investment and pricing into three segments: 1) land, 2) building, and 3) maintenance (including renovation). It views housing as a complex commodity rooted in land, influenced by shifts in land rent, and reliant on labor-intensive construction and ongoing maintenance. Housing is bought, sold, rented, and re-rented over time, creating a continuous flow of financial capital. Investment in land hinges on two factors: (a) subjective valuation of locations across the city, which can fluctuate with urban development, and (b) the performance of the construction sector relative to manufacturing (a macro-level factor). The first is subjective because a land plot deemed marginal today may become desirable in the future due to changes in accessibility to amenities, often driven by infrastructure investments or disinvestments. The second depends on fluctuations in profit rates across sectors. Building investments are influenced by labor costs and wages, as well as the costs of machinery, raw materials, and intermediate inputs, all of which are shaped by aggregate competitive relations and production conditions, including sectoral and national labor relations, minimum wage levels, labor laws, and other factors that influence labor costs. Competition between industries within the value chain affects the prices of inputs and machinery that circulate from other industries into the construction sector. Investments in maintenance and renovation depend on associated costs and inputs, which are affected by long-term wage rates, raw material prices, and short-term market expectations. Their impact on the final market price directly influences the supply and demand of the existing building stock, reflecting consumer preferences and speculative activities. Notably, fluctuations in maintenance and renovation directly influence housing prices via supply and demand, whereas land and building investments are driven more by macro-level capital flows and price formation.

A simplistic view of pricing neglects key factors that affect investment flows, including both reproducible and non-reproducible profit components within the sector and their roles in price formation. In this Shaikh-inspired model, the final price is determined by a weighted combination of (a) the profit-wage ratio—covering vertically integrated inter-sectoral profit-wage ratios—and (b) the relative price, defined as total industrial vertically integrated unit labor costs across all three investment types, acting as an overall indicator. Consequently, an essential element in housing prices is the total inflow (and outflow) of new investments into the housing sector, driven by the pursuit of higher profits. This continual reallocation of investments across sectors to achieve higher returns is often ignored by both neoclassical and heterodox housing price theories. Recognizing such movement helps clarify the timing of housing supply within broader economic interactions and forces. It also demonstrates that the overall performance of the economy and that of competing sectors strongly influence investment flows into or out of housing.

The three types of investment also involve different turnover times (i.e., the sum of production time and circulation time). Several factors influence these turnover times, with the durability of construction materials such as concrete, bricks, glass, and girders being a key element. This durability is affected by technological progress, innovation, climate conditions, and notably, the productivity of industries supplying intermediate inputs for construction. The overall circulation time depends on the interactions between these input-producing industries and the actual construction activities. However, the circulation times at different stages can vary considerably. Broader urbanization trends also affect the total circulation time in the construction sector, which, as Arboleda and Purcell (2021, 1603) show, is itself influenced by land relations and fluctuations in land rents. For instance, whether an investor chooses to demolish or renovate a building to boost its floor-space ratio depends on the pace of urbanization, investment flows into urban land, and the level of land rents that determine them. Ultimately, the realization of the initial investment depends on the total circulation time, the production time (for construction, maintenance, and related inputs), and the relational inter-sectoral dynamics that govern them.

Land rent is crucial for understanding capital flows in the housing construction sector because it reflects excess profits on investments and significantly influences overall profit rates (Farahani 2021; Moreno Zacarés 2024; Swyngedouw and Ward 2022; Ward and Aalbers 2016). Changes in land rent affect both the timing and volume of investments entering the sector. It operates in two main ways, each with distinct timing and economic triggers: first, the varying qualities of different plots produce differential rent (Harvey 2006 [1982]), shaping investor preferences based on location; second, a macro-level rent, discussed in Chapter 5, arises from all plots in the sector and is charged by landowners or landowning builders (Farahani 2025). This non-relative rent fluctuates with competition from other sectors, such as manufacturing. When land rents increase overall, profit rates in urban land projects also rise, fueling a construction boom. As a result, land investments are the most significant among the three types for understanding when investment flows occur and when construction becomes attractive to capital, as Harvey (1978) calls it, capital switching. For example, housing construction generally demands more labor than manufacturing (Bruegel 1975; Farahani 2025; Manning 2023). The impact of land rent as excess profit is so substantial that even with higher wages, it remains cost-effective for investors to spend less on machinery and still achieve high returns from land rent. During crises and periods of low manufacturing profits, construction can be a safer investment due to the potential for excess land rent profits, provided that sector-wide land rent rates remain high.

6.1.2 Existing Explanations and Debates on the Housing Shortage in Malmö

The policy recommendation for addressing Malmö's housing shortage—specifically, building high-rises and encouraging densification—aims to boost prices by increasing overall supply to meet rising demand (Malmö Municipality, 2021). This strategy is based on the neoclassical microeconomic principle (see Chapter 1) that the market price of housing, as a commodity, is affected by the quantity of housing supplied relative to demand and the law of marginal utility (Alonso 1964; Muth 1969). Widely discussed in New Urban Economics literature, this idea stems from the general equilibrium framework of the neoclassical model (McMaster and Watkins 2006, 904; Richardson 1976, 137). It holds that "relative (equilibrium) price magnitudes are determined by the relative amounts of a given product demanded and supplied, with these amounts seen as the total demand and supply from individuals and firms" (Nicholas 2012, 459). Consequently, this approach "usually begins with an explanation of individual demand and supply curves that connect prices to quantities demanded and supplied" (ibid.). In housing markets, it is suggested that market value reaches equilibrium when supply matches demand, and the marginal utility-price ratio stays consistent across all goods, enabling rational utility maximization (Bassett and Short 1980). In this context, land prices serve as an allocation mechanism, guiding resources to the most efficient bidders in housing and land markets (Alonso 1964; Mirowski 2006; Mooya 2016). Furthermore, consumer preferences and investor decisions are shaped by the trade-offs between housing costs and commuting expenses to employment centers (Bassett and Short 1980). As discussed in Chapter 2, heterodox urban social and economic geographers have critiqued this viewpoint over the past fifty years for not addressing persistent income and wealth inequalities, which cause temporary disequilibrium (Aalbers and Christophers 2014; Arundel 2017; Harvey 2006 [1982]; 1985; Kauko 2001; Revington 2015). Opponents claim that speculation on existing property for short-term financial gains inflates prices and diminishes effective demand. They also argue that government intervention is needed to lower barriers to entry and stimulate demand.

In Malmö, many scholars have used this critique to explain the housing shortage (Madureira and Baeten 2016). Concerning the aforementioned policy recommendation, main counterarguments include: a) questioning its ideological basis as neoliberal urban planning and entrepreneurial governance, b) highlighting its social impacts on low-income groups through rising prices and unaffordability, and c) warning of potential gentrification (Baeten 2012; Gustafsson 2021b). Likewise, research on densification primarily explores its social and environmental impacts and the struggles of local tenants against adverse effects (Gustafsson et al. 2019; Lisberg Jensen et al. 2023; Olsson et al. 2020). These studies reveal a notable gap in neoclassical (microeconomic) explanations, as they fail to consider income and wealth disparities as key factors influencing housing affordability (Listerborn and Baeten 2022; Madureira and Baeten 2016). They emphasize that the core issue is not a general housing shortage but a lack of affordable options. While increasing overall housing supply could, in the long term, help lower prices citywide, short-term challenges such as varying neighborhood prices and existing income gaps can hinder this. In fact, more supply might temporarily raise prices and intensify the probability of gentrification in low-income areas (Revington 2015). These studies often ignore the role of temporality, including fluctuations in new construction investments. They also leave unanswered two crucial questions: a) what economic factors initially made housing appear attractive? Furthermore, b) what causes disinvestment cycles, when housing stops attracting private investors?

6.2 Housing Shortage in Malmö—Empirical Evidence

6.2.1 Housing in Times of Crisis

Sweden was among the pioneer countries to implement a zero-interest rate policy from 2015 to 2016, followed by a negative interest rate policy from 2016 to 2019 (Riksbanken 2024). This aligned with a broader quantitative easing approach after the Great Recession. However, instead of generating significant real investments—the primary goal—these policies fueled speculative activities and increased trading in real estate markets (Roberts 2018), which significantly elevated the household debt-to-GDP ratio from 68% in 2008 to 94% in 2020 (SCB n.d.; 2023a). Since late 2021, rising inflation has prompted many central banks, including Sweden's Riksbank, to stop quantitative easing and sharply raise interest rates to curb demand and reduce inflation (Schnabel 2022). A significant result of this shift is that housing markets have become more volatile, driving up overall housing costs and rents, and making it more difficult for low-income households—including first-time working class homeowners—to manage mortgage and rental market fluctuations.

The root of this issue is evident. Since the deregulation of housing rents in 2011 (Sveriges Allmännytta n.d.), many middle- and low-income households in Malmö have increasingly moved toward homeownership. The annual sales of tenant-owned dwellings—the primary form of homeownership in multi-unit buildings—rose from 8,000 in 2008 to over 12,000 in 2021 (SCB 2022). The total number of these dwellings also grew, from 54,000 in 2008 to over 70,000 in 2022 (SCB 2023b). As shown in Figure 40, the share of tenant-owned units within multi-dwelling buildings—which accounted for 78% of the total housing stock—increased significantly. At the same time, the number of rental units decreased following the policy changes in 2011 (SCB 2023b). The recent changes in monetary policy, combined with stagnant wages and rising living

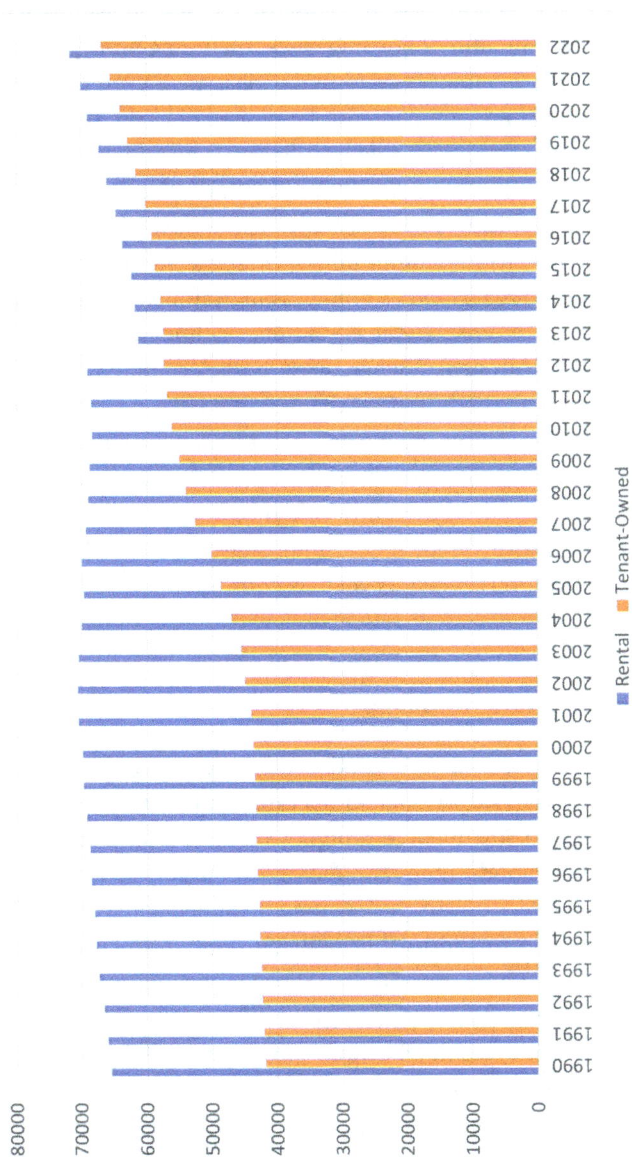

FIGURE 40 Malmö—tenure types in multi-dwelling buildings 1990–2022 (Source: SCB (my calculation))

costs—including energy prices—have jeopardized these households' ability to retain their homes. The ratio of housing costs (including mortgage payments) to disposable income has sharply increased. This issue is even more critical for renters, as rising rents are coupled with landlords' periodic disinvestment in property maintenance, often justified by inflation (Gustafsson 2021a).

This situation directly affects the shortage of affordable housing (Tenants Association 2016), resulting in increased housing costs, homelessness, and overcrowding in low-income communities. In 2023, municipal data indicate that 1,610 people were registered as homeless in Malmö (Malmö Municipality 2023), including 322 minors and 1,288 adults. Although these figures have improved from the 2018 peak—when 5,883 homeless individuals, including 2,499 minors, were recorded (ibid.)—the ongoing housing crisis exacerbates long-term affordability issues, now worsened by rising inflation and interest rates. Two main lessons emerge: a) macroeconomic factors like changes in inflation and interest rates significantly influence housing costs and consumption; and b) cyclical investment flows in housing and their impact on prices further affect micro-level behaviors such as consumer preferences and investor choices.

6.2.2 Housing Shortage in Malmö

As others have shown and as Malmö Municipality (2021) acknowledges, housing shortages are tied to broader socio-economic inequalities that disproportionately affect low-income groups (Madureira and Baeten 2016). In higher-cost neighborhoods, there is often an oversupply of housing, particularly in rental markets. Conversely, low-income areas face a starkly low ratio of dwellings available for affordable housing relative to residents (Malmö Municipality 2024). In 2021, the city had 165,133 dwellings and 174,413 households (Malmö Municipality 2024). This overall data suggests that the city does not face a significant housing shortage. However, breaking down the data reveals a different reality. Over the past decade, more than 40% of households in Malmö have been single-person households. Currently, households with three or four members are fewer than two-person households, which make up 27% (Malmö Municipality 2024). Larger families, with five or more members, account for only about 6–7% of all households (ibid.). The lack of affordable housing is particularly acute for low-income households with one or two people, including students and young adults (Grander 2023; Tykesson 2021). For younger individuals with lower incomes, high rents are compounded by long waits for publicly owned housing. Average public housing waiting times in the low-income area of Rosengård increased from 2.6 years in 2011 to

4 years in 2019 (Listerborn 2021, 1308; Grander 2023; Tenants Association 2021, 2). If we categorize dwellings into five types—1) less than 40 square meters, 2) 41–60 square meters, 3) 61–90 square meters, 4) 91–120 square meters, and 5) over 121 square meters—we can use Swedish minimum housing standards (Bengtson 1974) to assume that the first category suits single-person households, the second for two-person households, the third for three, the fourth for four, and the fifth for households with five or more members. This categorization shows that the most significant shortage of apartments—whether for rent or ownership—is among single-person households, followed by two-person households and those with more than five members (Figure 41). The latter group does not immediately threaten the supply of single-family homes, such as detached or semi-detached houses (Figure 42).

As shown above, multi-dwelling buildings make up 78% of the city's total housing stock. Figure 43 shows that rental dwellings house the majority of residents (over 40%).

When we compare this data to the real estate price index (Figure 44) and income levels (Figure 46), it becomes clear that the low-income population bears the brunt of the housing shortage.

The effectiveness of the policy mentioned above largely depends on the spatial variation of land values. More densification and high-rise building projects tend to be concentrated in lower-land-value areas, such as Rosengård. Conversely, many upscale high-rises are developed in wealthier parts of the city, including Western Harbor and New Harbor. This trend aligns with the interests of private investors, who prioritize short-term cost-return ratios. Additionally, with limited regulation of housing prices—including rents—affordability and quality have become directly linked to income levels. As expected in the heterodox explanations mentioned earlier, increasing income and wealth inequalities in recent years have significantly worsened housing inequality (Euronews 2024). Several examples illustrate this point. Figures 45 and 46 show a correlation between income levels, unemployment rates, and the ratio of residential areas to residents, indicating high density and shortages in low-income neighborhoods such as Rosengård, Fosie, and Hyllie (Boverket 2024a; Sandberg and Grander 2021). These areas have proportionately higher rental rates and lower-priced owner-occupied properties. The residential area per person in Örtagården, one of the poorest neighborhoods in Rosengård, is 26 square meters. By comparison, the figures are 44 square meters in the Old Town and 41 square meters in Western Harbor (Boverket 2024a). Western Harbor is known for its affluent, highly skilled professionals and a sizable expatriate population—27% of its residents were foreign-born in 2022, and overall, 35% were either foreign-born or had foreign-born parents (Malmö

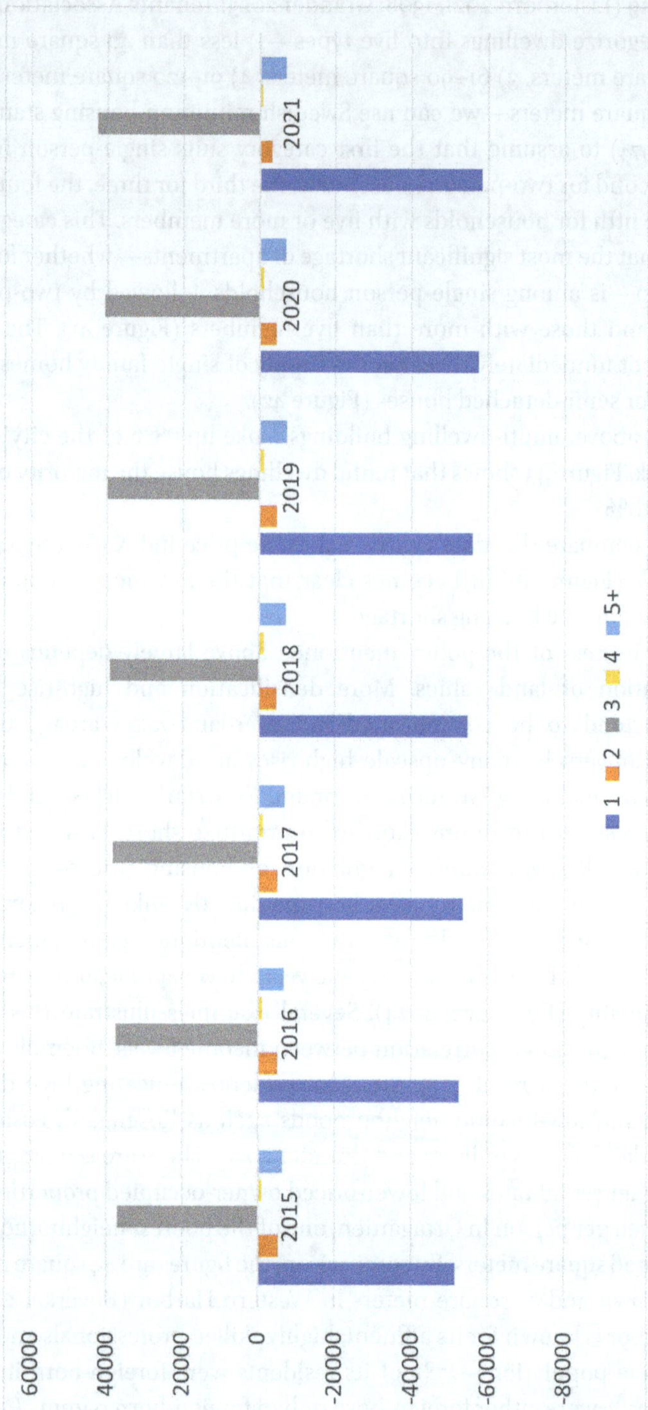

FIGURE 41 Malmö—number of adequately sized apartments per household size 2015–2021 (Source: SCB and Malmö Municipality (my calculation))

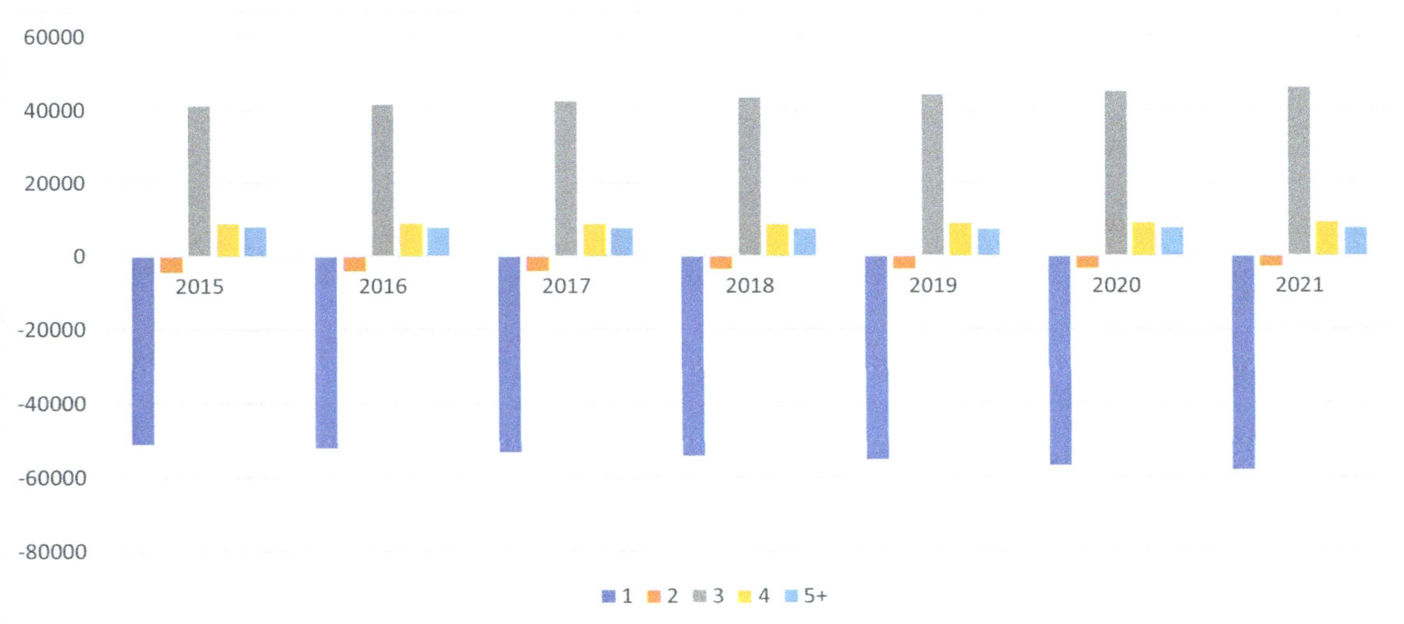

FIGURE 42 Number of all available adequately sized housing (apartments and houses) per household size, 2015–2021 (Source: SCB and Malmö Municipality (my calculation))

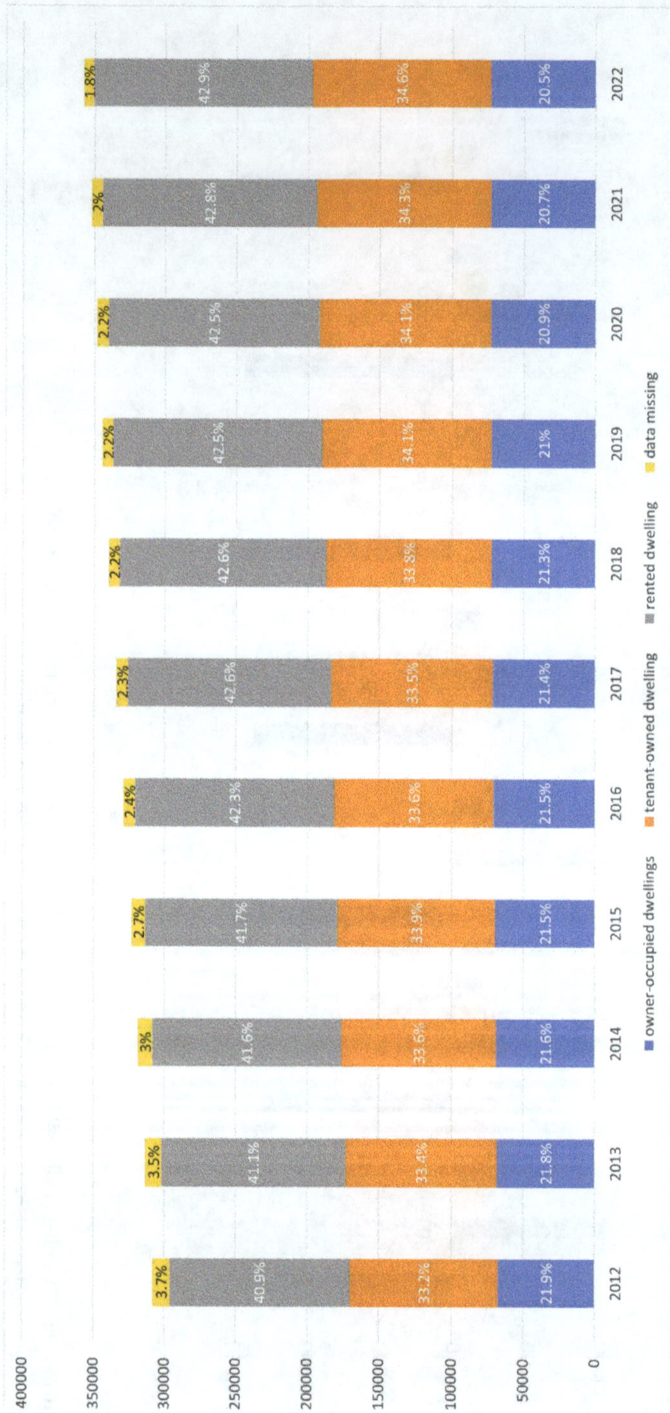

FIGURE 43 Malmö—number of people by tenure 2012–2022 (Source: SCB (my calculation))

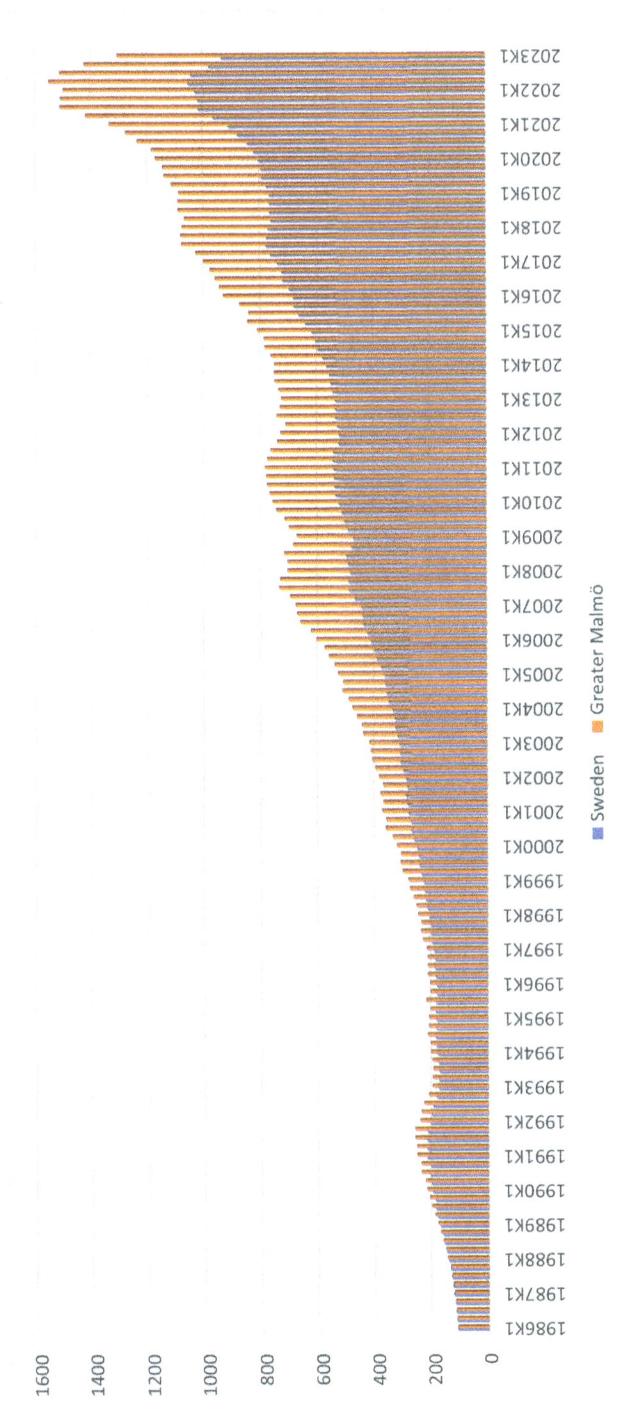

FIGURE 44 Sweden and Greater Malmö—real estate price index for one- and two-dwelling buildings for permanent living (1980 = 100) 1986–2022 (Source: SCB (my calculation))

FIGURE 45 Malmö—average living area per person (Source: Boverket's interactive Segregationsbarometern, https://segregationsbarometern.boverket.se/ (accessed 27 May 2024) (my modification))

FIGURE 46 Malmö—disposable income per unit of consumption (median) (Source: Boverket's interactive Segregationsbarometern, https://segregationsbarometern.boverket.se/ (accessed 27 May 2024) (my modification))

Municipality 2022). In Örtagården, these figures are much higher at 58% and 92%, respectively (ibid.).

The average income in the neighborhoods examined is 140,000 SEK, 296,000 SEK, and 359,000 SEK (see Figure 46). These figures exclude capital gains, which significantly impact the overall picture when included, as reported recently (UBS 2025). In 2021, the average annual capital income was 167,438 SEK for Örtagården and 478,802 SEK for Western Harbor (Malmö Municipality 2024). The active workforce, ages 16 to 74, comprises 70% of Western Harbor's population but only 40% in Örtagården (ibid.). In Western Harbor, professionals in law, economics, science, and technology make up the largest occupational group at 15%, while in Örtagården, the primary employment sectors are public healthcare at 23.2% and public education at 11.7% (ibid.). Housing tenure also varies greatly: all housing in Örtagården is rental, whereas 78% of housing in Western Harbor is tenant-owned (Boverket 2024a). Long-term unemployment rates reflect these differences as well; Örtagården has a rate of 9%, compared to 2% in Western Harbor and the Old Town (ibid.).

The key takeaway from this evidence, as some heterodox scholars note, is that a housing shortage exists for two main groups: low-income and low- to middle-income families with 1–2 members, and those with five or more. More appropriate housing should be developed in areas such as Rosengård. The question remains: why does this increase in supply not occur?

6.3 Implications of the TILR for Housing Shortage in Malmö

I begin with Rosengård, home to some of the city's poorest neighborhoods, including Örtagården, characterized by high unemployment rates and entirely rental housing. The key property owners here are the municipal housing company MKB and the private firm Victoriahem. A controversial high-rise project called Culture Casbah has been planned in response to the noted policy recommendation (Baeten et al. 2016; MKB Fastigheter 2017; Gustafsson 2022, 20). This initiative is a partnership between MKB and its public-private partner, Rosengårdfastigheter, founded in 2017 following a merger with three private firms: Fastighets AB Balder, Heimstaden AB, and Victoriahem AB. Rosengårdfastigheter acquired 7% of MKB's units in Rosengård as part of this deal. Initially conceived as a high-rise development, Culture Casbah aims to introduce new housing, offices, meeting spaces, daycare centers, shops, and venues for services, sports, and culture (Rosengårdfastigheter n.d.). After extensive debates on the project specifics and based on earlier evidence (Figure 41), a recent plan has been proposed that prioritizes larger homes for families of five or more, along with smaller units for individual households (SKD 2024).

As discussed in the previous chapter, the construction industry is highly concentrated by four major companies: Skanska, NCC, Peab, and JM (Blackwell, Holgersen, Wallstam 2023). In Scania County, where Malmö is the largest metropolitan area, these companies control 30% of all urban residential land, with Skanska and NCC being particularly influential (SOU 2018, 157). In 2018, they acquired more than 1.3 million square meters of urban residential land nationwide (ibid. 156), roughly equivalent to 16,500 homes (ibid. 155–156). According to the TILR, this ownership grants them excess profits on land, as they benefit from lower-cost development conditions. Meanwhile, land appears as an expense for construction firms that do not own it. In Malmö, the municipal company MKB and the private firm Victoriahem are active in the land market, although they are not primarily involved in construction, unlike Skanska.

As demonstrated in Chapter 5, understanding fluctuations in aggregate land rents is essential for grasping changes in housing construction investments in Sweden over recent years (Farahani 2025). In 2020, during the COVID-19 pandemic, Sweden saw a 29% increase in new construction investments, even as manufacturing profits declined (Farahani 2021; Tykesson 2022). However, after the pandemic, this trend reversed. The total number of permits for new construction, especially in Greater Malmö, dropped from 507 in 2020 to 482 in 2021, then to 334 in 2022, and further down to 204 in 2023 (SCB 2024a). A similar decline was seen in newly built dwellings, which rose from 1,920 in 2019 to 3,262 in 2021, then decreased to 1,382 in 2022 and 522 in 2023 (SCB 2024b). Several factors contribute to this situation: 1) rising interest rates have increased borrowing costs, 2) government support for rental and student housing has ended (Boverket 2024b), and 3) many construction companies have paused building projects while holding onto their land, waiting for higher profit margins (as confirmed through my email exchanges with the Malmö municipality's City Planning Department). In this environment, land hoarding—anticipating higher future land rents (a significant part of their overall profit)—has become a practical investment strategy.

The curse of low-income residential areas is that differential rents therein persistently tend to stay low. Private investment tends to flow into these areas only when sectoral land rents (absolute rents) are relatively high, thereby raising expected profits for landowning investors. Fluctuations in these rents are beyond municipal control. This context explains the rationale behind projects like Culture Casbah: beyond increasing supply to restore balance, these initiatives, regardless of ideological views, aim to boost differential rents to attract private investment. However, they also have limitations; when sector-wide land rents are low, these neighborhoods often experience disinvestment in new development, rendering projects like Culture Casbah and related infrastructure improvements largely ineffective. For instance, in Rosengård, hopes that the December 2018 opening of the metro line would attract private investment have not materialized. The municipality has struggled to attract investors, with only one land allocation call issued since 2019, announced for 2025 (Malmö Municipality 2025). Two agreements with MKB's Rosengårdfastigheter have been signed—mainly concerning Culture Casbah—in Törnrosen and Örtagården, in 2019 (now expired) and 2023. Currently, there is no investor interest for 2025, as confirmed by my email exchanges with the department (also, Friberg 2025).

Addressing the shortage of affordable housing in this context calls for systematic public intervention that goes beyond current institutional arrangements for land market regulation and management. As Grander (2018) highlights, despite decades of privatization, Sweden's public housing system (*Allmännyttan*) remains essential in reducing housing inequalities. Presently, MKB owns and manages 16% of all multi-family buildings in Malmö, totaling 23,000 units (SCB 2023c). However, market-driven tenant cooperatives, which account for over 34% of all apartments in the city (Figure 43), limit the public sector's economic influence, particularly on land prices. Additionally, EU competition laws mandate that public companies generate positive annual revenue and restrict market interventions that threaten free competition (Kommunförbundet n.d.; EUR-Lex 2003). Municipal firms like MKB are required to operate according to market principles to comply with these regulations and can only undertake construction projects when it makes economic sense (Salonen et al. 2019). Given the current circumstances and limited municipal land resources, addressing the unequal distribution and scarcity of affordable housing—primarily dependent on new construction investments—will continue to rely on private sector investments driven by broader macroeconomic forces.

6.4 Concluding Remarks

The shortage of affordable housing in Malmö is most acutely felt by the low-income population. In the context of limited municipal land ownership, this shortage is driven by the cyclical movement of private investments, especially in new construction within the sector. Unlike neoclassical and heterodox approaches, the shortage is not solely due to temporary disequilibrium in either the supply or demand structures. Instead, as indicated by the TILR and the underlying real competition theory, it is driven by the withdrawal of investment from the housing sector in a marketized land-and-property system. In this context, densification and high-rise development strategies, although economically sensible and realistic given current market conditions, can only succeed if they are part of a broader, more organized social and economic plan aimed at regulating land rents and increasing wages. Otherwise, as heterodox critics warn, such policies are likely to worsen spatial inequalities. Assuming current conditions, especially in low-income neighborhoods where shortages are most severe, the increase in supply depends on a temporary rise in sector-wide absolute rents (i.e., excess profits) that attract new investment across the entire sector. Without decisive, direct public intervention in land markets and new construction, private investment to supply housing will remain low in these areas. Effective reform in the housing market, to address the housing problems faced by the urban poor, must focus on: a) going beyond simply fixing the unequal distribution of existing housing and taking control of housing production and prices by regulating land markets, and b) combining these strategies with other welfare measures, especially raising wages and ideally transforming the entire urban land ownership system and removing land from the market.

CHAPTER 7

The Decline of Iran's First Public Housing Program

The following two chapters expand my operationalization of the TILR to the context of the Global South, starting with the implications for the Iranian housing sector at the national level. Following the same scalar order as in the Swedish cases discussed above, the next chapter explores the model's implications for the urban context. My goal in both cases is to analyze different ways in which the housing sector, as a whole, relates to the rest of the economy. This chapter presents my analysis of the Iranian housing sector, focusing on the failure of Iran's first and only state-led housing program, the Mehr Housing Program. The analysis incorporates the concept of absolute rent as a structural mechanism for controlling capital flows into urban land investments, using the inter-sectoral and multi-scalar framework outlined in the TILR. It aims to challenge the traditional linear approach that relates macro-level (global) similarities with micro-level (local) differences. The case of Iran is interesting because it introduces complexity into the spatiotemporal analysis of aggregate and inter-sectoral rates of return, which are central to measuring land rent creation and appropriation in the TILR. Existing analyses tend to explain Iran's situation through exogenous mechanisms, such as the backwardness of its political and governmental systems, the underdevelopment of capitalist political and economic relations, limited expertise, and the restricted influence of technocrats due to political interference by undemocratic and religious forces. In contrast, this chapter offers a structural alternative by highlighting the repercussions of the actually-existing Iranian capitalism and its economic and geopolitical limitations.

7.1 Iranian Capitalism, State, and Public Economy

I start with a brief historical overview of capitalist urbanization in Iran. The urban population accounts for 73.4 percent of approximately 82 million people (World Bank 2018). The national tenancy rate has stayed between 15 and 25 percent over the past fifty years (SCI 2014), while the owner-occupancy rate decreased from 70 percent in the mid-1970s to 50 percent (SCI 2016–2017). The remaining dwellings are classified as "dwellings for government and military employees" (ibid.). More significantly, "an overwhelming majority of tenants are working class (ca. six million households)" (Farahani and Yousefi 2021, 46). Around 40 percent of household expenses in urban areas go toward housing; in Tehran, the figure rises to 50 percent (approximately twice the minimum wage) (SCI 2014; CBI 2017a; TMICTO 2014–2015). Independent estimates are naturally much higher—at least 70 percent—for low-income working families (Farahani 2013; Raisdana 2001; Yousefi and Farahani 2019).

What makes the Iranian housing sector intriguing compared to many advanced capitalist economies is its consistent lack of direct involvement from both central and local governments in systematically providing low-income, de-commodified housing. I will save the discussion of the challenges faced by local governments and municipalities for the next chapter and instead focus solely on how the central state operates in the Iranian capitalist system in this chapter. The absence of direct state intervention is not uncommon among countries of the Global South (Frieden 1981; Glinavos 2008; Hewison 1988; Newell 2008; Topal et al. 2018). The contrast is most noticeable when compared to a country like Sweden, as discussed earlier (Chapter 5). However, it also applies to other countries in the Global North, where state interventions are much less extensive but rarely non-existent. At the conceptual level, this observation has implications for the debate over privatization, and specifically, the common conflation of privatization and commodification in anti-neoliberal literature. The assumption, here, is "if goods and services are privately owned or produced, they are commodified, and if not, they are necessarily de-commodified" (Farahani and Yousefi 2021, 48). What such (superficial) explanations overlook is the role of profit in commodity production, no matter if the producer is a state entity or a private one.

Iranian state-owned companies are active in the economy, but not in a Keynesian welfare-state fashion. They are involved in for-profit practices. In the case of urban development (including residential development), the services provided by state-owned companies are commodified. The role of the state is crucial, as it enables lower production costs by using state-owned resources or outsourcing to private developers at negotiated lower prices, with the expectation that the final price will be reduced. As I will discuss in the next chapter, this outsourcing practice is vital for municipalities to remain active in urban development, especially in the absence of reliable taxation. Iranian taxation is characterized by hidden corporate income and an exemption system designed to benefit favored companies, including all state or military-affiliated ones, which "allegedly are involved in 60% of the total economies activity" (ibid. also, INTA 2015). This common practice of "relying on the 'natural market mechanism' for provisioning public goods and then using price mechanisms to overcome potential conflicts arising because of competition is best categorized as commodified provision even if it is led by the state" (Harvey 2009 [1973], 88 in Farahani and Yousefi 2021, 50; also, La Grange and Pretorius 2005).

Housing has largely been excluded from Iranian state regulations and control, as "the central state assumes no obligation to initiate public housing provision" (Farahani and Yousefi 2021, 46). Instead, this allows the private sector to dominate through market forces. This trend is reflected in national accounts and central and local policy documents on land, investment, and housing spending throughout most of the 20th century (Bharier 1971; Raisdana 2001; Sadvandian and Etehadieh 1989; Tehran Municipality 2019). In response, the army and industries took over financing, planning, and developing company towns and similar projects to house their employees, including many working families (Yousefi and Farahani 2022). That is not to say the government has entirely ignored this potentially explosive social issue. Instead, over the last fifty years, most administrations have typically subsidized land and construction materials (such as concrete, girders, etc.) for private developers to promote lower-cost housing construction, balance supply and demand, and indirectly help lower housing prices (Farahani and Yousefi 2021, 46). In other words, the aim of housing subsidies is "to attract private developers and subcontractors to invest in residential development and not secure housing for the poor" (ibid. 50). In this context, residential land plots mostly remain privately owned. Market forces of supply and demand mainly determine rent and property values. Dwellings are typically developed by individual homeowners and small-scale developers, who then sell or rent them out (ibid. 46). A few medium- and large-scale developers also participate in the owner-occupied market (ibid.; Yousefi and Farahani 2019). However, homeowners are "solely responsible for maintenance [through informal verbal agreements between owners], which, particularly for rentals, has proven problematic, as it has repeatedly caused tensions between tenants and single-dwelling owners" (Farahani and Yousefi 2021, 46).

The government's lack of interest in housing investment is evident in final consumption expenditure data from 1960 to 2013. The highest spending categories are defense and police, followed by economic affairs and the ideologically charged social and cultural sectors (Figure 47). Apart from two brief periods—the early 1970s, due to mass rural-to-urban migration after land reforms in the early 1960s, and the early 1990s, following the Iran-Iraq war of 1980–1989—housing consistently ranked as the lowest category (at 2.7% on average). Limited state regulations on the housing market partly explain the high official return rates in real estate (consistently around 15–20 percent over the last 30 years) and risky, speculative investments that have led to subpar

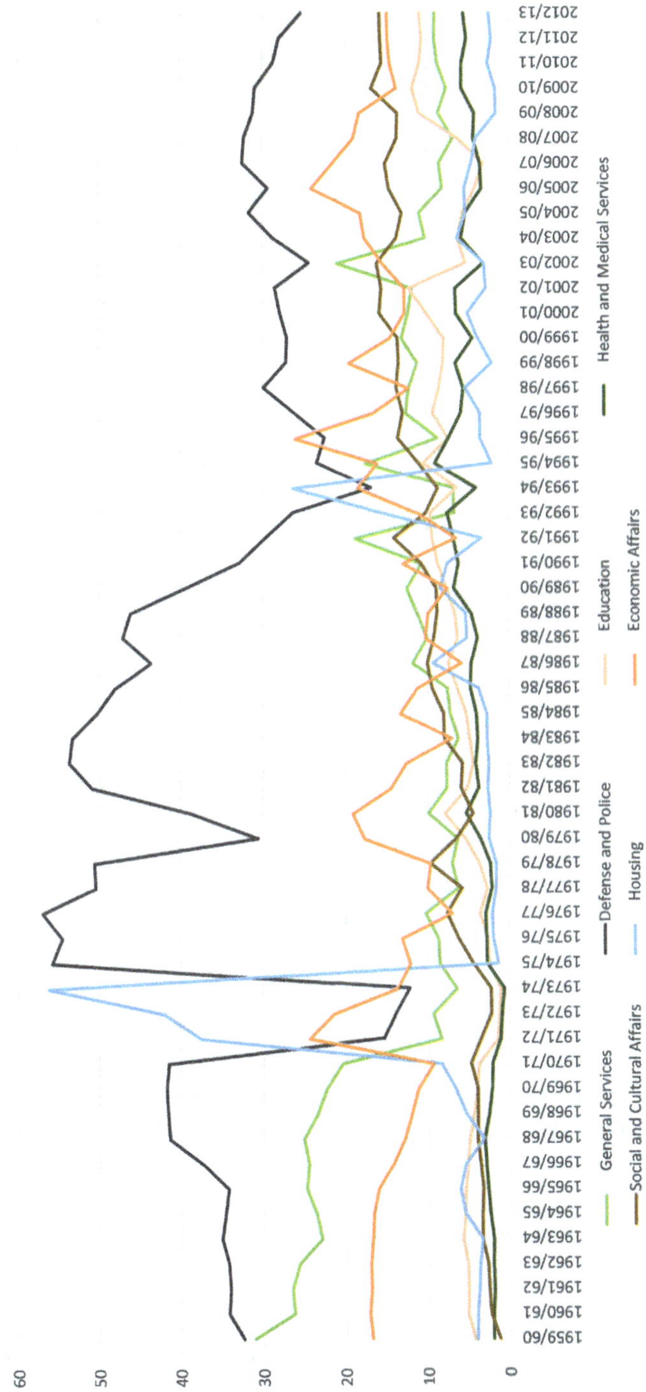

FIGURE 47 Iran—government final expenditure by type (%) (Source: CBI (2013a) (my calculation))

constructions (CBI 2013a). While this pattern might support the exogenous explanation, alluded to above, of how Iranian capitalism functions, as we will explore further below, it does not tell the entire story because it obscures the role of profits in investments in urban land.

7.2 Labor Relations and the Aggregate Rate of Profit

As noted above, the housing sector in Iran is "predominantly private … with high levels of individual (even atomistic) ownership, development, sale, and renting out of land and dwellings" (Farahani and Yousefi 2021, 50; also, Behdad and Nomani 2009, 97; Behdad and Nomani 2011). Two distinctive features characterize the sector: a) the absence of active state regulations culminated in the absence of any public (low-income) housing provisions, and b) the super-exploitation of workers, not least in the construction sector (Farahani and Yousefi 2021, 50; Yousefi and Farahani 2019, 3). The latter feature needs further exploration. Both the manufacturing and construction sectors have been struggling with low economies of scale over the last few decades. However, this has been generally overcome in the housing sector in general and construction in particular, by "incorporating low-skilled, cheap, almost entirely unorganized, and largely (including illegal) migrant and seasonal labor" that stands at around 70% of the sectoral work force (Farahani and Yousefi 2021, 50; also Behdad and Nomani 2011; Raisdana 2001; Sepehrdoust 2013, 70; Zakeri et al. 1996, 419). Even in highly moderated official data (and this cannot be overstated[1]), the average wage of a low-skilled construction worker has "consistently been around 30 percent below the national minimum wage" for the past twenty years (SCI 2019; Farahani and Yousefi 2021, 50). The Iranian housing sector, labor-intensive, minimally mechanized, and heavily dependent on cheap labor and long hours, exemplifies this issue. In 2016, unskilled construction workers outnumbered high-skilled workers by a factor of 10, with high-skilled workers accounting for only 4% of total employment in the sector (SCI 2016). Meanwhile, high-skilled workers in the manufacturing industry have consistently represented about 40–45 percent over the last twenty years (SCI 2015) (Farahani and Yousefi 2021, 50). The labor relations are characterized by a) the dominance of verbal contracts, b) the absence of labor benefits

1 It is a well-known fact that the official data in Iran is adjusted to downplay the extent of inequalities. However, using the official data as a baseline in a consistent empirical approach remains valid, as long as we consciously acknowledge that the actual conditions are likely much more severe.

like health insurance, unemployment benefits, and pensions, c) the systematically discriminatory contracts, particularly for ethnic, national minorities (Kurds in particular) as well as women, and d) severely restricted political (and individual) freedoms, as indicated by the imprisonment of many union leaders and labor activists (Farahani and Yousefi 2021, 50). The latter is crucial for sustaining the extreme levels of inequality mentioned above and for limiting the constant risk of popular uprisings. It also clearly positions the state (as well as its security forces and, say, morality police) alongside the capitalists in day-to-day class struggle, and, interestingly, ties struggles for recognition and political freedoms to struggles against exploitation.

These are reflected in the capital cost-labor cost ratio. Figure 48 shows that the organic composition of capital (as net capital stock divided by compensation of employees) in the construction sector has been significantly lower than in the manufacturing sector. Data on employee compensation is available only for the 13 years shown in the graph. Nevertheless, the trend is consistent with the rest of the data I use and present in this chapter. Crucial is the relation between the organic composition of capital and technology. For Marx, the organic composition of capital is to be understood in terms of the use of labor-efficient technologies. The long working days in Iranian industries (up to 2–3 shifts a day) (Farahani 2013) indicate persistently low rates of profit (see Figure 53). That is partly due to difficulties in importing frontier technologies (due to US-led sanctions), without which the organic composition of capital fluctuates much less frequently than it would if labor-efficient technologies were more easily acquired. The state's attack on labor, which includes slashing wages and criminalizing unionization, greatly contributes to the continuous exploitation of labor under such circumstances and helps the capitalists maintain profitability, regardless of the limits on the import of frontier technologies. I will discuss this further in Section 7.5 below.

We get a clearer picture if we triangulate this data with sectoral data on gross investment in machinery. Figure 49 shows this data at constant prices, and Figures 50, 50, and 52 show it at current prices. In both cases, regardless of the calculation method, we see a general tendency to invest less in the construction sector machinery. That is consistent with the organic composition data. Furthermore, as Figures 50, 51, and 52 show, as the economy entered the crisis in 1974, the two began to diverge, with a dramatic take-off by the late 1990s.

Similarly, the low aggregate rate of profit (Figure 53) should be analyzed in context. As Figure 53 shows, profit rates (as net operating surplus divided by net capital stock in current costs) began to fall in 1974, with two slight recovery periods in 1990–1993 and 1997–2004. Overall, the trend has been downward over the last 40 years, with a significant decline in the late 1970s following the

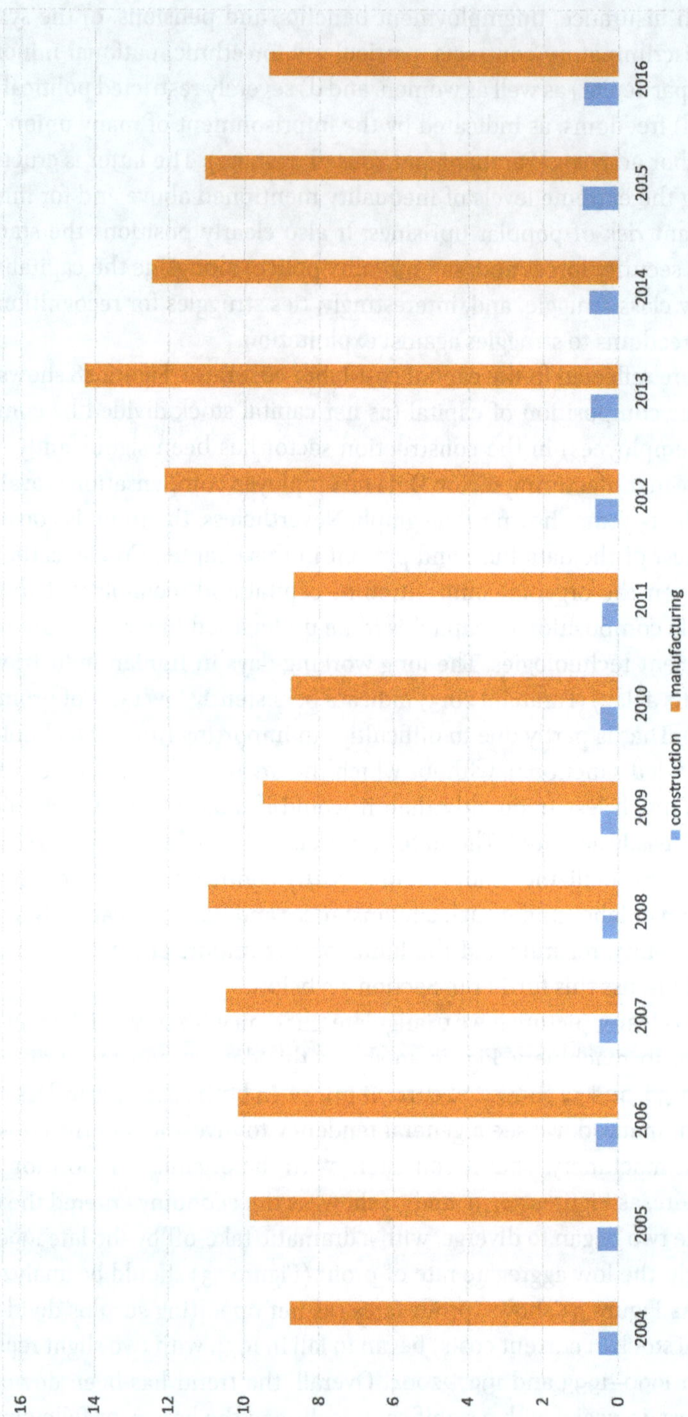

FIGURE 48 Iran—organic composition of capital (Source: SCI (2020) (my calculation))

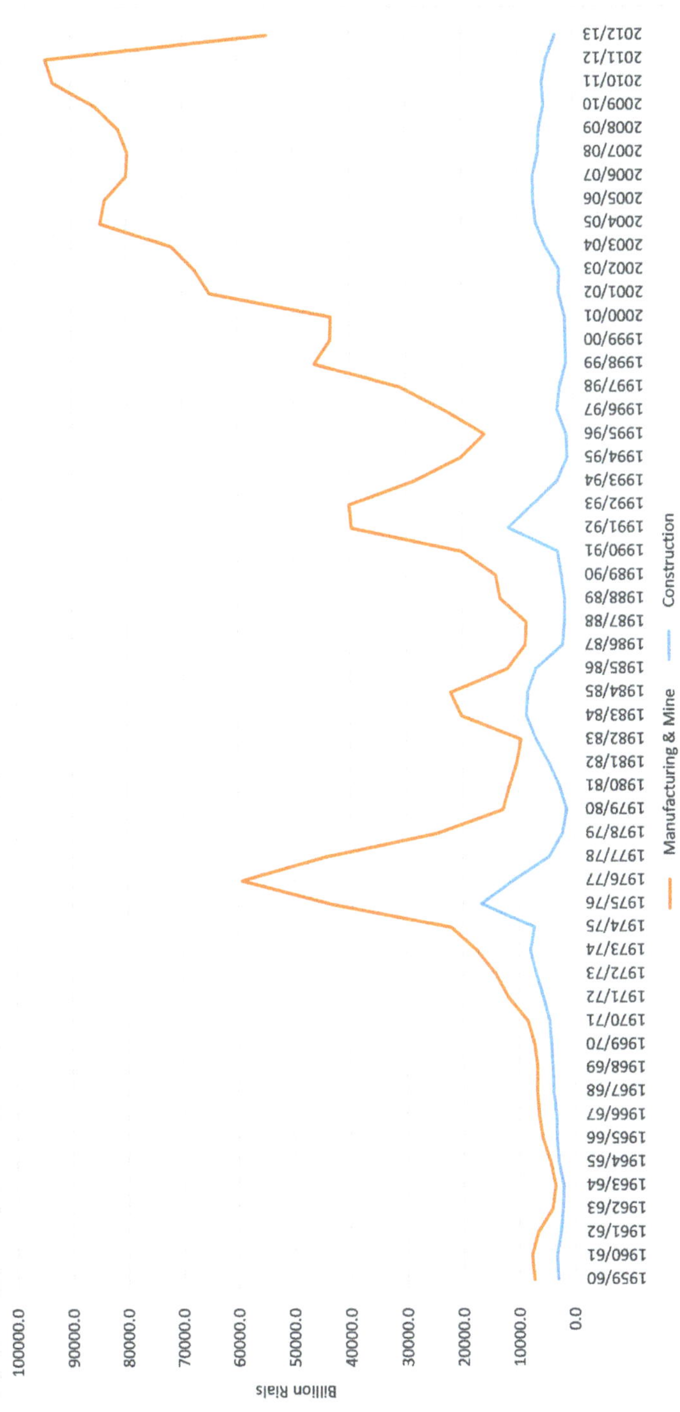

FIGURE 49 Iran—Private sector's gross fixed capital formation in machinery by sector, constant 2004/2005 prices (Source: CBI (2013b) (my calculation))

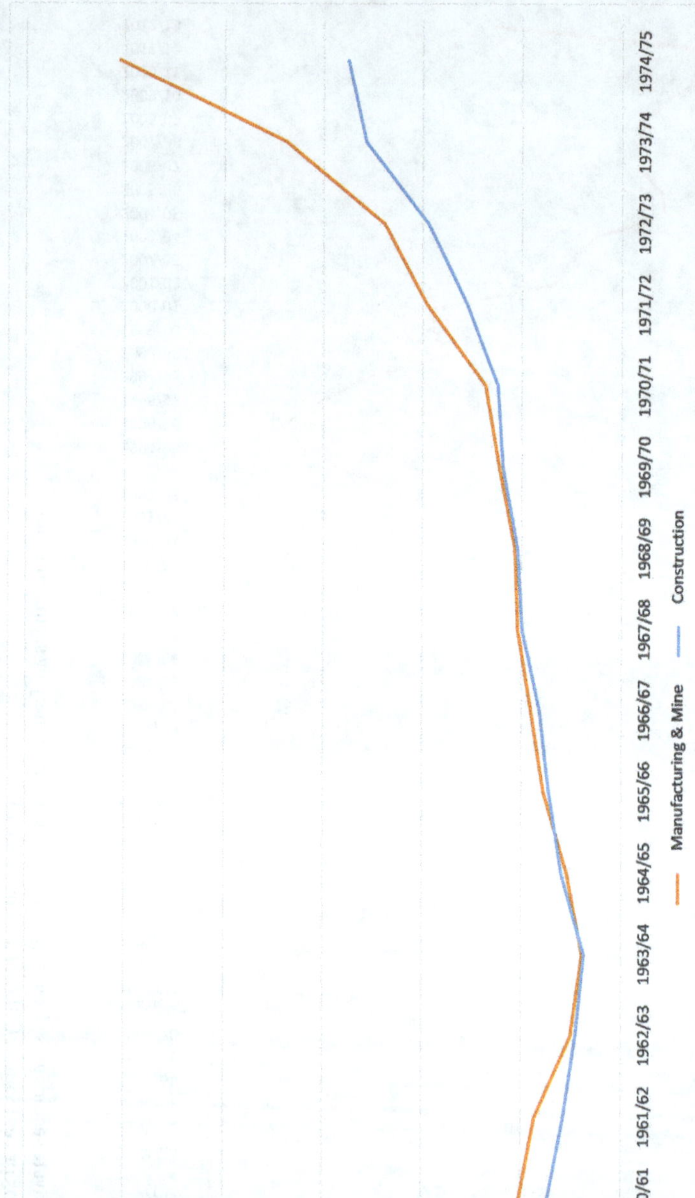

FIGURE 50 Iran gross fixed capital formation in machinery by sector, current prices 1959–1974 (Source: CBI (2013b) (my calculation))

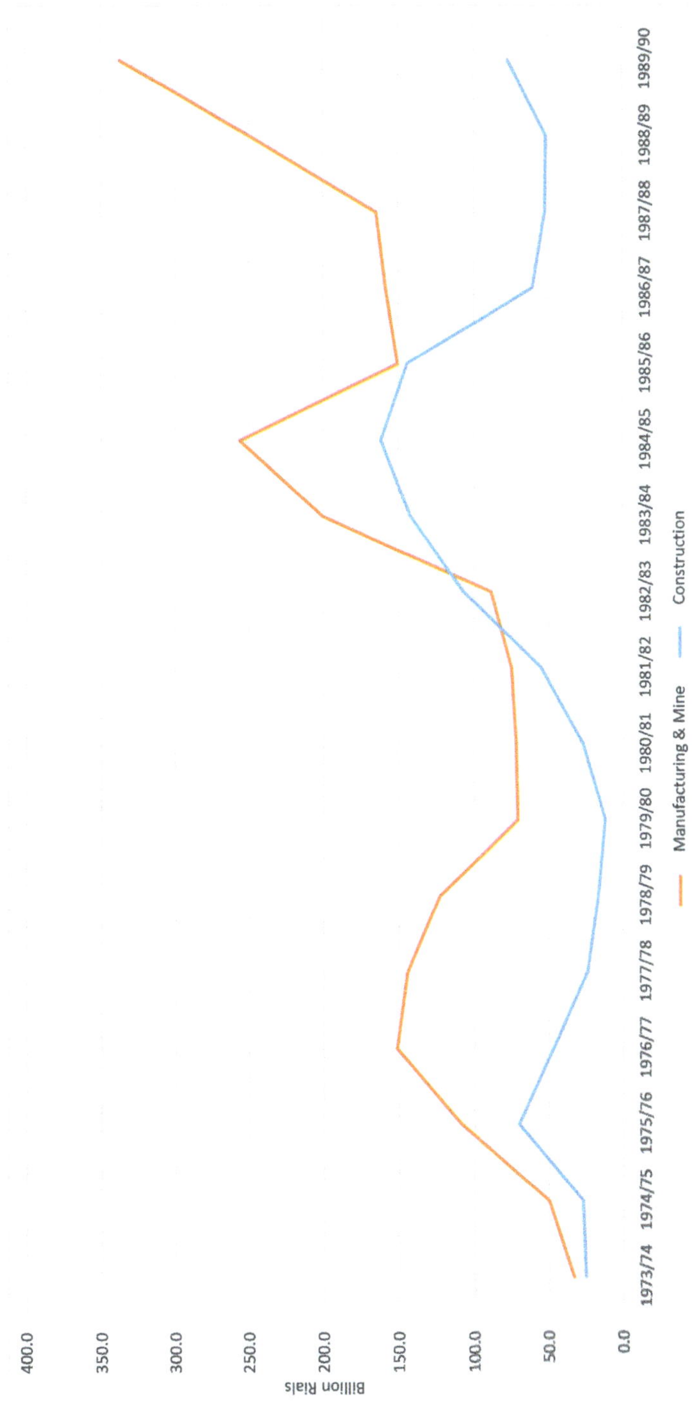

FIGURE 51 Iran gross fixed capital formation in machinery by sector, current prices 1974–1990 (Source: CBI (2013b) (my calculation))

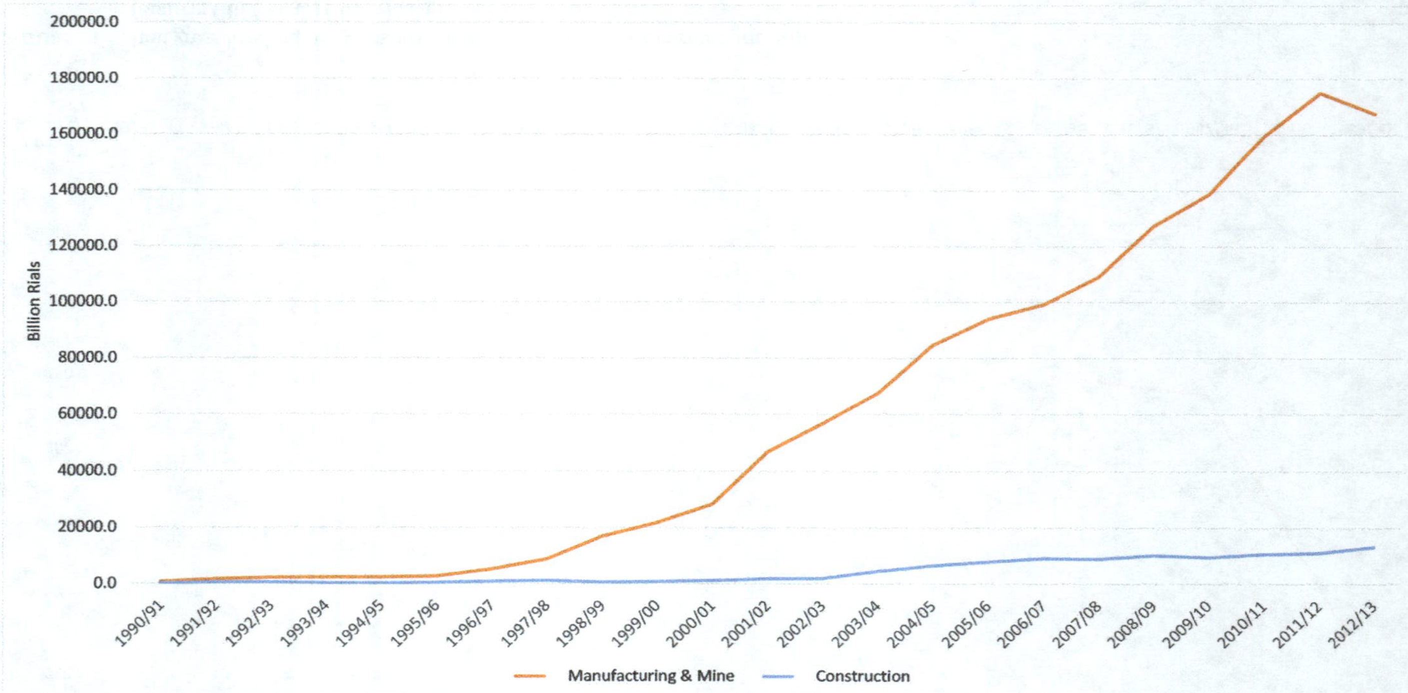

FIGURE 52 Iran gross fixed capital formation in machinery by sector, current prices 1990–2013 (Source: CBI (2013b) (my calculation))

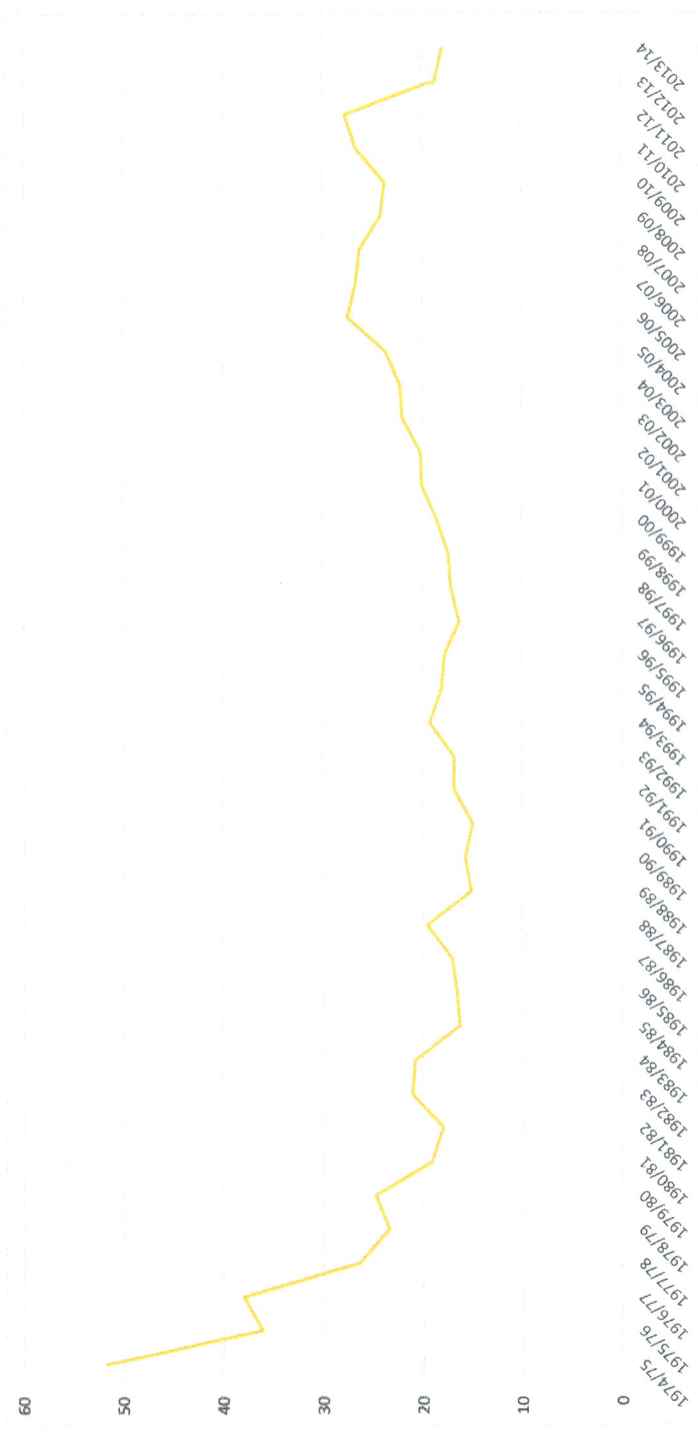

FIGURE 53 Iran—aggregate rate of profit 1974–2014 (Source: CBI (2016) (my calculation))

1979 Revolution, a major extra-economic event expected to have immediate economic implications.

What is interesting is the apparent inability of the economy (in terms of aggregate profitability) to bounce back. Nevertheless, it somehow managed to grow during a secular decline in aggregate figures. To explain, we should note that although the overall trend is downward, the profit rate level compared to international levels is not very low (Roberts 2020b). This prompts a further question: what has been keeping the profit rate high? And the answer lies in an inter-sectoral comparison. Again, it should be clarified that data on employee compensation is available only for 13 years. But that only means the values are to be assumed to be lower. A more accurate calculation for those 13 years is shown in Figure 55. Figure 55 shows that construction profits not only compensate for almost every decline in manufacturing profits (including the crucial decline in the late 1970s), but also account for the two recoveries in the early 1990s and the period from 1997 to 2004 (Figure 56). During two periods (a recovery in the late 1980s and a decline since 1997) of manufacturing profit rates, construction profit rates remained constant and upward. These points, as anticipated in the TILR, indicate differential profitability between the two sectors and suggest the presence of absolute rent.

These figures, it is to be noted, are to be cautiously taken. My calculations of net profits are inevitably inaccurate due to the absence of sectoral depreciation and compensation data for the entire period. However, a triangulation of this data and investments (presented in Figure 61 below) cautiously corroborates my overall assessment. An accurate calculation of the sectoral profit rates is only possible for an arbitrary sequence of seven years, during which both sectoral data for compensation of employees and depreciation are available. The results, as shown in Figure 57, are again generally consistent with the less accurate ones. Here, the data show that, while in both 1986 and 1999 manufacturing profits overtook construction profits, the difference between the two sectors has ballooned since the beginning of the 21st century.

That, in turn, indicates that the recovery from the general slump in the profit rate in 1997 (Figure 53) could be attributed to the potential shift toward construction and built environments. This recovery occurred during the 'Reformist' turn of the regime, as their hopes of normalization and the end of their relative marginalization in the global markets began to fade. In the case of capital switching (as incremental profit rates), the data again lacks values for the compensation of employees. But overall, it is consistent with the other data (Figures 58, 59, 60). Here, we see a more turbulent portrait of the situation. During the first phase of the modernization process in the 1960s, the profits in the two sectors were much closer in magnitude. However, in

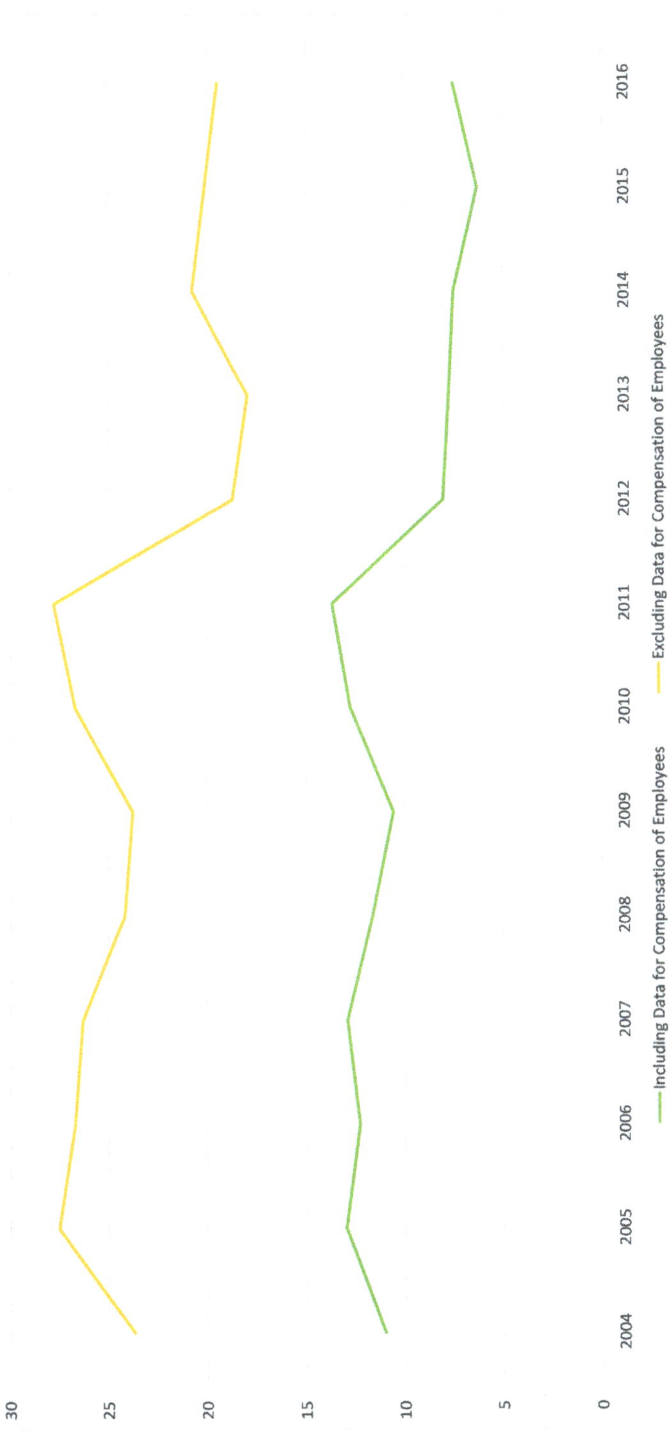

FIGURE 54 Iran—aggregate rate of profit with/out compensation of employees (Source: CBI (2013b) (my calculation))

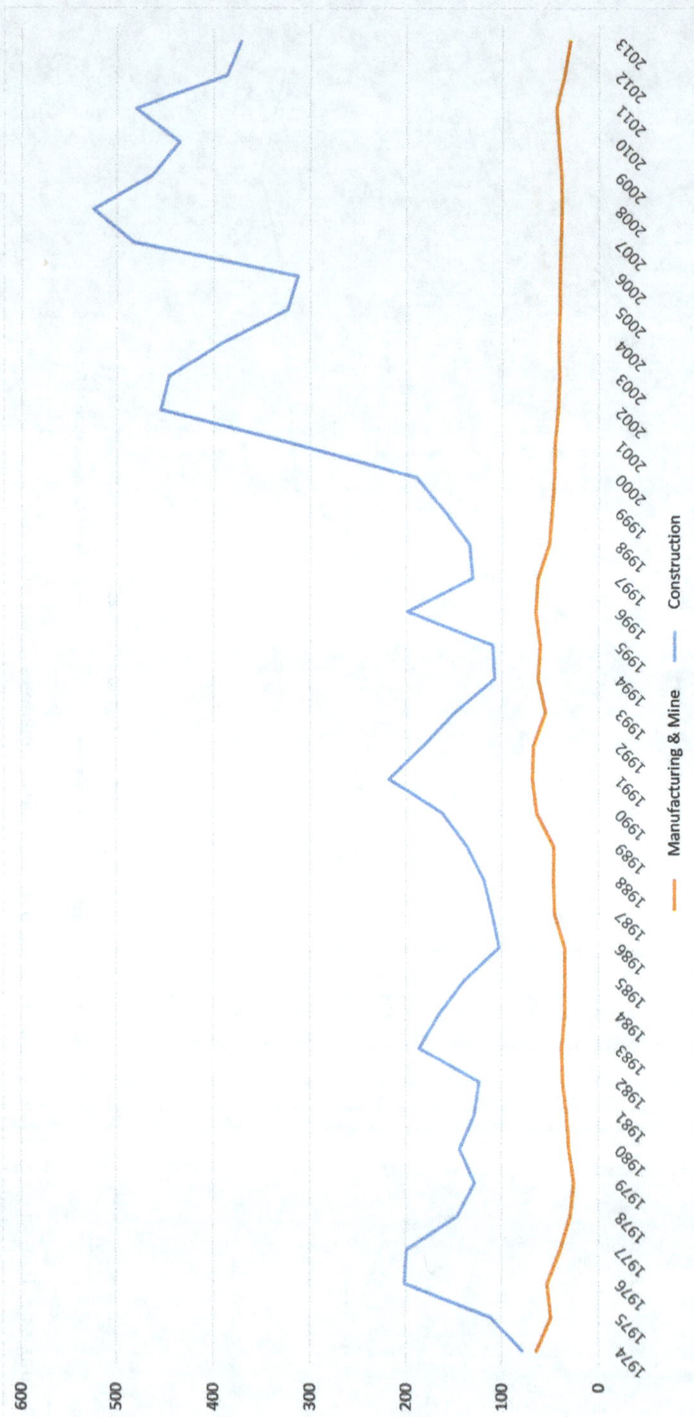

FIGURE 55 Iran—sectoral profit rates 1974–2013 (Source: CBI (2013b) (my calculation))

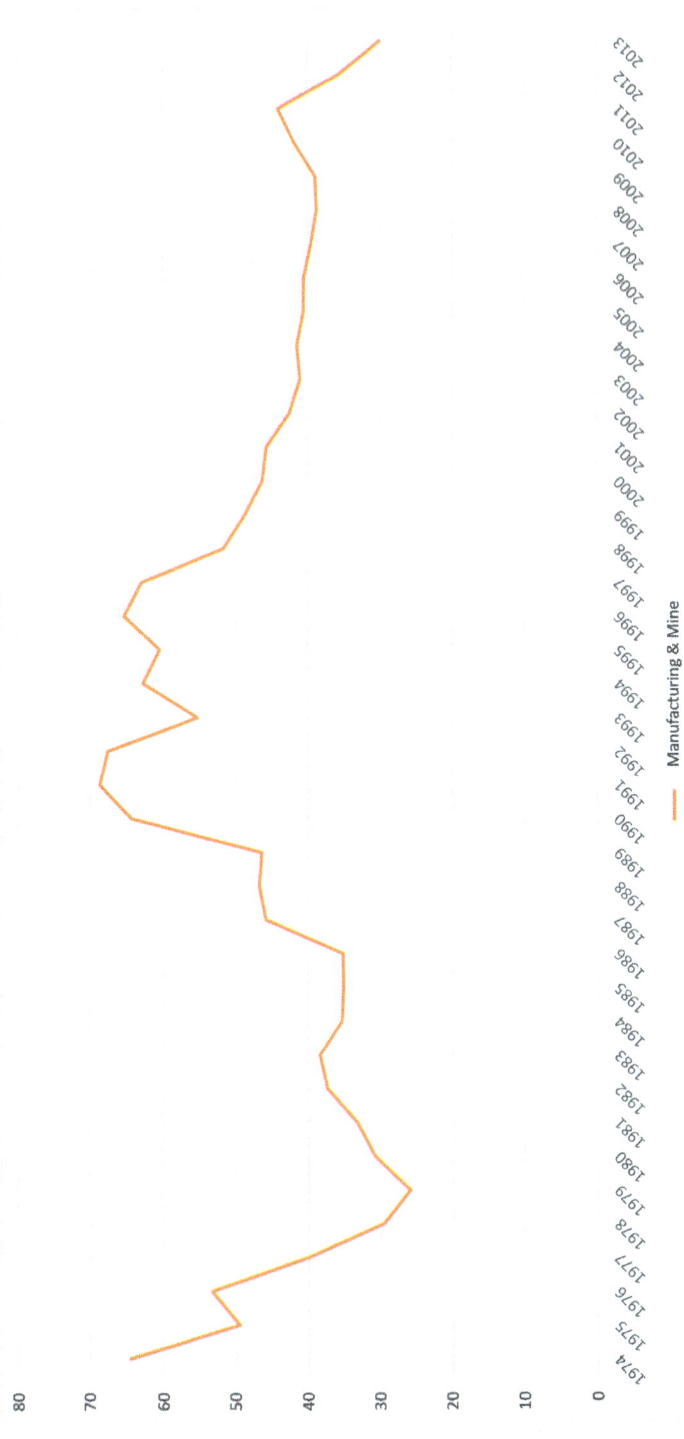

FIGURE 56 Iran—manufacturing profit rate 1974–2013 (Source: CBI (2013b) (my calculation))

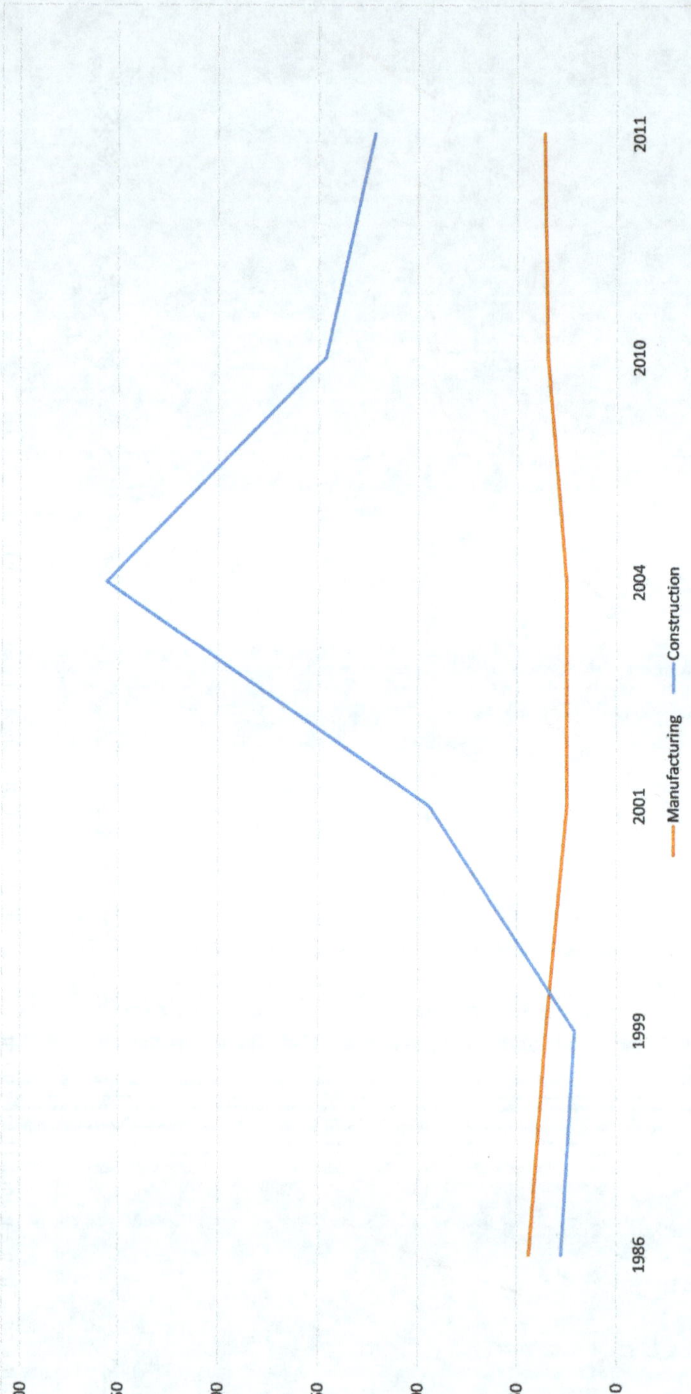

FIGURE 57 Iran—sectoral profit rates, selected years (Source: CBI (2013b) (my calculation))

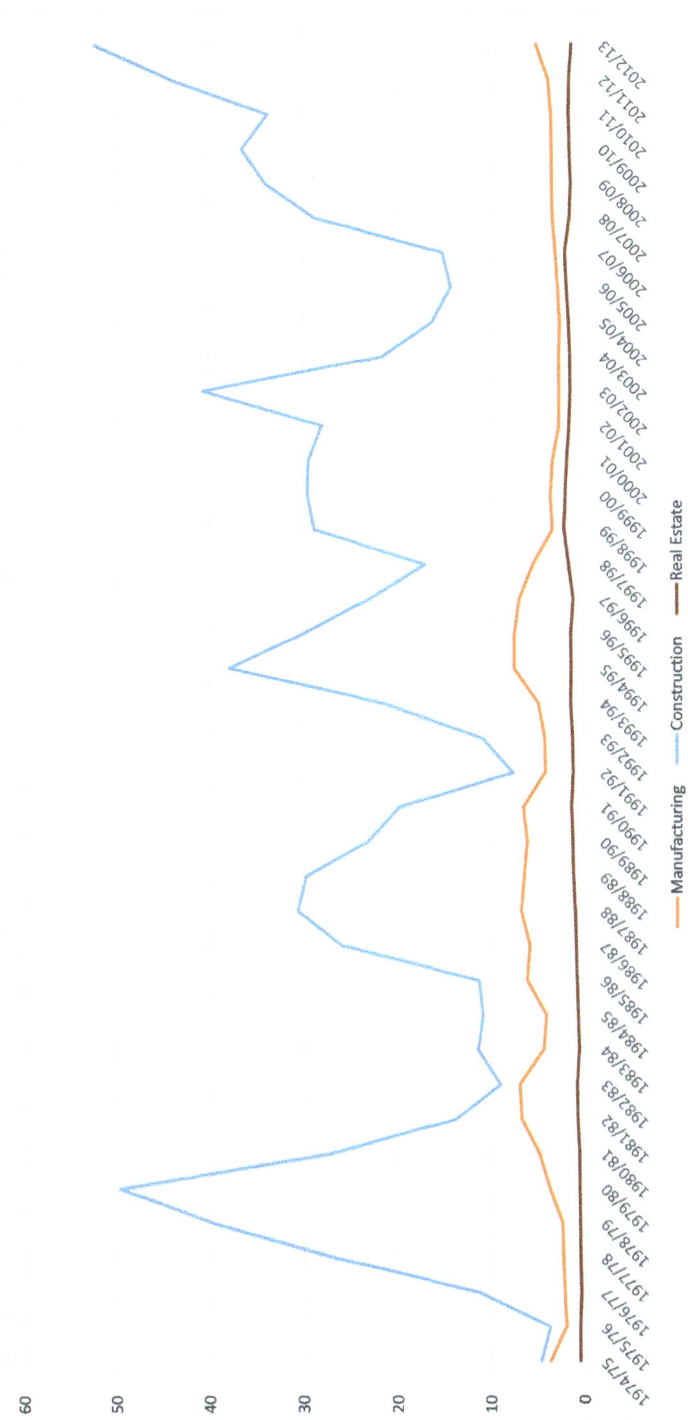

FIGURE 58 Iran—incremental profit rates 1974–2013 (Source: CBI (2013b) (my calculation))

FIGURE 59 Iran—incremental profit rates, manufacturing sector 1974–2013 (Source: CBI (2013b) (my calculation))

FIGURE 60 Iran—incremental profit rates, real estate business 1974–2013 (Source: CBI (2013b) (my calculation))

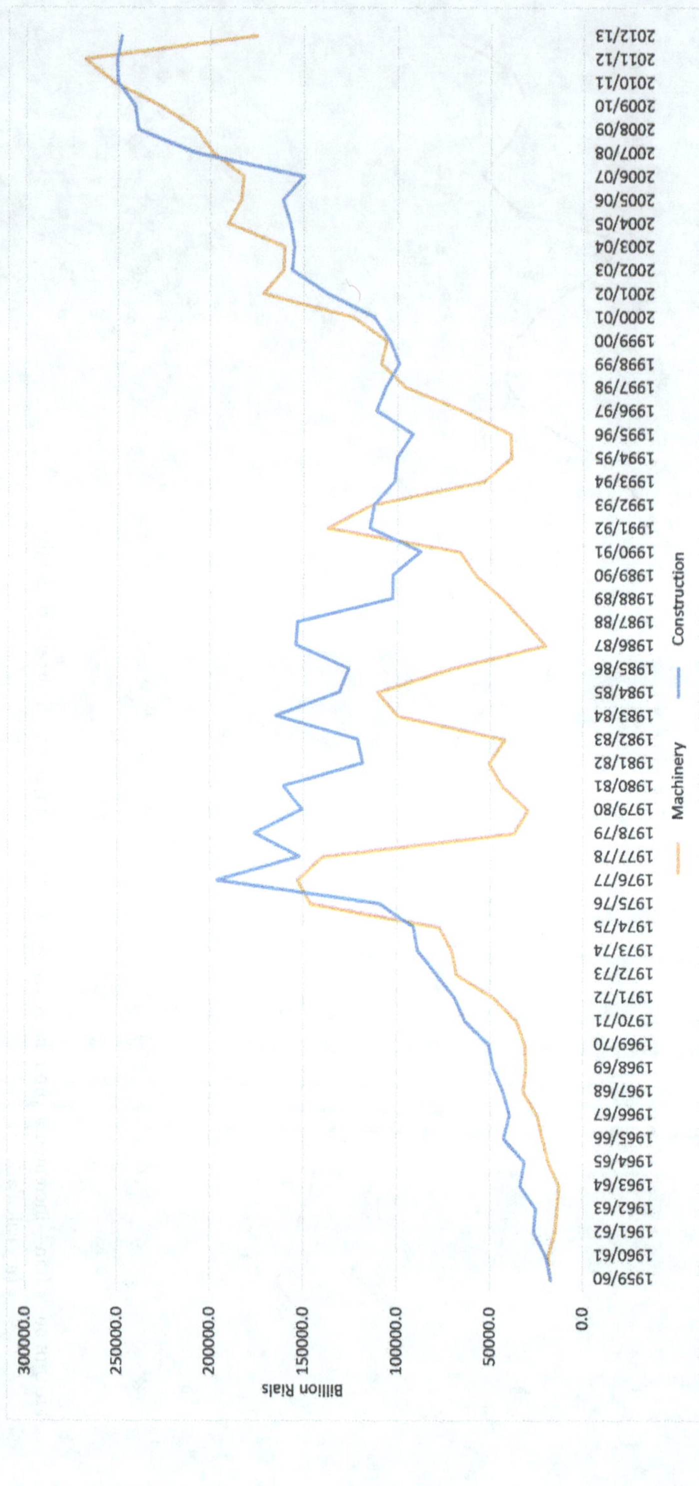

FIGURE 61 Iran—private sector's gross fixed capital formation in machinery and construction 1959–2013, constant prices (2004/2005) (Source: CBI (2013b) (my calculation))

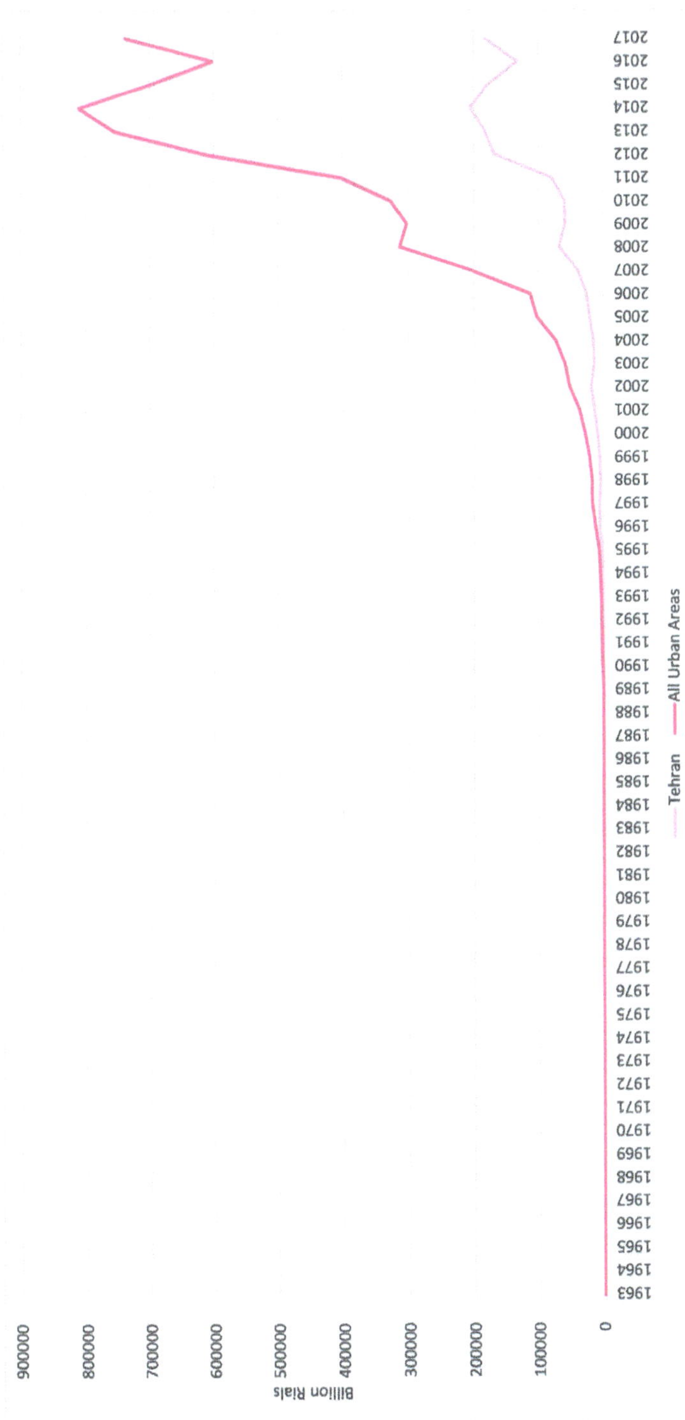

FIGURE 62 Iran—private sector's investment in new buildings in urban areas 1963–2017 (Source: SCI (2020) (my calculation))

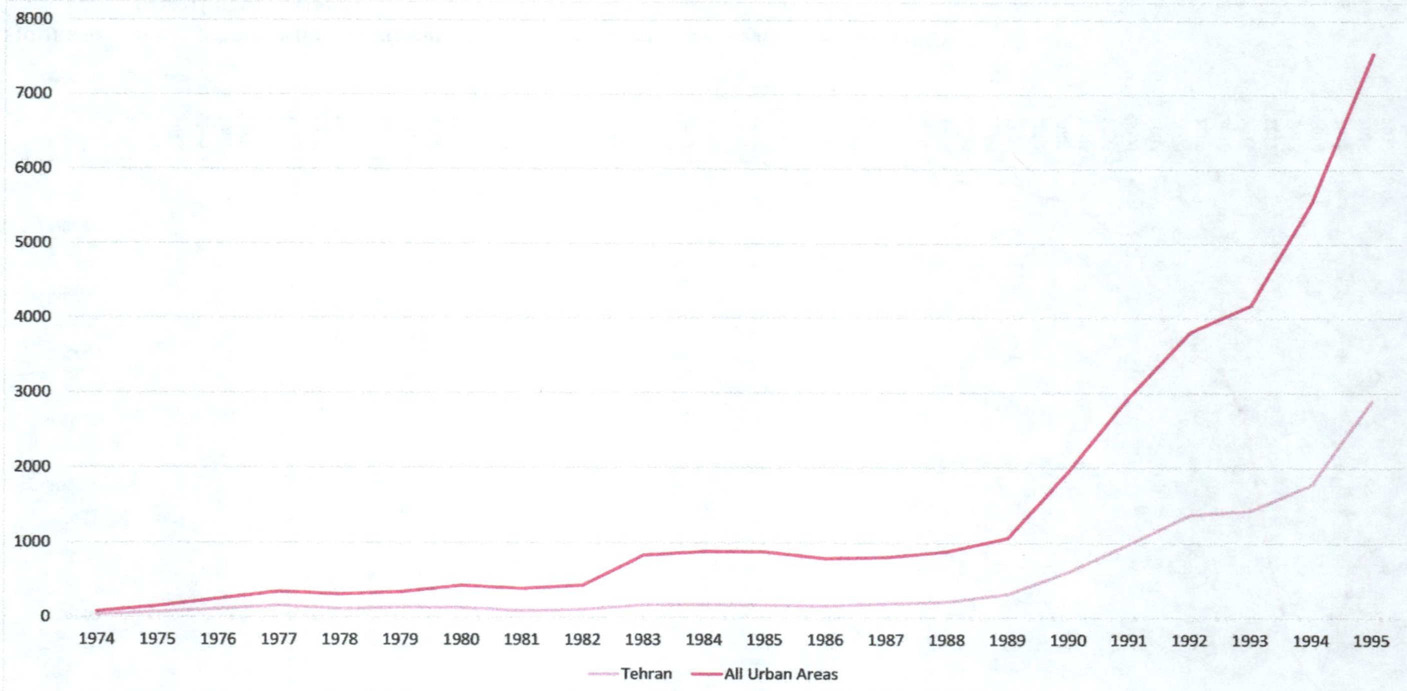

FIGURE 63 Iran—private sector's investment in new buildings in urban areas 1974–1995 (Source: SCI (2020) (my calculation))

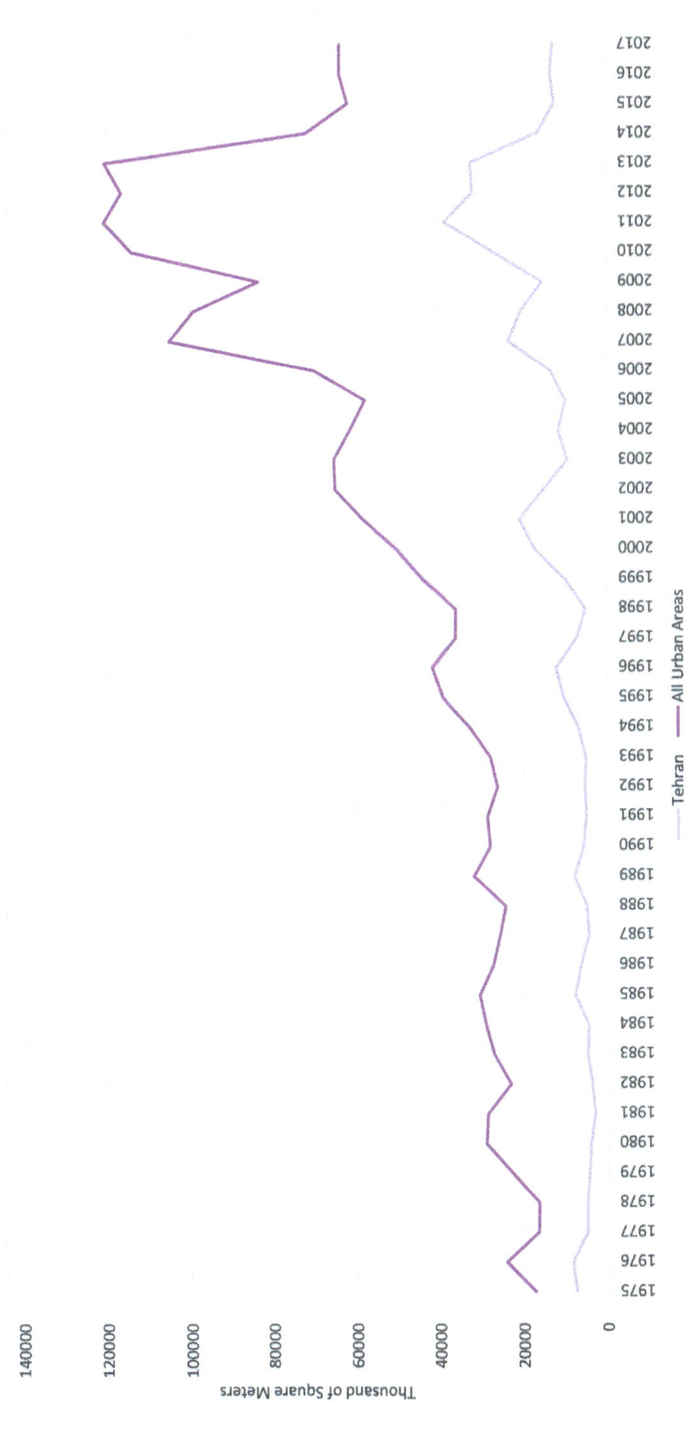

FIGURE 64 Iran—construction permits in urban areas 1975–2017, thousands of square meters (Source: SCI (2020) (my calculation))

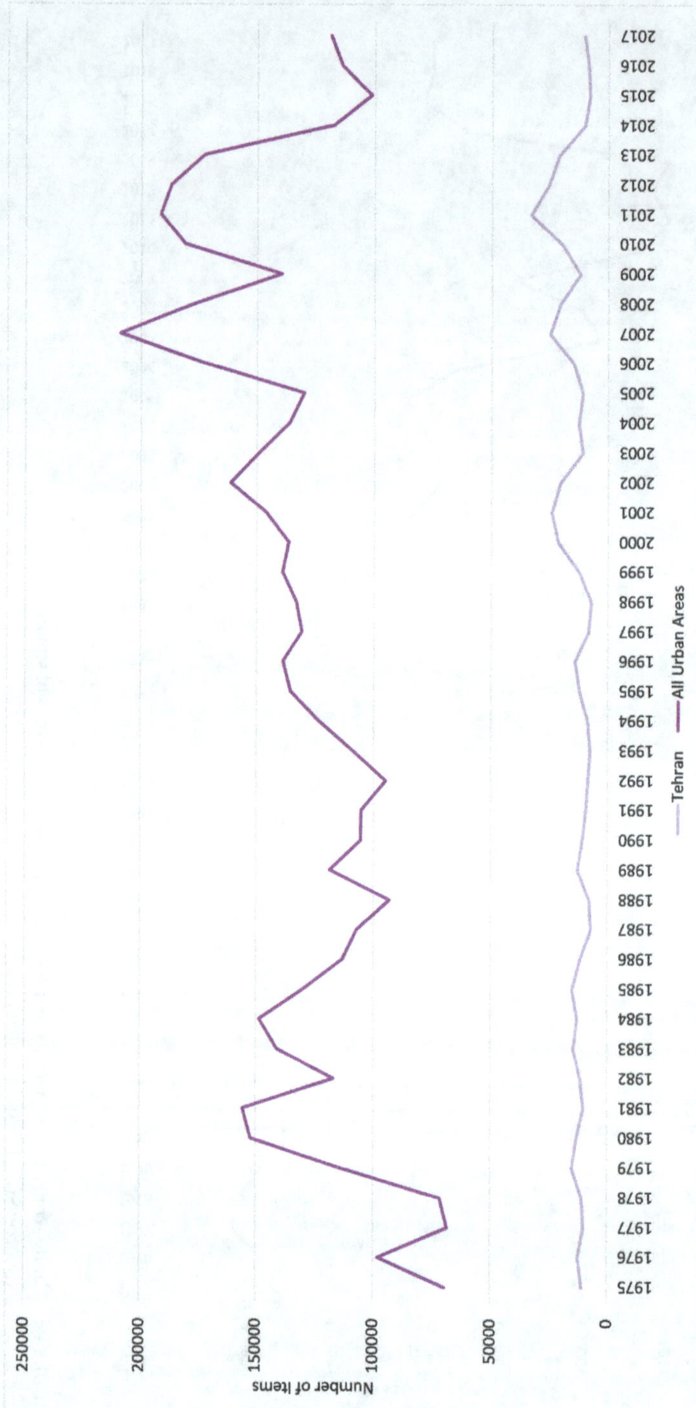

FIGURE 65 Iran—construction permits in urban areas 1975–2017 number of units (Source: SCI (2020) (my calculation))

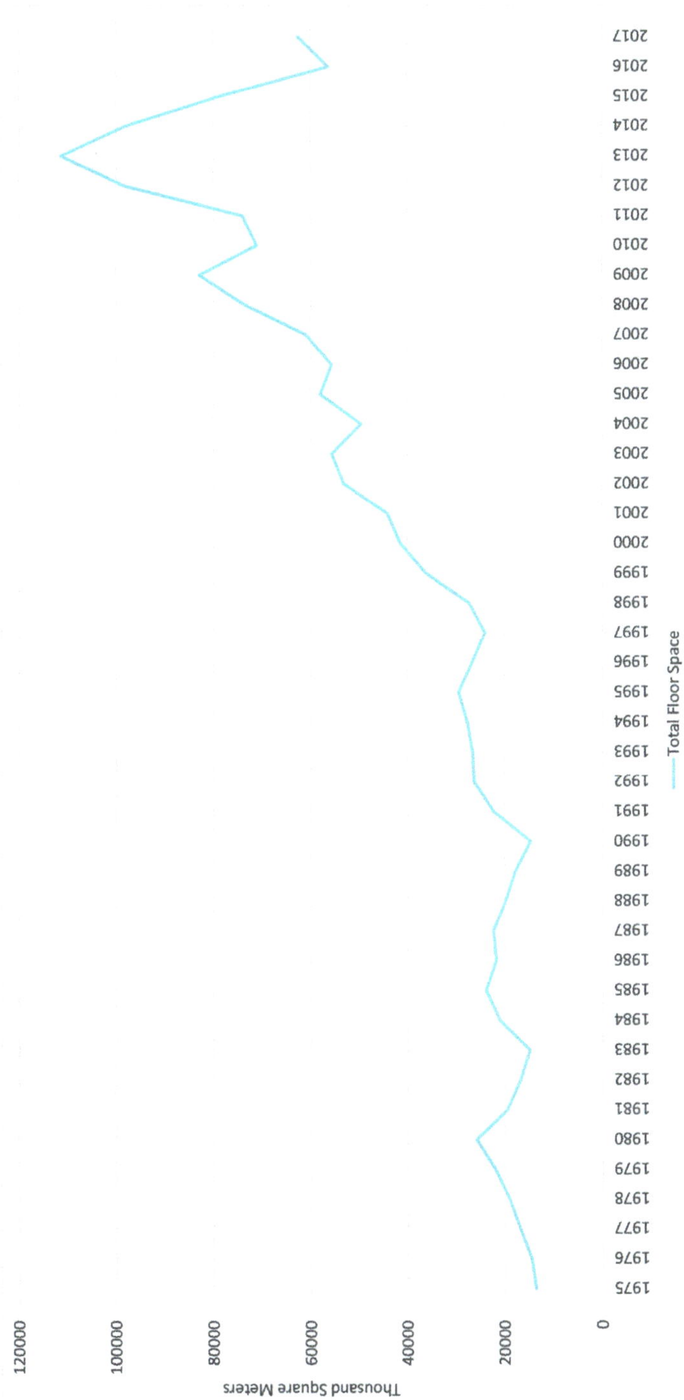

FIGURE 66 Iran—residential units completed by the private sector in urban areas 1975–2017, thousands of square meters (Source: SCI (2020) (my calculation))

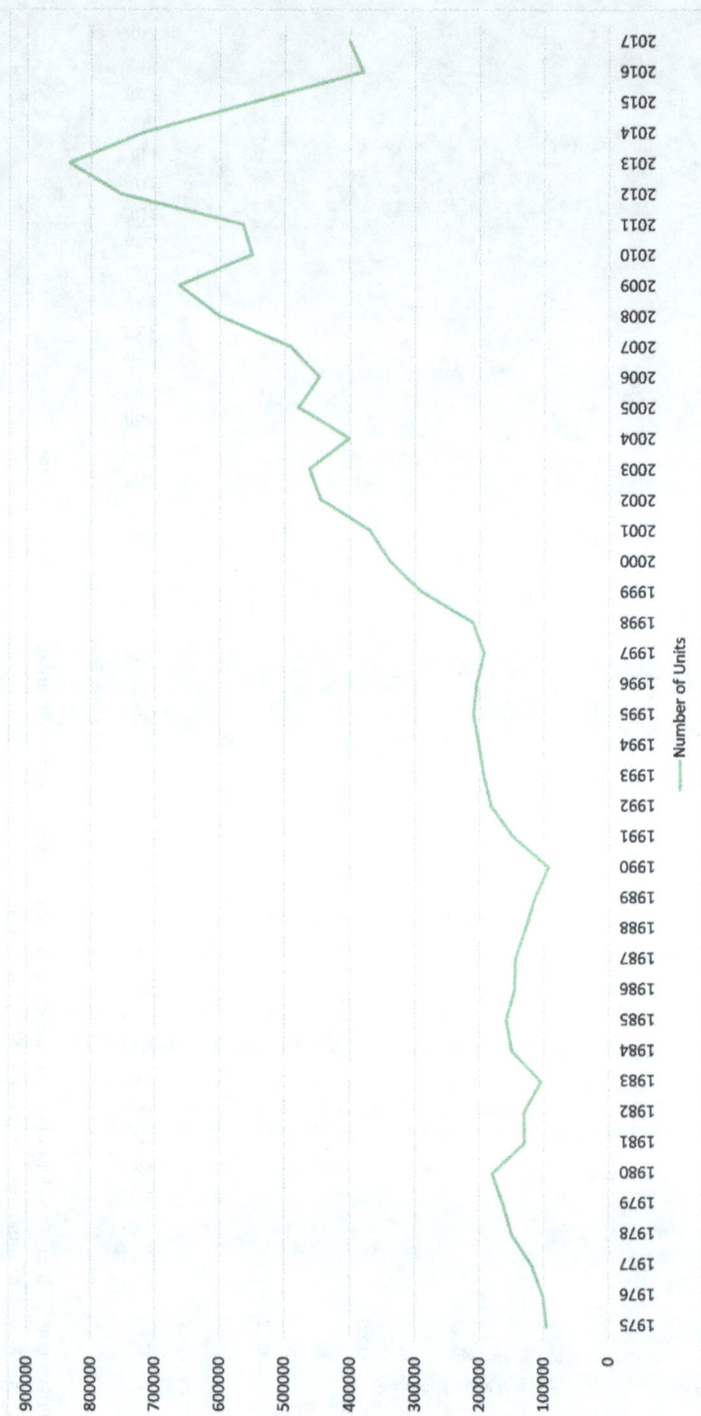

FIGURE 67 Iran—residential units completed by the private sector in urban areas 1975–2017, number of units (Source: SCI (2020) (my calculation))

the late 1970s, as manufacturing profits began to fall, construction profits rose abruptly (Figure 59). That is partly due to a rapid rise in migration to Tehran and a few other large cities in the 1970s (Dehesh 1994). This trend generally holds, except for three periods: 1986–1991 and 1993–1998, when both rise, and 2002–2008, when both fall. However, first, even in those three periods, the difference between the two rates is significant. Furthermore, second, at least in downward cycles, real estate profits had been rising (Figure 60). This latter case involves speculative investment in residential markets.

Let me now contrast these data with investment data and see their impacts on investments. Figure 61 shows that fluctuations in sectoral profit rates correspond to fluctuations in gross investment, and that investors generally prefer construction to machinery.

The (private) construction data in Tehran and across all urban areas (Figures 62 and 63) generally show an upward trend. However, all three dramatic increases (the early 1980s, the early 1990s, and the early 2000s) correspond to the respective peaks in construction profits.

Similar patterns (with similar peaks) can be observed for both construction permits (Figures 64 and 65) and completed buildings (Figures 66 and 67).

7.3 Financial System, Manufacturing Sector, Technology, and Geopolitical Conflicts

The Iranian financial system is characterized by underdeveloped financial institutions and instruments, which, in the case of housing, means the absence of mortgage markets. It limits "the possibility of homeownership for most of the population, who are required to finance their purchase" in cash and seek support from "various personal loans (with high interest rates) from banks or informal sources such as family members and relatives" (Farahani and Yousefi 2021, 50) (cf., most advanced capitalist economies in which mortgage markets are dominant (Aalbers 2012)). This underdevelopment of the financial system is indicated (Orhangazi 2008; Palley 2013) by a) a relatively low (around three percent) contribution of finance in GDP (CBI 2012; 2016) (Figure 68); b) a low (roughly three percent) contribution of finance in GNP (Figure 69); c) insignificant contribution of financial companies to overall employment (ibid.) (Figure 70); d) the lack of developed financial institutions including hedge funds, equity funds, and others (CBI 2012; 2016); e) primitive financial instruments such as derivatives, leverages, and a severely limited credit system isolated from global markets (ibid.); f) extremely high interest rates at 14 percent (ibid. Farahani and Yousefi 2021, 50).

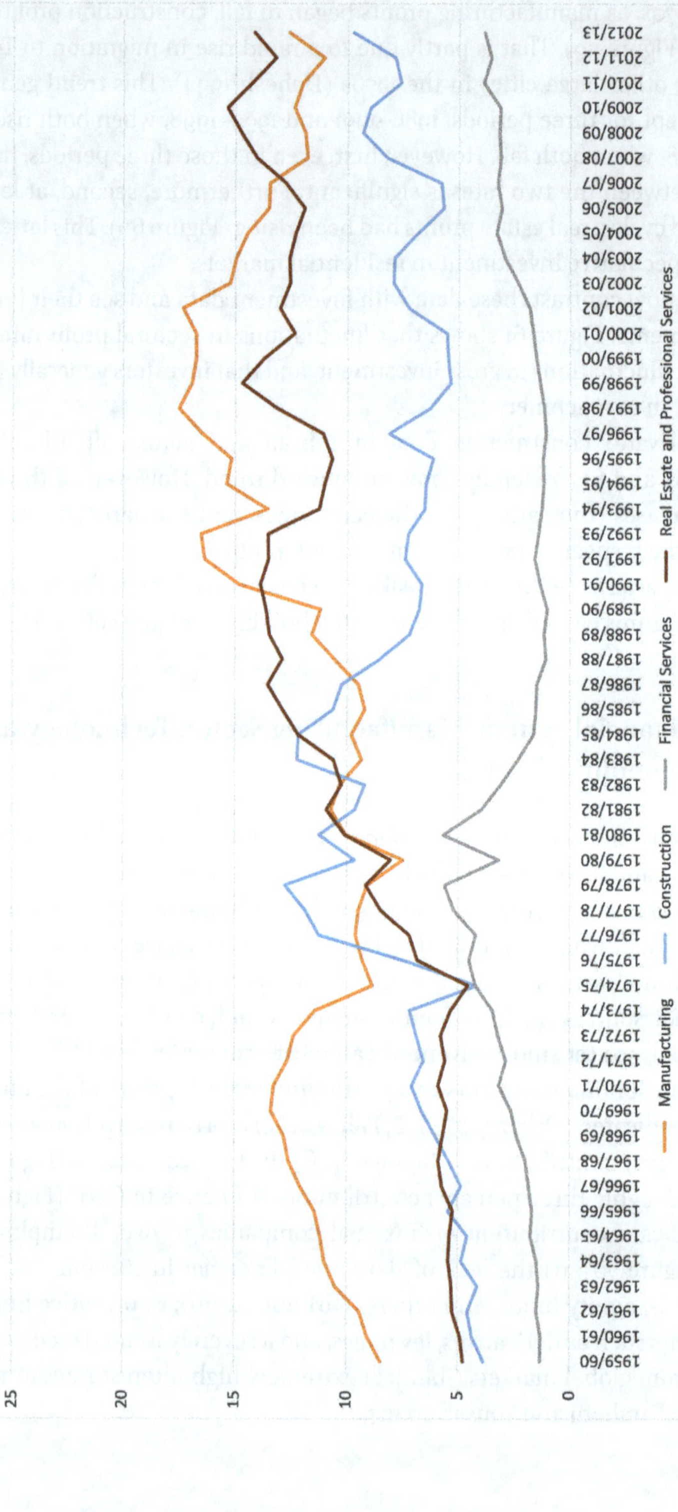

FIGURE 68 Iran—share of sectors in GDP (%) (Source: CBI (2013a) (my calculation))

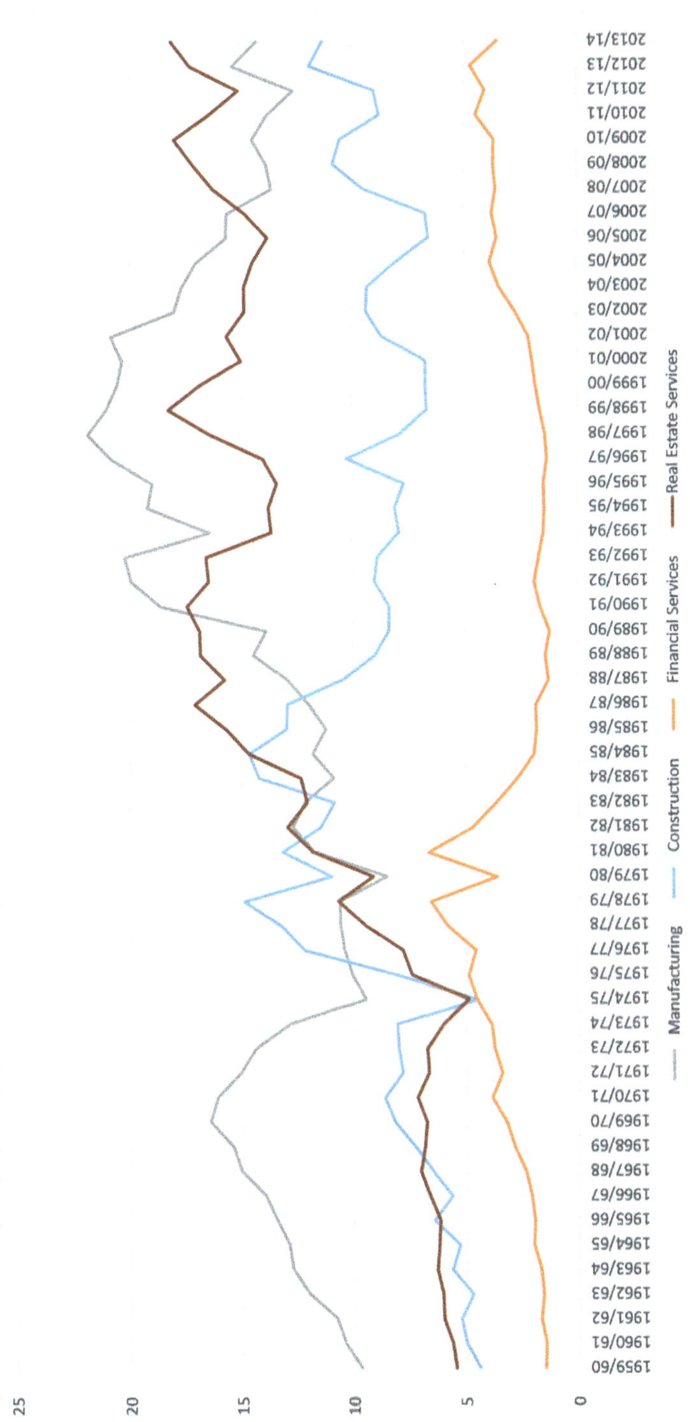

FIGURE 69 Iran—share of sectors in GNP (%) (Source: CBI (2013a) (my calculation))

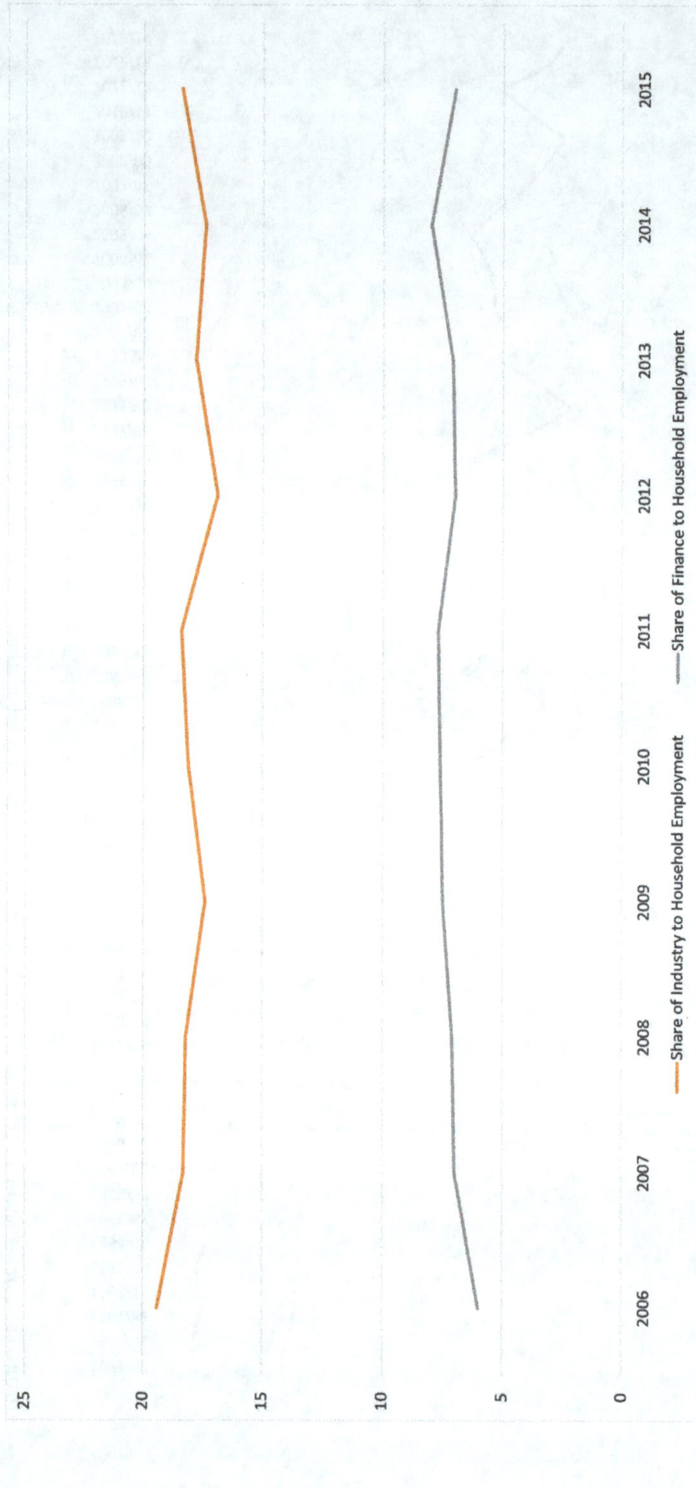

FIGURE 70 Iran—household employment by sector (Source: CBI (2013a) (my calculation))

This predicament stems from the relative isolation of the Iranian economy from international trade and financial markets. The regime's expanded regional (imperialist) interventions, most recognizably since the aftermath of the US war in Iraq and its failure, contributed to this situation. These interventions, no matter how modest compared to the regime's more powerful regional rivals (specifically, Israel, Turkey, and to a lesser extent, Saudi Arabia), promised relative domestic economic stability to Iranian capitalists. This is evident in the ability to stave off direct military confrontations for almost forty years, from 1989 to 2025, in one of the world's most militarily volatile regions—a region characterized by continuous and intensive inter-imperialist (both global and regional) rivalries without a clear regional hegemon effectively since the end of the Nixon Doctrine. But, somewhat paradoxically, the regime's regional strategy simultaneously intensified tensions with the US and its allies, leading to dire (unintended) economic consequences. For the present discussion, the most significant ones include semi-isolation from international markets and sanctions on technologies. The US-led sanctions of the past 40 years or so, "especially on the import of labor-efficient technology, intertwined with various regional geopolitical conflicts," that continue to destabilize the region (to say the least) since the end of the Cold War, contributed significantly to both low productivity and economies of scale in the Iranian economy (Farahani and Yousefi 2021, 51; also Schott 2006). Labor input to productivity can be increased in two ways: "the length of the working day … and the intensity of the working day" (Farahani and Yousefi 2021, 55). The length of the working day can be "prolonged as far as labor laws allow it … The intensity of the working day, however, depends on the ability of capital to maximize the output through technological advancement" (ibid.). The rapid growth of labor input in productivity "from less than 20 percent of the US level in 1990 to close to 40 percent in 2011" (at PPP exchange rates) (IMF 2015, 19) has been achieved on account of "very long working days, systematic wage cuts, and suppression of independent labor organizations" (Farahani and Yousefi 2021, 55). Capital input to productivity that requires adopting labor-efficient technologies, on the other hand, "has remained strikingly constant, as 'Iran's industry sectors do not operate with frontier technology'" (IMF 2015, 25 in Farahani and Yousefi 2021, 55). The (aggregate) manufacturing economies of scale have been rapidly declining from 0.0.8 to –0.16 in the last 20 years (Ashrafzadeh and Alaedini 2018), primarily due to "technological deficit and low productivity" (Farahani and Yousefi 2021, 55). In this context, thanks to the state's continuous and intense pressure to slash wages, prolong the working day, and criminalize unionization, the Iranian manufacturing sector has managed to secure profitability. However, this strategy has reached its absolute physical limits as workers' capacity to work 2–3 shifts a day with extremely low wages and high inflation has begun to diminish significantly (Farahani 2013). Additionally, by isolating the economy from global markets, regional geopolitical conflicts hinder the alternative strategy (assuming capitalists are willing to pursue it) of technological development.

7.4 The Mehr Housing Program, an Overview[2]

Let me now revisit a national housing initiative in Iran and discuss the various ways its demise was rooted in the aforementioned forces and processes. In 2007, the Mahmoud Ahmadinejad government launched the Mehr Housing Program to develop 2.3 million apartments nationwide. As a means-tested plan, it aimed to make homeownership affordable for the poorest ten percent of the population—those with a monthly income less than twice the minimum wage, who owned no property, were registered as families, and had been residing in the city where they applied for at least five years (MCLS 2008). Applicants had to form cooperatives to build the housing (MCLS 2008). This involved buying units off-plan—before construction—with the cooperatives using members' collected funds to either build the homes or sell them to private subcontractors if necessary. The Ministry of Cooperatives, Labour, and Social Welfare (MCLS) provided templates for cooperative statutes, and applicants had to pay their share of site preparation costs before establishing their cooperatives (MCLS 2008). The MCLS does not mediate disputes between subcontractors and cooperatives if conflicts arise (ibid.). The MCLS identified and secured state-owned lands and some private plots to develop the Mehr Housing Program townships (NTOIR 2014a; 2014b; NOLH 2017). To reduce prices and lower costs without causing market disruption or overburdening government finances, the government committed to acquiring the cheapest land parcels and offering them to applicants for the construction of apartment blocks. Consequently, most townships are located on the outskirts of cities, often in relatively remote areas (see Figure 71). The Housing Foundation of the Islamic Revolution (HFIR) oversaw this process (HFIR 2017). Although land was initially allocated through 99-year leases, this did not legally prohibit applicants from selling or renting out their units (HFIR 2017; NTOIR 2014b).

2 This section relies heavily on Farahani and Yousefi (2021) with modifications.

FIGURE 71 Location of three townships in Tehran Province

The state-owned Bank-e-Maskan (Housing Bank) was responsible for providing personal loans to applicants for off-plan purchases, covering up to 30 percent of the final apartment price at a 9 percent interest rate (Housing Bank, 2017a). Applicants had to pay the remaining amount in installments, with the first installment being as high as 50 percent of the unit's value (NTOIR 2014b). The fixed personal loan by the Housing Bank covered around 10 percent of the market value of an average property in a city like Tehran, requiring the borrower to offer collateral equal to the property's value (Housing Bank 2017b). Later, the bank introduced an alternative private loan for wealthier households, allowing loan amounts up to four times the primary loan, with a 9.5% interest rate and monthly payments twice the minimum wage (ibid.). The government also committed to reducing administrative costs—offering a 50 percent discount on construction permits and permits for electricity, gas, and water supply, with payments spread over two years (NTOIR 2014b). Additionally, it provided partial subsidies for administrative costs related to architectural and project planning (ibid.).

Without a functioning public economy, the Mehr Housing Program homes were sold at market prices. The prices listed in the program's townships were about 40 percent lower than the city-wide market rates for similar units in Tehran. However, given their location, these prices are not particularly low; they remain roughly 15 percent above the average unit prices in the most affordable inner-city neighborhoods. Out of the promised 2.3 million units, only 500,000 were completed in the first eight years, and by the last year of Ahmadinejad's administration (Hamshahri Online 2016). Due to various administrative and financial constraints, cooperatives were forced to auction construction tasks to subcontractors, some of whom sold their rights to other subcontractors. Due to the low volume of construction and rising program costs, the newly elected Rouhani administration abandoned the entire program despite continued support in parliament (Ayar Online 2015; Jahan News 2013). The Ministry of Roads and Urban Development was tasked with completing units under construction and stopping the construction of new ones (Ayar Online, 2015). As one of the initial steps to ease pressure on the central government, in 2014, the government ended the 99-year land-leasing policy and sold the land directly to applicants (Donya-e-Eqtesad 2014).

Facing unforeseen financial burdens on applicants, the administration actively intervened in the market through two key actions. First, it enlisted two major companies—Iran's Kayson Inc. and Turkey's Kuzu Group—as subcontractors to carry out construction work. Second, it promoted the development of alternative townships within inner cities, starting with two in Tehran, diverging from the initial plan for low-income, property-less applicants (Consbank 2012). The first action resulted in increased costs because of subpar construction by small local subcontractors, which raised unit prices. To calm dissatisfied applicants and sell surplus units, the government boosted personal loans from the Housing Bank, initially doubling and then tripling the amount (Ibena News 2017). However, these loans never exceeded 30% of the final price demanded by the companies. Consequently, many were unable to afford the rising costs, so they sold their units and exited the program, while some who could afford the higher prices rented them out. The second action also spurred middle-income families to seek units as secondary rental properties. Ultimately, the government's efforts failed to achieve its intended goals. The larger developers also failed to meet applicants' expectations. Despite prices continuously rising, many units lack basic facilities. Kuzu was found to have delivered 60-square-meter units to buyers who paid for 80 square meters (Asr-e-Sakhteman 2016). In two larger townships in Tehran Province, Pardis and Parand, Kayson Inc. is building new residential complexes with higher quality and notably higher prices (Kayson-ir.com). This trend extends beyond large developers. Smaller developers and realtors have also entered the townships to capitalize on the booming market amid a changing socio-economic landscape (Figure 72).

By 2016, the government claimed that 90% of the units had been handed over to applicants (Pirasteh News 2017). However, objections from angry applicants protesting the handling of the process dispute this, revealing that only about 1.3 million units—roughly 60%—were completed (Pirasteh

FIGURE 72 The physical condition of Mehr Housing Programs buildings. Examples from two townships near Tehran. From top left clockwise: 1) A Mehr Block in Parand Township, 2) and 3) Two Mehr Blocks in Abshenasan Township, 4) a non-Mehr Block in Parand Township

News 2017). Many of these units lack essential facilities like electricity and water (Donya-e-Eqtesad 2010; Eghtesad Online 2018; Mehr News Agency 2018). Since residents of the Mehr Housing Program are legal owners, subcontractors are not easily held responsible for missing facilities, as owners are accountable for securing and maintaining them. This has increased tension between homeowners and tenants, especially in rented dwellings, leading to approximately 118,000 vacant units (Entekhab 2016). Though applicants' social status has improved, many still cannot afford current prices (Aftab News, 2013; Iran File News, 2017). After the November 2017 earthquake in Kermanshah province, 90% of two newly built Mehr Housing townships were destroyed, prompting President Rouhani to criticize state involvement in housing development (BBC Persian 2017; Radio Farda 2017).

The Mehr Housing Program did not fulfill its initial promises regarding both quality and quantity. Many in the target group could not afford the construction costs, and the government was unable to provide subsidies. Consequently, the area now features abandoned Mehr Housing developments amidst relatively expensive non-Mehr Housing buildings. These new neighborhoods attracted private developers, as land prices were expected to increase. The limited public economy, combined with the program's market-oriented approach, explains why it failed to serve low-income populations effectively. Without a robust public economy, creating effective public or de-commodified housing in Iran remains unlikely. The program's failure was due to insufficient public economic support and its design to operate within Iran's market and structural housing constraints.

7.5 Inter-sectoral Analysis and Urban Land Rent in the Iranian Housing Sector

In recent literature on heterodox urban economic geography, finance, insurance, and real estate (the so-called FIRE sectors) are the most discussed destinations of capital moving away from the manufacturing sector in pursuit of higher returns (Orhangazi 2008; 2017, 545). The underdevelopment and international isolation of Iranian finance capital contribute to the tendency to shift investments from manufacturing to construction and housing development. As Figures 49 and 58 show, capital formation in construction is at least twice as significant as in machinery, and both sectors offer substantially higher rates of return than manufacturing. Higher profit rates in construction (reflected in comparative rates of return) drive the investment shift (as shown by the share in capital formation) (Figures 55 and 61). Data disaggregated into residential and non-residential construction reveal that investment in residential construction is notably higher. In 2017 alone, residential construction accounted for 70 percent of all investment in the construction sector across urban areas (CBI 2017b). Fluctuations in profit rates within manufacturing help explain the macro-level pattern of capital flow into the housing sector, as discussed in the TILR.

The Mehr Housing Program, promoted by the state as the country's long-awaited and overdue public housing initiative, began in 2007 with a commitment to build 2.3 million units nationwide, mainly on the outskirts of medium- to large-sized cities. However, due to its anticipated failure, the program was officially terminated in 2013 (Farahani and Yousefi 2021). The government typically planned to subsidize land, particularly in remote areas, as well as construction materials such as concrete and girders. These resources would be provided to private developers to create townships, which would then be sold at relatively affordable prices to low-income families. Nonetheless, as construction costs rose, the target demographic (low-income residents) became increasingly unable to access the program. In individual plots within the Mehr Housing Program, the flow of capital is primarily influenced by two factors: first, the interaction between differential rent I and II, which impacts investment choices such as expanding land development or boosting investments in construction; and second, the level of competition among developers or firms involved (ibid. 56). This dynamic is exemplified by Keyson Inc., a private developer subcontracted by the government to develop townships for the program. The company soon started constructing upscale complexes, including a 552-unit residential project in Parand township (near Tehran), adjacent to Mehr Housing blocks. "The new, more intensive investments not only increase rents for the new complex but also pressure existing Mehr Housing units' rents and raise the overall township's value, benefiting developers and multi-dwelling owners" (ibid.).

The inexpensive land plots initially allocated for the program's development attracted private developers who hoped to build cheaply, sell at market price, and pocket the rent. "The remote location of the townships did not prevent businesses and affluent residents from seeking new investment opportunities, as it most commonly happened in Tehran's satellite townships Parand and Pardis, a process that increased land values" (ibid. 57). This supports the argument made by supporters of the program that developing Mehr Housing Program townships would eventually stimulate growth in the surrounding areas by attracting local businesses. In other words, "as far as small-scale developers and multi-dwelling owners are concerned, the program has not entirely failed" (ibid.). The interplay between differential rent I and II was responsible for both the rise in prices and the further development of Mehr Housing Program townships. Absolute rent at the macro level contributed to high land rent in remote areas and exceptionally marginal plots. On the micro level, the interplay between differential rent I and II—created and appropriated through changes in relative space due to nearby economic development—further raised total land rent. However, the maximum and overall rates of land rent are influenced by inter-sectoral competition and differences in sectoral profitability. "[I]nvestment in capital-intensive industries (e.g., manufacturing, which needs more advanced technology or a higher organic composition of capital) in Iran has become less profitable over recent decades, leading to shifts toward labor-intensive sectors (such as construction and extraction), which have a lower organic composition of capital" (ibid. 56).

Four structural features of Iranian capitalism shape rent creation and appropriation. First, extensive private ownership of urban land results in a large class of urban landowners who are atomistic, intensely competitive, and only loosely aligned by an abstract class interest. Second, financial capital is underdeveloped. Third, labor-efficient technologies remain underdeveloped. Fourth, the manufacturing sector has low profitability (Farahani and Yousefi 2021, 56–57). Additionally, this process is supported by unregulated labor conditions, an unorganized labor force, and an unregulated housing market (ibid. 57). National-level inter-sectoral competition influences sectoral rates of return, with the difference between profits in the manufacturing and construction sectors determining the maximum land rent. When manufacturing profits decline, the gap between overall profits and construction sector profits—manifested as excess sectoral profit—becomes a source of rent. This is intensified by the suppression of organized labor and low wages in the construction sector, which heavily depend on weakened (domestic and international) migrant and seasonal labor (ibid. 56). As a result, due to high rates of absolute rent and the shift to urban residential construction, Iranian capitalists can refuse to invest in labor-efficient technologies, even when US-led sanctions do not prevent them to do so, and still enjoy relatively high returns. When manufacturing profits fall, many industrialists abandon underperforming factories to invest in housing, even on marginal plots like those in the Mehr Housing Program (ibid.). This allows them to offset declining manufacturing returns by increasing the aggregate profit rates that include land rents. In this way, Iranian capitalists and the state go hand in hand in the exploitation of labor. The case of Iran's construction industry and the decline of the Mehr Housing Program, therefore, presents another empirical challenge to Harvey's SMLR. In the case of the discontinuation of the Swedish Municipal Site Leasehold (Chapter 5), there was no switch to built environments, as absolute rents were low and capital shifted to the financial sector instead. In Iran, switching to built environments and land markets does occur, but within the context of limited financial development (contra Harvey's financialization thesis) and highly competitive atomistic land ownership (contra his monopolistic land ownership thesis). The next chapter extends this analysis to the urban scale and discusses how such processes translate into spatial inequalities at the municipal level.

CHAPTER 8

Spatial Inequality and Gentrification in Tehran

This chapter[1] builds on the analysis of capital switching and land rent in the Iranian housing sector in the previous chapter to explain the role municipalities play in this process. It also encompasses analysis of some implications for spatial planning and their social ramifications, spatial inequalities, and gentrification. I aim to elaborate on the mechanisms that connect the economic structural forces explained in the previous chapter (and anticipated in the TILR) to spatial planning and their subsequent repercussions in the city of Tehran. The analysis, therefore, relies on the conclusions drawn in the previous chapter regarding the Iranian economy, the most germane of which are: a) lack of a functioning public economy to provide for the poor, b) an extensively privatized housing sector with atomistic ownership and development, c) high rate of return for residential development with an average of 20% for the 1990–2013 period (CBI 2013a), d) persistently low wages, low manufacturing economies of scale, high unemployment (12.1% in 2018) (SCI 2018), e) underdeveloped financial system that is semi-isolated from international markets, f) a relatively high rate of absolute rent in the construction sector that drive the capital switching from the manufacturing sector.

8.1 Housing and Spatial Inequality in Tehran

8.1.1 Geographies of Housing in Tehran

Tehran, covering 700 km^2 and housing over 12 million residents, is a highly densely populated city. The city is spatially divided between the affluent north and the underserved south. Public transportation is generally limited, and economic and administrative centers are primarily concentrated in the north and central areas, which also have higher land values. In this context, the lack of reliable public (including low-income or affordable) housing options means that housing costs in the city account for 48% of average household expenses and are 2.2 times the national average (CBI 2017a; TMICTO 2014–2015). Around six million working families live in rental housing (average household size in

1 This chapter relies on the arguments and evidence presented in Yousefi and Farhani (2022) and Farahani (2013).

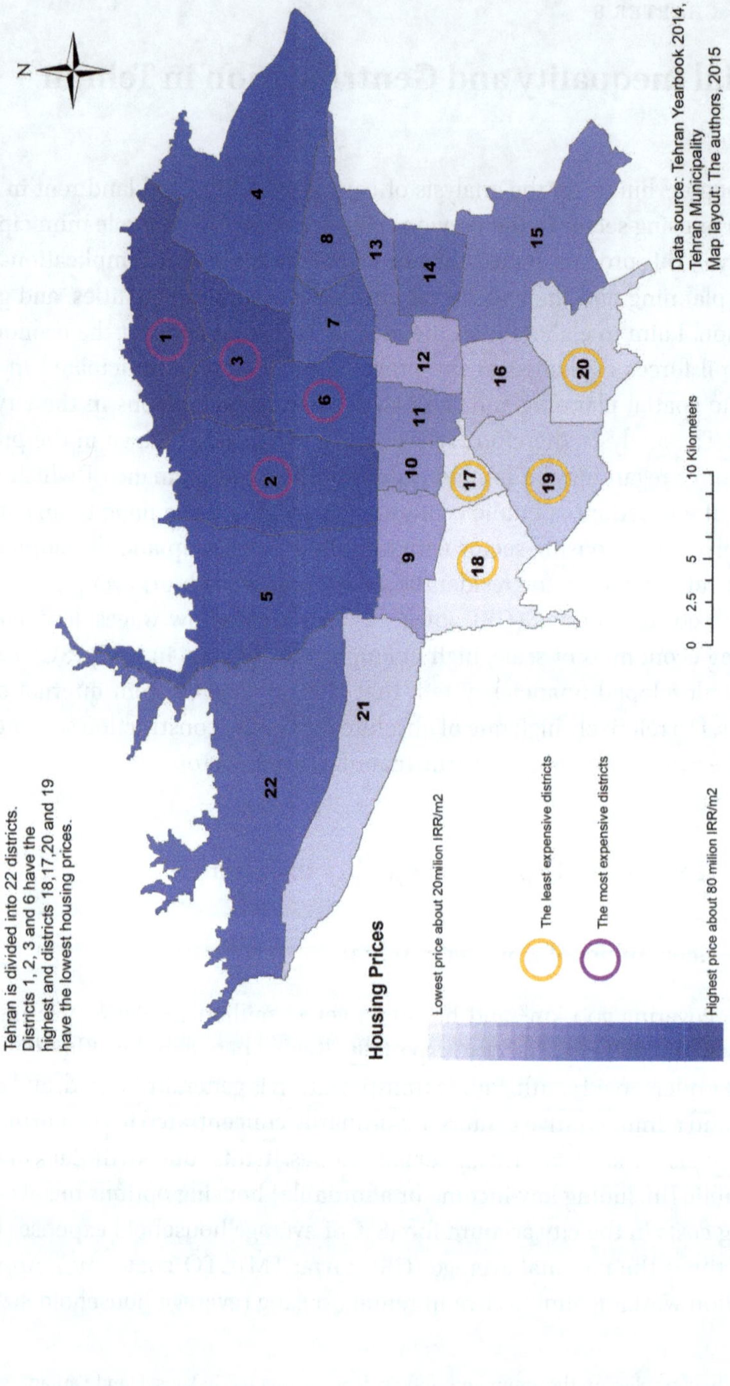

FIGURE 73 Housing prices in Tehran (Source: Yousefi and Farahani (2022))

2017 was 3.3) (SCI 2017). For many of them, concentrated in the southern areas and more recently in low-income outer neighborhoods, housing costs can consume all their initial disposable income (Raisdana 2001; SCI 2017).

Housing expenses serve as an indicator of income levels and help evaluate spatial inequality in the city. Since official data on income distribution is unavailable, analyzing geographic patterns in housing prices provides a helpful way to examine this inequality. In 2016, District 18 had the lowest average housing price at about 20 million IRR per square meter, while the minimum wage was 8.1 million IRR monthly (Yousefi and Farahani 2022, 27). Conversely, District 1 had the most expensive housing, roughly four times that of District 18, at 80 million IRR per square meter (ibid.). Online realtor portals also help to clarify these figures. In 2016, prices in northern Tehran, such as districts 1 and 3, ranged from 140 to 250 million IRR per square meter (www.iranfile.ir; www.melkeman.com). Figure 73 illustrates the distribution of housing prices across districts, based on the average price per square meter. While official data only show district averages and do not reflect intra-district price variations, significant differences between northern and southern Tehran remain (Yousefi and Farahani 2022, 27). Low-income residents primarily live in the southern and western parts of the city. Interestingly, the spatial distribution of publicly owned primary schools, general hospitals, and metro stations also follows this pattern: more schools, hospitals, and stations are highly concentrated in wealthier areas (ibid.).

8.1.2 Municipalities and the Outsourcing Practice

Municipal responsibilities in Iran are confined to administrative tasks, such as issuing construction permits and approving floor plans, with no direct involvement in housing services. Developers—individuals and companies—are responsible for building, redeveloping, and selling or renting apartment units at market rates. While municipalities issue building permits, they do not have a mandate to develop or plan housing, nor do they have much control over urban land and resources. Municipal finances and administration are primarily dependent on the central government, which can contract during periods of economic downturn (Farahani and Yousefi 2021). In Tehran, for example, the municipality relies heavily on outsourcing urban and residential development to private developers. These developers are compensated through a floor-space-ratio allowance system that permits buildings to be taller than the district land policy allows (MRUD 2017). Essentially, demolishing and rebuilding a block adheres to the neighborhood's floor-space ratio, which is based on the area's average land value, unless the municipality grants exceptions

(Yousefi and Farahani 2022). The value of outsourced projects similarly depends on local land prices, which are reflected in floor-space-ratio allowances. This means that more costly outsourced projects for private developers, such as road construction and metro stations, are paid for by the municipality through these allowances for residential development in higher-value areas. Municipalities are increasingly generating revenue by selling these allowances to developers, shaping future market-driven planning strategies (ibid.). As a result, the floor-space-ratio allowance becomes the primary mechanism for marketizing municipal activities and leaving the housing market unregulated. Indeed, this lack of regulation in the housing market creates opportunities for corruption, which is often cited as the reason for the Iranian state's insufficient response to housing problems, as alluded to in the previous chapter. What this explanation is silent about is the role of spatial planning that favors market forces, land policies designed to promote rent-based profit-making, and the economic forces that contextualize them.

8.1.3 A Story of Gentrification[2]

An interesting transformation of Peykan-Shahr, Iran's first industrial township located 24 kilometers west of Tehran in 2011, may help illustrate the argument above (Farahani 2013). The 42-kilometer Tehran-Karaj Freeway, built in 1966, connects Tehran to Karaj and passes through the township. The Peykan-Shahr neighborhood is on the northern side, while the company's main site is on the southern side of the freeway. Established in 1969, the township was designed to provide housing for workers of Iran's first and largest automaker, Iran National (ibid. 401). Founded in 1962, Iran National directly benefited from the 1962 land reforms, which designated marginal wastelands along what today is the Tehran-Karaj Freeway as dedicated industrial land. Later, the company grew to become Iran's leading automaker, producing about 50 percent of the country's cars, and Peykan-Shahr became a prominent suburb on Tehran's outskirts. Before the 1979 Revolution, the company's ownership was 51 percent private and 49 percent state-owned. After the Revolution, it was nationalized. By 2005, as part of a privatization effort, 49 percent of its stock was sold to private investors (ibid.).

The township was initially created to accommodate seasonal workers (primarily migrant workers) during the company's construction phase. Later, it was allocated to the company's employees, including night shift and on-call staff, with a capacity of about 6,000 residents (ibid. 401). Tenancy was

2 The section is a summary of an earlier interview-based study (Farahani 2013).

restricted to firm employees, but starting in 1996, some homes were renovated for white-collar workers. Since then, the population has gradually increased. The township includes 50 four-story residential apartment blocks. Half of these have eight units per floor, and the other half have six. Small flats measure 40 square meters, while large flats are 60 square meters. All large flats are duplexes, divided into 25 or 30 square meters per floor. Flat allocation depended on family size, job roles, and work experience. The firm owned the land and buildings, and when it began the partial sell-off of residential units in 2004, it offered significant rental discounts to existing tenants (ibid.). Property values in the township surged significantly from 2004 to 2011, after decades in which the company had withheld properties from the market (ibid. 403).

The working conditions were characterized by typically long hours, including significant overtime, with up to three shifts a day (about 18 hours) and shifts on holidays and weekends (ibid. 402). Low wages and rising living costs pushed women and children into the growing black market, primarily working in domestic services for wealthier families, as well as engaging in peddling, drug dealing, and prostitution. After the 1979 Revolution, building maintenance was largely neglected. In the absence of basic municipal urban services, the company provided free transportation four times daily between the main site and Peykan-Shahr for both day and night shifts (ibid.). Some buses also transported township residents to Tehran. Although Peykan-Shahr has only primary schools, free transportation to secondary schools in nearby towns was provided. The company also ran an affordable kindergarten for tenants, oversaw all installation services, and managed major repairs. Additionally, a daytime charity healthcare clinic, funded by the company, provided general and emergency services, including vaccinations (ibid.). The company allowed the employee cooperative to operate a grocery store supplying necessities at low prices. Later, as the local market grew, new stores were rented out to non-local shopkeepers.

Between 2002 and 2004, the firm decided to sell the residential units and later the land. The units were sold with priority to occupying tenants (ibid. 403). Tenants had the option to purchase their flats at 60 percent of market price, which ranged from approximately 80 million to 110 million IRR for 40- to 60-square-meter flats. The firm also promised a 70 million IRR private loan, though buyers were required to repay these loans upon retirement. Many residents, however, only received about 20 million IRR of the loan before retiring (ibid.). Flats not bought by tenants were sold to local shopkeepers, garage owners, plumbers, tenants' relatives, and others at current market prices. Many of these new owners rent out the flats rather than living in them. After the sell-offs, some changes occurred in the township: the kindergarten was closed, and the healthcare clinic was sold to the firm's private Healthcare Center. As expected, property prices doubled within the first two years and increased twelvefold by 2011. The average annual price increase was 164 percent, significantly higher than the 16.7 percent average annual inflation rate (ibid.).

By 2011, there were no recorded changes in the physical environment, meaning no investments in physical space had materialized. This temporarily excludes the influence of differential rent II. However, the price rise could not be attributed solely to changes in tenure, even though they played a role. The physical transformation of the surrounding area, particularly regarding relative space—as expected in both the SMLR and the TILR—was a key factor in increasing differential rent I. I noted three spatial developments in the region (ibid. 403): "First, by 2005, Iran Khodro Metro Station on the Tehran-Karaj metro line was established. Second, in 2006, the Hemmat Expressway, which connects Tehran east to west, was extended to Peykan-Shahr. Third, in 2010, a slum around the township called Azad-Shahr was successfully redeveloped and gentrified" (ibid.). All these initiatives put pressure on land and building values in Peykan-Shahr. As neighboring areas began to redevelop, planning for Peykan-Shahr's redevelopment finally started in 2019.

8.2 Social Demand, Profitability, and Land Rent

One interesting implication of these processes is in the case of effective demand (Yousefi and Farahani 2022, 38–39). Indeed, with extensive inequalities, a degree of low effective demand can be expected. The income ratio between the top 10% and the bottom 10% is officially 12 (TCCIMA 2014). The total expenditure of the wealthiest 8% can be as much as 45 times higher than that of the poorest 15% (Ansari 2015, 34). The total gross expenditure of the lowest decile is five times less than the national average, while it is three times higher than the national average for the highest decile (CBI 2017a). On the other hand, over the past 13 years, especially during a period of strict economic sanctions, luxury product consumption surged to new heights (Yousefi and Farahani 2022, 39). This trend also extends to lavish real estate, particularly in districts 1 and 3, where prices are often kept undisclosed. Private jets—at least 200 registered with the Customs Administration (IRICA)—are also common among the wealthy (Mehr News Agency 2017). In 2013, luxury car imports ranked second among the most profitable import sectors in Iran (Taraz News 2013), and they were the fourth-largest import category overall, after rice, soy, corn, and wheat (IRICA 2013). By 2016, IRICA had registered 392 Porsche vehicles (IRICA 2016). Overall, the import of consumer products, excluding basic goods, has increased dramatically over the past four decades (rising five-fold between 2000 and 2017), with luxury product imports averaging 10% (or 10–12 billion USD) of total imports since 2004 (CBI 2019a). This contributes to the increase in aggregate demand, which rose eightfold between 2000 and 2013, as high luxury consumption and spending offset the decline in effective (social) demand among low-income groups (CBI 2019b).

As noted in the previous chapter, extra-economic geopolitical tensions and the resulting US-led sanctions greatly influence the current trajectory of the Iranian economy. In this context, the state actively seeks to maintain the profitability of investments by keeping wages suppressed and political (and individual) freedoms restricted. At the same time, high unemployment rates further reinforce social and spatial inequalities. The role of the state—especially local governments—is not entirely passive in land markets either. Outsourcing practices and their payment methods for urban development projects, such as the floor-space-ratio allowance, alongside leaving land markets unregulated, actively encourage greater private involvement in residential development and the extraction of absolute rents, as per the TILR. Interestingly, both the SMLR and the rentier state literature (Bina 2006; Coronil 1997) overlook the active role of the state in land rent extraction to promote *productive* capital accumulation. Spatial inequality is an inevitable outcome that both the state and capitalists must reproduce to keep this system functioning (i.e., maintain high overall investment levels, thereby helping the economy grow). Residents in northern and central districts, where land and housing prices are highest, have access to all urban amenities that are lacking in southern and western districts (Yousefi and Farahani 2022, 37). As significant new investments, such as malls and commercial properties, began moving to the southern areas of the city, residents were further pushed outward, often renting second-hand apartments in Mehr Housing Program townships. This triggered a dispersal process, supported by targeted infrastructure investments.

CHAPTER 9

Concluding Remarks on Empirical Comparisons of the Two Models

The empirical studies presented in Part 2 allow us to compare the explanatory power of the TILR and the SMLR. After the first study, which was limited to countering the empirical gaps and tensions in Harvey's own original empirical studies that informed his theory of urban land rent, four empirical studies were presented to discuss the relevance of the TILR and the concept of absolute rent in both the Global North and the Global South, at both national and city scales. Using Lakatos's postulates, these studies allow us to evaluate whether the TILR explains everything that the SMLR successfully explains, addresses the aforementioned conceptual anomalies, and perhaps explains some 'novel' facts, above all, the relevance of the concept of absolute rent for urban research. If that is true, then it can be argued that it has 'excess empirical content' over the SMLR.

I would argue that the SMLR's analytical tools are limited because, beyond the monopoly pricing mechanism (which explains the level of rent with the power of the landlord class), the model fails to provide tools to measure and explain rates, ceilings, and magnitudes of land rent. Moreover, the model fails to relate rent creation and appropriation processes to the rest of the economy, limiting the analysis to the micro-level (that is, the single economic sector of land, and specifically the ownership aspect of land), e.g., with the housing submarket, and isolated from the whole-economy level trends and structures. The SMLR analyzes capital's movement from the primary (productive investments) to the secondary (investments in built environments) circuits, conceptualized as capital switching, in a somewhat ahistorical manner. Regarding empirical anomalies, the SMLR relies on inadequate indicators, such as transfer payments and direct rental returns, to explain land rent relations. It should incorporate more comprehensive indicators to measure excess returns as the source of rent, without conditioning on landlords' monopoly power. Harvey argued that neoclassical models are "special cases, which describe conditions when absolute and monopoly rents are insignificant, when absolute and relational concepts of time and space are irrelevant, and when the institution of private property is notably quiescent in the land and property markets" (Harvey 1973, 188). I would argue that his SMLR, too, must be viewed as a special case, describing conditions in which land and property markets are highly financialized, class-monopoly relations over land vigorously dominate rent business, and profitability, inter-sectoral competition, and multi-scalar dynamics are irrelevant.

The TILR explains economic urbanization processes with contextual economic mechanisms. It explains the macro (whole-economy) level source of rent with differential inter-sectoral rates of return. Then, it demonstrates the cyclical nature of rent creation and appropriation, corresponding to profit rate cycles, by empirically using incremental profit rates to indicate capital switching. Crucial in its endogenously structural analysis of economic urbanization processes is the dynamics between national economic trends and local-level economic relations. National economic trends govern (macro-level) rent rates and ceilings, and local-level economic relations determine (micro-level) rent rates and magnitudes. The TILR proposes differential inter-sectoral and intra-sectoral rates of profit as analytical tools, conceptualized in terms of absolute rent and differential rent I and II. In other words, I would contend that the TILR explains everything that the SMLR explains, without the anomalies mentioned above, by introducing the concept of absolute rent.

Nevertheless, two further questions are to be addressed. First, if bringing in the concept of absolute rent can resolve the SMLR's conceptual and empirical anomalies, why have Harvey and Harvey-inspired urban economic geographers opted against incorporating and operationalizing it? Furthermore, second, why can the SMLR not be easily appended with the analytical tools anticipated in the TILR, such as inter-sectoral and incremental rates of return, without generating more theoretical inconsistencies and tensions? Answering these questions requires further analysis of the SMLR's internal theoretical tensions, which limit its ability to address the empirical evidence presented in Part 2. That will be the task of Part 3.

PART 3

Theoretical Foundations of the Two Models

CHAPTER 10

The SMLR, TILR, and Theories of Competition

Lakatos rejects the empiricist claim that an isolated crucial experiment "can instantly overthrow a research programme" (Lakatos 1978, 86). Instead, he emphasizes how scientists often persist in ignoring crucial experiments that challenge the hard cores of their research programs and the empirical evidence incompatible with their theoretical frameworks. This collective resistance, which can take years to break, relies on the heuristic power of the criticized research program—derived from its underlying theories—to address anomalies by repeatedly developing new auxiliary hypotheses as protective belts around its core assumptions. Part 2 of this book showed that incorporating the concept of absolute rent into the analysis and using alternative tools to measure and explain rent rates, ceilings, and magnitudes—including inter-sectoral and incremental rates of return as projected in the TILR—can fill empirical and conceptual gaps in Harvey's SMLR. In this chapter, I explore the theoretical underpinnings of the SMLR to answer two additional questions: First, why have Harvey and other urban economic geographers, inspired by Harvey, dismissed the concept of absolute rent over the last fifty years, even though doing so has limited their ability to develop a fully endogenous, structural explanation of rent creation and appropriation? Second, why can alternative tools proposed in the TILR not serve as a protective belt around the SMLR without generating further internal tensions? Despite the empirical evidence supporting the importance of absolute rent (as shown in Part 2), I believe practitioners of the SMLR will tenaciously resist its inclusion. This resistance is rooted in the model's underlying economic theory, which considers both the concept of absolute rent and the analytical tools of the TILR as theoretically inconsistent with its core assumptions. Therefore, examining the model's theoretical consistency is essential to assess how well the SMLR might respond to my empirical critique from Part 2—and to determine whether this critique could be considered a 'crucial experiment' in the Lakatosian sense.

The SMLR and TILR are based on two different yet equally valid interpretations of Marx's economic theory. These interpretations are developed by Paul M. Sweezy (1970 [1942]) and Anwar M. Shaikh (2016).[1] Harvey acknowledges the

1 Other prominent interpretations of Marx's economic theory, for example, include Moishe Postone's value-form interpretation, Elmar Altvater and Paul Mattick's logic of capital interpretation, Fred Moseley's macro-monetary interpretation, and, closer to Shaikh's

Sweezyan influences on his interpretation of Marx's theory and its integration into geographic analysis. For the TILR, among various classic interpretations that incorporate the concept of absolute rent, I turned to Shaikh. His interpretation is important for the TILR and its application to geographic research because it includes analytical tools for the structural analysis of the historical contingency of inter-sectoral competition for capital switching and the varying inter-sectoral profitability, which explain macro-level relations involved in rent creation and appropriation. More significantly, Shaikh offers robust tools for the theoretical comparison of the two models. I use Shaikh's (2016) typology of economic theories—based on their competition theories—to explain the roots of the SMLR. Instead of highlighting the differences between Harvey's (and Sweezy's) and Marx's original project, Shaikh's typology helps clarify the methodological roots of Harvey's approach, its internal consistency, and its explanatory power. In this chapter, I supplement Shaikh's typology of economic theories with a typology of rent theories to explain the theoretical basis for rejecting the concept of absolute rent in the SMLR.

10.1 Competition Theories and Economic Theories

Shaikh (2016; 2019; 2022) classified the most presently dominant theories of competition in economics as a) the theory of perfect competition that underpins neoclassical approaches, b) the theory of imperfect competition that informs heterodox approaches, and c) the theory of real competition that underlies classical political economy.

10.1.1 The Theory of Perfect Competition

Shaikh argues that the economic theory linked to perfect competition is neoclassical economics. As a descendant of Walrasian general equilibrium theory, neoclassical economics portrays an idealized view of the capitalist economy (Shaikh 2016; Zachariah 2020). In its theory of the firm, companies compete as 'rational' (but passive) price-takers and cost cutters, assuming that demand will balance supply through general equilibrium (Shaikh 2016). Shaikh explains, "[t]rading began with an announced market price that elicited buy or sell offers for quantities of individual commodities and labor power; this price being in accordance with the assumed utility-maximizing behavior of individual

interpretation, Guglielmo Carchedi, Alan Freeman, and Andrew Kliman's temporal, single-system interpretation.

participants" (ibid. 342). He states that, in perfect competition, firms enter the market with perfect knowledge and free entry and exit for both capital and labor. They operate within an equilibrium and tend to ignore demand. The model describes an ideal form of capitalist competition characterized by free entry and exit and perfect knowledge among an infinite number of small firms operating within a supply-and-demand equilibrium (ibid.). Anomalies and counterexamples are viewed as imperfections, which, in turn, are addressed by widening and deepening (free) markets (ibid.). Shaikh notes that the theory "assumes that all firms are exactly the same and like modern Major-Generals, that they have perfect knowledge of all relevant economic circumstances ... These two assumptions turn out to contradict one another so that price-taking behavior turns out to require that firms hold irrational expectations" (ibid. 346). The theory has also been criticized for basing prices on subjective preferences and scarcity (ibid. 328; also, Inoua and Smith 2022). In summary, Shaikh critiques perfect competition theory for: a) describing competitive firms as "price-takers" if perfect conditions exist and "passive price-setters" if they do not, b) portraying cost-cutting firms as "oligopolists," c) defining equilibrium as "a state-of-rest" where supply equals demand, d) interpreting profit as "short-term maximum profit," and e) assuming free competition "only if there is a multitude of small [price-taking] firms," with perfect knowledge and no barriers to entry or exit (Shaikh 2016, 17; 314).

10.1.2 Theories of Imperfect and Monopolistic Competition

The theory of imperfect competition,[2] according to Shaikh, diverges from and relies on similar ('irrational') assumptions (ibid. 357). Profit-maximizing, passive price-taking, cost-cutting firms enter the market with imperfect knowledge, with entry and exit barriers tied to imperfect competitive relations (i.e., monopolistic or oligopolistic competition) (ibid.). He (ibid.) states that over time, firms face shrinking market shares, diminishing returns, and a downward-sloping demand curve. Nevertheless, the equilibrium remains plausible because external forces, such as regulations and government spending, boost investment and help recover falling effective demand (ibid.). The imperfect competition theory emphasizes that the capitalist economy is constantly imperfect, and that perfect competition belongs to a distant past (ibid.). Thus,

2 Keynesian (e.g., Keynes 1964; Krugman 1991; Samuelson 1969), Sraffian (e.g., Sraffa 1926; Steedman 1977), and Post-Keynesian (e.g., Kalecki 2009 [1969]; Robinson 1970 [1933]) theories, according to Shaikh, are quintessential economic theories of the theory of imperfect competition.

in contrast to perfect competition theory, anomalies are treated as rules rather than exceptions (ibid.). Furthermore, like in the perfect competition theory, firms here are passive price-takers. But unlike in perfect competition, because firms are not all the same size, the demand curve is downward-sloping (ibid.). Shaikh highlights that firms still aim to maximize profit within this framework. Nevertheless, because firms vary in size, competition tends to be oligopolistic or monopolistic (ibid.). Firms may switch between markets to adapt to changing demand, which influences the scope of fiscal policy to increase effective demand (ibid.). The theory of imperfect competition, therefore, "proceeds by relaxing one or more of the assumptions of the theory of perfect competition: perfect knowledge, maximizing behavior of consumers and firms, perfect mobility of labor and capital (perfect entry and exit), large number of consumers and firms (to justify price-taking), diminishing returns at some point so that the average cost curve is U-shaped, and no consumption or production externalities" (ibid. 357).

In the Marxian economics tradition, Shaikh (ibid. 353) describes a similar response that arose from a neo-Ricardian critique of Marx by Ladislaus Bortkiewicz (1952 [1906, 1907]), who argued that Marx's analysis of the transformation from values to prices is internally inconsistent (the transformation problem[3]). As a result, his labor theory of value is considered unreliable. Sweezy (1970 [1942]) incorporated Bortkiewicz's critique of Marx's labor theory of value and Hilferding's theory of finance capital (1981 [1910]) to develop an economic theory of monopoly capitalism. His theory suggests that it is not value and profitability but prices and overaccumulation that drive capitalist development in the current stage of monopoly, which has persisted since the early 20th century (also Baran and Sweezy 1966). According to Hilferding, "[c]artelized industries are said to achieve higher profit rates by raising prices and limiting the growth of supply" (Shaikh 2016, 353). Hilferding further states that "the need for cartels to limit the growth of their own supply in the face

3 Moseley (2011, 186, emphasis in original) summarizes the 'problem' as: "in Marx's theory of prices of production in volume 3 of *Capital*, he '*failed to transform the inputs*' of constant and variable capital from values to prices of production". It is argued that "constant and variable capital are derived from given physical quantities of means of production and means of subsistence, and are first determined as the values of these groups of commodities in volume 1 and then determined as their prices of production in volume 3. The criticism is that Marx failed to make this transformation of constant and variable capital in volume 3, but instead left these inputs in value terms" (ibid.). Hence, Marx's theory, so the argument goes, is logically inconsistent. Suffice it to note that Bortkiewicz's critique has been widely contested on both theoretical and empirical grounds since the 1970s (see e.g., Freeman and Carchedi 1996; Foley 1982; Freeman 2010; Kliman 2007; Mattick 1981; Moseley 1991; 2016; Shaikh 1977; 2016; Yaffe 1976).

of their 'exceptionally large profits ... makes the export of capital an urgent matter'" (Hilferding 1981 [1910], 233–234; Zoninsein 1990, 19–20 in Shaikh 2016, 353–354). Sweezy's theory, which Shaikh classifies as the theory of monopolistic competition, "builds on Marx's argument that the scale and capital intensity of production and the centralization of ownership increase as capitalism develops" (Shaikh 2016, 353). Capitalist development "leads to a growing monopolization of capital, so that at some point in the late nineteenth century monopoly supersedes competition and ushers in a new stage of capitalism" (ibid.). In this context, Shaikh explains, "objective laws of prices and profit rates [of competition] give way to power-driven outcomes [of monopoly]" (ibid. 353). According to Shaikh, the theory presents an equilibrium view of monopoly capitalism, assuming a golden age of the free market in the 19th century, which ended with the Long Depression (1873–1896). Since then, capitalism has entered a monopoly stage, mainly with finance capital overtaking productive sectors (i.e., the real economy).

According to Shaikh (ibid. 354), "Sweezy accepts Hilferding's claim that rising scale, capital intensity, and centralization of capital lead away from 'free competition' toward monopolies" (Sweezy 1970 [1942], 254 in Shaikh 2016, 354). The difference is that, for Sweezy, "the dominance of big banks in the early stages was merely a 'passing phase'" (ibid.). This led Sweezy to suggest "the term 'monopoly capital' over Hilferding's 'finance capital'" to describe the current stage of capitalist development (Shaikh 2016, 354). Sweezy (1970 [1942], 258 in Shaikh 2016, 354) agrees with "Hilferding's central point" that "the objective laws of competition are superseded by contingent outcomes based on various degrees of monopoly power." Monopoly power allows monopolies "to limit supply and hence to raise price," which results in "higher profits at the expense of the competitive sector, prompting the rise of monopolies in that sector so that monopolization spreads" (ibid.). Ideally, a "uniform degree of monopoly could conceivably bring about roughly equal profit rates" (ibid.). However, the unequal nature of monopolization in practice leads to "a hierarchy of profit rates that are highest in the most monopolized (large-scale) sectors and lowest in the most competitive (small-scale) ones" (ibid.). Shaikh (ibid.) explains, "[m]onopolies slow down the expansion of their productive capacity 'in order to maintain their higher rates of profit' (Sweezy 1981, 302) so that 'capital crowds into more competitive areas'" (Sweezy 1970 [1942], 285 in Shaikh 2016, 354). Furthermore, "'the level of income and employment under monopoly capitalism is lower than it would be in a more competitive environment'" (Sweezy 1981, 285, 302, in Shaikh 2016, 354).

In the absence of the labor theory of value, Shaikh argues that, in the Sweezyan interpretation, profits are disconnected from the production process. Instead, they are linked to barriers to trade and firms' sizes, affecting their ability to manipulate supply and decelerate "the expansion of their production capacity" to enforce (excess) monopoly prices and sustain (excess) monopoly profits (Shaikh 2016, 354). A monopoly price depends on the Kaleckian concept of the "degree of monopoly," which is the "power of a firm to impose a [monopoly] price markup[4] on prime production costs" (Foster and McChesney 2012, 85 in Shaikh 2016, 356). According to Shaikh, the Sweezyan theory of monopolistic competition is a politically radical branch of imperfect competition theory. The main obstacle to free entry and exit, as well as the primary cause of shrinking investment opportunities, is monopoly relations primarily controlled (and exploited) by finance capital. Like the perfect competition model, an economy is considered competitive only when there are an infinite number of small firms (ibid. 355). In other words, the Sweezyan interpretation sees competition as a "large number and small size of firms" to minimize the effects of monopoly prices and monopolistic superprofits (Shaikh 2016, 355). However, Shaikh emphasizes that "it is solely within the theory of perfect competition that an industry is deemed fully competitive only when its firms are infinitesimal price-takers, identical in cost structure and infinite in number" (Shaikh 2016, 355).

Both Marxist and non-Marxist theorists have discussed gaps and tensions in Sweezy's theory, from Schumpeter (1950) to Mattick (1981). Shaikh provided one of the most systematic methodological appraisals of Sweezy's model. Two key anomalies with monopoly capitalism theory, as identified by Shaikh, are pertinent to my analysis. First, the Sweezyan interpretation requires an exogenous (i.e., political, institutional) explanation to understand monopoly relations. That is, it explains monopoly relations exogenously and through the actions of the agent. Second, monopoly relations should be explained, not assumed: suppose we have an economy in which all firms are monopolies; then we have competition between monopolies, but competition never stops being relevant.

10.1.3 The Theory of Real Competition

Classical political economists, Shaikh argues, are distinguished from post-classical political economists by their 'realistic' perspective on capitalist

4 For Kalecki, a monopoly price markup is "determined by 'the degree of concentration, the relation of transport costs to price, the degree of standardization of price, the organization of commodity exchange, and so on'" (Kriesler 1988, 111 in Shaikh 2016, 360). And market prices "depend on the markup over prime costs ([degree of monopoly over material and labor costs]) and the average price (degree of competition)" (ibid.; also Kalecki 2009 [1969], 14).

competition and growth. Marx, in particular, developed a theory of "anarchical" competition where "competitive firms are active price-setters and aggressive cost-cutters (unlike the passive price-taking firms assumed in perfect competition), and the creation of techniques with lower production costs generally requires greater investment in fixed capital per unit" (Shaikh 2016, 327). In other words, the basis for the theory of turbulent (real) competition, as revived and expanded by Shaikh, is not ideal, 'pure' competition, nor is it the supposed imperfections that might distort that idealized image (whether as exceptions or rules), but an actual disequilibrium where few firms succeed and most fail. A Marxian concept of real competition "brings about a constant fluctuation whose 'disorder is its order', and 'anarchical movement, in which rise is compensated by fall and fall by rise, which ... bring with them the most fearful devastations and, like earthquakes, cause bourgeois society to tremble to its foundations'" (Marx 1847, 174–175 [203–217] in Shaikh 2016, 356).

Shaikh distinguishes Marx's theory of competition from those of Smith and Ricardo in several ways. First, for Marx, the logic of capital is "to invest money to make more money," meaning profit-seeking (Shaikh 2016, 333). Second, based on Marx's arguments in Capital, Volume Three, he argues that capital acts as 'many capitals' competing for higher profits and lower costs in the real world. Third, market prices are determined by average production conditions, which are set by and tend to revolve around the most productive, regulating capitals (ibid. 336). Firms compete (both within and between sectors) in turbulent disequilibrium conditions to become new 'regulating capitals,' aware that the demand curve slopes and their profit share is constantly at risk (ibid.). Fourth, "the mobility of capital equalizes profit rates of the regulating capitals" both within and across sectors (ibid. 567). This causes supply to grow faster than demand in those industries, which will "drive down their prices and profits" (ibid. 260). Fifth, Shaikh clarifies that Marx's development of his theory of competition is based on "differential [sectoral] profitability" (ibid. 336), which stems from his critique of Ricardo's differential rent in agriculture. Sixth, Marx's theory of crisis—that is, the law of the tendency of the rate of profit to fall—incorporates labor costs, technology choices, and time paths to explain why and how crises happen (ibid.). In the theory of real competition, according to Shaikh, regardless of the number and sizes of active firms, firms are profit-seeking, price-setting, and cost-cutting actors who aggressively invest in labor-efficient technologies to set new prices and become new regulating capitals. They operate in a turbulent disequilibrium in which their profits gravitate around prices set by regulating capitals. Shaikh explains that regulating capital is the most efficient form of capital in the manufacturing sector. However, in extractive, rent-bearing industries, competition is governed by the least efficient production conditions due to land rent components of total returns, allowing (non-regulating) capitals to invest less aggressively in labor-efficient technologies while still enjoying relatively high returns (ibid.). I will return to this in the next chapter.

10.2 Harvey and Theories of Competition

Harvey has faced criticism for ambiguities in his economic analyses since the 1970s from both Marxists and non-Marxists (e.g., Bruegel 1975; Evans 1991; Kliman 2015; Mattick Jr. 2008; Murray 1977, 1978; Roberts 2014, 2016b). But especially in recent years, this has become a growing debate over Harvey's economic theory of choice. The reason is that, particularly recently, he has failed to present a coherent economic theoretical framework for his analysis of the spatiality of capitalist development and its recurring overaccumulation crises, nor has he provided a consistent basis for his sometimes not-well-supported critique of Marx's analysis of capitalist development and its recurrent profitability crises (Harvey 2018; 2021; Roberts 2020a). Thus, it is argued that when it comes to economic theory, Harvey appears inconsistent.

I have a fourfold argument regarding this line of critique. First, the alleged inconsistency is not monolithic throughout Harvey's career. Harvey appears to rely more consistently on Sweezy's theory of monopoly capitalism in his early works. Sweezy's influence is evident in his publications during the 1970s and 1980s (e.g., Harvey 1973; (with Chatterjee) 1974; 1974a; 1978; 2006 [1982]; 1985; 1989). His groundbreaking intervention in relating the spatial dynamics of capitalist development to those of capital accumulation culminated in this period (the 1970s and 1980s). The critique of inconsistency seems especially applicable to his later (more polemical) works, but it does not pertain to the purpose of this study. Second, and more significantly, he maintains consistency in his interpretation of rent theory, and once again, his SMLR aligns with Sweezy's interpretation. Third, all this indicates that, among the available (scientifically valid) interpretations of Marx's economic theory, Harvey chose the one suggested by Sweezy, which he believed was more analytically suited to explain the geographical dynamics of capitalist development. Fourth, the methodological validity of the critique depends on empirical evidence demonstrating that his economic theory could produce anomalous results for geographic research (Harvey's subject matter). Such empirical (geographical) implications have rarely been provided by Marxist critics of Harvey, no matter how accurate they might have been at the level of economic theory.

Harvey might seem inconsistent in his popular science works in recent years. But this was not the case from the 1970s until the early 1990s, when he established his model for urban land rent. As for those early (yet more substantial) academic works, his economic theory is pretty straightforward. This has been addressed in most commentary and critiques raised by other Marxists (e.g., Callinicos 2009). Sweezy's influence, particularly Luxemburg/Sweezy's interpretation of Marx's theory of accumulation that emphasizes the circulation and realization sphere, is prominent and clear in Harvey's works throughout the 1970s and 1980s (e.g., Murray 1977). That does not mean Harvey accepted Luxemburg (1951) or Sweezy uncritically. On the contrary, Sweezy elevated Luxemburg's (and Bortkiewicz's (1952 [1906, 1907])) interpretation by connecting both under-consumption and overaccumulation processes to monopolistic and oligopolistic competition, which supposedly dominated capitalism since the end of the 19th century (Baran and Sweezy 1966; Sweezy 1970 [1942]). In his critique of neoclassical theories of urbanization, Harvey revived and advanced the Sweezyan interpretation, linking economic processes of urbanization and geographical unevenness to overaccumulation and monopolistic relations.

Harvey (2006 [1982], 144) criticizes neoclassical economics for idealizing "firms in ways that never existed and fetishiz[ing] the small-scale enterprise, which lacks any degree of monopolistic market power, as the ideal agent for achieving competitive equilibrium." He (ibid. 144) argues that "[i]n the supposedly 'competitive' stage of capitalism, when firms were indeed relatively small, the law of value operated imperfectly and the laws of motion were but partially felt." In the mid-19th century, the main economic goal "was to perfect competition, enhance the operation of the law of value and continue to increase the productivity of labour so that accumulation could be sustained" (ibid. 144–145). The objective was to remove barriers to capital circulation and eliminate "local monopolies … through spatial integration" (ibid. 145). By spatial integration, he means that "[t]ransaction costs had to be much reduced, mechanisms for the collection and dissemination of information improved, and an institutional structure to facilitate money payments, capital flows, etc., had to be created" (ibid.). Harvey contrasts this idealized neoclassical view of capitalist urbanization with the realities of imperfect, monopolistic relations (ibid.). He states, "[t]o some extent the barriers to competition were reduced by massive improvements in transport, communications, and banking techniques" (ibid.). However, "the rise of large-scale, quasi-monopolistic forms of organization with quite immense market power by nineteenth-century standards" limits the success of the strategy in each sector. Regarding the railroads,

> [t]he 'organizational revolution' that took place at the end of the nineteenth century, and which culminated in the emergence of trusts and cartels, can in part be seen as an attempt to deal with all of these barriers to competition by replacing the family business by modern business enterprise. This replacement occurred ... when 'administrative coordination permitted greater productivity, lower costs, and higher profits than coordination by market mechanisms.' (ibid.)

Harvey does not directly reference Sweezy in the passages mentioned above. However, the case he presents is a classic example of both imperfect and monopolistic competition theories, as discussed by Shaikh (2016). It illustrates that all barriers to a perfectly competitive economy, governed by the free movement of an infinite number of small firms, are effectively no exceptions to free-market principles. Harvey (2006 [1982]) emphasizes that monopoly relations are embedded in every aspect of the capitalist market and production. Additionally, as with Sweezy (1970 [1942]), the emergence of such monopoly relations can be traced back to the late nineteenth century. The passages also reflect another interesting theoretical rivalry. Here, Harvey presents his methodologically superior alternative to neoclassical location theory and introduces early ideas for his theory of uneven geographical development (see Chapter 1 above). Highlighting the importance of "spatial competition and the resulting geographical mobility of capitalist production," Harvey (2006 [1982], 389) states, "[u]nder competition, relative locational advantage translates into excess profit." Similar to technological advantage, the excess profit from locational advantage "accrues to individual capitalists who sell at the social average but produce at local costs which are lower than the social average" (ibid.). Long-term monopolies over prime locations are "taxed away as land (location) rent ... The rate of profit to capitalist producers tends to be equalized across locations either through the appropriation of rent or through the geographical mobility of production capital" (ibid.).

To clarify his critique, using "a highly simplified model" inspired by perfect competition theory, he assumes: a) "all capitalists turn over all elements of their capital on an annual basis and that they are free to change location without incurring any devaluation at the end of each year," b) "a closed plain upon which competing capitalists with identical technologies accumulate capital through the production and exchange of a homogeneous product," and c) "all capitalists have perfect information about profit opportunities on the plain" (ibid.). To equalize profit rates, "[a]t the end of each year, capitalists can shift into a spatial configuration of production locations" (ibid.). To explain the barriers to continuous accumulation, he further assumes, "[i]f one capitalist expands output and shifts location to maximize the prospects of realizing values (in both production and exchange), then other capitalists are forced to follow suit in order to defend their competitive position" (ibid. 389). Thus, he concludes, "[t]he aggregate long-run effect on a closed plain is that the search for individual excess profits from location forces the average profit rate closer and closer to zero" (ibid. 389). This hypothetical situation means "that competition for relative locational advantage on a closed plain under conditions of accumulation tends to produce a landscape of production that is antithetical to further accumulation" (ibid. 389). Capitalists "tend to expand production and shift locations up to the point where the capacity to produce further surplus value disappears" (ibid. 389–390). Harvey calls this "a spatial version of Marx's falling rate of profit thesis" (ibid. 390). That hypothesis follows from two additional hypotheses. The first suggests that "the processes making for 'spatial equilibrium'—broadly spelled out in bourgeois location theory—are, from the Marxian perspective to be seen as part and parcel of the processes which lead to crises of accumulation" (ibid.). The second indicates that "those countervailing forces (including those unleashed in the course of crises), which push the space economy of production into some seeming state of chronic disequilibrium, have a potentially important role to play in staving off, limiting, or resolving aggregate spatial crises of accumulation" (ibid.). These hypotheses lead Harvey to move away from Marx's 'thesis' and develop his alternative model for explaining the spatial crisis of overaccumulation, which includes two mechanisms for "crisis formation and resolution" expressed as uneven geographical development and spatial fix to highlight the importance of space and location in the "circulation and accumulation of capital" (ibid.).

Sweezy's interpretation depended on Bortkiewicz's critical review of Marx's labor theory of value. Bortkiewicz (1952 [1906, 1907]) contended that Marx's explanation for transforming values into prices of production was inconsistent—a critique that Harvey (2006 [1982], 351) considers valid. Therefore, both Sweezy and Harvey view Marx's calculation of profit rates, based on values—and consequently his entire crisis theory, which relies on the law of the tendency of profit rates to fall—as unreliable.[5] Instead, to explain periodic drops in demand, the Sweezyan perspective highlights a significant shift in capitalist competition since the late 19th century, marked by the rise of monopolies. Monopolistic competition, primarily controlled by a limited number of large firms, results in surplus capital and overaccumulation. Capital must find new externalities—and investment opportunities—to resolve these contradictions and absorb surplus capital. Sweezy examines these externalities, notably

5 This argument was also echoed by Marxist and non-Marxist economists such as Sraffa (1926) and Robinson (1970 [1933]).

with the growth of luxury production, including large-scale military production (Baran and Sweezy 1966). According to Harvey (2006 [1982]), urban built environments—characterized by long turnover times—constitute the most notable externalities capable of gradually absorbing surplus and potentially spatially resolving overaccumulation crises. Harvey's SMLR aligns consistently with the core assumptions of the Sweezyan interpretation. The model is also, to some degree, externally explanatory. Scientists, as Lakatos noted, tenaciously defend these two qualities of a scientific model against external anomalies arising from newly discovered evidence and competing theoretical explanations. The SMLR has faced such criticisms since it became prominent in Marxist geography. However, it withstood these critiques due to its remarkable ability to explain particular (mainly neoliberal) urban economic processes through the monopolistic dynamics of capital.

10.3 Competition Theories and Rent Theories

Let me now extend Shaikh's typology of competition theories to theories of land rent.

Regarding the theory of perfect competition, I believe the solution to the land rent problem is clear. Since rent is an anomaly caused by monopolies, it should be eliminated for a perfectly competitive market to function properly. Yes, rent might still exist, but its value should be determined according to Say's Law—that is, supply creates its own demand. Therefore, as long as market forces set rent rates and levels, the rent problem will be resolved. As we saw in Chapter 1, neoclassical urban economic geographers like Alonso see rent as a tool for the rational allocation of resources in land and housing markets. In other words, the perfect competition theory views rent as an imperfection that arises from firm monopolies in sectors that generate rent based on land. For example, in the oil industry, national governments and international cartels like OPEC have created sectoral quasi-monopolies to secure the land-rent component of their profits. To counter this effect, efforts should focus on widening and deepening the market against sectoral monopolies, such as through antitrust laws. The theory of imperfect competition also considers land rent as an imperfection caused by firm monopolies, such as monopolistic land ownership. However, unlike the theory of perfect competition, imperfection is viewed as the normal condition. Both branches of imperfect competition theory, as explained by Shaikh, suggest that external forces must be applied to lessen the adverse effects of land rent. Since non-productive sectors like finance exploit the rising rent, the public sector and civil society should regulate rent creation and distribution. They should also curb speculative investments and other unproductive economic activities, including monopolistic ownership, through measures like broad anti-monopoly alliances and similar efforts to unite small capitalists and the poor against finance capital and monopoly landowners. Once again, the theory relies on external explanations to analyze monopoly relations as preconditions for rent creation.

Inspired by the theory of imperfect competition, the SMLR views rent as a barrier to the free flow of capital caused by the monopolization of land. The creation and control of rent are linked to monopolistic property relations, which restrict the circulation of capital and its movement across space. Rent, therefore, emerges from the strong presence of landowners and developers, who team up with finance to liquidate land as a spatially fixed asset. This partnership (between speculators and developers) appropriates the rent, with market-friendly urban policies and governance serving as the catalysts of the entire process. Harvey (2006 [1982], 73) states rent arises due to "[t]he monopoly power that accrues to landowners through the private ownership of land." This privilege itself stems from land being "an indispensable condition of production in general" (ibid.). Landed property acts as a barrier to the circulation of capital (ibid.), and land rent is paid "for the use of the land as a condition or means of production" (ibid.). The level of rent depends on the landlord class's power to set monopoly prices on land,[6] which is influenced by the broader social context, described as "a pattern of social relationships that penetrate willy-nilly into the heart of the production process and condition its organization and form" (ibid.)

This perspective on land rent as a common feature of capitalist economies is also shared by Shaikh's real competition theory, which informs the TILR. Here, the source of rent is understood as the excess sectoral profit rate present in rent-bearing sectors. Rent arises from turbulent macro-level inter-sectoral and micro-level intra-sectoral competitive dynamics, which, in turn, set its limits (rates and ceilings) and determine its magnitudes. Historical and geographical contexts play a crucial role in determining when and where investments

6 Later, Harvey seems to equate rent with all sorts of monopoly pricing, and more specifically, in the art market (Harvey 2002). Following Shaikh, the TILR would consider that analogy problematic because it views rent extracted from resources as nonreproducible conditions of production, rather than as scarce commodities (such as paintings) whose prices rise according to demand. Marx (1991 [1894], 770) also distinguishes between surplus product and land rent, which, for example, applies to vacant dwellings that some scholars equate with land rent (cf. Bradley 2023).

shift to rent-bearing sectors, making rent creation and appropriation historically contingent. When present, the excess sectoral profit in rent-bearing sectors drives capital movement. "[G]iven that competition among producers will enforce a common price, lower-cost producers will tend to have higher profit margins and higher profit rates … This means that better mines and lands will earn excess profit for their producers simply because their conditions are not reproducible" (Shaikh 2016, 266; also see Chapter 1 above). Rent is appropriated by the landlord when and where the landlord and the capitalist are separate. It is appropriated by capitalists when and where they invest in and own land (e.g., in modern capitalism). In that case, "[e]ven if the capitalist and the landlord are the same, one persona gets the normal profit and the other gets the rent" (ibid. 333). Rent stays "in the pockets of the firms operating the land if they own it themselves, it can be shared between the firms and the actual landowners if the two are different entities, or can even be appropriated entirely by the latter if they have the power to rent their land to the highest bidder" (ibid. 266).

The underlying economic theories that inform the two models discussed in this study—Sweezy's theory of monopolistic competition and Shaikh's theory of real competition—conceptualize distinct categories of land rent. The SMLR includes differential rent I, differential rent II, and class-monopoly rent, while the TILR consists of differential rent I, differential rent II, and absolute rent. The key distinction lies in two macro-level categories: class-monopoly rent and absolute rent. Class-monopoly rent refers to the social (monopolistic) patterns of land ownership within class structures that give rise to rent and spatial monopoly (a relative locational advantage). Absolute rent, on the other hand, presents a different perspective. It is equally indifferent to the immediate natural characteristics of the land (in terms of differential fertility or relative space), which are central to differential rent I and II. Instead, absolute rent depends on inter-sectoral competition, which determines excess profits across sectors. Fluctuations in profitability within other sectors, especially manufacturing, and the overall state of inter-sectoral competition determine whether rent exists, as well as its ceiling and rate at the macro level. That is to say, the concepts of differential rent I and II explain variations in rent magnitudes and rates within individual sectors at the micro level. Meanwhile, the concept of absolute rent explains the rent's ceiling and rate at the macro level, along with the rent magnitude on the marginal land plot when differential rents are zero. When differential rents are nonzero, provided that absolute rent exists at the macro level, the total land rent equals the sum of the differential and absolute rents.

10.4 Harvey's Argument against the Concept of Absolute Rent

Harvey's engagement with the concept of absolute rent has never been straightforward. Absolute rent is indeed the central concept of his article with Chatterjee (1974), whose empirical evidence, as previously mentioned, underpins his entire theory of urban land rent. Nevertheless, the definitions, mechanisms, and determinants they present never fully align with what Marx described in Capital. "Absolute rent implies class monopoly power of some sort", write Harvey and Chatterjee (1974, 32) in one instance. They clarify their point by stating, "by 'class monopoly' we mean a class of producers (or consumers) who have power over a class of consumers (or producers) in a situation of structured scarcity" (ibid.). According to them, absolute rent "accrues to the monopoly power of landlords as a class vis-à-vis the collective power and condition of the tenantry" (ibid. 33). Absolute rent, therefore, results from "a 'class' conflict within a restricted geographical area (within an absolute space)" (ibid. 33). They interpret Marx's explanation of the mechanisms responsible for creating absolute rent, i.e., barriers to the equalization process, as "absolute limits of some sort operating over different segments of the housing market" (ibid.). "'Absolute limits' means in this case the creation of absolute urban spaces within which producers and consumers of housing services face each other as classes in conflict" (ibid.). Rent appropriation depends on a) "the internal conditions within that sub-market" and b) "the interaction between sub-markets" (ibid.). They define class-monopoly power as "the relative power of those supplying housing and those consuming it, as that relative power is mediated by institutional policies (legal, political, financial, governmental, etc.)" (ibid. 34). Harvey later elaborates on these power relations by stating that landed property "entails an *absolute* conception of space, one of the most important properties of which is a principle of individuation established through exclusivity of occupation of a certain portion of space—no two people can occupy exactly the same location in this space and be considered two separate people" (Harvey 2006 [1982], 338–339, emphasis in original).

In a likely response to that conceptual tension, Harvey famously diverges from the definitions presented in his article with Chatterjee by renaming the category of rent analyzed there (using the same empirical evidence) as class-monopoly rent (Harvey 1974a, 241). Other geographers have viewed this conceptual shift as a rejection of the relevance of absolute rent in geographic research, especially in urban contexts. Sheppard and Barnes note that Harvey "quickly realized, though, that absolute rent was inappropriate, substituting the term 'class monopoly rent'" (Sheppard and Barnes in Barnes and Sheppard

2019, 207 footnotes, my emphasis). Later, Harvey more explicitly dismissed the concept of absolute rent. He states, "absolute rent is not an important category" in Marx's critique of Ricardo; it serves only as a prelude to his main critique and the development of the two concepts of differential rent (2006 [1982], 353). More recently, Harvey (2010, 81) explicitly states, "I discount here a third category that Marx proposed called 'absolute rent' because, frankly, *I do not think it works*" (emphasis added). Elsewhere, he notes, "'I now think that Marx's theory of absolute rent is *meaningless* and *irrelevant*. Marx does not develop monopoly rent but mentions it on the edges. But it has a clear relevance in urban situations'" (Harvey 2013 interview in Barnes and Sheppard 2019, 207, my emphasis).

As noted in Chapter 1, Harvey's decision to omit the concept of absolute rent from his SMLR is puzzling, given that it played a significant role in Marx's analysis of ground rent in Capital, Volume Three. To address this potential tension, Harvey singles out an empirical anomaly and a theoretical inconsistency in Marx's original formulation of the concept of absolute rent. These are: a) that Marx's argument for the low organic composition of capital in agriculture is inconclusive, and b) that Marx's explanation of the source of absolute rent (i.e., the excess inter-sectoral profit rate) suffers from "the transformation problem." Let me explore these two points in more detail and discuss how they relate to Harvey's underlying economic theory.

10.4.1 The Organic Composition of Capital Problem

Harvey begins his critique of the concept of absolute rent by reexamining Marx's conceptualization, focusing on his analysis of the technical prerequisites for the emergence of absolute rent in agriculture and other labor-intensive, rent-bearing sectors. This critique starts with a potential dilemma: if absolute rent rises in sectors with a lower relative organic composition of capital, then it could also disappear and become irrelevant if the sector's low organic composition of capital improves due to historical and technological developments (Harvey 2006 [1982], 352).[7] Harvey (2006 [1982], 352) says, "[t]he low value composition of capital in agriculture is attributable more to technological and scientific lag in that sector than to anything else. Once agriculture catches up, which at some point it must, then absolute rent disappears, leaving the landowners to take monopoly rents if they can". This, according to Harvey, gives more prominence to monopoly rent, especially if landlords can

7 This argument is also shared by institutionalist and Ricardian urban critics of absolute rent such as Ball (1977; 1985), Economakis (2003), Evans (1988; 1991; 1999a), and Scott (1976).

"artificially withdraw land from production and so raise the rents on the remainder" (Harvey 2006 [1982], 353). This argument suggests that, under financialized monopoly over urban land, landed property, even in marginal lands, can perpetually extract a surplus through monopoly pricing without being affected by the fluctuations of absolute rent. However, as noted in Chapter 1 and by Edel (1992, 76), Harvey never supported this assumption with evidence. Without robust empirical support, it is not easy to agree with him that a unified, fully financialized, and monopolized land market across all urban areas worldwide is feasible.[8] Without that exceptional condition, the effect of monopoly rents will be minimal and difficult to generalize.

In the TILR, the existence of absolute rent depends on inter-sectoral competitive dynamics at the whole-economy level, which secure excess sectoral profits by incorporating labor-efficient technologies (maximizing the rate of exploitation). If inter-sectoral competition indicates higher expected rates of return in the manufacturing sector (or even in finance), alternatively, if inter-sectoral differential profitability or technological difference between sectors were minimal, of course, absolute rent would be minimized (as Davis (2006) observed in the Dubai real estate market prior to the Great Recession). In other words, at the macro level, in the presence of absolute rent, firms can refuse to invest in labor-efficient technologies (leading to a lower organic composition of capital) and still pocket high rates of return. But that is spatiotemporally determined and depends on the empirical study of each case, as noted in two opposite cases in Chapters 5 and 7. For example, suppose absolute rent diminishes due to relatively lower sectoral rates of return. In that case, the same firms have no choice but to invest heavily in labor-efficient technologies to remain competitive, leading to an increasing sectoral organic composition of capital. Thus, agriculture's 'catching up' is not a one-time development. Instead, it is a consequence of a long-term, turbulent inter-sectoral competitive process through which rent-bearing sectors might reflect a high or low organic composition of capital at a given time and place.

---

8 A similar overly generalized version of the financialization thesis is also visible in some financialization literature, which ignores the massive increase of global merchandise output (compared to pre-1990s levels) due to offshoring practices (Peck 2017) of the globalization era, which allowed some regions to be more financialized and others more industrialized in this global division of labor and its associated market specialization. For a critique, see Subasat and Mavroudeas (2023), Neel (2018), and Kliman and Williams (2015). This global dimension is central to Marx's analysis of interest-bearing capital and profitability in Capital, Volume Three.

More important, inspired by the Sweezyan interpretation and in the absence of the labor theory of value[9] (Bruegel 1975; Edel 1992; Kliman 2015; Murray 1977; Roberts 2020a), Harvey's favored mechanism to determine the level of both absolute and monopoly rents is monopoly pricing (the manipulation of supply by landed monopolies). He (2006 [1982], 351) writes, "[t]he level of absolute rent depends upon supply and demand conditions as well as upon the area of new land taken into cultivation". The two categories differ as "[w]ith absolute rent, landlords do not interfere with surplus value production directly" (ibid. 353). However, "[m]onopoly rent actively curtails surplus value production (though not, of course, when levied on consumption) and forces a redistribution of surplus value from other sectors not into agriculture but into the hands of the landlords" (ibid.). And he concludes, "[b]oth kinds of rent depend, however, upon the ability of the capitalist producers to realize monopoly prices" (ibid.). The monopoly pricing mechanism, by definition, is dissociated from production processes and is therefore independent of the dynamics of the organic composition of capital. Harvey justifies his methodological choice by critiquing Marx's notion of the organic composition of capital. However, as shown in Part 2, Harvey's argument against the organic composition of capital does not exhaust the empirical evidence. While following a cyclical pattern, the organic composition of capital in the construction sector remains generally lower than in manufacturing, primarily due to land rent. Harvey's decision to separate housing and urban development from the dynamics of the construction sector (as noted in Chapter 1), and to limit the analysis to the activities of financiers, developers, and landowners, influenced his conclusions. Nonetheless, these do not necessarily render the rival explanation invalid.

10.4.2 The Transformation Problem

Harvey's rejection of the category of absolute rent is primarily concerned with its urban applications. But he extends this critique to practically any reliable application of the concept, even in agriculture, where there seems to be less controversy regarding its relevance among economic geographers and political economists, and conditions the validity of the concept to "the successful resolution of the so-called 'transformation problem'" (Harvey 2006 [1982], 351). The concept of absolute rent and the transformation problem are both closely

9 Of course, Harvey has reviewed different conceptualizations of value and value theory throughout his illustrious career (e.g., Harvey 2006 [1982]; 2017). The point herein is that he has not empirically incorporated the labor theory of value into his SMLR analyses of urban land rent.

related to the question of value. If the transformation problem is valid, the labor theory of value will be rejected, and so will be absolute rent, which is what Bortkiewicz (Bortkiewicz 1919, 173 in Fratini 2018, 972) did. All these seeming theoretical tensions in Marx's economic theory lead Harvey to conclude, "Rey's (1973) characterization of Marx's theory of absolute rent as a 'fiasco' is partially correct in the sense that there is a lot of elaborate theorization about what ends up being of minor importance" (Harvey 2006 [1982], 352, footnote).

One point that needs to be addressed early on concerns Harvey's perspective on (and application of) 'the transformation problem'. For Bortkiewicz and later the neo-Ricardians and Sweezy, the 'problem' is primarily mathematical and is thus expressed in terms of modeling consistency (Shaikh 1982a). Both Sraffa (1926) and Sweezy (1970 [1942]) later tried to reformulate 'the problem' within their respective analytical frameworks to explain prices, demand, and monopolies. However, that does not seem to be the case for Harvey. Harvey shows no effort to extend 'the problem' into a geographic research question. Instead, he accepts it as a starting point. Harvey begins his discussion with an interesting (though not exhaustive) introduction to the debate (2006 [1982], 64–68). After that brief introduction, he does not revisit it until he states that the validity of absolute rent depends on "the successful resolution of the so-called 'transformation problem'" (ibid. 351). His critique suggests that because absolute rent requires an analysis of values, it cannot be applied within a framework that sees 'the transformation problem' as a valid critique of Marx's theory of value. And if that is true—and if one agrees with that critique—then class-monopoly rent should instead be analyzed in terms of monopoly rent and the monopoly pricing mechanism (Harvey 1974a, 241). This is a valid and logically consistent conclusion.

The transformation problem, if proven, is significant (as argued by others such as Bandyopadhyay 1982b, 186–187; Fratini 2018, 962; Harvey 2006 [1982], 355; Ramirez 2009; Scott 1976), because it would eliminate even the possibility of absolute rent. Excess profits in rent-earning sectors, caused by a lower sectoral organic composition of capital and thus lower prices than values, would become irrelevant if the transformation problem is confirmed and Marx's labor theory of value is refuted. Bortkiewicz argued that "Marx was not able to prove in any way that the concept of absolute ground-rent he formulated, understood as an excess of the value above the price of production of the agricultural products, corresponds to something real in the process of price formation" (Bortkiewicz 1919, in Fratini 2018, 972). If this critique is valid, then, as Fratini concludes, the concept of absolute rent becomes "theoretically unsound" (ibid.). Moreover, as Fratini (2018, 962) argues, the difference between sectoral values and prices of production, determined by inter-sectoral competition, sets "the upper limit of absolute rent." Therefore, the absence of such a difference means no excess sectoral profit rates in extractive sectors—meaning no absolute rent. This point is essential if both the concept of absolute rent and the transformation problem are considered valid. In that case, absolute rent would have no upper limit (or ceiling). Instead, absolute rent would appear as a form of rent imposed solely because landed property is a barrier to the free flow of capital between plots, with no ceiling. In other words, it would be "essentially equivalent to monopoly rent," meaning rent that arises from monopoly prices over land plots (Fratini 2018, 962). In other words, without the labor theory of value, "if the class of landowners has the power to interfere with the normal capitalistic process of price formation and earn rent from that, this rent must be deemed due to monopoly pricing" (ibid.). However, Fratini contends that even without the upper limit, one cannot conclude that absolute rent is merely another term for monopoly rent or can be measured using monopoly prices (cf. Harvey's (1974a) argument for class-monopoly rent). In contrast to monopoly rent payment, "the payment of absolute rent is exactly what allows capitalists to remove the barrier raised by landed property" (Fratini 2018, 981).

The concept of absolute rent suggests that analyzing intra-sectoral dynamics (through differential rents) alone is inadequate for understanding what determines rent rates and ceilings at the sectoral and whole-economy levels. Going beyond sectoral boundaries and investigating inter-sectoral interactions and competition is essential to grasp the processes that control rent rates (Fine 2019). In this way, rent creation and appropriation are fundamentally linked to the dynamics of productive capital at both micro and macro scales. The importance of the labor theory of value to rent theory is evident. Not only does the labor theory of value operate at a higher level of abstraction than market prices, but it also empirically explains long-term overall trends and patterns of price fluctuations. Additionally, by clarifying sectoral profit rate expectations based on the varying degrees of fixed capital in use, the labor theory of value also accounts for the movement of capital between branches and its structural connection to labor exploitation. The concept of absolute rent has a similar function. All rents (as the relative price of land) at a market price level result from monopolies. It reflects "the common character" of all rents (Marx 1991 [1894], 772). Monopoly pricing may exist at individual sites or plots, but inter-sectoral competition is needed to reveal the forces and conditions that drive rent creation and appropriation. Rejecting the concept of absolute rent based on the transformation problem, as theoretically justified as it is, strips the subsequent rent theory of such empirical sophistication.

Furthermore, Bortkiewicz's thesis is not universally accepted and has been subject to significant criticism. These criticisms can be divided into two groups.

The first group claims that 'the problem' is not mathematical or even theoretical but at least partly a misinterpretation of Marx's theory of value. Their main critique of Bortkiewicz's thesis is based on the straightforward fact that production takes time, and the input and output values cannot be treated as equal (Kliman 2007); therefore, there is no transformation problem. As Kliman (2007, 21) states,

> a commodity's value is determined by the average amount of labor currently needed to produce it … the phrase 'currently needed to produce' reflects the idea that the value of newly-produced items determines the value of already-existing ones … the phrase 'average amount of labor' [means] any labor spent on the production of a commodity in excess of what [Marx] calls the socially necessary labor-time does not count as value-creating labor.

This point is important because it explains the competitive relationship between less- and more-efficient producers, which prevents them from charging prices above or below the social average. In other words, what they earn or lose is based on profit, not price. For Marx, Kliman continues (ibid.), an increase in productivity lowers the value of labor time, thus lowering the value of production prices and profits. Kliman (ibid.) further elaborates that "a commodity's value is the sum of two components": a) "value transferred from used-up means of production", and b) new value added by living labor. The first refers to "the amount of value that is needed to acquire the means of production (rather than their own value)" (ibid. 22). This 'needed' amount of value transferred "depends upon [a)] the current cost, rather than the historical cost, or original cost, of the means of production, and [b)] the socially average expenditure on the means of production" (ibid.). Thus, Kliman concludes, "if the efficiency with which a particular firm uses inputs is greater than (less than) the industry average, its actual expenditure will be less than (greater than) the sum of value transferred to its products" (ibid. 22). Measuring the amount of value transferred lies at the heart of the controversy. As proponents of the transformation problem consider the value of inputs and outputs simultaneously, they argue that Marx's 'solution' is inconsistent because it is unclear how prices of production can be consistently transformed into values, rendering the numbers incoherent.

The second group of critics challenges Bortkiewicz's thesis on methodological grounds. Shaikh (1977; 1978; 1982; 2016) argues that all comparisons between prices, regardless of the theory, face problems, as "any pair of comparisons gives rise to a transformation problem" (Shaikh 2016, 224). Transformation problems similarly arise in Sraffian approaches when comparing production prices, or market and monopoly prices (ibid. 212). As a result, proponents of 'the problem' face inconsistencies because their starting points are based on different economic theories. In other words, methodologically speaking, the assumptions behind the transformation problem are incompatible with Marx's competition theory and align more closely with an imperfect competition theory. Therefore, instead of providing a 'solution' to the problem (ibid. 242), he considers their critique, along with their entire presumption (that transforming inputs and outputs must be simultaneous), methodologically invalid.

10.4.3 Harvey's Solution: Abandoning Absolute Rent

Harvey's solution to the noted problems in incorporating the concept of absolute rent is to propose an alternative category, class-monopoly rent, which serves as a novel auxiliary hypothesis in the Lakatosian sense. The concept of class-monopoly rent is used to explain monopoly prices in land markets at the macro level, complementing analyses of plot-level differential (relative) rents. However, a class monopoly does not account for rent rates, ceilings, or levels, nor does it explain the drivers and mechanisms behind those monopoly prices without considering the influence of landlords and agential power relations. Therefore, it must include external forces to do so. Harvey ties this to the power of a class of speculator-developers over land markets through institutional and regulatory "arrangements" (Harvey 1974a, 243). Such arrangements are necessary to ensure "certain minimum rates of return" below which speculator-developers would not be willing to enter the market (ibid.).

In his empirical studies, he fails to explain the drivers of sectoral (monopolistic) rates of return. He writes, "[w]hat the minimum must be is difficult to say—but in the United States a 40 per cent rate of return is not regarded as abnormal" (ibid.). He adds that his observations suggest it is unlikely the rent could benefit low-income tenants. Instead, he assumes "an hierarchical structure of some sort through which class-monopoly rents percolate upwards but not downwards" (ibid.). All is to the benefit of finance capital, as "[a]t the top of this hierarchy sit the financial institutions" (ibid.). The role of finance is to ensure that spatially fixed assets in urban land markets are liquidated for further speculation. The whole arrangement explains capitalist urbanization as an outcome of the circulation of capital through which developers and speculators go hand in hand to maintain the exploitation of low-income tenants. Furthermore, since it occurs outside the production sphere, manufacturing capital is not the agent of exploitation in this process because values and profits are not involved. Whereas, for the TILR, the concept of absolute rent was articulated as an economic mediator with the help of which industrial capital is just as much involved in the exploitation in the social reproduction sphere, here the urban social life, because land rent is regulated by fluctuations of inter-sectoral profit rates at the whole-economy level. The minimum level below which investors refuse to invest in land is determined by the interest rate, not an arbitrary 40 percent figure. Keynes' argument for the relation between marginal efficiency of capital (i.e., expected profit rate) and interest rate will be a better starting point, even though it is inadequate as it lacks the variable of rent (see Chapter 11).

Harvey's critique of the concept of absolute rent is weak on both counts. That is, he ignores empirical evidence and refuses to engage both theoretically and empirically with the questions of the organic composition of capital in rent-bearing sectors and the transformation problem. This makes it more likely that his rejection of the concept is just a strategy to avoid inconsistency, which is all well and good, but much less compelling than he suggests. His claim that the category of absolute rent is irrelevant for urban research is only valid if one accepts all of Harvey's assumptions. Like any other model, his SMLR depends on the validity of these assumptions. The real question is whether those assumptions are justified, which the empirical evidence in Part 2 sought to challenge.

10.5 Concluding Remarks

All that is to say, the exclusion of the concept of absolute rent in Harvey's SMLR is a methodological choice aimed at maintaining internal consistency. It is undoubtedly not a methodological 'error'. If this proposition holds, then incorporating the concept demands an alternative economic theory. The competition theory used in the SMLR, borrowing Shaikh's lexicon, is monopolistic competition. The concept of absolute rent is inconsistent with that theory. Harvey struggled with incorporating the concept of absolute rent into his model in the 1970s (Harvey and Chatterjee 1974). He ultimately decided against it (Harvey 1974a; 2006 [1982]) to stay internally consistent. This is a scientifically valid and rational decision. Nevertheless, this analysis refutes the argument that the notion of absolute rent is categorically and empirically irrelevant for urban research. This brings us back to the typology of rent theories. The types of rent each of the two interpretations of Marx's economic theory, discussed here, derive from their respective competition theories. Shaikh's theory of real competition permits Marx's original categories of differential rent I, differential rent II, and absolute rent. The Sweezyan theory of monopolistic competition, which influences Harvey's SMLR, allows for differential rent I, differential rent II, and class-monopoly rent.

The Harveyan interpretation of Marx's rent theory, as seen in the SMLR, is consistent with the core assumptions of the theory of monopoly capitalism. Therefore, rejecting the category of absolute rent stems from a paradigmatic choice, a valid scientific decision aimed at maintaining internal consistency. Turbulent inter-sectoral competition is key to the concept of absolute rent. However, it conflicts with the fundamental assumptions of any theory of imperfect competition, including monopoly capitalism. This explains a) why Harvey and urban economic geographers, inspired by Harvey, have not included the concept of absolute rent over the past fifty years, and b) why, in some cases, they have favored *ad hoc* dismissals of the structural analysis altogether. It also suggests why the SMLR cannot be easily appended with the concept of absolute rent and the TILR's alternative analytical tools, which I discussed in Part 2, without making the SMLR inconsistent with its underlying economic theory.

The critique does not need to engage in an esoteric Marxological debate to disprove Bortkiewicz's neo-Ricardian critique. Textual and conceptual analyses, though essential for establishing the groundwork, are insufficient to challenge that critique. As Bruegel (1975), Ive (1976), Yaffe (1976), Murray (1977; 1978), Sandemose (2006), Das (2017), and others have demonstrated, a thorough methodological and empirical critique is instead necessary. Shaikh argues that the neo-Ricardian critique is internally inconsistent because a) it depends on exogenous (political, institutional) forces to explain monopolies, b) it fails to explain how monopolies or oligopolies compete, c) it is based on the same assumptions it seeks to refute, namely, perfect competition, and d) it relies on neoclassical presumptions for empirical analysis. Notwithstanding, Sweezy's monopoly capital school is a legitimate tradition that offers a valid interpretation of Marx's economic theory. The question is whether it can provide a comprehensive and consistently structural explanation of capitalist urbanization processes using Marxian rent theory. The weakness of the SMLR is not that it differs from other (more orthodox) interpretations of Marx's economic theory. But that, in the absence of the concept of absolute rent, it relates spatial dynamics to exogenous monopoly relations (shaped by ideological and policy choices) rather than to endogenous inter-sectoral dynamics driven by productive capital. This contradicts its original promise to explain urban spatial dynamics structurally—i.e., in terms of the inner workings of the capitalist economic system. The SMLR's underlying economic theory prevents it from providing a consistently endogenous structural explanation, on the one hand, and from incorporating the TILR's solutions as a protective belt, on the other.

CHAPTER 11

The Turbulent Inter-sectoral Model of Land Rent (TILR)

The TILR rivals the SMLR by a) offering analytical tools for pinpointing the presence of absolute rent and measuring and explaining its rate, ceiling, and magnitude, b) explaining the historical contingency of rent creation and appropriation and capital switching, c) incorporating a multi-scalar analysis with the dynamics of the local and the national, and d) explaining rent creation and appropriation structurally and in terms of the dynamics of productive capital. The source of land rent, according to the TILR, is excess sectoral profits (determined by the state of turbulent inter-sectoral and intra-sectoral competition), and capital moves to rent-bearing sectors when differential inter-sectoral profit rates rise in those sectors. The TILR does all this by bringing in the concept of absolute rent (dismissed in Harvey's model on grounds of internal consistency) to analyze economic urbanization processes under capitalism.

The most influential non-Marxist critics of the notion of absolute rent in particular and Marx's rent theory in general (i.e., Ball 1977; 1985; Evans 1991; 1999a; Haila 1988; 1989; 1990; Scott 1976) highlight three (one theoretical and two empirical) inconsistencies in Marx's concept of absolute rent, with the first two also shared by Harvey. They argue that the concept of absolute rent becomes irrelevant to urban research 1) if the conceptualization presupposes Marx's 'inconsistent' transformation of input and output prices, known as the transformation problem; 2) if one does not consider the organic composition of capital to be low in construction and built environments; and 3) if the landed property itself does not appear as a barrier preventing the movement of capital onto the land. More importantly, according to them, the main issue with the concept is that it cannot be applied to the concrete analysis of fluctuations in land markets and property values (i.e., market prices). In other words, the Marxian rent theory (especially its category of absolute rent) seems too theoretical to be practically used in real estate and housing economics. Haila (1990, 282) notably cites Harvey as an example of this intellectual tendency. Their critique of the Marxian rent theory challenges its radical stance on spatial inequalities in the capitalist city, thereby highlighting social conflicts over land relations. They consider it normative and not sufficiently economic. The

TILR seeks to complement Marxist scholarship on urban land rent in response to such critiques.

As Marx (1991 [1894], 772) argues, the nature of all rent is monopoly. All modern rent theories—whether Marxian, Ricardian, or neoclassical—explain, to some degree, the economic forces behind rent and the structures involved in its creation and appropriation beyond that monopolistic *appearance*. Rent theories seek to explain the character (or 'form') of rent—such as differential, absolute, or class monopoly—and to measure and clarify its magnitude, rate, and maximum level. Harvey's SMLR goes beyond the neoclassical and institutionalist approaches mentioned above, but only partially. It does not adequately address macro-level rates and ceilings of land rent, nor does it provide proper analytical tools for measuring and explaining rent rates and magnitudes. The TILR, informed by an alternative economic theory capable of analyzing the turbulent nature of capitalist competition, improves upon the SMLR in this regard. The model incorporates the concept of absolute rent to structurally explain the processes of capitalist urbanization and urban land markets, focusing on the macro-dynamics of capital accumulation and productive capital. To do so, it introduces empirical tools for measuring rent rates and ceilings, and explaining how land rent creation and appropriation relate to inter-sectoral competition at the whole-economy level. Modern capitalist relations in land have created opportunities for land ownership, allowing capital to secure rent as part of the excess returns on land investments, which offset periodic declines in manufacturing profitability. This occurs independently of the influence of non-productive financial and commercial interests or the collusions of landlords, or of assuming "a purely arbitrary determination of price" made up in "the heads of the agents of circulation" (Marx 1991 [1894], 428). This is crucial for understanding rent in modern urban settings, where, notwithstanding the presence of the state (either national or local) and a few large-scale landowners, most land plots are owned by industrial investor-capitalists (Murray 1977; Shaikh 2016). The TILR provides a multidimensional view of the land market, incorporating long-term, inter-sectoral, and multi-scalar dynamics.

My point is fairly straightforward. The three economic categories—profit, interest, and rent—should be viewed in the context of intra- and inter-sectoral competition. This assumption enables the analysis of the overall average profit, which is a combination of the profit of the enterprise, interest, and land rent (Marx 1991 [1894], 474). This 'overall average profit' refers to "average total" sectoral capital, meaning "the normal, average situation for capital invested" in that branch, which in modern terms relates to sectoral expectations (ibid. 243). In the final analysis, the overall rate of profit "depends on the level of exploitation of labour as a whole by capital as a whole" (ibid. 298–299). Specifically, in the case of land rent, this assumption allows for explaining the rise in land rent "as a result of the overall social labour" (ibid. 775). The assumption, according to Marx (ibid. 774), enables us to view both the economy as a whole and its individual sectors in their totality. It reflects (ibid.),

> the law of value as it makes itself felt, not only in relation to the individual commodities or articles, but rather to the total products at a given time of particular sphere of social production autonomized by the division of labour; so that not only is no more labour-time devoted to each individual commodity than necessary, but out of the total social labour-time only the proportionate quantity needed is devoted to the various types of commodity.

Regarding housing and the built environment, the assumption enables viewing the housing sector as a whole industry that includes all primary actors Harvey identifies for the sector, i.e., "landlords, developers, financiers, builders, and state" (Harvey 2006 [1982], 397), and explaining each one in relation to the others. This implies that while some actors, such as developers, are more susceptible to financial fluctuations and influence, others, like construction, are more influenced by inter-sectoral competition.

The rates of profit, interest, and rent are determined by their competitive interplay. This means that, depending on historical and geographic context, one or two of these components—part of sectoral investment return rates—may fall below the others. Capital tends to flow toward sectors with higher expected returns. Shaikh traces this to Keynes (1964), who showed that interest rates are linked to fluctuations in profit rates, so interest rate cycles typically follow profit rate cycles. However, rent rate cycles, which influence investment in land, can move in the opposite direction. Investment in land generally involves productive use rather than pure speculation, which anticipates higher future prices (i.e., land hoarding). The overall sectoral return rate in rent-bearing sectors combines the return on production and the land rent component. When we incorporate scale and multi-scalar relations into the model, it captures the spatial effects of long-term capital movement both horizontally and vertically. Including time allows the flow of capital to be placed within a historical and geographic context, illustrating various scenarios of vertical and horizontal capital flows. Including the whole economy (or national) level allows explaining the relationship between capital flows into land and the rest of the economy, just as, for instance, having a national minimum wage indicates that sectoral wage rates are meant to be equalized across the economy. In this framework, rent is generated endogenously, through the dynamics of productive capital driven by long-term vertical (scalar) and horizontal (sectoral) movements at the macro level. Therefore, rent creation and appropriation are internally linked to the rest of the economy rather than determined exogenously, as the SMLR suggests. It is important to recognize that the sectoral distinctions discussed are conceptual. Even in large-scale manufacturing industries involved in financial and land markets, the profit, rent, and interest components of total return are heavily influenced by their own sectoral profit formation and circulation. This means, for example, that the financial division of a large corporation must compete with other active financial firms in the market and cannot rely solely on the overall profitability of the parent corporation.

At the same time, this argument suggests that if (aggregate) rents decline to a level where the total rate of return on investment in rent-based sectors drops below the industrial profit rate and the financial interest rate, there will be no capital flow into land, as seen in Dubai's land markets in the mid-2000s (Davis 2006).[1] It also indicates that if profits fall below rents but rents fall below interest rates, capital will not flow into land but instead move toward finance, as observed in Sweden during the mid to late 1980s in Chapter 5. If profits do not decrease at all, capital continues to favor the manufacturing sector. Overall, to accurately understand capital movements, one must empirically study the barriers to movement across all three branches of capital and interpret the results within multi-scalar relations to predict movements at the plot, regional, national, and international levels. This is particularly important when tracing the origins of the type of capital in question. An example is the United States since the Great Recession, when, following a decline in US manufacturing profit rates, capital first migrated to finance (through hedge funds), then to private rental housing markets in other countries, such as Spain, or to large-scale land acquisitions (or land grabbing) in the developing world (Yrigoy 2020). A city-level or even national-level analysis alone cannot fully explain such processes. These scalar dynamics are especially critical in housing, where local dynamics are heavily influenced and conditioned by nationally determined land policies and economic structures. Moreover, these macro-level structures shape the options and decisions of local agents, including government and social movements. All of this, of course, is explained at a capital-as-such (i.e., aggregate) level. Individual capitals (especially smaller

1 In another example, following the supply shock caused by the COVID-19 pandemic in some countries, capital flowed into land markets. For instance, in Sweden, building permits for new construction increased 29 percent in 2020 (rising from a total of 3500 and 3550 in 2018 and 2019 to 4600 in 2020) (SCB 2021), whereas, in other countries such as the United States and China, capital flowed into fictitious cryptocurrency and non-fungible token markets (Mariana et al. 2021; Chen et al. 2021).

ones) might still feel pressure to move or stay put, even when the comparative relation described here is not at play. In other words, if the return on investment for the current investment (for each individual capital) drops below the expected profit, they would move to other sectors or choose not to move at all. What influences high returns at the micro-level is essentially demand. Rent theory aims to explain (contra neoclassical economics) why there could be such high demand in specific sectors or plots. The concept of absolute rent also offers a way to analyze long-term, structural land relations under capitalism in a dynamic, non-static manner.

Harvey's SMLR elaborates and explains a structural scenario for how capital flows onto land by adding a spatial dimension to Marx's analysis of capital movement between branches in Capital, Volume Three. At the risk of oversimplification, this scenario suggests that the overaccumulation crisis necessitates spatial expansion (through the production of space), which results in inequality and low effective demand. A competing scenario for capital flows onto land (presented by the TILR) considers comparative sectoral rates of return. The sector with the higher potential rates (according to investors' expectations) attracts a large share of investments, thereby directing capital flows. Profit rates and the manufacturing sector are central to this dynamic, as Keynes also confirmed. Other sectors attract capital when and where expected profit rates fall below expected rent or interest rates. Depending on the historical and geographical context, this may lead to increased land or financial investments to stave off deeper slumps. Overaccumulation might happen in response to a decline in overall profits. However, a) it is not the leading cause of capitalist crises, and b) it does not primarily drive or influence the flow of capital onto land as much as inter-sectoral competition and profitability cycles do.

Expected profit rate (similar to Keynes' marginal efficiency of capital) must be higher than the interest rate for real (productive) investment to occur. This is because the present value of expected returns on capital needs to exceed the current cost of capital. In other words, the marginal efficiency of capital must surpass the interest rate; otherwise, investors tend to hoard money or save. Shaikh explains that the difference with Marx is that "Keynes takes the expected rate of profit (marginal efficiency of capital) as exogenous in the short run" (Shaikh 2016, 577, footnote). At the same time, for Marx, "it is regulated by the actual rate of profit over the longer run" (ibid.). Finance is understood as the mobilization of total surplus and its allocation to the most efficient investment opportunities. In this context, fluctuations in the interest rate are linked to fluctuations in the profit rate. The TILR indicates that the expected profit rate must be higher than both the interest rate and the rent rate for productive investment to take place. Moreover, the differential inter-sectoral profitability determines the rate and ceiling of land rents. Therefore, Keynes' equation can be updated to include three variables: the expected profit rates (Pr), the expected interest rates (r), and the expected rent rates (Lr). In other words, productive investment requires that the expected profit rate exceeds both the interest rate and the land rent rate (i.e., Pr > r > Lr).

But there is more complexity in this process when it comes to imposing capital switching. According to Shaikh, the theory of real competition "conceives of profit rate equalization as a dynamic and turbulent process" (Shaikh 2008, 167). He elaborates, "[i]nvestment flows into an industry are motivated by the expected rates of return on those potential new investments that embody the best-practice conditions of production" (ibid.). Shaikh refers to these new investments as regulating capitals. He argues that "[t]here is no single expected rate of return in any given industry, but rather a diverse set of expected returns that are revised continually in the light of actual outcomes" (ibid. 168). So he elaborates, "if the regulating profit rates in a given industry are higher than the economy-wide average, production in this industry will accelerate until the supply in the industry grows more rapidly than its demand" (ibid.). In the construction sector, this process is evident in the rise in new construction. The process implies that competition is led by lower-cost regulating capitals (who set expectations for rates of return), leaving aside higher-cost capitals. It also implies that "there is never a moment in which all capitals within an industry operate under the same conditions of production" (ibid. 169). That is why "competition between industries leads to a process of entry and exit of capital in search of higher profit rates" (ibid.). All of this indicates that an average profit rate would be insufficient for assessing the influence (in terms of profit rate) of regulating capital. Instead, Shaikh recommends measuring the rates of return on the most recent investment, which he refers to as the incremental rate of profit (ibid. 171; 174). It is this incremental profit rate across different industries that reveals the frequent capital switching between sectors, corresponding to variations in stock market returns (ibid. 174; also Shaikh 1998, 371), and which Harvey (1974a; 1978; 1989) describes (and expands upon) as moving from the primary to the secondary circuit of capital.

The organic composition of capital (as the ratio of capital cost to labor cost) explains why land (and extractive sectors in general) can generate higher expected returns on investment when and where profits are low. It also clarifies the competitive relationship between manufacturing and extractive (rent-bearing) sectors. High rent levels in rent-bearing sectors mean that capitalists can avoid investing in labor-efficient technologies and still achieve relatively high returns. This implies that, in the absence of absolute rent, a new investor must meet the technological frontier set by existing regulating capital, around which sectoral competition gravitates, to survive. This survival means they need to operate at low cost and aim for high expected profits relative to the current regulating capital. Conversely, when absolute rent exists (i.e., total manufacturing profit rates are lower than total rent rates), a newcomer can bypass meeting the technological frontier, operate with a lower technological level than the sector's regulating capital, and still enjoy high returns due to land rents. Of course, as we saw in Chapter 7, in the case of Iran, this depends on the ability to acquire land, which is a scarce and non-reproducible condition of production. In other words, even if, at a given time and place, technological innovations offer reasonably priced, labor-efficient technologies for constructing five-story buildings, if profit rates are comparatively lower than rent rates, capitalists in the construction sector might choose not to invest in that technology, instead relying heavily on cheap labor (i.e., to operate labor-intensively), and still, pocket excess returns (in the form of profit rates on the construction process plus land rents).

At the local level, when macro-level rents exist, the primary influence on land use would be differential rent I and II, and how they interact through extensive and intensive investment strategies. Their magnitudes will be combined with the absolute rent to determine the total land rent. The existence of rent explains why prices in rent-bearing sectors are controlled by the regulating capital operating under the worst production conditions. In contrast, prices in the manufacturing sector are controlled by the regulating capital operating under the best, most efficient production conditions. The absence of rent in manufacturing means that capitalists compete intensely over the most valuable and efficient use of resources. This involves pursuing the highest possible profits and the lowest costs, employing the most recent labor-efficient technologies already established by the current regulating capital, and heavily investing in innovative labor-efficient technologies through research and development. Harvey (following Marx) conceptually replaced soil fertility in Ricardo's rent theory with the favored location, viewing it as a relative locational advantage in urban space. However, location does not carry the same material significance as fertility, and 'favored location' is largely subjective. Nonetheless, this favored location can be explained in two ways: 1) what Harvey calls relative space, meaning its relation to what occurs in the surrounding area in terms of geographical (spatial) development; 2) regional inter-sectoral relations, meaning its relation to economic development in the surrounding area, or the economic aspect of the location. The TILR enhances the SMLR with this second point. Analyzing relative space is essential for understanding the strength of intra-sectoral competition that influences differential rent I and II. Absolute rent indicates the amount of rent when differential rent is zero (at the margin). Conversely, when differential rent is not zero, absolute rent contributes to the total rent.

Absolute rent will accrue to the state if land is nationalized. The municipalization of land has a similar effect but yields fewer returns for the government. Absolute rent can be minimized if profit rates are restored and rent rates fall below them. In that case, individual plots could still generate rent, but rent cannot be the primary strategy (whether state or corporate). For Marx, the idea of absolute rent suggests that if perfect competition theory were correct, capitalism should have nationalized land long ago. It has not (and perhaps could not) because rent extraction helps when manufacturing profits decline. In this sense, rent is a real and necessary part of modern capitalism, helping to offset falling profit rates and prevent system collapse. Therefore, instead of advocating for land nationalization, capitalists encouraged land acquisitions to redirect land rents to themselves rather than traditional landowners.

The TILR improves on the SMLR by 1) proposing a comprehensive analysis at the whole-economy level that explains historical contexts, such as the historical contingency of rent creation and appropriation; 2) developing an empirical strategy to measure and explain land rent rates, ceilings, and magnitudes at both macro and micro levels; 3) providing an analysis of differential rent I and II and their interaction with macro-level rent dynamics, in terms of economic and spatial development; and 4) presenting a consistently structural analysis of urban capitalist land relations that connects rent's creation and appropriation to the dynamics of productive capital.

Summary and Conclusions

Housing in contemporary urban economies remains a commodity out of reach for millions of low- to middle-income households. As the cases I opened this book with show, this is primarily due to consistently high prices and periodic shortfalls in public and private investment. The economic forces and determinants behind temporal rhythms of investments and prices are frequently obscured by "innumerable different empirical circumstances, natural conditions, racial relations, historical influences acting from outside, etc." (Marx 1991 [1894], 927). However, if all that is to be known are differences, then there is little point in theorizing. The role of economic theories is to identify and explain the economic forces at play in contemporary capitalist cities, debate their conceptualizations, and suggest strategies to address housing problems. The common factor among these theories is that investments in housing production, like any other commodity, depend on profit expectations. The source of this profit is explained differently across theories, from efficiency to monopolies and exploitation. Since housing is based on land, and the profitability of investments in it always includes a land-rent component, the conceptualizations of the source of profit in the competing economic theories naturally extend to their respective theories of land rent.

In urban economic geography, the political economy approach to explaining urban land and housing problems is most systematically developed by Harvey. He advances his analysis of economic urbanization processes by critiquing neoclassical explanations that focus on investment choices driven by investor behavior and consumer preferences. He emphasizes the importance of economic structural relations that determine land relations, thereby influencing location and investment decisions (see Chapter 1). In this structural account, crises of overaccumulation generate and worsen uneven geographies of capitalist development. In response, capital often switches from the primary circuit (productive investments) to the secondary circuit (investments in built environments) to create new spaces of accumulation and absorb surplus capital. Land rent, arising from monopolistic land ownership, is crucial to Harvey because it acts as a barrier to the free flow of capital, i.e., capital switching. Overcoming this barrier requires an influx of finance capital, which, in turn, raises the risk of speculative activity in the built environment, making housing even less affordable for low-income households.

In this book, I have reconstructed Harvey's interpretation of rent theory as the Spatial Monopoly Model of Land Rent (SMLR). The SMLR primarily builds on Marx's rent theory and the categories he proposed. However,

Harvey considers Marx's third category, absolute rent (Appendix 1.2), irrelevant to urban research and introduces an alternative, class-monopoly rent (Appendix 1.4), to replace it in his model. This methodological and conceptual approach, however, does not exhaust all available empirical evidence (see Part 2). Reflecting on the reasons for this failure to explain empirical evidence, I have elucidated some limitations and weaknesses of the SMLR. The most important among them are:

1) Above and beyond a monopoly pricing mechanism, it offers limited analytical tools for empirical research on rent rates, ceilings, and magnitudes.
2) It offers inadequate economic mechanisms for macro-level (i.e., whole-economy level) patterns of rent creation and appropriation.
3) It offers an inadequate explanation for the historical contingency of macro and micro-level rent creation and appropriation, and capital switching.
4) It breaks with its structural starting points and does not offer a consistently endogenous structural analysis of rent creation and appropriation (see Chapter 1).

The alternative Turbulent Inter-Sectoral Model of Land Rent (TILR), which I propose in this book, improves upon the SMLR and addresses its conceptual and empirical inconsistencies by reintroducing the often-overlooked concept of absolute rent (Chapters 1 and 11). The model incorporates long-term inter-sectoral and multi-scalar dynamics of capital. Supported by analytical tools for measuring and explaining rent rates, ceilings, and magnitudes at both macro and micro levels, it also considers the historical contingency of rent creation, appropriation, and capital switching. According to the TILR, expected sector-wide profit rates guide capital movement between branches. In the built environment, the sectoral profit rate encompasses absolute (or sector-wide) land rent. The level and rate of this land rent, along with its temporal rhythm, are influenced by competition across sectors. High sectoral land rent levels promote investment and accelerate supply, while low rent levels discourage investment. This means Harvey's two core conditions for the rise of land rent (monopolization and financialization) should be understood as exceptional cases of this general tendency. By linking rent creation and appropriation to macro-level productive capital dynamics, the model provides a consistently endogenous structural explanation that Harvey's initial promise ultimately failed to deliver.

The two models' explanatory powers in addressing the anomalies have been empirically compared across five studies. The first study (see Chapter 4) involves a critical reevaluation of Harvey's two seminal empirical analyses of Baltimore. It aims to compare the analytical tools provided by each model at a conceptual level. These tools are also used to compare the historical contingencies of rent creation and appropriation, as well as capital switching. The remaining four studies primarily seek to demonstrate the relevance of the concept of absolute rent and the implications of using the TILR model, which incorporates it, for urban analysis at two scales—national and urban—and across both the Global North and the Global South. The second and third studies (see Chapters 5 and 6) provide empirical evidence of absolute rent and capital switching at the national (land policy) and urban (housing shortage) levels in Sweden. This is followed by the fourth and fifth studies (see Chapters 7 and 8), which expand this discussion to the Global South, examining the importance of the category of absolute rent for analyzing national housing strategies and city-level processes of gentrification and spatial inequalities in Iran. These two countries are notable for our current purpose, as they both pose empirical challenges to Harvey's explanation despite their historical and geographical differences. They both highlight the importance of profit cycles and the crisis of profitability in the creation and appropriation of land rents. This is especially evident in Iran, where its semi-isolation from global financial markets and the absence of financialized speculative activity in the housing market are characterized by fierce competition among atomistic landlords. The two national-level studies (Chapters 5 and 7) explore the effects of land rents and subsequent capital switching in two contrasting cases: low land rents with a shift away from built environments in Chapter 5, and high land rents with a shift toward built environments in Chapter 7. The two city-level studies (Chapters 6 and 8) examine how land rents influence investment and how temporal rhythms of investment shape gentrification and filtering processes in Tehran and Malmö—two cities with different recent experiences: one with a consistently profitable construction industry and the other facing more fluctuating fortunes.

The empirical analyses in Part 2 aimed to demonstrate the importance of the concept of absolute rent in urban research. However, further analysis of theoretical inconsistencies was necessary to a) explain why the SMLR and its advocates continue to dismiss the idea of absolute rent and b) clarify why the SMLR cannot be easily combined with the analytical tools of the TILR without inflicting additional theoretical tensions (see Chapter 10). Inspired by Shaikh's typology, I argued that both models are based on similarly sophisticated interpretations of Marx's economic theory. The influence of the Sweezyan theory of monopolistic competition on the SMLR is well-known. The concept of absolute rent is methodologically inconsistent with the core assumptions of the theory of monopolistic competition. This theory depends on exogenous, or extra-economic, barriers to the free movement of capital (the power of the landlord class) to explain excess returns and rent levels. Conversely, the concept of absolute rent is based on inter-sectoral competition, the creation of surplus value, and profit rate cycles. Drawing on this theory of monopolistic competition, Harvey identifies an empirical anomaly and a theoretical inconsistency to critique the concept of absolute rent. First, Harvey argues that the concept relies on a problematic idea: sectors that generate rent have lower organic compositions of capital. Second, he claims that Marx's argument for transforming values into prices of production is internally consistent. I considered and rejected Harvey's two objections to absolute rent in this book: the first anomaly is addressed empirically in Part 2 (see Section 4.3), and the second on methodological grounds in Part 3 (see Section 10.4). The logical question, then, is: why not simply incorporate the category of absolute rent into Harvey's SMLR model? I argued (see Chapter 10) that what the TILR offers in response to SMLR's weaknesses—providing alternative analytical tools and introducing the concept of absolute rent—is incompatible with the core assumptions of Harvey's underlying economic theory. In this sense, despite its internal consistency, the SMLR contains internal tensions that prevent it from offering a fully endogenous structural explanation of rent creation and appropriation. The TILR offers a different perspective, grounded in a competing interpretation of Marx's economic theory, rooted in classical political economy, and recently reaffirmed by Shaikh as the theory of real competition. Further research is required to explore the geographies of real competition in other areas of economic geography. Here, the theory allows the TILR to incorporate the concept of absolute rent in a consistent manner and to provide an endogenous structural explanation of how rent is created and appropriated. It uses the above-mentioned analytical tools to measure and explain rent rates, ceilings, and magnitudes.

The findings of this study have implications for both theory and practice. Some theoretical implications are self-evident, as they emphasize the need to expand the scope of heterodox urban economic geography beyond Harvey's interpretation, especially to acknowledge the diversity of approaches and scientific pluralism. In an academic and disciplinary sense, Harvey's goal has been to maintain the internal consistency of his model for urbanization processes under capitalism. This often results in neglecting the changing realities of contemporary capitalism and the new forms it has taken recently. This is particularly important since the start of the Great Recession and is even more evident in the current phase of deglobalization (or slowbalization) and its associated policies (such as tariffs, reshoring, and industrial policies). As shown earlier (Chapter 1), Harvey's analysis of urbanization is also quite narrow, focusing mainly on specific features of neoliberal (and heavily financialized) capitalism, particularly in some areas of the Global North. The evolving landscape of the global capitalist economy over the last decade challenges these assumptions. However, this changing context should not render Marxist political-economic geography irrelevant. This study contributes by broadening the scope of the Marxist theory of urban land rent and placing the analysis within larger debates in Marxist political economy and Marxist geography. Marxist scholarship in political economy has grown substantially since Marx's time, extending Marx's economic theory and competing with other (orthodox and heterodox) explanations since the early 20th century. I believe this scientific legacy should be our main reference point, rather than the supposed accuracy of this or that reading of Marx's texts, especially if our primary goal is to extrapolate these ideas across disciplines, like urban economic geography, to explain phenomena as complex as urbanization. As noted in Chapter 1, Harvey's work has been informed by a similar interdisciplinary understanding, at least early in his career, even though he has recently favored textual and Marxological debates over which reading is more accurate.

The two main components of this watershed moment—the simultaneous decline of globalization and neoliberalism—require a reevaluation of traditional urban geography concepts influenced by anti-neoliberal Marxist scholarship, with Harvey's work being the most notable example. The multi-scalar and inter-sectoral approach I propose here adds empirical value by bringing the national scale back into urban analysis. Many urban economic geographers from the globalization era categorically dismissed the importance (sometimes even the relevance) of the national scale in their critique of methodological nationalism. Not that the national scale was ever entirely irrelevant in practice, but now that neoliberal globalization is in the rear-view mirror, it is experiencing a noticeable comeback. The new era is characterized by national industrial policies, restructuring, and trade protectionism, all of which critically influence urban and regional economic development and investment patterns across cities in both the Global North and South. Including economic structural analysis at the national level offers context for micro-level investment activities on individual land parcels by different investors. Urban economies are shaped by broader economic forces beyond the city's boundaries. Governing them is conditioned by pressures from these economic forces at both national and international levels. The process is indeed context-sensitive, as the links between local policymaking and national or international economic dynamics vary from case to case. Cities depend on context-specific financial support from central governments for social and welfare programs, as well as on local trends in employment structures and income levels, which are, by definition, beyond immediate municipal control. Therefore, the general principle remains that policies must continually adapt to sustain a healthy capitalist economy—ensuring profitability in manufacturing, high overall investment, and economic growth. The same logic applies to the housing sector, with its persistent, multifaceted, and scalar problems, some of which I mentioned at the beginning of this book. Tackling these issues requires considering them in tandem with broader socio-economic developments, such as improving wages, generating employment opportunities, attracting investment, and analyzing producers' and consumers' expectations beyond sectoral boundaries. This means viewing the housing sector in its totality and as part of the capitalist economy in its totality. Understanding these relational dynamics within and between sectors—driven not just by speculative activities but mainly by profit motives in productive branches of the economy—has implications for both structural reform programs and anti-capitalist strategies at the practical level. This point is especially critical today, as persistent affordability issues are compounded by financial and regulatory turbulence, including rising interest rates and inflation, amid stagnant wages and disinvestment in construction. Unlike structure-less localist perspectives, the alternative presented here emphasizes the importance of integrating national and local dynamics, as national economic structures shape and influence local investments, disinvestments, and inequalities. Ignoring economic structural forces at both levels diminishes the effectiveness of regional and municipal policies and strategies of urban movements. All these points underscore the importance of absolute rent as a key concept in urban economic geography and the inter-sectoral and multi-scalar competition that drives its fluctuations. The main practical implication of this alternative explanation of capitalist urbanization is to show that the distribution of surplus value between branches and the formation of the average profit rate—quoting Marx one last time—demonstrate how the entire capitalist class "participates in the exploitation of the entire working class" (Marx 1991 [1894], 298–299).

APPENDIX 1

Rent Categories: an Overview

Empirically, all rent appears in the accounts as a total sum ("a lump sum" as Ward and Aalbers 2016, 1764 specify). Different rent theorists categorize various types of rent, highlighting the nature of land rent as differential, absolute, monopoly, and class-monopoly, among others. Each category entails variables that explain its relationship with other economic and institutional forces shaping rent and its role in the overall total. For example, on marginal plots where differential rents are zero, absolute rent accounts for most of the total rent, whereas on other plots, both differential and absolute rents contribute. However, this does not mean that magnitudes and rates of rent cannot be calculated. On the contrary, they can and should be, as shown in Part 2.

1.1 Differential Rent

Ricardo viewed land rent as differential rent, calculated as the difference between the total (or aggregate) price of production and the total regulating price. The total production price is the price at which the product must be sold to ensure a normal profit for that type of capital, while the total regulating price is the price at which the product will be sold. Lands with better soil fertility have lower production costs and higher potential yields, so the level of rent is determined by differential fertility. Survival conditions refer to the best generally available land (or the marginal land in use) and determine the expansion of supply, as this land provides the minimum production needed to meet demand and earns a normal profit. All other plots earn a higher profit rate. Moreover, since the survival condition of production in the marginal plot, in terms of rates of return, regulates the produce's price, Ricardo argues, the least fertile plot earns no rent, while all other (more fertile) plots earn excess profits, which constitute rent—the highest excess profits, or highest rent level, will be in the most fertile plot with the highest yield. Therefore, differential natural conditions of production in agriculture guarantee that rent is paid in the more fertile plots. Social arrangements are necessary for the landlord to refuse to lease the land (or demand higher rent) and for the capitalist to refuse to invest in it (or seek higher profits). Empirically, if the same capital is invested in different plots, the total production price for all will be the same. However, individual production prices will vary, centered around the conditions of the marginal plot. Differential natural conditions lead to high rents in the best plots. As the economy expands, more land will be cultivated. The least fertile lands require more labor for cultivation, which in turn increases produce prices and ultimately decreases demand (Ricardo 2004 [1911], 69). This falling demand might cause workers to demand higher wages, which can lower profits and potentially trigger an economic crisis.

In contrast to "vulgar economists" who see rent as a direct factor of production (i.e., as the market price of land), Ricardo argues, "[w]hen land of an inferior quality is taken into cultivation, the exchangeable value of raw produce will rise, because more labour is required to produce it" (ibid. 37). For "the exchangeable value" of the products is determined by the amount of labor time needed to produce them in "the most unfavourable circumstances" (ibid.). Ricardo defines differential rent as "a surplus accruing to landlords because of different fertilities" (Murray 1977, 103). It results from the proprietor's monopoly control over the fertile plots (Ricardo 2004 [1911], 39). Shaikh argues, "Ricardo assumes that over time this process extends to ever-worse land, with ever-higher (relative) prices of corn" (Shaikh 2016, 333). As inferior plots enter production, the market price of the product will increase to cover the higher natural (or production) prices of plots with lower quality. Thus, the process contributes to higher average prices of agricultural products, which indirectly causes wages to fall as workers' demand decreases, leading to a decline in overall profit shares (Ricardo 2004 [1911], 41). This is what leads to the crisis. For Ricardo, in other words, differential rent is understood as a result of "diminishing returns to soil" (Economakis 2003, 341).

Marx critically improves on Ricardo's concept of differential rent. First, Marx (1969, 247–249; (with Engels) 2010 [1982], 260–262) explains that it is not the labor time spent on a single commodity, but the socially necessary labor time required to produce that commodity across the entire economy that determines its value. Socially necessary labor time is understood as the expected labor time above which the labor process is considered unproductive. Second, Marx argues that a flawed labor theory of value—one that fails to distinguish between constant and variable capital—causes Ricardo to attribute profits to a natural factor, such as fertility. Third, Marx contends that Ricardo fails to recognize fertility as a social process that depends on technological development and the level of capital investment. Fourth, Marx elaborates that the excess yield and the resulting excess profit that form rent could be generated by either expanding land in use or investing more intensively in technology. Fifth, there is no evidence to support Ricardo's claim that "economic growth leads to the use of land of ever-poorer quality" (Shaikh 2016, 336, footnote). Sixth, Marx notes that in practice, rising rents do not necessarily lead to falling profits; they may instead cause profits to rise, fall, or remain unchanged (Murray 1977).

All this led Marx (1991 [1894]) to identify two categories of differential rents. Differential rent I is generated by equal quantities of capital invested in plots with varying fertility levels (i.e., expanding land to increase yield or the extensive margin). Differential rent II is produced by successive quantities of capital invested in plots with the same fertility level (i.e., intensive investment in the same plot, or the intensive margin), such as with the aid of chemical fertilizers. (Shaikh Unpublished Lecture Notes[1]). Shaikh explains differential rent I and II as investment strategies, meaning that depending on which one appears more economical (in terms of expected profit for a respective type of capital), the capital either engages in extensive movement (more acquisitions or mergers) or invests more intensively (incorporating more technologies to extract additional value from the land) (ibid.). The competition between differential rent I and II as investment strategies is determined by regulating production conditions, specifically by focusing on the worst available conditions of production rather than the worst available land (ibid.). This means that moving to the next land (as in differential rent I) or going deeper (as in differential rent II) depends on which strategy the investor considers cheaper (lower costs) (ibid.). Empirically, especially with differential rent I, the strategy depends on external circumstances, such as the condition of other available plots. In both cases, the capitalist would not invest or lease if the expected profit rate is lower than the normal rate (i.e., below the interest rate) for a capital of its type.

Differential Rent I and II are essential in urban economic geography and political-economic analyses of urbanization, especially concerning residential and commercial development (Harvey 2006 [1982]; 1985; also Edel 1976; 1992). Harvey's key contribution lies in his interpretation of how Differential Rent I and II function within the urban space. To do so, he builds on Marx's (1991 [1894], 871) analysis of a dialectical interaction between the two types of differential rent interacts with capital flows onto land parcels. This interaction allows the two types of differential rent to set limits and impose conditions on one another (Harvey 2006 [1982], 354–356). As Fine explains, "Marx's theory of [Differential Rent] (1 and 2) is built around intra-sectoral competition to establish the value of differential productivity of capitals across the lands in use, thereby realizing these rents" (Fine 2019, 454). In terms of TILR, the

1 Notes from Shaikh's transcribed lectures on rent theory (Shaikh 1982b; 1984; 1994) digitized by Bard Digital Commons.

intra-sectoral competition among firms within a region determines the limits and conditions for rent levels and regulates the interaction Harvey describes.

1.2 Absolute Rent

Marx further criticizes Ricardo by incorporating the roles of competition and inter-sectoral dynamics. He contends that there is a relationship between rents and profits. However, unlike Ricardo's assertion, this relationship operates not at the micro (i.e., firm) level but across the entire economy within an inter-sectoral competitive context. In other words, rent may increase due to a decline in profits in other sectors, but this rise does not necessarily reduce profits within the same sector, as Ricardo assumes. Marx thus develops a concept that explains the structural connection between the rise of rent at the macro level and long-term sectoral competition, which he calls absolute (i.e., non-relative) rent. The variation in sectoral profitability across the entire economy determines the rate and level of absolute rent (Marx 1991 [1894]; Murray 1977). According to Marx, at the macro level, the equalization of rates of return among sectors produces rent, and the competitive dynamics between sectors define its limits.

> Absolute rent depends on three things:
> i) The tendency of commodities to exchange at their value, and the modification of this tendency towards exchange at prices of production as a result of the free flow of capital between branches.
> ii) The presence of low organic composition of capital in those branches yielding absolute rent.
> iii) The reproduction of comparative monopoly power of landed property against capital in those branches. (Murray 1977, 109)

It starts with the difference between the product's value and its production prices. The product's value is set by the socially necessary labor time needed to produce it in a specific economy. Meanwhile, production prices reflect long-term, competitive, average prices that also include material costs (Shaikh 2016). Although the total value determines the total production price in each economy (Marx 1991 [1894], 892), the actual production prices can be higher or lower than the value of the products made in each sector. This is because different sectors require varying amounts of labor time to produce. Marx (1991 [1894], 892) states that labor-intensive sectors that need less machinery, equipment, etc. (i.e., the lower capital-labor ratio, or the organic composition of capital) than capital-intensive sectors can sell their products at their actual value, not at the average price (also Sheppard and Barnes 1990, 130). Rent is the difference between these two prices, which appears as excess profit (Murray 1977, 107). Typical examples include agriculture, mining, other extractive sectors (forestry and fisheries), and construction.

A type of rent that, on a macro level, determines landlords' demand for payment in such sectors is called "independent of the differences in fertility between types of land or successive investment of capital on the same land" (Marx 1991 [1894], 894). Absolute rent "arises out of inter-sectoral competition to equalize the rate of profit across sectors via flows of capital to and from higher and lower rates of profit" (Fine 2019, 454). In the TILR, the level of competition between sectors determines the excess profit (the source of rent). Rent, therefore, increases in proportion to the total excess profit (driven by differential profitability between sectors). This process is historically contingent, as macro-level rent effects could be reduced if excess profits in extractive sectors disappear and their overall sectoral profit falls below that of manufacturing. However, Harvey finds this category "irrelevant" and "meaningless" for urban research (Harvey 2013 interview in Barnes and Sheppard 2019, 207; also Harvey 2010, 81).

1.3 Monopoly Rent

Harvey says, "Marx does not develop monopoly rent but mentions it on the edges. But it has a clear relevance in urban situations" (Harvey 2013 interview in Barnes and Sheppard 2019, 207). Harvey considers monopoly rent relevant in two cases: a) "property owners who control land of such special quality or location in relation to a certain kind of activity may be able to extract monopoly rents from those desiring to use that land," and b) "landowners may refuse to release the unused land under their control unless paid such a high rent that the market prices of commodities produced on that land are forced above value" (Harvey 2006 [1982], 350). Marx develops three rent categories: differential rent I and II, and absolute rent. Many geographers and urban researchers also include monopoly rent among rent categories (Ball 1977; 1985; Edel 1976; Evans 1988; 1991; 1993; 1999a; 1999b; Harvey 1973; 1974a; 2006 [1982]; 1985; Houghton 1993; Markusen 1978; Scott 1976; Swyngedouw 2012). As Harvey states (Harvey 2013 interview in Barnes and Sheppard 2019, 207), for Marx (1991 [1894], 772), monopoly rent is not developed as a separate category. Instead, it is seen as a universal feature of all land ownership, therefore a form of rent, and is defined in terms of monopoly pricing detached from the overall dynamics of capitalist land production (Marx 1991 [1894], 971; 910).

1.4 Class-Monopoly Rent

Harvey introduces a fourth category to Marx's three categories to explain social conflicts and power relations related to the monopoly pricing of land. He considers it relevant in "any situation in which the rate of return to a class of providers of an urban resource (such as housing) is set by the outcome of conflict with a class of consumers of that resource" (Harvey 1974a, 239). Rent, in this context, is "the outcome of the conflict of interest" between a class of owners and a class of users (ibid. 243). Class-monopoly rent also helps incorporate finance capital into the analysis. "When trade in land is reduced to a special branch of the circulation of interest-bearing capital," Harvey states, "then, I shall argue, land ownership has achieved its true capitalistic form" (Harvey 2006 [1982], 347). This concept allows for examining the conflictual economic relationship over land in terms of class. Landlords and developers can claim land rent and extract excess returns only if they act as a unified class. Land rent occurs when landowners manipulate supply, such as by keeping dwellings vacant in housing cases. Doing so requires a favorable legal and regulatory environment and a well-developed financial market that offers instruments to liquidate a fixed spatial asset, such as land. Essentially, class monopoly is the condition regulating this category of rent. Class-monopoly rent is especially important in spaces of social reproduction (including housing) and the redistribution of resources (Harvey 2006 [1982], 350).

APPENDIX 2

Data Sources

2.1 Data Sources Used for Chapter 4

Rates of return data are sourced from BEA's interactive data platforms, including NIPA, Asset/Wealth tables, industry tables, and regional accounts (accessed September 9–23, 2020).
BEA. National Data, GDP & Personal Income. https://apps.bea.gov/iTable/iTable.cfm?reqid=19&step=2#reqid=19&step=2&isuri=1&1921=survey;
BEA. National Data, Fixed Assets. https://apps.bea.gov/iTable/iTable.cfm?ReqID=10&step=2;
BEA. Industry Data, GDP-by-Industry. https://apps.bea.gov/iTable/iTable.cfm?ReqID=51&step=1;
And https://apps.bea.gov/iTable/iTable.cfm?reqid=147&step=2&isuri=1;
BEA. Regional Data, GDP & Personal Income https://apps.bea.gov/itable/iTable.cfm?ReqID=70&step=1

Definitions:
Gross value added: GDP minus taxes on production and imports less subsidies
Gross operating surplus (gross profit): Gross value added minus compensation of employees
Net operating surplus (net profit): Gross operating surplus minus depreciation (of fixed assets)
National income: GDP minus depreciation (Consumption of fixed capital)
Gross investment: Investment in private fixed assets (historical or current cost)
Kliman's property income: GVA minus depreciation of private fixed assets (historical cost) minus compensation of employees
Kliman's rate of profit: Property income (or net operating surplus) divided by net stock of fixed private capital (historical cost)
Roberts' rate of profit: National income less compensation of employees divided by (net stock of private nonresidential fixed assets divided by compensation of employees plus 1)
Shaikh's rate of profit: Net operating surplus divided by net stock of capital
Shaikh's incremental rate of profit: The change in gross profit divided by lagged nominal gross investment (the previous year)

NIPA Tables:
Table 1.10. Gross Domestic Income by Type of Income
Table 1.12. National Income by Type of Income
Table 1.17.5. Gross Domestic Product, Gross Domestic Income, and Other Major NIPA Aggregates
Table 1.3.5. Gross Value Added by Sector
Table 5.4.3. Real Private Fixed Investment in Structures by Type, Quantity Indexes
Table 5.4.5. Private Fixed Investment in Structures by Type
Table 6.2 A, B, C, D. Compensation of Employees by Industry
Table 6.17A. Corporate Profits Before Tax by Industry
Table 7.5. Consumption of Fixed Capital by Legal Form of Organization and Type of Income

Asset/Wealth Tables:
Table 1.3. Current-Cost Depreciation of Fixed Assets and Consumer Durable Goods
Table 3.1ESI. Current-Cost Net Stock of Private Fixed Assets by Industry
Table 3.3ESI. Historical-Cost Net Stock of Private Fixed Assets by Industry
Table 3.4ESI. Current-Cost Depreciation of Private Fixed Assets by Industry
Table 3.6ESI. Historical-Cost Depreciation of Private Fixed Assets by Industry
Table 3.7ESI. Investment in Private Fixed Assets by Industry
Table 3.8ESI. Chain-Type Quantity Indexes for Investment in Private Fixed Assets by Industry
Table 4.1. Current-Cost Net Stock of Private Nonresidential Fixed Assets by Industry Group and Legal Form of Organization
Table 4.3. Historical-Cost Net Stock of Private Nonresidential Fixed Assets by Industry Group and Legal Form of Organization
Table 6.1. Current-Cost Net Stock of Private Fixed Assets by Industry Group and Legal Form of Organization
Table 6.3. Historical-Cost Net Stock of Private Fixed Assets by Industry Group and Legal Form of Organization
Table 6.6. Historical-Cost Depreciation of Private Fixed Assets by Industry Group and Legal Form of Organization

Regional Tables:
SAGDP3S Taxes on Production and Imports less Subsidies (National and regional; Total and Sectoral)

SAGDP7S Gross Operating Surplus (for regional and national GOS, total and sectoral)
CAINC30 Economic Profile

Industrial tables (GDP-by-Industry):
Value Added industry
Components of Value Added by Industry

Figures:
Corporate profits before tax by industry (Figure 2): Table 6.17A, lines 1, 12, 13, 53
Sectoral fixed investment in structures (Figures 3 and 4): Tables 5.4.5 lines 14, 35; 5.4.3 lines 14, 35
Kliman-inspired corporate profits (Figure 5): Tables 1.3.5 lines 1, 4, and 8; 6.3 line 2; 6.6 line 2
Kliman-inspired aggregate private profit rates (Figure 6): Tables 1.3.5 lines 1, 5; 1.10 line 10; 6.3 line 1; 6.6 line 1; 6.2 line 3
Kliman-inspired sectoral profit rates (Figure 7): Tables 3.3 ESI lines 10, 11, 49, 55; 3.6ESI lines 10, 11, 49, 55; 6.2 lines 12, 13, 52; SAGDP3S lines 10, 11, 49, 55; value added by industry lines 11, 12, 54
Roberts-inspired total rate of profit (Figure 8): Tables 1.17.5 line 1; 4.3 line 1; 7.5 line 1; 1.12 lines 1, 2; 4.1 line 1
Roberts-inspired sectoral profit rates (Figure 9): Tables 6.2 lines 12, 13, 52; value added by industry lines 11, 12, 54; 3.4ESI lines 10, 11, 49, 55; 3.1 ESI lines 10, 11, 49, 55
Shaikh-inspired aggregate rate of profit (Figure 10): Tables 6.1 line 16; 1.10 line 9
Shaikh-inspired private sector rate of profit (Figure 11): Tables 6.1 line 1; 1.10 lines 10, 21
Shaikh-inspired corporate rate of profit (Figure 4.12): Tables 6.1 line 2; 1.3.5 line 8
Shaikh-inspired sectoral profit rates (Figures 13 and 14): Tables 6.2 lines 12, 13, 52; 3.4ESI lines 10, 11, 49, 55; 3.1 ESI lines 10, 11, 49, 55; SAGDP3S lines 10, 11, 49, 55; SAGDP7S lines 11, 12, 49
Shaikh-inspired incremental sectoral profit rates (Figures 15–17): Tables 3.8ESI and 3.7ESI lines 10, 11, 12, 17, 20, 24, 30, 49, 55; SAGDP7S lines 11, 12, 19, 21, 25, 33, 49, 55; also, Tables 3.7ESI lines 10, 11, 49, 55; SAGDP7S lines 11, 12, 49, 55
Baltimore metropolitan area income (Figure 18): Table CAINC30, Lines 90, 230
The organic composition of capital (Figure 19): Tables 3.1 ESI lines 10, 11; 6.2 lines 12, 13

Construction investment data is taken from the United States Census Bureau Construction Spending accounts. https://www.census.gov/construction/c30/oldtc.html (accessed September 28, 2020)
Figure 20–23: Value of Construction Put in Place Statistics; Table 1 Annual Value of Construction Put in Place in the United States Current Dollars

2.2 Data Sources Used for Chapters 5 and 6

Data are from Statistics Sweden (SCB) and the OECD. Stats interactive tables, and The Conference Board Tables (CBT).
https://scb.se/en/finding-statistics/statistics-by-subject-area/national-accounts/
https://stats.oecd.org/# (accessed October 26, 27, 29, 2020)
https://www.conference-board.org/ilcprogram/productivityandulc (accessed November 5, 2020)
Malmö's data is taken from the municipality's economic and population database:
https://malmo.se/Fakta-och-statistik/Statistik-for-Malmos-omraden.html (accessed February 5, 2024)
For Maps: Boverket's interactive Segregationsbarometern:
https://segregationsbarometern.boverket.se/ (accessed 27 May 2024)

Definitions:
Gross value added: GDP minus taxes on production and imports less subsidies
Gross operating surplus (gross profit): Gross value added minus compensation of employees
Net operating surplus (net profit): Gross operating surplus minus depreciation (of fixed assets)
National income: GDP minus depreciation (Consumption of fixed capital)
Gross investment: Investment in private fixed assets, i.e., gross fixed capital formation
Net Capital Stock: Net fixed assets
Shaikh's rate of profit: Net operating surplus divided by net stock of capital
Shaikh's incremental rate of profit: The change in gross profit divided by lagged nominal gross investment (the previous year)
Kliman's rate of profit: Property income (or net operating surplus) divided by net stock of fixed private capital (historical cost)

Roberts' rate of profit: National income less compensation of employees divided by (net stock of private nonresidential fixed assets divided by compensation of employees plus 1)

SCB Tables:

National Accounts:
GDP: production approach (ESA2010), current prices, SEK million by industrial classification NACE Rev. 2 and year, lines C10–C33 Manufacturing, F41–F43 Construction, J61 Telecommunication, K64–K66 Financial Services and Insurance Activities, L68 Real Estate Activities
Bruttoinvesteringar (SNA68), löpande priser, mkr efter näringsgren SNI69 och kvartal [Gross Investment by Industry] lines, 2000 Extractive, 3000 Manufacturing, 5000 Construction, 7000 Communication, 8000 Finance
Value-added, detail components (ESA2010), current prices, SEK million by industrial classification NACE Rev. 2, transaction item and year (Net Operating Surplus, Consumption of Fixed Capital), lines C13–C15 (Manufacturing), F41–F43 (Construction), J61 (Telecommunications), K64–K66 (Financial Services and Insurance Activities)
Labor costs (ESA2010), current prices, SEK million by industrial classification NACE Rev. 2, observations and year, Compensation of Employees, lines C10–C33 Manufacturing, F41–F43 Construction, A01–T98 Market producers and producers for own final use total
Labour productivity by industrial classification (ESA2010) SNI 2007, seasonally adjusted. Quarter 1993K1–2020K2
Multifactor productivity (MFP). Yearly growth in percent units by industrial classification NACE Rev. 2, Yearly growth rates for the base variables and year, line A01–T98 Market producers and producers for own final use total
Fixed capital formation (ESA2010), current prices, SEK million by industrial classification NACE Rev. 2, type of asset and year, lines 1.1.1 Dwellings, 1.1.1.1 Dwellings, new constructions, 1.1.1.2 Dwellings, reconstructions, 1.1.2 Other buildings and structures

Wealth Accounts:
Balance sheets (ESA2010), end of year, net, current prices in SEK million by sector, type of asset, and year (lines S1 Total Economy, S11 Non-Financial Corporations, S12 Financial Corporations)

Stocks of fixed assets, net, January 1st each year (ESA2010), current prices, SEK million by industrial classification NACE Rev. 2, type of asset, and year lines, 0002 Total Economy, C10–C33 Manufacturing, F41–F43 Construction, J58–J63 Information and Communication, K64–K66 Financial Services and Insurance Activities, L68–N82 Real Estate, Renting, and Business Services
Lines S1, S11, S12: AN11M, AN11K; AN21, AN211, AN2111, AN2112
For Fixed Assets (Net): S1, S11, S12; AN11

Sector Accounts:
Institutional non-financial sector accounts (ESA2010), current prices, SEK million by sector, transaction item and year (S1, S11, S12), Lines 0.P5g Gross Capital Formation, II.1.1.B2g Gross Operating Surplus, II.1.1B2n Net Operating Surplus, III. 1.2.P51c Consumption of Fixed Capital, III.1.2.P51g Gross Fixed Capital Formation, II.1.1.D1 Compensation of Employees

Housing, Construction, and Building Tables:
Building permits for new construction, number by region, type of building, and quarter (Lines 010, 020, 030, 060)
Completed dwellings in newly constructed buildings by region, type of building, and year

OECD Tables:

14A. Non-financial accounts by sectors
6A. Value Added and its components by activity, ISIC rev4, 2019 archive (constant and current prices):
Net Operating Surplus by industry: lines, VTOT Total Activity, VC Manufacturing, VF Construction, VJ Information and Communication, VK Financial and Insurance Activities, VL Real Estate Activities
Gross Operating Surplus by Industry: lines VTOT, VC, V10–12, V13–15, V16–18, V19, V22–23, V24–25, V26, V27, V28, 29–30, V31033, VF, VJ, VK, VL
Gross Fixed Capital Formation: lines VTOT, VC, V10–12, V13–15, V16–18, V19, V22–23, V24–25, V26, V27, V28, 29–30, V31033, VF, VJ, VK, VL
6A. Value Added and its components by activity, ISIC rev4 (constant and current prices)
9A. Fixed assets by activity and by asset, ISIC rev4 (constant and current prices)

The Conference Board Tables:
International Comparisons of Manufacturing Productivity and Unit Labor Cost, Table 1: Manufacturing Sector Indexes

Malmö Statistical Tables:
Household Size (Table 3), Ethnic Background (Tables 5 and 6), Education (Table 7), Day-Time Population (Tables 9 and 10), Night-Time Population (Tables 11 and 12), Employment (Tables 13 and 14), Income (Tables 18, 19, 22, and 23), Capital Gains (Tables 20 and 21), Dwelling Type (Table 26)

2.3 Data Sources Used for Chapters 7 and 8

The data are sourced from the Central Bank of Iran (CBI) and the Statistical Center of Iran (SCI) online databases.
Central Bank of Iran:
Economic Time Series Database: https://tsd.cbi.ir/ (accessed November 13, 2020)
National Accounts: https://www.cbi.ir/simplelist/5796.aspx; (accessed November 12, 2020)
Statistical Center of Iran:
Input-Output Tables: https://amar.org.ir/دادهها-و-اطلاعات-آماری/حساب-های-
--ملی-و-منطقهای/جدول-داده-و-ستانده#5608761 (accessed November 13, 2020)

Definitions:
Gross value added: GDP minus taxes on production and imports less subsidies
Gross operating surplus (gross profit): Gross value added minus compensation of employees
Net operating surplus (net profit): Gross operating surplus minus depreciation (consumption of fixed capital)
Gross investment: Investment in private fixed assets, i.e., gross fixed capital formation
Shaikh's rate of profit: Net operating surplus divided by net capital stock at current costs
Shaikh's incremental rate of profit: The change in gross profit divided by lagged nominal gross investment (the previous year)

Tables:
Central Bank of Iran Tables:
From National Accounts Tables:
National Product—At Current Prices:
Table 1. Gross National Product (Income) by Activities—Billion Rials
Table 15. Value Added of Manufacture Industries at Basic Prices—Billion Rials
Table 21. Value Added of Construction at Basic Prices—Billion Rials

Table 39. Value Added of Real Estate & Professional Services at Basic Prices—Billion Rials

National Expenditure—At Constant 2004/05 Prices:
Table 13. Gross Fixed Capital Formation in Machinery and Construction—Billion Rials
Table 14. Gross Fixed Capital Formation by Private and Public Sectors—Billion Rials
Table 15. Gross Fixed Capital Formation in Machinery and Equipment by Activities—Billion Rials

National Expenditure—At current prices:
Table 15. Gross Fixed Capital Formation in Machinery and Equipment by Activities—Billion Rials
Table 17. Gross Fixed Capital Formation by Activities—Billion Rials
Table 18. Gross Fixed Capital Formation in Machinery by Activities from Domestic Production—Billion Rials
Table 20. Gross Fixed Capital Formation in Construction in Urban and Rural Areas by the Private Sector—Billion Rials

National Accounts Tables, by Sector, Current and Basic (2010 = 100) Prices (in Persian):
Table 1: Value Added by Economic Groups, Current Prices—Billion Rials
Table 17. Value Added and Operating Surplus, Whole Economy, at Current Prices—Billion Rials
Table 22. Value Added and Operating Surplus, Manufacturing, at Current Prices—Billion Rials
Table 24. Value Added and Operating Surplus, Construction, at Current Prices—Billion Rials

From Economic Time Series Database:

Net Capital Stock Tables:
Table 1 Net Capital Stock 1974–2014

Construction and Housing Sector Tables:
Private Sector Investment in New Buildings in Urban Areas / Investment by Urban Areas
Residential Units Completed by the Private Sector in Urban Areas
Construction Permits Issued by Municipalities in Urban Areas
Construction Permits Issued by Municipalities in Urban Areas

Statistical Center of Iran:

Input-Output Tables:
For net operating surplus, compensation of employees, consumption of fixed capital, gross fixed capital formation (by industry)

Table 1: [جدول داده ستانده اقتصاد ایران] Input-Output—Iranian Economy, 1986; 1991; 1999; 2004; 2011

[جدول مصرف اقتصاد ایران] Table 5. Consumption Table—Iranian Economy, 2001; [جدول مصرف اقتصاد ایران] Table 2. Consumption Table—Iranian Economy, 2010

References

Aalbers, M.B. (2008). The financialization of home and the mortgage market crisis. *Competition & Change, 12*(2), 148–166.

Aalbers, M.B. (2009a). Geographies of the financial crisis. *Area, 41*(1), 34–42.

Aalbers, M.B. (2009b). The sociology and geography of mortgage markets: Reflections on the financial crisis. *International Journal of Urban and Regional Research, 33*(2), 281–290.

Aalbers, M.B. (eds). (2012). *Subprime cities: The political economy of mortgage markets.* Chichester: Wiley-Blackwell.

Aalbers, M.B. (2017). The variegated financialization of housing. *International Journal of Urban and Regional Research, 41*(4), 542–554.

Aalbers, M.B., & Christophers, B. (2014). Centring housing in political economy. *Housing, Theory and Society, 31*(4), 373–394.

Ackerman, S. (2023, September 12). Robert Brenner's unprofitable theory of global stagnation. *Jacobin*. Available at: https://jacobin.com/2023/09/robert-brenner-marxist-economics-falling-rate-of-profit-stagnation-overcapacity-industrial-policy (accessed March 11, 2024).

Aftab News. (2013). قیمت مسکن مهر از ابتدا تا امروز [The Mehr Housing Program—prices]. Available at: http://aftabnews.ir/fa/news/192016 (accessed November 20, 2017).

Alami, I. (2023). Ten theses on the new state capitalism and its futures. *Environment and Planning A: Economy and Space, 55*(3), 764–769.

Alami, I. & Dixon, A.D. (2024). *Spectre of state capitalism.* Oxford: Oxford University Press, Incorporated.

Albalate, D., Bel, G., Gradus, R. & Reeves, E. (2021). Re-municipalization of local public services: incidence, causes and prospects. *International Review of Administrative Sciences, 87*(3), 419–424.

Alonso, W. (1964). *Location and land use: toward a general theory of land rent.* Cambridge, Mass.: Harvard University Press.

Anderson, M.B. (2014). Class monopoly rent and the contemporary neoliberal city. *Geography Compass, 8*(1), 13–24.

Anderson, M.B. (2019). Class monopoly rent and the redevelopment of Portland's Pearl District. *Antipode, 51*(4), 1035–1056.

Anderson, M.B., Zickefoose, G., Andrie, T., & Newton, T. (2024). Landlord opposition to rent control and the politics of class monopoly rent. *Human Geography*, DOI: 19427786241234546.

Ansari, A. (2015). نابرابری های آموزشی در حال تشدید است [Educational inequalities are increasing]. *Shargh Special Issue: Economics. 2529*, 34–37.

Arboleda, M., & Purcell, T.F. (2021). The turbulent circulation of rent: towards a political economy of property and ownership in supply chain capitalism. *Antipode*, *53*(6), 1599–1618.

Arundel, R. (2017). Equity inequity: Housing wealth inequality, inter and intragenerational divergences, and the rise of private landlordism. *Housing, Theory and Society*, *34*(2), 176–200.

Ashrafzadeh, H.R., & Alaedini, P. (2018). Manufacturing exports and employment in Iran: the role of economies of scale and human capital. In: Alaedini, P. & Razavi, M. (eds), *Industrial, trade, and employment policies in Iran*. Cham: Springer, pp. 55–76.

Asr-e-Sakhteman. (2016). کم فروشی در واحدهای مسکن مهر پردیس [Fraud in the MHP units in Pardis township]. Available at: http://www.asresakhteman.com/News/3517 (accessed November 20, 2017).

Ayar Online. (2015). عملکرد آخوندی، وزیر راه و شهرسازی در سال دوم دولت یازدهم [Evaluating Akhoundi's time in office as the minister of Roads and Urban Development]. Available at: http://ayaronline.ir/1394/06/146418.html (accessed November 20, 2017).

Baeten, G. (2017). Neoliberal planning. In: Gunder M, Madanipour A and Watson V (eds) *The Routledge Handbook of Planning Theory*. Routledge. pp. 105–117. DOI: 10.4324/9781315696072.

Baeten, G. (2012). Normalising neoliberal planning: the case of Malmö, Sweden. In: Tasan-Kok, T. & G. Baeten. (eds). *Contradictions of neoliberal planning: cities, policies, and politics*, pp. 21–42. Dordrecht: Springer Netherlands.

Baeten, G., Brunnström, P., Dahlstedt, M., Grundström, K., Gustafsson, J., Larsen, H.G., Thörn, C. (2016). Debattinlägg: Att ett projekt som Culture Casbah skulle bryta segregationen finns det inte mycket som stödjer. *Sydsvenskan*. Available at: https://www.sydsvenskan.se/2016-11-15/att-ett-projekt-som-culture-casbah-skulle-bryta-segregationen-finns-det-inte-mycket-som-stodjer (accessed April 19, 2024).

Ball, M. (1977). Differential rent and the role of landed property. *International Journal of Urban and Regional Research*, *1*(1–4), 380–403.

Ball, M. (1985). The urban rent question. *Environment and Planning A*, *17*(4), 503–525.

Ball, M. (1998). Institutions in British property research: A review. *Urban Studies*, *35*(9), 1501–1517.

Balta, M.O., & Eke, F. (2011). Spatial reflection of urban planning in metropolitan areas and urban rent; a case study of Çayyolu, Ankara. *European Planning Studies*, *19*(10), 1817–1838.

Bandyopadhyay, P. (1982a). Neo-Ricardianism in urban analysis: Scott, A.J. *International Journal of Urban and Regional Research*, *6*(2), 277–282.

Bandyopadhyay, P. (1982b). Marxist urban analysis and the economic theory of rent. *Science & Society*, *46*(2), 162–196.

Barbesgaard, M., Zhang, H., Hertanti, R., Gagyi, A., & Vervest, P. (2024). The "new Darwinian world" of the energy transition. *Transnational Institute*. Available at: https://www.tni.org/en/article/the-new-darwinian-world-of-the-energy-transition (accessed October 31, 2024).

Baran, P.A., & Sweezy, P.M. (1966). *Monopoly capital: an essay on the American economic and social order*. New York: Monthly Review Press.

Barnes, T.J., & Sheppard, E.S. (2019). *Spatial histories of radical geography: North America and beyond [Electronic resource]*. Wiley.

Barnes, T.J. (1994). Functional metaphors: A reply to Richard Peet and David R. Reynolds. *Economic Geography*, *70*(3), 308–313.

Bassett, K., & Short, J.R. (1980). *Housing and residential structure: Alternative approaches*. London: Routledge & Kegan Paul.

BBC Persian. (2016). شعارهایی که انقلاب ایران را ساخت [1979 Revolution's slogans]. Available at: http://www.bbc.com/persian/blog-viewpoints-38905398 (accessed November 20, 2017).

Beauregard, R.A. (1991). Capital restructuring and the new built environment of global cities: New York and Los Angeles. *International Journal of Urban and Regional Research*, *15*, 90–105.

Beauregard, R.A. (1994). Capital switching and the built environment: United States, 1970–89. *Environment and Planning A*, *26*(5), 715–732.

Behdad, S., & Nomani, F. (2009). What a revolution! Thirty years of social class reshuffling in Iran. *Comparative Studies of South Asia, Africa and the Middle East*, *29*(1), 84–104.

Behdad, S., & Nomani. F. (2011, April 18). Iranian labor and the struggle for independent unions. Available at: https://www.pbs.org/wgbh/pages/frontline/tehranbureau/2011/04/labors-struggle-for-independent-unions.html (accessed November 13, 2019).

Beitel, K. (2016). Circuits of capital, ground rent and the production of the built environment: A (new) framework for analysis. *Human Geography*, *9*(3), 27–42.

Belina, B. (2025). Disentangling the secondary circuit of capital: The place of rental housing. In: Biagi, F. (eds). *Reimagining urban Marxisms*, pp. 147–162. London: Routledge.

Bengtson, S. (1974). Housing and planning in Sweden, In: Fuerst, J.S. (eds). *Public housing in Europe and America*, pp. 99–109. London: Routledge.

Berry, M. (2023). *A theory of housing provision under capitalism*. London: Palgrave Macmillan.

Bharier, J. (1971). *Economic development in Iran 1900–1970*. London: Oxford University Press.

Bina, C. (2006). The globalization of oil: A prelude to a critical political economy. *International Journal of Political Economy*, *35*(2), 4–34.

Blackwell, T., Holgersen, S. & Wallstam, M. (2023). Dreaming of efficient markets? Residential construction, competition, and affordability in the Swedish housing sector. *Housing Studies*, 1–24. DOI: 10.1080/02673037.2023.2256257.

Blücher, G. (2006). 1900-talet—det kommunala planmonopolets århundrade [The twentieth century—the century of the municipal planning monopoly]. In: Blücher, G. & Graninger, C. (eds). *Planering med Nya Förutsättningar* [Planning with new prerequisites]. Linköping: Stiftelsen Vadstena Forum för Samhällsbyggande and Linköpings Universitet.

Boda, C.S., & Faran, T. (2018). Paradigm found? Immanent critique to tackle interdisciplinarity and normativity in science for sustainable development. *Sustainability*, *10*(10), 3805. DOI: 10.3390/su10103805.

Borgegård, L.E., & Kemeny, J. (2004). High-rise housing in a low-density country, In: Turkington. R. (eds). *High-rise housing in Europe: current trends and future prospects*, pp. 31–48. Delft, the Netherlands: DUP Science.

Borsdorf, A., & Hidalgo, R. (2013). Revitalization and tugurization in the historical centre of Santiago de Chile. *Cities*, *31*, 96–104.

Bortkiewicz, L. von (1919). Zu den grundrententheorien von Rodbertus und Marx. *Archiv fur die Geschichte des Sozialismus und der Arbeiterbewegung*, *8*, 248–257.

Bortkiewicz, L. von (1952 [1906, 1907]). "Value and price in the Marxian system" (part I), in *International Economic Papers*, 1952, 2. Available at: http://classiques.uqac.ca/classiques/Bortkiewicz_ladislaus_von/value_and_price_marxian_system/value_price_marxian_system.pdf (accessed May 15, 2020).

Boverket. (2007). *Bostadspolitiken—Svensk politik för boende, planering och byggande under 130 år*. Karlskrona, Boverket.

Boverket. (2017). *Urban density done right—ideas on densification of cities and other communities*. Swedish National Board of Housing, Building and Planning.

Boverket. (2022). Acquisition of land. Available at: https://www.boverket.se/en/start/building-in-sweden/swedish-market/laws-and-regulations/building-process/ (accessed May 4, 2022).

Boverket. (2023). Grunddragen i den nya byggnadslagstiftningen utgiven av Kungliga byggnadsstyrelsen 1947. Available at: https://www.boverket.se/contentassets/22140678c50841128f99d542d6ab2eb7/1947-nya-bygglagstiftningen.pdf (accessed January 9, 2024).

Boverket. (2024a). Online interactive statistical lab [segregationsbarometer]. SCB data. Available at: https://segregationsbarometern.boverket.se/labbet/#/statistiklabbet/map?location=kommun-1280&indicator=25&bg=0 (accessed April 10, 2024).

Boverket. (2024b). *Discontinuation of the support for investments in rental and student housing*. Swedish National Board of Housing, Building and Planning. Available at: https://www.boverket.se/sv/bidrag--garantier/stod-for-hyresbostader-och-bostader-for-studerande/#:~:text=Riksdagen%20beslutade%20den%201%20december,2021%2F22%3ACU1 (accessed June 24, 2025).

Bourassa, S. (1993). The rent gap debunked. *Urban Studies, 30*(10), 1731–1744.

Bradley, Q. (2023). Artificial scarcity in housebuilding and the impact on affordability: the return of absolute rent. *Antipode*. DOI: 10.1111/anti.12925.

Brenner, R. (2006). *The economics of global turbulence: the advanced capitalist economies from long boom to long downturn, 1945–2005*. London: Verso.

Bruegel, I. (1975). The Marxist theory of rent and the contemporary city: A critique of Harvey. *Political Economy and the Housing Question: Bulletin of the Conference on Socialist Economics, 3*, 34–46.

Bryson, J. (1997). Obsolescence and the process of creative reconstruction. *Urban Studies, 34*(9), 1439–1458.

Bua, A. & Davies, J.S. (2023). Understanding the crisis of new municipalism in Spain: The struggle for urban regime power in A Coruña and Santiago de Compostela. *Urban Studies, 60*(11), 2054–2072.

Buchwalter, A. (2012). *Dialectics, politics, and the contemporary value of Hegel's practical philosophy*. London: Routledge.

Byrne, D., & Beirne, P. (1975). Towards a political economy of housing rent. *Political Economy and the Housing Question: Bulletin of the Conference on Socialist Economics, 3*, 47–67.

Caesar, C. (2016). *Municipal landownership and housing in Sweden: exploring links, supply and possibilities*. PhD Thesis, Kungliga Tekniska högskolan, Sweden.

Callinicos, A. (2009). *Imperialism and global political economy*. Cambridge: Polity.

Campling, L. (2025). Pelagic imperialism in the 21st century? A geopolitical economy of China's distant water fishing industry. *Journal of Agrarian Change, 25*(3), 1–12. DOI: 10.1111/joac.70005.

Carchedi, G. (1991). *Frontiers of political economy*. London: Verso.

Castree, N. (1995). On theory's subject and subject's theory: Harvey, capital, and the limits to classical Marxism. *Environment and Planning A, 27*(2), 269–297.

Castree, N. & Christophers, B. (2018). Banking spatially on the future: Capital switching, infrastructure, and the ecological fix. In: Braun, B. (eds) *Futures: Imagining Socioecological Transformation*. Routledge, pp. 154–162.

Castree, N. & Gregory, D. (eds) (2006). *David Harvey: a critical reader*. Oxford: Blackwell.

Castree, N., Kitchin, R., & Rogers, A. (2013). *A dictionary of human geography*. Oxford: Oxford University Press.

CBI (Central Bank of Iran). (2012). *Annual review*. Available at: http://www.cbi.ir/page/10567.aspx (accessed November 27, 2020).

CBI (Central Bank of Iran). (2013a). Annual national accounts. Available at: https://www.cbi.ir/simplelist/5796.aspx (accessed November 27, 2020).

CBI (Central Bank of Iran). (2013b). Economic report and balance sheet. Available at: https://www.cbi.ir/category/EconomicReport_en.aspx (accessed November 29, 2018).

CBI (Central Bank of Iran). (2016). *Annual review*. Available at: http://www.cbi.ir/page/16416.aspx (accessed November 20, 2017).

CBI (Central Bank of Iran). (2017a). نتایج بررسی بودجه خانوار [*Household budget survey*]. Available at: https://cbi.ir/simplelist/1600.aspx (accessed November 13, 2019).

CBI (Central Bank of Iran). (2017b). نتایج بررسی فعالیت های ساختمانی بخش خصوصی در مناطق شهری استان های مختلف ایران [*Private construction sector survey*]. Available at: https://www.cbi.ir/simplelist/17533.aspx (accessed November 13, 2019).

CBI (Central Bank of Iran). (2019a). Economic time series database. Available at: http://tsd.cbi.ir/Display/Content.aspx (accessed March 20, 2019).

CBI (Central Bank of Iran). (2019b). *National expenditure at current prices*. Available at: https://cbi.ir/simplelist/5796.aspx (accessed March 20, 2019).

Charney, I. (2001). Three dimensions of capital switching within the real estate sector: A Canadian case study. *International Journal of Urban and Regional Research, 25*(4), 740–758.

Charnock, G., Purcell, T.F., & Ribera-Fumaz, R. (2014). City of rents: The limits to the Barcelona model of urban competitiveness. *International Journal of Urban and Regional Research, 38*(1), 198–217.

Chen, T., Lau, C.K.M., Cheema, S., & Koo, C.K. (2021). Economic policy uncertainty in China and bitcoin returns: Evidence from the covid-19 period. *Frontiers in Public Health, 9*, 1–7. DOI: https://doi.org/10.3389/fpubh.2021.651051.

Christophers, B. (2010). On voodoo economics: theorising relations of property, value and contemporary capitalism. *Transactions of the Institute of British Geographers, 35*(1), 94–108.

Christophers, B. (2011). Revisiting the urbanization of capital. *Annals of the Association of American Geographers, 101*(6), 1347–1364.

Christophers, B. (2014). From Marx to market and back again: Performing the economy. *Geoforum, 57*, 12–20.

Christophers, B. (2016). For real: Land as capital and commodity. *Transactions of the Institute of British Geographers, 41*(2), 134–148.

Christophers, B. (2019). The problem of rent. *Critical Historical Studies, 6*(2), 303–323.

Christophers, B. (2020). *Rentier capitalism: Who owns the economy, and who pays for it?*. London: Verso.

Christophers, B. (2021). A tale of two inequalities: Housing-wealth inequality and tenure inequality. *Environment and Planning A: Economy and Space, 53*(3), 573–594.

Christophers, B. (2024). *The price is wrong: why capitalism won't save the planet*. London: Verso.

Clark, E. (1987). A critical note on Ball's reformulation of the role of urban land rent. *Environment and Planning A, 19*(2), 263–267.

Clark, E. (1988). The rent gap and transformation of the built environment: Case studies in Malmö 1860–1985. *Geografiska Annaler: Series B, Human Geography*, *70*(2), 241–254.

Clark, E. (1992). On gaps in gentrification theory. *Housing Studies*, *7*(1), 16–26.

Clark, E. (1995a). An arrow-cycle interpretation of the redevelopment of Stockholm's central business district. *Geografisk Tidsskrift-Danish Journal of Geography*, *95*(1), 83–91.

Clark, E. (1995b). The rent gap re-examined. *Urban Studies*, *32*(9), 1489–1503.

Clark, E. (2004). Rent rhythm in the flamenco of urban change. In: Mels, T. (eds). *Reanimating places: A geography of rhythms*. Aldershot: Ashgate, pp. 147–160.

Clark, E. (2014). Good urban governance: making rent gap theory not true, *Geografiska Annaler: Series B, Human Geography*, *96*(4), 392–395.

Clark, E. (2018). Making rent gap theory not true. In: Albet, A., & Benach, N. (eds). *Gentrification as a global strategy: Neil Smith and beyond*. London: Routledge, pp. 71–84.

Clark, E. & Hedin, K. (2009). Circumventing circumscribed neoliberalism: The 'system switch' in Swedish housing. In: Glynn, S. (eds). *Where the other half lives: Lower income housing in a neoliberal world*. Pluto Press, pp. 173–194.

Clark, E., & Gullberg, A. (1991). Long swings, rent gaps and structures of building provision-the postwar transformation of Stockholm's inner city. *International Journal of Urban and Regional Research*, *15*(4), 492–504.

Clark, E. & Gullberg, A. (1997). Power struggles in the making and taking of rent gaps: The transformation of Stockholm city. In: Källtorp, O. (eds). *Cities in transformation—transformation in cities: Social and symbolic change of urban space*. Aldershot: Avebury, pp. 248–265.

Clark, E., & Pissin, A. (2020). Potential rents vs. potential lives. *Environment and Planning A*, 1–21. DOI: 10.1177/0308518X20971308.

Clark, E., & Runesson, L. (1996). Municipal site leasehold in Sweden: a land policy instrument in decay. *European Planning Studies*, *4*(2), 203–216.

Clarke, S., & Ginsburg, N. (1975). The political economy of housing. *Political Economy and the Housing Question: Bulletin of the Conference on Socialist Economics*, *3*, 1–33.

Clifton, J., Warner, M.E., Gradus, R. & Bel, G. (2021). Re-municipalization of public services: trend or hype?. *Journal of Economic Policy Reform*, *24*(3), 293–304.

Copley, J. (2022). *Governing financialization: The tangled politics of financial liberalization in Britain*. Oxford University Press.

Consbank. (2012). شرایط مسکن مهر ویژه تهران [Special MHP for Tehran—requirements]. Available at: http://www.consbank.com/fa/news/11734 (accessed November 20, 2017).

Considine, M. & Dukelow, F. (2010). Introduction: boom to bust, Irish social policy in challenging times. *Irish Journal of Public Policy*, *2*(1), 1–3.

Coronil, F. (1997). *The magical state: nature, money, and modernity in Venezuela.* Chicago: University of Chicago Press.

Cox, K.R. (1982). Housing tenure and neighborhood activism. *Urban Affairs Quarterly, 18*(1), 107–129.

Cox, K.R. (2013). Notes on a brief encounter: critical realism, historical materialism and human geography. *Dialogues in Human Geography, 3*(1), 3–21.

Cox, K.R. (2016). Geographies, critical and Marxist, and lessons from South Africa. *Human Geography, 9*(3), 10–26.

Cox, K.R., & Mair, A. (1991). From localised social structures to localities as agents. *Environment and Planning A, 23*(2), 197–213.

Cox, K.R., & Wood, A. (1997). Competition and cooperation in mediating the global: the case of local economic development. *Competition & Change, 2*(1), 65–94.

Darling, E. (2005). The city in the country: Wilderness gentrification and the rent gap. *Environment and Planning A, 37*(6), 1015–1032.

Das, R. (2017a). David Harvey's theory of accumulation by dispossession: A Marxist critique. *World Review of Political Economy, 8*(4), 590–616.

Das, R. (2017b). David Harvey's theory of uneven geographical development: A Marxist critique. *Capital & Class, 41*(3), 511–536.

Das, R. (2023). The good and the bad in David Harvey's popular Marxism. *Critical Sociology, 49*(7–8), 1079–1094.

Davis, M. (2006). Fear and money in Dubai. *New Left Review, 41*, 47.

Dehesh, A. (1994). Developmental instability in Iran: its impact on housing since 1962. *Cities, 11*(6), 409–424.

Diappi, L., & Bolchi, P. (2008). Smith's rent gap theory and local real estate dynamics: A multi-agent model. *Computers, Environment and Urban Systems, 32*(1), 6–18.

Dikeç, M. (2016). Rage and fire in the French Banlieues. In: Mayer, M., Thörn, H., & Thörn, C. (eds). *Urban uprisings*. London: Palgrave Macmillan, pp. 95–119. DOI: 10.1057/2F978-1-137-50509-5.

Dikeç, M., & Swyngedouw, E. (2017). Theorizing the politicizing city. *International Journal of Urban and Regional Research, 41*(1), 1–18.

Donya-e-Eqtesad. (2010). تصاویر مسکن مهر بدون آب [Lack of water supply in the MHP Units—pictures]. Available at: http://donya-e-eqtesad.com/news/634393# (accessed November 20, 2017).

Donya-e-Eqtesad. (2014). دستورالعمل فروش زمین ۹۹ ساله به صاحب مسکن [99-year lease sales—instructions]. Available at: https://www.donya-e-eqtesad.com/fa/tiny/news-811440 (accessed January 4, 2018).

Duman, A. & Tonak, E.A. (2024). Clarification and application of the category profit on alienation. *Review of Radical Political Economics, 56*(2), 233–246.

Duncan, S. (1985). Land policy in Sweden: separating ownership from development. In: Barrett, S. & Healey, P. (eds). *Land policy: problems and alternatives*. Aldershot: Gower.

Duncan, S. (1986). House building, profits and social efficiency in Sweden and Britain. *Housing Studies*, *1*(1), 11–33.

Duncan, S. (1989). Development gains and housing provision in Britain and Sweden. *Transactions of the Institute of British Geographers*, 157–172.

Economakis, G.E. (2003). On absolute rent: Theoretical remarks on Marx's analysis. *Science & Society*, *67*(3), 339–348.

Edel, M. (1976). Marx's theory of rent: urban applications. *Kapitalistate*, *4–5*, 100–124.

Edel, M. (1977). Rent theory and working class strategy: Marx, George and the urban crisis. *Review of Radical Political Economics*, *9*(4), 1–15.

Edel, M. (1992). *Urban and regional economics, Marxist perspectives*. Chur: Harwood Academic Publishers.

Ekers, M. & Prudham, S. (2017). The metabolism of socioecological fixes: Capital switching, spatial fixes, and the production of nature. *Annals of the American Association of Geographers*, *107*(6), 1370–1388.

Eghtesad Online. (2018). عدم تحویل ۲۶۶هزار مسکن مهر به دلیل نبود انشعابات. [266 thousand Mehr dwellings not handed over due to lack of infrastructure]. Available at: https://www.eghtesadonline.com/n/1bWZ (accessed April 14, 2020).

Englund, P. (2015). The Swedish 1990s banking crisis: a revisit in the light of recent experience. Riksbank Macroprudential Conference, Stockholm June 23–24, 2015. Available at: http://archive.riksbank.se/Documents/Avdelningar/AFS/2015/Session1-Englund.pdf (accessed December 18, 2024).

Entekhab. (2016). آمارهای مسکن مهر. [The Mehr Housing Program—statistics]. Available at: http://www.entekhab.ir/fa/news/326572 (accessed November 20, 2017).

Evans, A.W. (1988). *On absolute rent*. Department of Economics, University of Reading. Discussion paper in urban and regional economics, Series C, No 36.

Evans, A.W. (1991). On monopoly rent. *Land Economics*, *67*(1), 1–14.

Evans, A.W. (1993). On monopoly rent: Reply. *Land Economics*, *69*(1), 111.

Evans, A.W. (1999a). On minimum rents: Part 1, Marx and absolute rent. *Urban Studies*, *36*(12), 2111–2120.

Evans, A.W. (1999b). On minimum rents: Part 2, a modern interpretation. *Urban Studies*, *36*(13), 2305–2315.

EUR-Lex (2003). *Council regulation (EC) No 1/2003 of 16 December 2002 on the implementation of the rules on competition laid down in Articles 81 and 82 of the Treaty*. Available at: https://eur-lex.europa.eu/legal-content/EN/TXT/?uri=OJ%3AC_202401645 (accessed May 21, 2024).

Euronews. (2024). Where in Europe has the most wealth inequality?. *Euronews*. https://www.euronews.com/business/2024/04/01/wealth-inequality-where-in-europe

-is-wealth-most-unfairly-distributed#:~:text=Huge%20disparities%20among%20the%20richest&text=Looking%20at%20the%20richest%20decile,every%20country%20except%20for%20Belgium (accessed April 12, 2024).

Farahani, I. (2013). Vanished in gaps, vanquished in rifts: The social ecology of urban spatial change in a working class residential area, Peykan-Shahr, Tehran, Iran. *Journal of Political Ecology*, 20, 395–412.

Farahani, I. (2021). *Land rent, capital, rate of profit: a critique of Harvey's model of urban land rent.* (Doctoral Dissertation, LU (Lund University)).

Farahani, I. (2024). Capitalist urbanization in the post-neoliberal and de-globalizing world economy: A minor critical engagement with VIP-Urbanism literature. *Human Geography*, *17*(3), 353–358.

Farahani, I. (2025). Capital switching, economic crisis, and land rent: Examining discontinuation of Swedish municipal site leasehold in the 1980s. *Human Geography*, 19427786251332583.

Farahani, I. (Forthcoming). Shortage of affordable housing in Malmö: Implications of Shaikh's theory of real competition.

Farahani, I. Barbesgaard, M. Jakobsen, J. (2026). Political economy in geographic research: Institutionalist versus Marxist approaches. In: Das, R., Latham, R., & Fasenfest, D. (eds). The power of Marxist thought. Leiden: Brill Publishers., pp. pp. 85–108.

Farahani, I., & Yousefi, S. (2021). Public housing, intersectoral competition, and urban ground rent: Iran's first public housing program that never was. *Human Geography*, *14*(1), 45–61.

Feldman, M. (2017). Ground rent in the circuit of capital: time, space, and macroeconomic geography. Presented at: 7th Nordic Geographers Meeting, Stockholm, Sweden, June 18–21, 2017.

Fine, B. (2019). Marx's rent theory revisited? Landed property, nature and value. *Economy and Society*, *48*(3), 450–461.

Flamant, C. (2021). Elements for a coherent theory of rent. *World Review of Political Economy*, *12*(3), 395–427.

Foley, D.K. (1982). The value of money the value of labor power and the Marxian transformation problem. *Review of Radical Political Economics*, *14*(2), 37–47.

Foster, J.B., & McChesney, R.W. (2012). *The endless crisis: How monopoly-finance capital produces stagnation and upheaval from the USA to China.* New York: Monthly Review Press.

Fratini, S.M. (2018). Is Marx's absolute rent due to a monopoly price?. *The European Journal of the History of Economic Thought*, *25*(5), 961–985.

Freeman, A. (2010). Trends in value theory since 1881. *World Review of Political Economy*, *1*(4), 567–605.

Freeman, A., & Carchedi, G. (eds). (1996). *Marx and non-equilibrium economics.* Cheltenham: Elgar.

Friberg, V. (2025). *Malmös stadsbyggnadsdirektör: Vi Måste Kroka Arm I Utvalda geografier. Bostadspolitik*. Available at: https://www.bostadspolitik.se/2025/06/09/malmos-stadsbyggnadsdirektor-vi-maste-kroka-arm-i-utvalda-geografier/ (accessed June 23, 2025).

Frieden, J. (1981). Third World indebted industrialization: international finance and state capitalism in Mexico, Brazil, Algeria, and South Korea. *International Organization, 35*(3), 407–431.

Friedmann, J. (2002). *The prospect of cities*. Minneapolis: University of Minnesota Press.

Gilmore, R.W. (2007). *Golden gulag: Prisons, surplus, crisis, and opposition in globalizing California*. Berkeley: University of California Press.

Glinavos, I. (2008). Neoliberal Law: unintended consequences of market-friendly law reforms. *Third World Quarterly, 29*(6), 1087–1099.

Gotham, K.F. (2006). The secondary circuit of capital reconsidered: Globalization and the US real estate sector. *American Journal of Sociology, 112*(1), 231–275.

Gotham, K.F. (2009). Creating liquidity out of spatial fixity: The secondary circuit of capital and the subprime mortgage crisis. *International Journal of Urban and Regional Research, 33*(2), 355–371.

Gradus, R. & Budding, T. (2020). Political and institutional explanations for increasing re-municipalization. *Urban Affairs Review, 56*(2), 538–564.

Grander, M. (2018). *For the benefit of everyone? Explaining the significance of Swedish public housing for urban housing inequality* (Doctoral dissertation, Malmö University).

Grander, M. (2023). The inbetweeners of the housing markets—young adults facing housing inequality in Malmö, Sweden. *Housing Studies, 38*(3), 505–522.

Gregory, D. (2006). Introduction: troubling geographies. In: Castree, N. & Gregory, D. (eds) *David Harvey: a critical reader*. Oxford: Blackwell, pp. 1–25.

Gregory, D., Johnston, R.J., Pratt, G., Watts, M., & Whatmore, S. (eds) (2009). *The dictionary of human geography*. (5th ed.) Malden, MA: Wiley-Blackwell.

Gustafsson, J. (2021a). Renovations as an investment strategy: circumscribing the right to housing in Sweden. *Housing Studies*, 1–22.

Gustafsson, J. (2021b). Spatial, financial and ideological trajectories of public housing in Malmö, Sweden. *Housing, Theory and Society, 38*(1), 95–114.

Gustafsson, J. (2022). *The state of tenancy: Rental housing and municipal statecraft in Malmö, Sweden* (Doctoral dissertation, Department of Human Geography, Stockholm University).

Gustafsson, J., Hellström, E., Richard, Å., & Springfeldt, S. (2019). The right to stay put: resistance and organizing in the wake of changing housing policies in Sweden. *Radical Housing Journal, 1*(2), 191–200.

Gustafsson, B., Johansson, M. & Palmer, E. (2009). The welfare of Sweden's old-age pensioners in times of bust and boom from 1990. *Ageing & Society, 29*(4), 539–561.

Guy, S., & Henneberry, J. (2000). Understanding urban development processes: Integrating the economic and the social in property research. *Urban Studies*, *37*(13), 2399–2416.

Haila, A. (1988). Land as a financial asset: The theory of urban rent as a mirror of economic transformation. *Antipode*, *20*(2), 79–101.

Haila, A. (1989). Misguided rhetoric on rent: A comment on Ball and Clark. *Environment and Planning A*, *21*(11), 1525–1532.

Haila, A. (1990). The theory of land rent at the crossroads. *Environment and Planning D: Society and Space*, *8*(3), 275–296.

Haila, A. (2015). *Urban land rent: Singapore as a property state*. Oxford: Wiley-Blackwell.

Hall, P. (1980). Does land matter?. *Built Environment*, *6*(4), 229.

Hall, T. & Vidén, S. (2005). The million homes programme: a review of the great Swedish planning project. *Planning Perspectives*, *20*(3), 301–328.

Hammel, D.J. (1998). Re-establishing the rent gap: An alternative view of capitalised land rent. *Urban Studies*, *36*(8), 1283–1293.

Hammel, D.J. (1999). Gentrification and land rent: A historical view of the rent gap in Minneapolis. *Urban Geography*, *20*(2), 116–145.

Hamshahri Online. (2016). آخرین امار مسکن مهر [The Mehr Housing Program—statistics]. Available at: http://www.hamshahrionline.ir/details/359173/Economy/House (accessed November 20, 2017).

Harris, R., & Lewis, R. (2001). The geography of North American cities and suburbs, 1900–1950: A new synthesis. *Journal of Urban History*, *27*(3), 262–292.

Harvey, D. (1969). *Explanation in geography*. London: Arnold.

Harvey, D. (1974a). Class-monopoly rent, finance capital and the urban revolution. *Regional Studies*, *8*(3–4), 239–255.

Harvey, D. (1974b). Population, resources, and the ideology of science. *Economic Geography*, *50*(3), 256–277. DOI: 10.2307/142863.

Harvey, D. (1975). Class structure in a capitalist society and the theory of residential differentiation. In: Peel, R., Chisholm, M., & Haggett, P. (eds). *Processes in physical and human geography: Bristol essays*. London, UK: Heinemann Educational Books, Ltd., pp. 354–369.

Harvey, D. (1976). Labor, capital, and class struggle around the built environment in advanced capitalist societies. *Politics & Society*, *6*(3), 265–295.

Harvey, D. (1978). The urban process under capitalism: A framework for analysis. *International Journal of Urban and Regional Research*, *2*(1–3), 101–131.

Harvey, D. (1981). The spatial fix—Hegel, von Thunen, and Marx. *Antipode*, *13*(3), 1–12.

Harvey, D. (1982). Land rent and the transition to the capitalist mode of production. *Antipode*, *14*(3), 17–25.

Harvey, D. (1985). *The urbanization of capital*. Oxford: Blackwell.

Harvey, D. (1989). *The urban experience.* Baltimore: Johns Hopkins University Press.

Harvey, D. (1993). Class relations, social justice and the politics of difference. In: Keith, M. & Pile, S. (eds). *Place and the politics of identity.* London: Routledge, pp. 41–65.

Harvey, D. (1995). Militant particularism and global ambition: the conceptual politics of place, space, and environment in the work of Raymond Williams. *Social Text, 42,* 69–98.

Harvey, D. (2000). Reinventing geography. *New Left Review, 4,* 75–97.

Harvey, D. (2002). The art of rent: Globalisation, monopoly and the commodification of culture. *Socialist Register, 38*(38), 93–110.

Harvey, D. (2003). *The new imperialism.* Oxford: Oxford University Press.

Harvey, D. (2005). *A brief history of neoliberalism.* Oxford: Oxford University Press.

Harvey, D. (2006 [1982]). *The limits to capital.* (New and fully updated ed., [2006 Verso ed.].). London: Verso.

Harvey, D. (2006). *Spaces of global capitalism: Towards a theory of uneven geographical development.* London: Verso.

Harvey, D. (2008). The right to the city. *New Left Review, 53,* 23–40.

Harvey, D. (2009). Their crisis, our challenge. Interview with Marco Berlinguer and Hilary Wainwright. Available at: https://links.org.au/david-harvey-their-crisis-our-challenge (accessed October 21, 2024).

Harvey, D. (2009 [1973]). *Social justice and the city.* London: Edward Arnold.

Harvey, D. (2010). *The enigma of capital and the crises of capitalism.* Oxford: Oxford University Press.

Harvey, D. (2012). The urban roots of financial crises: Reclaiming the city for anti-capitalist struggle. *Socialist Register, 48.*

Harvey, D. (2014). *Seventeen contradictions and the end of capitalism.* London: Profile Books.

Harvey, D. (2016). Crisis theory and the falling rate of profit. In: Subasat, T. (eds). *The great financial meltdown: Systemic, conjunctural or policy created?*, Cheltenham, UK: Edward Elgar Publishing, pp. 37–54.

Harvey, D. (2017). *Marx, capital and the madness of economic reason.* London: Profile Books.

Harvey, D. (2018, March 14). Marx's refusal of the labour theory of value. *David Harvey Website.* Available at: http://davidharvey.org/2018/03/marxs-refusal-of-the-labour-theory-of-value-by-david-harvey/ (accessed May 19, 2021).

Harvey, D. (2021). Rate and mass. *New Left Review, 130,* 73–98. DOI: 10.64590/my8.

Harvey, D. (2023). *A companion to Marx's Grundrisse.* London: Verso.

Harvey, D., & Chatterjee, L. (1974). Absolute rent and the structuring of space by governmental and financial institutions. *Antipode, 6*(1), 22–36.

Healey, P., & Barrett, S. (1990). Structure and agency in land and property development processes: Some ideas for research. *Urban Studies, 27*(1), 89–103.

Hedin, K., Clark, E., Lundholm, E., & Malmberg, G. (2012). Neoliberalization of housing in Sweden: Gentrification, filtering, and social polarization. *Annals of the Association of American Geographers, 102*(2), 443–463.

Hewison, K. (1988). The state and capitalist development in Thailand. In: Taylor, J.G. and Turton, A. (eds). *Southeast Asia: Sociology of "developing societies"*. London: Palgrave. pp. 73–83.

HFIR. (Housing Foundation of the Iranian Revolution). (2017). گزارش اقدامات انجام شده مسکن مهر [The Mehr Housing Program—development report]. Available at: http://bonyadmaskan.ir/Pages/MaskanMehr.aspx (accessed November 20, 2017).

Hilferding, R. (1981 [1910]). *Finance capital: A study of the latest phase of capitalist development.* Edited by Tom Bottomore. London: Routledge & Kegan Paul.

Houghton, T. (1993). On the nature of real estate, monopoly and the fallacies of 'monopoly rent'. *International Journal of Urban and Regional Research, 17*(2), 260–273.

Housing Bank. (2017a). مسکن مهر [The Mehr Housing Program]. Available at: http://bank-maskan.ir/5957/index.aspx (accessed November 20, 2017).

Housing Bank. (2017b). تسهیلات مسکن [Housing personal loans—instruction]. Available at: http://bank-maskan.ir/6056/index.aspx (accessed November 20, 2017).

Huber, M.T. (2022). Resource geography III: Rentier natures and the renewal of class struggle. *Progress in Human Geography, 46*(4), 1095–1105.

Hård, M. (2010). The good apartment: the social (democratic) construction of Swedish homes. *Home Cultures, 7*(2), 117–133.

Ibena News. (2017). وام مسکن مهر افزایش یافت [Higher loans for the MHP applicants]. Available at: https://tinyurl.com/ror7djy (accessed November 20, 2017).

IMF (International Monetary Fund). (2015). *Islamic Republic of Iran.* IMF Staff Country Reports. *2015/350*, 1–28.

Inoua, S.M., & Smith, V.L. (2022). Neoclassical supply and demand, experiments, and the classical theory of price formation. *History of Political Economy, 54*(1), 37–73.

INTA (Iranian National Tax Administration). (2015). قانون مالیات های مستقیم [Direct tax law]. Available at: http://download.tax.gov.ir/GeneralDownloads/DirectTaxLaw13940431.pdf (accessed April 6, 2018).

Iran File News. (2017). نیمه پنهان مسکن مهر [The dark side of the Mehr Housing Program]. Available at: http://news.iranfile.ir/News/4058 (accessed November 20, 2017).

IRICA (Islamic Republic of Iran Customs Administration). (2013). سالنامه آماری تجارت خارجی [*Annual statistical report—international trade*]. Available at: http://www.irica.gov.ir/Portal/file/?36121/salnameh-1392.zip (accessed January 16, 2018).

IRICA (Islamic Republic of Iran Customs Administration). (2016). واردات- جداول [*Imports—tables*]. Available at: http://www.irica.gov.ir/Portal/home/?report/4599/5139/251687/1395 (accessed January 16, 2018).

Ive, G. (1975). Walker and the "new conceptual framework" of urban rent. *Antipode*, *7*(1), 20–30.

Jahan News. (2013). مسکن مهر آخوندی را به مجلس کشاند [The Mehr Housing Program led to Akhoundi impeachment]. Available at: http://www.jahannews.com/phototitr/322324 (accessed November 20, 2017).

Jones, P. (2021). *The falling rate of profit and the Great Recession of 2007–2009*. Leiden, The Netherlands: Brill. DOI: 10.1163/9789004398320.

Kalecki, M. (2009 [1969]). *Theory of economic dynamics an essay on cyclical and long run changes in capitalist economy*. New York: Monthly Review Press.

Kauko, T. (2001). Combining theoretical approaches: the case of urban land value and housing market dynamics. *Housing, Theory and Society*, *18*(3–4), 167–173.

Kerr, D. (1996). The theory of rent: From crossroads to the magic roundabout. *Capital & Class*, *20*(1), 59–88.

Keynes, J.M. (1964). *The general theory of employment, interest and money*. (1. Harbinger ed.) New York: Harcourt, Brace, Jovanovich.

King, R.J. (1987). Monopoly rent, residential differentiation and the second global crisis of capitalism the case of Melbourne. *Progress in Planning*, *28*, 195–298.

King, R.J. (1989a). Capital switching and the role of ground rent: 1 Theoretical problems. *Environment and Planning A*, *21*(4), 445–462.

King, R.J. (1989b). Capital switching and the role of ground rent: 2 Switching between circuits and switching between submarkets. *Environment and Planning A*, *21*(6), 711–738.

King, R.J. (1989c). Capital switching and the role of ground rent: 3 Switching between circuits, switching between submarkets, and social change. *Environment and Planning A*, *21*(7), 853–880.

Kliman, A. (2007). *Reclaiming Marx's "Capital": A refutation of the myth of inconsistency*. Lanham, MD: Lexington Books.

Kliman, A. (2011). Marx's reproduction schemes as an unbalanced-growth model. *Critique of Political Economy*, (1), 33–61. Available at: https://copejournal.com/wp-content/uploads/2015/12/andrew-kliman-marx_s-reproduction-schemes-as-an-unbalanced-growth-model.pdf (accessed March 11, 2024).

Kliman, A. (2012). *The failure of capitalist production: Underlying causes of the Great Recession*. London: Pluto Press.

Kliman, A. (2015). Harvey versus Marx on capitalism's crises part 1: Getting Marx wrong. *New Left Project*. Available at: http://www.newleftproject.org/index.php/site/article_comments/harvey_versus_marx_on_capitalisms_crises_part_1_getting_marx_wrong (accessed November 24, 2017).

Kliman, A., & Williams, S.D. (2015). Why 'financialisation' hasn't depressed US productive investment. *Cambridge Journal of Economics*, *39*(1), 67–92.

Kommunförbundet. (n.d.). *Konkurrensneutralitet* [*Competitive neutrality*]. Available at: https://www.kommunforbundet.fi/juridik/kommunerna-bolagen-och-marknaden/konkurrensneutralitet (accessed May 21, 2024).

Konkurensverket (n.d.). Konkurrensbegränsande offentlig säljverksamhet | Konkurrensverket [Anti-competitive public sales operations]. Available at: https://www.konkurrensverket.se/konkurrens/lagar-och-regler/konkurrensbegransande-offentlig-saljverksamhet/ (accessed May 32, 2024).

Kriesler, P. (1988). Kalecki's pricing theory revisited. *Journal of Post Keynesian Economics*, *11*(1), 108–130.

Krijnen, M. (2018a). Gentrification and the creation and formation of rent gaps: Opening up gentrification theory to global forces of urban change. *City*, *22*(3), 437–446.

Krijnen, M. (2018b). Beirut and the creation of the rent gap. *Urban Geography*, *39*(7), 1041–1059.

Krugman, P. (1991). Myths and realities of US competitiveness. *Science*, *254*(5033), 811–815.

Kutz, W. (2016). The Eurozone crisis and emerging-market expansion: Capital switching and the uneven geographies of Spanish urbanization. *International Journal of Urban and Regional Research*, *40*(6), 1075–1093.

La Grange, A. & Pretorius, F. (2005). Shifts along the decommodification-commodification continuum: Housing delivery and state accumulation in Hong Kong. *Urban Studies*, *42*(13), 2471–2488.

Lakatos, I. (1978). *Philosophical papers. Vol. 1, The methodology of scientific research programmes*. Cambridge: Cambridge U.P.

Lambertini, L., Mendicino, C., & Punzi, M.T. (2013). Leaning against boom-bust cycles in credit and housing prices. *Journal of Economic Dynamics and Control*, *37*(8), 1500–1522.

Lauria, M. (1984). The implications of Marxian rent theory for community-controlled redevelopment strategies. *Journal of Planning Education and Research*, *4*(1), 16–24.

Lebowitz, M.A. (1986). David Harvey, the limits to capital (book review). *Economic Development and Cultural Change*, *34*(2), 385.

Lefebvre, H. (2003 [1970]). *The urban revolution*. Minneapolis, Minn.: University of Minnesota Press.

Lenin, V.I. (2004 [1899]). *The development of capitalism in Russia*. Honolulu: University Press of the Pacific.

Ley, D. (1987). Reply: The rent gap revisited. *Annals of the Association of American Geographers*, *77*(3), 465–468.

Lipsmeyer, C.S. (2011). Booms and busts: how parliamentary governments and economic context influence welfare policy. *International Studies Quarterly*, *55*(4), 959–980.

Lisberg Jensen, E., Malmqvist, E., & Olsson, A.J. (2023). Growing from Inside: Densification and Ecosystem Services in Three Comprehensive Plans from Southern Sweden. *Sustainability*, *15*(13), 9928, 1–14. DOI: https://doi.org/10.3390/su15139928.

Listerborn, C. (2021). The new housing precariat: experiences of precarious housing in Malmö, Sweden. *Housing Studies*, 1–19.

Listerborn, C., & Baeten, G. (2022). Struggling with conceptual framings to understand Swedish displacement processes, In: P. Jakobsen. E. Jönsson. H.G. Larsen. *Socio-spatial theory in Nordic geography: intellectual histories and critical interventions*, pp. 207–216. Cham: Springer International Publishing.

López-Morales, E. (2010). Real estate market, state-entrepreneurialism and urban policy in the 'gentrification by ground rent dispossession' of Santiago de Chile. *Journal of Latin American Geography*, 145–173.

López-Morales, E. (2011). Gentrification by ground rent dispossession: The shadows cast by large-scale urban renewal in Santiago de Chile. *International Journal of Urban and Regional Research*, *35*(2), 330–357.

López-Morales, E. (2013). Measuring the invisible: The dispossession of the rent gap as a form of displacement. *RC21, Session 8, Gentrification Revisited: New Methods to Research Displacement*, 1–23.

López-Morales, E. (2016a). Assessing exclusionary displacement through rent gap analysis in the high-rise redevelopment of Santiago, Chile. *Housing Studies*, *31*(5), 540–559.

López-Morales, E. (2016b). Gentrification in Santiago, Chile: A property-led process of dispossession and exclusion. *Urban Geography*, *37*(8), 1109–1131.

López-Morales, E., Sanhueza, C., Espinoza, S., Ordenes, F., & Orozco, H. (2019). Rent gap formation due to public infrastructure and planning policies: An analysis of Greater Santiago, Chile, 2008–2011. *Environment and Planning A*, *51*(7), 1536–1557.

Lundqvist, L.J., Elander, I. & Danermark, B. (1990). Housing policy in Sweden—still a success story?. *International Journal of Urban and Regional Research*, *14*(3), 445–467.

Lund Hansen, A., Larsen, H.G., Grydehøj, A. & Clark, E. (2015). Financialisation of the built environment in Stockholm and Copenhagen. *FESSUD Working Paper Series*, *115*.

Luxemburg, R. (1951). *The accumulation of capital*. London: Routledge and Kegan Paul.

Madureira, A.M., & Baeten, G. (2016). By invitation only: uses and users of the 'entrepreneurial city'. *International Planning Studies*, *21*(4), 362–376.

Malm, H., & Jenning, P. (2019). Cityfiction: scenarios for densification, In: *Proceedings of the symposium on simulation for architecture and urban design*, pp. 121–128. Available at: https://media1.fojab.se/2019/06/SimAUD2019_Proceedings_MalmJenning.pdf (accessed April 17, 2024).

MKB Fastigheter AB. (2017). Balder, Heimstaden, MKB och Victoria Park har förvärvat bostadsbestånd—ska förverkliga Culture Casbah. Available at: https://www.mynewsdesk.com/se/mkb_fastighets_ab/pressreleases/balder-heimstaden-mkb-och-victoria-park-har-foervaervat-bostadsbestaand-ska-foerverkliga-culture-casbah-1715599 (accessed April 19, 2024).

Malmö Municipality. (2021). *Bostadsförsörjningsprogram 2022–2026 för Malmö stad.* [Housing supply program for Malmö 2022–2026]. https://moten.lund.se/welcome-sv/namnder-styrelser/kommunstyrelsen/kommunstyrelsens-sammantrade-2021-12-01/agenda/bostadsforsorjningsprogram-2022-2026-for-malmo-stad-remisshandling pdf?downloadMode=open (accessed April 17, 2024).

Malmö Municipality. (2022). *Utländsk bakgrund—statistikunderlag för Malmös områden* [Population background database]. Dataplattform Malmö. Available at: https://ckan-malmo.dataplatform.se/dataset/utlandsk-bakgrund-statistikunderlag-for-malmos-omraden (accessed April 8, 2024).

Malmö Municipality. (2023). *Malmö stads kartläggning av hemlösheten år 2023.* [Homelessness data for 2023]. Available at: https://motenmedborgarportal.malmo.se/welcome-sv/namnder-styrelser/arbetsmarknads-och-socialnamnden/mote-2023-12-20/agenda/hemloshetskartlaggning-malmo-oktober-2023pdf?downloadMode=open (accessed April 10, 2024).

Malmö Municipality. (2024). Statistikunderlaget for Malmö. Available at: https://malmo.se/Fakta-och-statistik/Statistik-for-Malmos-omraden.html (accessed April 8, 2024).

Malmö Municipality. (2025). Avslutade markanvisningar. Available at: https://malmo.se/Stadsutveckling/For-dig-som-bygger-och-utvecklar/Markanvisning/Avslutade-markanvisningar.html (accessed May 6, 2025).

Manning, F.T.C. (2020). *A defense and expansion of the theory of capitalist ground rent: Speculation, securitization, and struggles over land and housing* (Doctoral Dissertation, CUNY (The City University of New York)).

Manning, F.T.C. (2023). Geographies of ground rent: Periodizing ground rent theory, spatializing ground rent refusal. *Human Geography, 16*(3), 355–369.

Markusen, A.R. (1978). Class, rent, and sectoral conflict: uneven development in western US boomtowns. *Review of Radical Political Economics, 10*(3), 117–129.

Mariana, C.D., Ekaputra, I.A., & Husodo, Z.A. (2021). Are Bitcoin and Ethereum safe havens for stocks during the COVID-19 pandemic?. *Finance research letters, 38*, 1–7. DOI: 10.1016/j.frl.2020.101798.

Maringanti, A., & Jonnalagadda, I. (2015). Rent gap, fluid infrastructure and population excess in a gentrifying neighbourhood. *City, 19*(2–3), 365–374.

Marx, K. (1847). Wage labour and capital. In: Tucker, R.C. The Marx-Engels reader. New York: W.W. Norton, pp. 174–175.

Marx, K. (1969). *Theories of surplus value. P. 2*. London: Lawrence & Wishart.

Marx, K. (1973). *Grundrisse: foundations of the critique of political economy: (rough draft)*. London: Penguin.

Marx, K. (1976 [1867]). *Capital: a critique of political economy. Vol. 1*. Harmondsworth: Penguin.

Marx, K. (1991 [1894]). *Capital: A critique of political economy, Vol. 3*. London: Penguin Books.

Marx, K. (1992 [1978]). *Capital: a critique of political economy. Vol. 2*. Harmondsworth: Penguin.

Marx, K., & Engels, F. (2010 [1982]). *Collected works. Vol. 38, Marx and Engels: 1844–51: [letters of Marx and Engels]*. London: Lawrence & Wishart.

Massey, D. (1985). New directions in space. In: Gregory, D., & Urry, J. (eds). *Social relations and spatial structures*. Basingstoke: Macmillan, pp. 9–20.

Massey, D., & Catalano, A. (1978). *Capital and land: Landownership by capital in Great Britain*. London: Edward Arnold.

Mattick, P. (1981). *Economic crisis and crisis theory*. London: The Merlin Press.

Mattick, P. Jr. (2008). The limits to capital. *Historical Materialism, 16*(4), 213–224.

Mattsson, H. (2006). Sweden. In: Williams, R.H. & Wood, B. (eds). *Industrial property markets in Western Europe*. Taylor & Francis.

McDonald, J.F. (2007). William Alonso, Richard Muth, resources for the future, and the founding of urban economics. *Journal of the History of Economic Thought, 29*(1), 67–84.

McDonald, D.A. (2024). Landscapes of remunicipalization: A critical literature review. *Urban Affairs Review, 60*(6), 1898–1930. DOI: 101177/10780874241233535.

MCLS (Ministry of Cooperatives, Labour, and Social Welfare). (2008). تعاونی های مسکن مهر [The Mehr Housing Program cooperatives act]. Available at: https://www.mcls.gov.ir/icm_content/media/image/2013/06/28840_orig.doc (accessed November 20, 2017).

McMaster, R., & Watkins, C. (2006). Economics and underdetermination: a case study of urban land and housing economics. *Cambridge Journal of Economics, 30*(6), 901–922.

Mehr News Agency. (2017). بازار داغ هواپیمای شخصی [The booming private jets market]. Available at: https://www.mehrnews.com/news/4011717/بازار-داغ-اجاره-هواپیماهای-شخصی-چگونه-هواپیمای-شخصی-بخریم- (accessed January 16, 2018).

Mehr News Agency. (2018). شانزده هزار ساکن مسکن مهر بروجرد همچنان از نبود امکانات رنج می برند [16 thousand Mehr dwellings in Boroujerd still lack basic facilities]. Available at: https://mehrnews.com/xLLhY (accessed April 14, 2020).

Meidner, R. (1993). Why did the Swedish model fail?. *Socialist Register*, *29*(29), 211–228.

Mironova, O. & Stein, S. (2018). Where does public land come from? Municipalization and privatization debates. *Métropolitiques*. Available at https://metropolitics.org/https:/metropolitics.org/Where-Does-Public-Land-Come-From-Municipalization-and-Privatization-Debates.html (accessed October 14, 2025).

Mirowski, P. (2006). Twelve theses concerning the history of postwar neoclassical price theory. *History of Political Economy*, *38*, 343.

Misgeld, K., Molin, K. & Åmark, K. (eds). (1992). *Creating social democracy: a century of the social democratic labor party in Sweden*. (English transl. and rev. ed.) University Park: Pennsylvania State University Press.

Mitchell, D. (1997). The annihilation of space by law: The roots and implications of anti-homeless laws in the United States. *Antipode*, *29*(3), 303–335.

Mitchell, D. (2003). *The right to the city: Social justice and the fight for public space*. New York: Guilford Press.

Mooya, M.M. (2016). Neoclassical economic theory and traditional valuation methods. *Real Estate Valuation Theory: A Critical Appraisal*, 43–63.

Moreno Zacarés, J. (2024). Residential Accumulation: A Political Economy Framework. *Housing, Theory and Society*, 1–23. DOI: 10.1080/14036096.2023.2292567.

Moseley, F. (1991). *The falling rate of profit in the postwar United States economy*. London: Palgrave Macmillan UK.

Moseley, F. (2011). Recent interpretations of the "transformation problem". *Rethinking Marxism*, *23*(2), 186–197.

Moseley, F. (2016). *Money and totality: A macro-monetary interpretation of Marx's logic in capital and the end of the 'transformation problem'*. Leiden: Brill.

MRUD (Ministry of Roads and Urban Development, News Agency). (2017). شهرداری ها برای کسب درآمد تراکم می فروشند [FSR allowances and municipalities]. Available at: http://news.mrud.ir/news/38270/شهرداری-ها-همچنان-برای-کسب-درآمد-تراکم-می-فروشند-خیابان-های- (accessed March 26, 2019).

Murray, R. (1977). Value and theory of rent: Part one. *Capital & Class*, *1*(3), 100–122.

Murray, R. (1978). Value and theory of rent: Part two. *Capital & Class*, *2*(1), 11–33.

Muth, R.F. (1969). *Cities and housing: The spatial pattern of urban residential land use*. Chicago: University of Chicago Press.

Muth, R.F. (1971). The derived demand for urban residential land. *Urban Studies*, *8*(3), 243–254.

Needham, B., Segeren, A., & Buitelaar, E. (2011). Institutions in theories of land markets: Illustrated by the Dutch market for agricultural land. *Urban Studies, 48*(1), 161–176.

Neel, P.A. (2018). *Hinterland: America's New Landscape of Class and Conflict.* Reaktion Books.

Neutze, M. (1989). A tale of two cities: public land ownership in Canberra and Stockholm to the early 1980s. *Scandinavian Housing and Planning Research, 6*(4), 189–199.

Newell, P. (2008). CSR and the limits of capital. *Development and Change, 39*(6), 1063–1078.

Nicholas, H. (2012). What is the problem with neoclassical price theory?. *World Review of Political Economy, 3*(4), 457–477.

NOLH (National Organization of Land and Housing). (2017). دستورالعمل اختصاص اراضی مسکن مهر [The Mehr Housing Program—land allocation instructions]. Available at: http://nlho.ir/index.jsp?fkeyid=&siteid=1&fkeyid=&siteid=1&pageid=140 (accessed November 15, 2017).

NTOIR (New Towns Development Company). (2014a). سند جامع مسکن [Comprehensive plan for housing]. Available at: http://www.ntoir.gov.ir/index.aspx?siteid=1&fkeyid=&siteid=1&pageid=301 (accessed November 20, 2017).

NTOIR (New Towns Development Company). (2014b). دستورالعمل واگذاری عرصه واحدهای مسکن مهر 99 ساله به متقاضیان [99 years lease—instructions]. Available at: http://www.ntoir.gov.ir/index.aspx?fkeyid=&siteid=1&fkeyid=&siteid=1&pageid=310 (accessed November 20, 2017).

OECD (2023). Draft OECD toolkit to combat homelessness. Available at: https://www.oecd.org/els/soc/workshop-homelessness-toolkit-29Nov2023.pdf (accessed April 17, 2024).

Ollman, B. (2003). *Dance of the dialectic: steps in Marx's method.* Urbana: University of Illinois Press.

Olsson, G., (1974). The dialectics of spatial analysis. *Antipode, 6*(3), 50–62.

Olsson, L. (2018). The neoliberalization of municipal land policy in Sweden. *International Journal of Urban and Regional Research, 42*(4), 633–650.

Olsson, J.A., Brunner, J., Nordin, A., & Hanson, H.I. (2020). A just urban ecosystem service governance at the neighbourhood-level perspectives from Sofielund, Malmö, Sweden. *Environmental Science & Policy, 112*, 305–313.

Orhangazi, Ö. (2008). *Financialization and the US economy.* Cheltenham: Edward Elgar.

Palley, T.I. (2013). *Financialization: The economics of finance capital domination.* Basingstoke: Palgrave Macmillan.

Park, J. (2011). *Spatial analysis of housing markets with land rent theory of political economy: The cases of London, Seoul and Los Angeles* (Doctoral dissertation, UCL (University College London)).

Park, J. (2014). Land rent theory revisited. *Science & Society, 78*(1), 88–109.

Park, J. (2023). The dynamics of land rents in housing submarkets: a Marxian perspective. *Tijdschrift voor economische en sociale geografie*. DOI: 10.1111/tesg.12599

Passow, S.S. (1970). Land reserves and teamwork in planning Stockholm. *Journal of the American Planning Association, 36*(3), 179–188.

Peck, J. (2010). Zombie neoliberalism and the ambidextrous state. *Theoretical Criminology*, 14(1): 104–110.

Peck, J. (2017). *Offshore: Exploring the worlds of global outsourcing*. Oxford University Press.

Pirasteh News. (2017). آمارهای مسکن مهر [The Mehr Housing Program—statistics]. Available at: http://www.pirastefar.ir/?p=10986 (accessed November 20, 2017).

Porter, M. (2010). The rent gap at the metropolitan scale: New York City's land-value valleys, 1990–2006. *Urban Geography, 31*(3), 385–405.

Pries, J. (2017). *Social neoliberalism through urban planning: Bureaucratic formations and contradictions in Malmö since 1985*. Doctoral dissertation, Lund University.

Pries, J. (2022). A technocratic road to spatial justice? The standard as planning knowledge and the making of postwar Sweden's welfare landscapes. *Geografiska Annaler: Series B, Human Geography, 104*(3), 285–305.

Purcell, T.F., Loftus, A., & March, H. (2020). Value—rent—finance. *Progress in Human Geography, 44*(3), 437–456.

Radio Farda. (2017). حسن روحانی می گوید مردم بهتر از دولت برای خود خانه می سازند [Rouhani: People are better constructors than the state]. https://www.radiofarda.com/a/28853580.html (accessed November 20, 2017).

Raisdana, F. (2001). بررسی های کاربردی توسعه و اقتصاد ایران [*Studies on Iranian economy and development*]. Tehran: Cheshmeh Publications.

Ramirez, M.D. (2009). Marx's theory of ground rent: A critical assessment. *Contributions to Political Economy, 28*(1), 71–91.

Ratzka, A.D. (1980). *Sixty years of municipal leasehold in Stockholm: An econometric and cost-revenue analysis*. Stockholm: Swedish Council for Building Research. Available at: http://pascal-francis.inist.fr/vibad/index.php?action=getRecordDetail&idt=PASCALBTP8080214352 (accessed April 14, 2021).

Ratzka, A.D. (1981). Land banking in Stockholm: An evaluation of municipal residential leasehold as a public finance and housing subsidy instrument. *Journal of the American Planning Association, 47*(3), 279–288.

Ricardo, D. (2004 [1911]). *The principles of political economy and taxation*. Mineola, N.Y.: Dover Publications.

Richardson, H.W. (1976). The new urban economics: an evaluation. *Socio-Economic Planning Sciences, 10*(4), 137–147.

Riksbanken. (n.d.). *1992 interest rate 500%—the Krona floats.* 1992 interest rate 500%—the Krona floats. *Sveriges Riksbank.* Available at: https://www.riksbank.se/en-gb/about-the-riksbank/history/historical-timeline/1900-1999/interest-rate-500--the-krona-floats/#:~:text=The%20real%20interest%20rate%20rose,contributing%20to%20a%20banking%20crisis. (accessed December 18, 2024).

Riksbanken. (2024). *The Riksbank's reference rate.* Sveriges Riksbank. https://www.riksbank.se/en-gb/statistics/search-interest--exchange-rates/reference-rate/ (accessed April 17, 2024).

Revington, N. (2015). Gentrification, transit, and land use: Moving beyond neoclassical theory. *Geography Compass*, *9*(3), 152–163.

Roberts, M. (2009). *The Great Recession. Profit cycles, economic crisis. A Marxist view.* London: Michael Roberts.

Roberts, M. (2014). David Harvey, monomaniacs and the rate of profit. *Michael Roberts Blog.* Available at: https://thenextrecession.wordpress.com/2014/12/17/david-harvey-monomaniacs-and-the-rate-of-profit/ (accessed November 24, 2017).

Roberts, M. (2016a). Transformation and realisation—no problem. *Michael Roberts Blog.* Available at: https://thenextrecession.wordpress.com/2016/11/14/transformation-and-realisation-no-problem/ (accessed May 27, 2020).

Roberts, M. (2016b). Monocausality and crisis theory: A reply to David Harvey. In: Subasat, T. (eds). *The great financial meltdown: Systemic, conjunctural or policy created?*, Cheltenham, UK: Edward Elgar Publishing, pp. 55–72.

Roberts, M. (2016c). *The long depression: Marxism and the global crisis of capitalism.* Chicago: Haymarket Books.

Roberts, M. (2017). The end of QE. *The Next Recession.* Available at: https://thenextrecession.wordpress.com/2017/09/21/the-end-of-qe/ (accessed April 17, 2024).

Roberts, M. (2018). Sweden in deadlock. *The Next Recession.* Available at: https://thenextrecession.wordpress.com/2018/09/10/sweden-in-deadlock/ (accessed June 24, 2025).

Roberts, M. (2019). The US rate of profit measure for 2018. *Michael Roberts Blog.* Available at: https://thenextrecession.wordpress.com/2018/11/02/the-us-rate-of-profit-in-2017/ (accessed September 29, 2020).

Roberts, M. (2020a). Marx's law of value: A critique of David Harvey. *Human Geography*, *13*(1), 95–98.

Roberts, M. (2020b). A world rate of profit—a new approach. *Michael Roberts Blog.* Available at: https://thenextrecession.wordpress.com/2020/07/25/a-world-rate-of-profit-a-new-approach/ (accessed December 3, 2020).

Roberts, M. (2021a). Is neoliberalism finished?. YouTube. (2021, 30 November). Haymarket Books. Available at: https://youtu.be/bzCjTUNrQRk (accessed February 9, 2024).

Roberts, M. (2021b). The rate and the mass of profit. In: Michael Roberts Blog. Available at: https://thenextrecession.wordpress.com/2021/08/25/the-rate-and-the-mass-of-profit/ (accessed April 8, 2022).

Roberts, M. (2021c). Marx's reproduction schema. *Michael Roberts Blog*. Available at: https://thenextrecession.wordpress.com/2021/07/06/marxs-reproduction-schema/ (accessed March 11, 2024).

Robinson, J. (1970 [1933]). *The economics of imperfect competition*. London: MacMillan.

Rosengårdfastigheter. (n.d.). *Culture Casbah*. Available at: https://www.rosengardfastigheter.se/en/culture-casbah (accessed May 21, 2024).

Runesson, L. (1997). *Tomträtt: ett markpolitiskt instrument i upplösning*. PhD Thesis, Lund University, Sweden.

Rutland, T. (2010). The financialization of urban redevelopment. *Geography Compass*, *4*(8), 1167–1178.

Sadvandian, S., & Etehadieh, M. (1989). آمار دارالخلافه تهران [*Tehran statistics, 19th century*]. Tehran: Tarikh Iran Press.

Salonen, T., Grander, M., & Rasmusson, M. (2019). *Segregation och segmentering i Malmö*. Malmö Stad.

Samuelson, P.A. (1969). Classical and neoclassical theory. In: Clower, R.W. (eds). *Monetary theory*. London: Penguin, pp. 1–15.

Sandberg, M., & Grander, M. (2021). Trångboddhet i Malmö : en studie av trångboddhetens ojämlika utbredning och konsekvenser. DOI: 10.24834/isbn.9789178771288.

Sandemose, J. (2006). Concerning absolute rent. *Science & Society*, *70*(3), 360–366.

Schnabel, I. (2022). Isabel Schnabel's interview with T-online. *European Central Bank*. https://www.ecb.europa.eu/press/inter/date/2022/html/ecb.in220922~0f586d9078.en.html (accessed April 5, 2024).

Schumpeter, J.A. (1950). *Capitalism, socialism and democracy*. (3rd ed.) New York: Harper & Row.

Scott, A.J. (1976). Land and Land rent: An Interpretative review of the French Literature. *Progress in Geography*, *9*, 102–45.

Scott, A. (1982). Locational patterns and dynamics of industrial activity in the modern metropolis. *Urban Studies*, *19*(2), 111–142.

Schott, J.J. (2006). Economic sanctions, oil, and Iran. *Washington: Peterson Institute for International Economics*. Available at: http://www.iranwatch.org/sites/default/files/us-congress-jec-schott-iran-energy-072506.pdf (accessed December 5, 2020).

SCB (Statistics Sweden). (n.d.). *Financial accounts, quarterly and annual*. Available at: https://www.scb.se/en/finding-statistics/statistics-by-subject-area/financial-markets/financial-accounts/financial-accounts-quarterly-and-annual/ (accessed May 27, 2024).

SCB (Statistics Sweden) (1991). Statistik *årsbok* [*Statistical yearbook*]. Stockholm: Statistics Sweden.

SCB (Statistics Sweden) (1996). Statistik *årsbok* [*Statistical yearbook*]. Stockholm: Statistics Sweden.

SCB (Statistics Sweden). (2021). *Building permits for new construction, summary table of preliminary figures.* Available at: https://www.scb.se/en/finding-statistics/statistics-by-subject-area/housing-construction-and-building/statistics-on-building-permits-for-housing-and-non-residential-buildings/statistics-on-building-permits-for-housing-and-non-residential-buildings/pong/tables-and-graphs/building-permits-for-new-construction-summary-table-of-preliminary-figures/ (accessed June 2, 2021).

SCB (Statistics Sweden). (2022). *Sold tenant-owned flats by region. Year 2000–2022.* Available at: https://www.statistikdatabasen.scb.se/pxweb/en/ssd/START__BO__BO0501__BO0501C/FastprisBRFRegionAr/ (accessed April 17, 2024).

SCB (Statistics Sweden). (2023a). *Balance sheets (ESA2010), end of year, net, current prices in SEK million by institutional sector and type of assets. 1980–2022.* Available at: https://www.statistikdatabasen.scb.se/pxweb/en/ssd/START__NR__NR0103__NR0103K/SektorENS2010ArBR/ [household debt total] (accessed April 17, 2024).

SCB (Statistics Sweden). (2023b). *Number of dwellings by region, type of building and tenure (including special housing). 1990–2022.* Available at: https://www.statistikdatabasen.scb.se/pxweb/en/ssd/START__BO__BO0104__BO0104D/BO0104T04/ (accessed April 8, 2024).

SCB (Statistics Sweden). (2023c). *Number of dwellings by region, type of building and type of ownership (including special housing). 2013–2023.* Available at: https://www.statistikdatabasen.scb.se/pxweb/en/ssd/START__BO__BO0104__BO0104D/BO0104T03/ (accessed April 18, 2024).

SCB (Statistics Sweden). (2024a). *Building permits for new construction, number and gross floor area by region and type of building, quarterly 1996Q1–2024Q1.* Available at: https://www.statistikdatabasen.scb.se/pxweb/en/ssd/START__BO__BO0101__BO0101G/BlovAreaHustypKv/ (accessed May 29, 2024).

SCB (Statistics Sweden). (2024b). *Dwellings in newly constructed buildings by region and type of building, quarterly 1975Q1–2024Q1.* Available at: https://www.statistikdatabasen.scb.se/pxweb/en/ssd/START__BO__BO0101__BO0101C/LagenhetNyKv16/ (accessed May 29, 2024).

SCB BO (Statistics Sweden) (1990). *Bostads-och byggnadsstatistisk (BO) årsbok* [*Housing and construction statistical yearbook*]. Stockholm: Statistics Sweden.

SCB BO (Statistics Sweden) (1995). *Bostads-och byggnadsstatistisk (BO) årsbok* [*Housing and construction statistical yearbook*]. Stockholm: Statistics Sweden.

SCB SM (Statistics Sweden) (1995). *Statistika medelanden (SM) bostadsbyggnadet* [*Housing construction*]. Stockholm: Statistics Sweden.

SOU (Statens Offentliga Utredningar). (2018). *Statens offentliga utredningar.* [The state's public reports]. Available at: https://www.regeringen.se/contentassets/60abea00bcff44df9deb2a3206323523/sou-2018_67_webb.pdf (accessed April 17, 2024).

SCI (Statistical Center of Iran). (2014). *Summary results of the Iranian urban and rural household income and expenditure survey.* Available at: https://www.amar.org.ir/Portals/1/releases/s_heis_ur_1392.pdf (accessed November 20, 2017).

SCI (Statistical Center of Iran). (2015). تعداد و سهم شاغلان کارگاه های صنعتی [Employed in manufacturing sector]. Available at: https://www.amar.org.ir/Portals/0/PropertyAgent/461/Files/6877/2401z120811394.xls (accessed November 13, 2019).

SCI (Statistical Center of Iran). (2016). گروه عمده فعالیت اقتصادی بر حسب وضع شغلی [Employment statistics]. Available at: https://www.amar.org.ir/Portals/0/PropertyAgent/461/Files/9255/Shaghel_10Sale_Vaz_Shoghli_Kol_Shahri_Roostaii_Sal95.xls (accessed November 13, 2019).

SCI (Statistical Center of Iran). (2016–2017). *Iran Statistical Yearbook 2016–2017.* Available at: https://www.amar.org.ir/Portals/1/yearbook/1395/10.pdf (accessed November 13, 2019).

SCI (Statistical Center of Iran). (2017). *Summary results of the Iranian urban and rural household income and expenditure survey.* Available at: https://www.amar.org.ir/Portals/1/releases/heis/Household_Income_and_Expenditure_Survey_1396.pdf (accessed March 20, 2019).

SCI (Statistical Center of Iran). (2018). نرخ بیکاری [Unemployment rate]. Available at: https://www.amar.org.ir/news/ID/5604/نرخ-بيكاري-بهار-1397-برابر-با-12.1-درصد-است (accessed March 20, 2019).

SCI (Statistical Center of Iran). (2019). دستمزد ساعتی نیروی انسانی [Hourly wages]. Available at: https://www.amar.org.ir/Portals/0/News/1398/dastmozd2-97.pdf (accessed November 13, 2019).

SCI (Statistical Center of Iran). (2020). جداول داده ستانده [Input-Output Tables] Available at: https://amar.org.ir/5608761#حساب/آماری-اطلاعات-و-دادهها-های-ملی-و-منطقهای/جدول-داده-و-ستانده- (accessed November 25, 2020).

Sepehrdoust, H. (2013). The impact of migrant labor force on housing construction of Iran. *Journal of Housing and the Built Environment*, *28*(1), 67–78.

SKD. (Skånska Dagbladet). (2024). *22 våningar blev 16—nytt förslag för flyttade huset.* Available at: https://www.skd.se/2024-01-12/22-vaningar-blev-16-nytt-forslag-for-flyttade-huset (accessed May 29, 2024).

Shaikh, A. (1977). Marx's theory of value and the transformation problem. In: Schwartz, J. (eds). *The subtle anatomy of capitalism.* Santa Monica, Calif.: Goodyear, pp. 106–139.

Shaikh, A. (1978). An introduction to the history of crisis theories. In: Steinberg, B. (eds). *US capitalism in crisis*, New York: URPE, pp. 219–241.

Shaikh, A. (1982a). Neo-Ricardian economics: A wealth of algebra, a poverty of theory. *Review of Radical Political Economics, 14*(2), 67–83.

Shaikh, A. (1982b). Regulating Capitals and Absolute Rent. *Archives of Anwar Shaikh*. Available at: https://digitalcommons.bard.edu/as_archive/404 (accessed October 23, 2025).

Shaikh, A. (1990). Market value and market price. In: Eatwell, J., Milgate, M., Newman, P. (eds) *Marxian Economics*. London: The New Palgrave. Palgrave Macmillan. DOI: 10.1007/978-1-349-20572-1_38.

Shaikh, A. (1994). Marxian Value, Wages, Money. *Archives of Anwar Shaikh*. Available at: https://digitalcommons.bard.edu/as_archive/449 (accessed October 23, 2025).

Shaikh, A. (1998). The stock market and the corporate sector: A profit-based approach. In: Sawyer, M., Arestis, P., & Palma, G. (eds). *Festschrift for Geoffrey Harcourt*. London: Routledge & Kegan Paul., pp. 389–404.

Shaikh, A. (2008). Competition and industrial rates of return. In: Arestis, P., & Eatwell, J. (eds). *Issues in economic development and globalisation, Festschrift in honor of Ajit Singh*. Houndmills, Basingstoke, UK: Palgrave Macmillan, pp. 167–194.

Shaikh, A. (2011). The first great depression of the 21st century. *Socialist Register, 47*(47), 44–63.

Shaikh, A. (2016). *Capitalism: competition, conflict, crises*. Oxford: Oxford University Press.

Shaikh, A. (2019). Toward a coherent framework for pluralism and economics. *American Review of Political Economy, 11*(2).

Shaikh, A. (2022). Marx, Sraffa and classical price theory. *Contributions to Political Economy, 41*(1), 58–76.

Shaikh, A., & Tonak, E.A. (1994). *Measuring the wealth of nations, the political economy of national accounts*. Cambridge: Cambridge University Press.

Sheppard, E.S., & Barnes, T.J. (1986). Instabilities in the geography of capitalist production: Collective vs. individual profit maximization. *Annals of the Association of American Geographers, 76*(4), 493–507.

Sheppard, E.S., & Barnes, T.J. (1990). *The capitalist space economy: Geographical analysis after Ricardo, Marx and Sraffa*. London: Routledge.

Slater, T. (2017). Planetary rent gaps. *Antipode, 49*, 114–137.

Smet, K. (2016). Housing prices in urban areas. *Progress in Human Geography, 40*(4), 495–510.

Smith, D.M. (1971). Radical geography: The next revolution?. *Area, 3*(3), 153–157.

Smith, N. (1979). Toward a theory of gentrification: A back to the city movement by capital, not people. *Journal of the American Planning Association, 45*(4), 538–548.

Smith, N. (1987). Gentrification and the rent gap. *Annals of the Association of American Geographers, 77*(3), 462–465.

Smith, N. (1996a). Of rent gaps and radical idealism: A reply to Steven Bourassa. *Urban Studies*, *33*(7), 1199–1203.

Smith, N. (1996b). *The new urban frontier: Gentrification and the revanchist city*. London: Routledge.

Sraffa, P. (1926). The laws of returns under competitive conditions. *The Economic Journal*, *36*(144), 535–550.

Steedman, I. (1977). *Marx after Sraffa*. London: NLB.

Stein, S. & Mironova, O. (2020). Public land revisited: municipalization and privatization in Newark and New York City. *International Planning Studies*, *25*(3), 247–260.

Subasat, T., & Mavroudeas, S. (2023). Financialization Hypothesis. *World Review of Political Economy*, *14*(2), 204–233.

Summers, E. (2006). The de-municipalization of social housing: changing the regional map. *Yorkshire and Humber Regional Review*, *16*(1), 13–17.

Sutterlüty, F. (2014). The hidden morale of the 2005 French and 2011 English riots. *Thesis Eleven*, *121*(1), 38–56.

Sveriges Allmännytta. (n.d.). *Hyresrätten och Lagstiftningen*. Sveriges Allmännytta. Available at: https://www.allmannyttan.se/historia/tidslinje/hyresratten-och-lagstiftningen/ (accessed April 8, 2024).

Swedish Parliament. [Riksdagen] (1981). Om mark- och konkurrensvillkoren för statliga bostadslån m.m. (1980/81:194). Civilutskottets Betänkande (1980/81:CU40). https://www.riksdagen.se/sv/dokument-lagar/arende/betankande/om-mark--och-konkurrensvillkoren-for-statliga_G401CU40/html (accessed May 25, 2023).

Sweezy, P.M. (1970 [1942]). *The theory of capitalist development: principles of Marxian political economy*. New York: Monthly Review Press.

Sweezy, P.M. (1981). *Four lectures on Marxism*. New York: Monthly Review Press.

Swenson, P.A. (2002). *Capitalists against markets: the making of labor markets and welfare states in the United States and Sweden*. New York: Oxford University Press.

Swyngedouw, E. (2000). The Marxian alternative: Historical-geographical materialism and political economy of capitalism. In: Sheppard, E.S., & Barnes, T.J. (eds). *A companion to economic geography*. Oxford: Blackwell, pp. 41–59.

Swyngedouw, E. (2012). Rent and landed property. In: Fine, B., Saad-Filho, A., & Boffo, M. (eds). *The Elgar companion to Marxist economics*. Cheltenham: Edward Elgar Publishing, pp. 310–315.

Swyngedouw, E., & Ward, C. (2022). Land as an Asset. In: Hyötyläinen, M., & Beauregard, R. (eds). *The political economy of land: Rent, financialization and resistance* (1st ed.). Routledge, pp. 40–55. DOI: 10.4324/9781003280255.

Taraz News. (2013). واردات چه کالایی بیشترین سود را دارد [Highest Yielding Product to Import]. Available at: http://www.taraznews.com/content/38547 (accessed August 16, 2016).

Tapia, J.A. (2018). Investment, profit and crises: theories and evidence. In: Carchedi, G. & Roberts, M. (eds). *World in crisis: a global analysis of Marx's law of profitability*. Chicago: Haymarket Books.

Tapia, J.A. (2023). *Six crises of the world economy: Globalization and economic turbulence from the 1970s to the COVID-19 pandemic* [*Electronic resource*]. Palgrave Macmillan Ltd.

Tapp, R. (2020). From the state to the shareholder: rent and the production of shareholder value in real estate. *Antipode*. DOI: 10.1111/anti.12618.

TCCIMA (Tehran Chamber of Commerce, Industries, Mines, and Agriculture). (2014). بررسی وضعیت هزینه و درآمد خانوار در استان تهران و کل کشور [*Survey of household expenditure and income in Tehran province and the country*]. Available at: http://tccim.ir/images/Docs/EcoReport36.pdf (accessed April 9, 2018).

Tehran Municipality. (2019). شرح وظایف [Duties and responsibilities]. Available at: http://region8.tehran.ir/Default.aspx?tabid=559 (accessed November 20, 2017).

Tenants Association. (2016). Bostadsbristen landskap i Skåne [Landscapes of housing shortage in Scania]. Available at: https://www.hyresgastforeningen.se/globalassets/bostadsfakta/rapporter/2016/bostadsbristens-landskap-i-skane-2016.pdf (accessed April 17, 2024).

Tenants Association. (2021). Marknadshyror i Malmö [The rental market i Malmö]. Available at: https://www.hyresgastforeningen.se/globalassets/bilder/regionernas-bilder/sodra-skanes-bilder/ovriga-bilder/rapport---marknadshyror-i-malmo.pdf (accessed April 17, 2024).

Teresa, B.F. (2016). Managing fictitious capital: The legal geography of investment and political struggle in rental housing in New York City. *Environment and Planning A*, *48*(3), 465–484.

TMICTO (Tehran Municipality ICT Organisation). (2014–2015). *1393* آمارنامه شهر تهران. [*Tehran statistical yearbook 2014–2015*]. Tehran: Tehran Municipality ICT Organisation.

Tomasson, R.F. (1969). The extraordinary success of the Swedish social democrats. *The Journal of Politics*, *31*(3), 772–798.

Topal, A. Yalman, G.L., & Çelik, Ö. (2018). Changing modalities of urban redevelopment and housing finance in Turkey: Three mass housing projects in Ankara. *Journal of Urban Affairs*, 1–24.

Tykesson, T. (2021). Barnfamiljer och ungdomar behöver bostäder i Malmö. [Small families and the youth need housing in Malmö]. *Sydsvenskan*. Available at: https://www.sydsvenskan.se/2021-09-25/barnfamiljer-och-ungdomar-behoverbostader-i-malmo (accessed April 17, 2024).

Tykesson, T. (2022). Byggtakten fortsatt hög i Malmö. Små lägenheter dominerar. [Construction remains high in Malmö, dominated by low-rises]. *Sydsvenskan*.

Available at: https://www.sydsvenskan.se/2022-03-21/byggtakten-i-malmo-fortsatt-hog--sma-lagenheter-dominerar (accessed April 17, 2024).

UBS. (2025). Global Wealth Report 2024. *UBS*. Available at: Global Wealth Report 2024—Crafted wealth intelligence (accessed April 28, 2025).

Vedung, E. (1993). *Statens markpolitik, kommunerna och historiens ironi*. Stockholm: SNS (Studieförb. Näringsliv och samhälle).

Voorn, B., Van Genetten, M.L. & Van Thiel, S. (2021). Re-interpreting re-municipalization: finding equilibrium. *Journal of Economic Policy Reform*, *24*(3), 305–318.

Wachsmuth, D., & Weisler, A. (2018). Airbnb and the rent gap: Gentrification through the sharing economy. *Environment and Planning A*, *50*(6), 1147–1170.

Waldron, R. (2023). Generation rent and housing precarity in 'post-crisis' Ireland. *Housing Studies*, *38*(2), 181–205.

Walker, R.A. (1974). Urban ground rent: Building a new conceptual framework. *Antipode*, *6*(1), 51–58.

Walker, R.A. (1975). Contentious issues in Marxian value and rent theory: A second and longer look. *Antipode*, *7*(1), 31–53.

Ward, C. (2021). Contradictions of financial capital switching: Reading the corporate leverage crisis through the Port of Liverpool's whole business securitization. *International Journal of Urban and Regional Research*, *45*(2), 249–265.

Ward, C., & Aalbers, M.B. (2016). Virtual special issue editorial essay: 'The shitty rent business': What's the point of land rent theory?, *Urban Studies*, 53(9), 1760–1783.

Warner, M.E. (2023). Pragmatic municipalism: Privatization and remunicipalisation in the US. *Local Government Studies*, 1–19.

Watterton, J. (2023). Military spending and economic development: a theoretical note. *Human Geography*, *16*(2), 187–192.

Webber, S., Nelson, S., Millington, N., Bryant, G. & Bigger, P. (2022). Financing reparative climate infrastructures: Capital switching, repair, and decommodification. *Antipode*, *54*(3), 934–958.

Weber, R. (2002). Extracting value from the city: Neoliberalism and urban redevelopment. *Antipode*, *34*(3), 519–540.

Weber, R. (2010). Selling city futures: The financialization of urban redevelopment policy. *Economic Geography*, *86*(3), 251–274.

Weiler, P. (2008). Labour and the land: from municipalization to the land commission, 1951–1971. *Twentieth Century British History*, *19*(3), 314–343.

Whitehead, J., & More, N. (2007). Revanchism in Mumbai? Political economy of rent gaps and urban restructuring in a global city. *Economic and Political Weekly*, 2428–2434.

Wolf, M. (1997). Fixed capital stock in the Swedish national accounts. *Paper presented at the capital stock conference, Agenda item III*. Available at: https://www.oecd.org/sdd/na/2666557.pdf (accessed October 28, 2020).

World Bank. (2018). *Urban population (% of total)*. Available at: https://data.worldbank.org/indicator/SP.URB.TOTL.IN.ZS?locations=IR (accessed April 18, 2018).

Wyly, E. (2002). Mortgaged metropolis: Evolving urban geographies of residential lending. *Urban Geography, 23*(1), 3–30.

Wyly, E. (2015). Gentrification on the planetary urban frontier: The evolution of Turner's noösphere. *Urban Studies, 52*(14), 2515–2550.

Wyly, E.K., & Hammel, D.J. (1999). Islands of decay in seas of renewal: Housing policy and the resurgence of gentrification. *Housing Policy Debate, 10*, 711–771.

Wyly, E.K., Atia, M., & Hammel, D.J. (2004). Has mortgage capital found an inner-city spatial fix?. *Housing Policy Debate, 15*(3), 623–685.

Wyly, E., Moos, M., Hammel, D., & Kabahizi, E. (2009). Cartographies of race and class: Mapping the class-monopoly rents of American subprime mortgage capital. *International Journal of Urban and Regional Research, 33*(2), 332–354.

Wyly, E., Moos, M., & Hammel, D. (2012). Race, class, and rent in America's subprime cities. In: Aalbers, M.B. (eds). *Subprime cities: The political economy of mortgage markets*. Oxford, UK: Wiley-Blackwell, pp. 242–290.

Yaffe, D. (1976). Value and price in Marx's capital. *Revolutionary Communist, 1*, 31–49.

Yousefi, S., & Farahani, I. (2022). Spatial inequality in Tehran: a structural explanation. *Urban Research & Practice, 15*(1), 25–46. DOI: 10.1080/17535069.2019.1699596.

Yrigoy, I. (2019). Rent gap reloaded: Airbnb and the shift from residential to touristic rental housing in the Palma Old Quarter in Mallorca, Spain. *Urban Studies, 56*(13), 2709–2726.

Yrigoy, I. (2020). The role of regulations in the Spanish housing dispossession crisis: Towards dispossession by regulations?. *Antipode, 52*(1), 316–336.

Yrigoy, I. (2023). Unpacking capital switching: Value, rentierism and displacement in absolute and relative forms of switching. *International Journal of Urban and Regional Research, 47*(6), 940–956.

Zachariah, D. (2020, April 6). Interview with Anwar Shaikh: "The fundamental questions about capitalism seem to be coming back". *Jacobin*. Available at: https://jacobinmag.com/2020/04/anwar-shaikh-interview-capitalism-competition-conflict-crises/ (accessed April 16, 2020).

Zakeri, M., Olomolaiye, P.O., Holt, G.D., & Harris, F.C. (1996). A survey of constraints on Iranian construction operatives' productivity. *Construction Management & Economics, 14*(5), 417–426.

Zetterlund, H. (2022). *The Landed Municipality: The Underlying Rationales for Swedish Public Landownership and their Implications for Policy*. Doctoral dissertation, Department of Social and Economic Geography, Uppsala University.

Zoninsein, J. (1990). *Monopoly capital theory: Hilferding and twentieth-century capitalism*. New York: Greenwood Press.

Ödmann, E. (1973). Some views on land ownership in urban planning and housing production in Sweden. *Geoforum, 4*(1), 31–41.

Name Index

Subject Index

www.ingramcontent.com/pod-product-compliance
Lightning Source LLC
LaVergne TN
LVHW020653300926
849161LV00004B/929
* 9 7 8 9 0 0 4 7 6 3 2 0 3 *